WOMEN'S SONGS *from* WEST AFRICA

Edited by
**THOMAS A. HALE
AND AISSATA G. SIDIKOU**

Indiana University Press
BLOOMINGTON AND INDIANAPOLIS

This book is a publication of

Indiana University Press
Office of Scholarly Publishing
Herman B Wells Library 350
1320 East 10th Street
Bloomington, Indiana 47405 USA

iupress.indiana.edu

Telephone orders   800-842-6796
Fax orders   812-855-7931

© 2014 by Indiana University Press

Manufactured in the United States of America

Library of Congress Cataloging-in-
Publication Data

Women's songs from West Africa / edited by
Thomas A. Hale and Aissata G. Sidikou.
    pages cm.
    Includes bibliographical references and
index.
    ISBN 978-0-253-01017-9 (cloth : alkaline
paper) — ISBN 978-0-253-01021-6 (ebook)
1. Music—Africa, West—History and
criticism. 2. Women musicians—Africa, West.
3. West Africans—Music. I. Hale, Thomas A.
(Thomas Albert), [date]- editor. II. Sidikou,
Aissata G., editor.
    ML3760.W66 2013
    782.42082ʹ0966—dc23
                                    2013012262

1 2 3 4 5 19 18 17 16 15 14

To the African women who helped make this volume possible

Contents

WOMEN'S SONGS
FROM WEST AFRICA

Introduction ⟶☙

NEW PERSPECTIVES ON WOMEN'S SONGS
AND SINGING IN WEST AFRICA

Thomas A. Hale and Aissata G. Sidikou

The essays in this volume are the result of research presented at a conference titled "Women's Songs from West Africa" held at Princeton University. For the conference organizers, the event was the climax of a long effort to bring together researchers in a variety of disciplines who had worked for years and in some cases decades on song, a genre that reveals much about the world of women in West Africa.

To a large extent, the focus of both the conference and the project out of which it grew was the content rather than the sound or form of these songs. Although it is difficult to dissociate form from meaning, both in song and in literature, the organizers, specialists in African literature and related fields, believe that song constitutes the most widespread form of verbal art produced by women in Africa. The lyrics cannot be ignored in our efforts to understand and communicate to others the richness of African literature today.

The conference organizers embarked on this project after recording songs by women in West Africa during the 1980s and 1990s. Aissata G. Sidikou, author of *Recreating Words, Reshaping Worlds: The Verbal Art of Women from Niger, Mali and Senegal* (2001), collected songs in Niger and then compared them with lyrics sung by other women in Mali and Senegal that had been recorded and published by researchers as part of larger projects. Although other scholars have published works that include a focus on the songs of women in particular contexts—for example, Karin Barber's landmark study of songs by Yoruba women, *I Could Speak until Tomorrow: Oriki, Women and the Past in a Yoruba Town* (1991)—the study by Sidikou was the first to take a regional approach to the genre for woman singers. Thomas A. Hale, author of *Griots and*

Griottes: Masters of Words and Music (1998), studied professional artisans of the word, both male and female, from a regional perspective in Niger, Mali, Senegal, the Gambia, and other Sahelian countries. Although he, too, recorded songs by women, and produced a short video about griottes in one country, *Griottes of the Sahel: Female Keepers of the Songhay Oral Tradition in Niger,* distributed by the Pennsylvania State University, his approach was focused as much on the history and social functions of the performers as on the lyrics.

In the course of presentations of the results of their work at professional meetings, both Sidikou and Hale encountered other researchers—North American, European, and African—who were also studying songs by West African women. In some cases—for example, Beverly Mack of the University of Kansas and Susan Rasmussen from the University of Houston—these colleagues had been recording songs as well as other forms since the 1970s.

The long-term efforts of these researchers yielded greater understanding of women's complex and subtle roles in diverse societies as well as a corpus of many songs. But the outcomes of these projects remained to a large extent in isolation. For Beverly Mack, whose lifetime has been spent studying the verbal art, both oral and written, of Hausa women, it would have been impossible to carry out research of equal depth among, for example, a half-dozen other peoples in the region, because she would have had to learn many more languages—and devote several more lifetimes to the task.

As significant as these ethno-specific analyses were for scholars interested in learning more about the lives of women in West Africa, there was a clear need for a complementary regional approach. In her comparisons of songs across the Sahel, Sidikou discovered differences rooted in culture as well as many similarities based on common concerns of women. In his study of griots and griottes in the same region, Hale encountered a similar phenomenon: many differences stemming from the diversity of cultures, but also similarities based on traditions that go back many centuries and span a vast area from Senegal to Lake Chad.

It is because of these emerging regional similarities that we decided to limit the focus of this project to the Sahel region. It is made up of diverse peoples who nevertheless share common climatic, historical, and cultural experiences that include cycles of drought, the rise and fall of vast empires, highly stratified social structures, historical traditions maintained by griots, male and female, and systems of belief overlaid by Islam, a religion introduced into the region a millennium ago. Given these similar cultural features across the Sahel, a series of questions emerged:

Do women have a significant public voice through the medium of song? If so, what are women saying in their song lyrics? What links between these songs appear across the Sahel, both formal and thematic? Where does the genre of song fit into African literature?

The danger in such a comparative approach, of course, was that in making comparisons across cultures, we might elide differences and specificities to such an extent as to render the project meaningless. We do not want to end up with the kinds of generalizations one finds in some collections of verbal art from Africa.

Our solution is to produce two volumes. The first is *Women's Voices from West Africa: An Anthology of Songs from the Sahel* (Indiana University Press, 2011). The purpose is to identify common themes across the Sahel without losing sight of the cultural differences. The sources are diverse: archives, journals, books, and collections by researchers. The lyrics enable the reader to discern the many links between the songs of women from different societies in the region. The most striking example is the theme of marriage.

The second volume, this collection of seventeen essays presented by eighteen researchers at the Princeton conference and contributed to since then, offers insights into the specifics of cultures represented by the songs in the anthology.

It is important to point out here that there is not a one-to-one link between each of these papers and a song or group of songs in the anthology. Some essays provide context for particular genres—e.g., wedding songs. In these cases there is a very direct link, and these ties are often indicated in the first volume. But others inform the larger project. They provide information about singers, the financial aspects of their lives, and the impact of infertility on a woman's social status. As a collection, the essays provide both more specific analyses of particular traditions and additional evidence to answer the larger questions raised by the project.

The two-pronged approach represented by these books will give readers a multidimensional perspective on what women are expressing in their songs. Although there is thematic and formal overlap in the papers, they may be best read in groups of two, three, or four based on common features found across the Sahel.

The contributors to this volume come from the United States, Holland, France, Italy, Niger, Senegal, and Mali. But one participant at the Princeton conference who came from Guinea did not present a paper. Aicha Kouyaté, a griotte or *jelimuso* from Guinea, was a special invitee who commented on papers and also was the featured performer at a concert that featured singers and instrumentalists from the Gambia led by Al Haji Papa Susso. The concert attracted a full house in Taplin Hall, and served to mark the end of the conference in a lively fashion that saw many of the researchers on stage with the performers by the end of the evening.

The themes of the songs performed by Aicha Kouyaté resonate with those the team of researchers has recorded from Senegal to Niger—family, children, men, marriage, and self-respect. We believe that the lyrics of these songs must be viewed not simply as a way for women to pass the time of day while pounding millet, but as a form of expression that should be included in the larger picture of literature from Africa, oral and written.

Among those oral forms are epics, the best-known and most widely distributed texts because they are long, deal with heroes of the past, and are traditionally narrated by men. Women play a key role in many of them. For example, epics contain a veritable catalog of other forms, including songs. They are sung by both men and women. In fact, the two often perform together, with men and women alternating between narration and song. But women also tell stories and compose or perform other forms such as stories, riddles, proverbs, and praises. Although men and women do not always perform together, the evidence indicates that songs by women singers are central to the oral tradition in the Sahel—and in other parts of Africa.

The relationship of songs to written literature by women is more complex. Both oral and written media are part of a larger category of verbal art. They may overlap—for example, in the songs and poems analyzed by Beverly Mack, where the frontier between the written and oral forms is quite permeable. Songs become poems and poems become songs. But women who write novels, plays, and poems in European or African languages have benefited from education or training in these languages. The relationship between artist and audience is quite different from that of singer or singers and listeners. The result is that while one may find common themes in each medium—for example, children, marriage, and men—literature in written form, especially in European languages, is often informed by new formulations of these concerns, what is often called feminism.

Some might describe the women who perform these songs as feminists. But these singers see themselves simply as bold, accomplished, self-determined women who preserve and sustain women's values and the collective identity. "Feminism" is better known as a theme in African literature written in European languages. It is not likely that one can transfer the debate over feminism in contemporary African literature to the singers of these songs. We are in fact very much concerned with the application, or misapplication, of Western literary theory to African texts. There is a debate on this subject, with some scholars of literature composed in European languages arguing that one cannot avoid the use of Western literary theory. Others insist that one should rely only on African literary theories. The nexus of this debate is feminist theories. Female scholars from Africa have proposed their own, including "womanism," "nego-feminism," and "stiwanism." One of the concerns in these theories is how to deal with men. Are women complementary to men, should they support men, or should they attack patriarchy? These diverse views emerge in analyses of African literature written in European languages, but there are hardly any references in debates about feminist theory to what form of criticism should be applied to oral compositions. One scholar who has examined oral art by women is Mary E. Modupe Kolawole in her book *Womanism and African Consciousness*. Her chapter on "Women's Oral Genres and Ambivalent Literary Heroinism" is of interest in this debate, though it is largely descriptive. But the focus here is on the lyrics. In the end our concern is not on the singers and the songs as objects for theoretical analysis, but as subjects and as exemplars of the humanity of women.

The essays in this volume represent, then, a first effort not only to bring research on women's songs to a wider audience, but also, in tandem with the anthology that we have published, to introduce to the canon of African literature the genre of songs by women. Song as a verbal form is not limited to women, but there are many reasons for our focus on women's songs rather than on song in general.

First, in the patriarchal and largely Islamic region of the Sahel, women do not seem to have a public voice. Men dominate public discourse and women most often remain in the domestic sphere.

Second, men have tended, until recently, to dominate the written literary scene. It is only in the last twenty-five years that women, long denied full access to Western-style education, have entered the literary world thanks to changes in attitudes and policies concerning the importance of literacy for women.

The novels, plays, and poetry by women that have appeared since the late 1970s constitute the cutting edge in African literature today, a trend that is attested to by the number of books and theses devoted to writing by women. But we believe that interest in female authors should be matched by an equal focus on the oral art of women who have chosen the medium of song either because it is the means of expression with which they are most familiar or because they have not enjoyed the benefits of formal schooling. As we have indicated elsewhere, we do not accept the notion that there is an evolution of literature from the oral to the written. Both forms coexist today, and the practitioners of the written medium cannot claim superiority over those whose verbal art happens to be composed and performed orally.

Stepping back from both the songs presented in the anthology and the papers contributed to this volume, we can revisit the questions posed at the beginning of the introduction to draw several conclusions. The diverse evidence makes clear that women do have a powerful voice in their songs. They demand respect and agency in societies dominated by men. They offer their views on topics ranging from love to relations to men, from sports to politics. Their opinions are sharpest, however, in those songs that focus on marriage. These are concerns expressed in diverse cultures from Senegal to Niger. Hale and Stoller (1985) have referred to the concept of a deep Sahelian civilization based on a common history marked by empires, Islam, patriarchy, and cultural customs such as the maintenance of the collective conscience in narrations by male griots. As a result of our team's research on women's songs, we may also speak of a deep women's culture in the Sahel evidenced in the songs they sing to express their views. But we have only scratched the surface of this phenomenon. We hope that the songs in the anthology and the essays in this volume will inspire a new generation of researchers to study in greater depth the forms of verbal art composed and performed by women in the Sahel—and in other parts of Africa.

Before concluding, we want to touch on five topics concerning the presentation of work contained in this volume.

The first is audience. There is great variety in the audiences for the songs analyzed by the contributors. They range from large groups to an audience composed only of the researcher. In some cases he or she has identified the audience, in other cases not. On occasion, the researcher has created what folklorists call an induced natural context. This occurs when the performance occurs upon the request of the collector, who invites local listeners to attend. We are conscious of the fact, however, that these arrangements do not always reflect the reality of an event organized by the local people for their own purposes. But for lyrics found in archival sources, it is sometimes impossible to obtain information about the audience. An understanding of the audience—and this is especially the case for epic—is essential for deeper, more performance-based analyses of the song genre. Our interest here is in the content of the songs, but we are also acutely aware that meaning depends to some extent on context. In fact, four chapters here deal with aspects of performance.

The second is terminology for the singers, in particular words for professional female and male performers. The distinction is important because the focus here is on female singers. Some languages have not been codified into uniform writing systems, contributors have adopted different terms or spellings for performers, and there is not always agreement among researchers on which terms are appropriate. We have attempted to provide some uniformity, but the reader may find the terminology confusing at first, in particular the difference between the regional term, griot, which can refer to both sexes, and local terms that may also refer to both sexes or offer particular words for each gender.

Griot is of uncertain origin. One can find many etymologies for the term. They range from *jalolu,* the plural of the Mandinka term *jali* (Bird 1971) to Hale's more complex theory (1998). He traces the word back in French from the nineteenth-century *griot* to the early-seventeenth-century *guiriote,* then to the sixteenth-century Spanish *guineo,* and finally to the eleventh-century Tamazigh (Berber) *agenaou,* used by North African speakers for slaves taken from the kingdom of Ghana to Morocco. Whatever the origin, today *griot* is a widespread West African term used by people who have attended French schools to refer to male and female griots. When the subject is only female singers, the term *griotte* is now commonly used in trans-ethnic and local contexts.

Where possible, we will follow the usage of contributors by maintaining local terms, especially since the papers focus almost exclusively on particular peoples. In Bamana or Bamankan, for example, a people and language that are part of the vast Mande world, one finds both a general term, *jeli,* for men and women, and the gender-specific *jelikè* (pl. *jelikèw*) for a male and *jelimuso* (pl. *jelimusow*) for a woman. In Wolof, by contrast, the term *guewel* refers to men and women. (For a fuller analysis of these terms, see Hale 1998, appendix F: "Ethno-Specific Terms for Griots.") The result is that when referring to performers in both regional and local contexts, one finds that there is not always a neat one-to-one comparison between African languages and the terms *griot/ griotte.*

When referring, then, to both genders on a regional basis, we will use *griot.* When there is a need to distinguish between the genders we will adopt *male griot* and *female griot.* If the focus is only on women, we will use either *female griot* or *griotte.* To the extent possible, context will resolve any ambiguity.

Third, we will follow contributor usage in the spelling of ethnic groups. There are numerous variations, especially between French and English. The differences are not always significant, and it is unlikely the reader will encounter difficulty between, for example, Songhaï and Songhay, two different spellings adopted by different contributors.

Fourth, the reader will also find variations in the formatting of lyrics. Each contributor has adopted his or her own format, in both the spacing and numbering of lines. We have not attempted to impose a common format. The reader, in any case, should not encounter any difficulty in reading the lyrics.

Finally, we have avoided the term tribe, no longer used by most Africanists to describe African peoples because it is so imprecise. But in its narrowest definition, it refers to clans or extended families with a common language, culture and ancestor. In the case of Mauritania, tribe reflects the social structure of many peoples there, and for this reason it appears in the paper on women in Mauritania by Aline Tauzin.

We thank those who participated in the conference on Women's Songs from West Africa either in person or by sending essays and, above all, by contributing to the corpus of women's songs. We also thank the Office of the President at Princeton as well as the departments of French and Italian, Music, and History, the African Studies Program, and the Shelby Cullom Davis Center for Historical Studies; and, at Penn State, the College of the Liberal Arts, the Liberal Arts Research and Graduate Studies Office, and the Department of Comparative Literature for their support of the conference. Finally, we thank the Collaborative Research Program of the National Endowment for the Humanities, which provided funds for the direction of this project as well as for field research. In particular, we thank Senior Program Officer Elizabeth Arndt. She not only offered much useful guidance as we prepared the successive versions of the grant proposal, but she also demonstrated great interest in the project by attending the conference and the Aicha Kouyaté concert.

WORKS CITED

Barber, Karin. *I Could Speak until Tomorrow: Oriki, Women and the Past in a Yoruba Town.* Edinburgh: Edinburgh University Press, 1991.

Bird, Charles S. 1971. Oral Art in the Mande. In *Papers on the Manding,* ed. Carleton T. Hodge, 15–23. Bloomington: Research Center for the Language Sciences, Indiana University.

Hale, Thomas A. *Griottes of the Sahel: Female Keepers of the Songhay Oral Tradition in Niger.* University Park: Pennsylvania State University, 1990.

——. *Griots and Griottes: Masters of Words and Music.* Bloomington: Indiana University Press, 1998.

Hale, Thomas A., and Paul Stoller. Oral Art, Society, and Survival in the Sahel Zone. In *African Literature Studies: The Present State/l'Etat présent,* ed. Stephen Arnold, 163–169. Washington: Three Continents Press, 1985.

Modupe Kolawole, Mary E. *Womanism and African Consciousness.* Trenton, N.J.: Africa World Press, 1997.

Sidikou, Aissata G. *Recreating Words, Reshaping Worlds: The Verbal Art of Women from Niger, Mali and Senegal.* Trenton, N.J.: Africa World Press, 2001.

Sidikou, Aissata G., and Thomas A. Hale. *Women's Voices from West Africa: An Anthology of Songs from the Sahel.* Bloomington: Indiana University Press, 2011.

1

Wolof Women Break the Taboo of Sex through Songs

Marame Gueye

One of the most important but often neglected subjects in the preparation of children for adulthood is sex education, a topic that seems to preoccupy parents in a variety of cultures around the world. In many African societies, sex education is more a collective activity than an individual parental duty, and the medium is song. The question is just how this ubiquitous genre can serve to inform youths about such a private topic. The example of Wolof society offers a variety of insights into how the community employs song for teaching about sex and sexuality.

In Wolof culture, sex education occurs during weddings, where one hears a variety of songs. One particular sub-ceremony within Wolof weddings is *laabaan,* reserved exclusively for women and conducted by them. The purpose is to celebrate the bride's virginity. *Laabaan* is the term both for the ceremony and for the genre of songs sung at this event.

For the researcher, however, even one who comes from Wolof society, the songs marking the *laabaan* ceremony are the most difficult not only to understand but also to record. In my case, although I began research on wedding songs in 1996, I did not record a single *laabaan* song or performance until 1998. My paternal aunts, who are performing *guewel,* the Wolof term for griots of both sexes, sang *laabaan* songs, but they refused to let me enter the space where these songs are sung because it is reserved exclusively for married or divorced women. The result was that I had to enlist the help of *neenyo*[1] who were not family members and who were much younger than my aunts.

Before turning to the lyrics of the songs, it is important to explain the circumstances of the recordings. As an unmarried graduate student conducting research for a doctoral dissertation, I had to rely on someone my own age. Although I had attended several *laabaan* ceremonies in the past, including one with Adji Diara, I did not record those songs in the field because the public circumstances of the ceremonies were in general not conducive or appropriate to field recording. There was too much noise and movement during the event. Also, while the bride's friends are invited, they are asked to cover their ears because of the sexual nature of the songs. These conditions differ markedly from those in which epics are often recorded. In many cases, the epics are recorded in private venues such as the home of the performer. Although I did manage to record some songs in poor audio conditions at public events for the corpus collected for the women's songs project, I was most interested in those sung by Adji Diara because they were the most poignant. That is why I asked her to sing them again for me in a private context.

The 1998 recording of songs by the *neenyo* took place at my apartment in Dakar. Both of the singers were, like me, in their twenties. Although they felt at ease in discussions with me about sex, they insisted that the door of the apartment be closed because they did not want other people to attend the performance.

In the case of songs analyzed here, three women—Adji Diara as well as two *neenyo* from Dakar, Amy Thiam and Khady Thiam—allowed me to make my first recordings. I was introduced to these *neenyo* by one of my neighbors in Medina, one of the oldest neighborhoods in Dakar.

Once I had recorded songs from them, I was able to interview my mother (Diouf 2003a and 2003b), who gave me other *laabaan* songs and sayings. But our interaction illustrates the delicate nature of the subject. I should explain that we conducted these conversations on the phone, she in Senegal and I in the United States, thus creating some distance between the two of us. She would not have been comfortable with me in a discussion face-to-face in our home, where we had never had a conversation about sex. She was amazed, in fact, that I was interested in this subject and that I came all the way from the United States to conduct research on it.

During the phone interview, she emphasized to me the importance of virginity for a woman. She told me that nowadays women tend to believe that virginity is not important for the success of their marriage. But she said that men still want their brides to be virgins even though they say otherwise (Diouf 2003b). In her view, despite the Senegalese claim that some practices have been abandoned and that rituals such as the virginity test are now viewed as outmoded activities from the past, men still want virgin brides even if they do not say so openly.

Laabaan songs are traditionally performed by *neenyo* today, but women from other social groups can also sing them. As mistress of the ceremony, the family griotte is the one who most often leads the *laabaan* ceremony. However, any other griotte can also attend and make her contribution. They receive presents and money during and at the end of the ceremony. Other women can take part by giving testimonies or contributing to the singing, or by sharing their sexual tips.

Like the other sub-ceremonies of the wedding, *laabaan* constitutes a space for women's expression. However, I find it the most ambiguous site for the negotiation of power. The songs are sexually charged and speak mainly to the necessity for young women to remain virgins until marriage. Their messages do not seem to contest the sexualization and commodification of the female body. However, if one examines the lyrics more closely, the messages clearly show a break from the stereotypical silencing of African women. *Laabaan* ceremonies provide a place for Wolof women to transgress both Islamic and traditional modes of speech that advise "good women" not to use "bad" language. *Laabaan* songs also help listeners understand society's perception of the female body and its gender biases toward sex and sexuality.

VIRGINITY TEST: ALIEN OR INDIGENOUS?

Virginity is a subject that is central to the *laabaan* ceremony. As in many patriarchal societies, virginity was once a prerequisite for marriage for Wolof women. Although the tradition continues today, it appears that fewer women are virgins when they marry.

A ceremony is organized as part of the many other events that mark the wedding. The purpose is to highlight the abstinence of the bride and to celebrate her purity. It is not clear whether the Wolof conducted a virginity test before the arrival of Islam and European colonization, but some people claim that in any case the practice is alien to the culture. Writing about ancient African cultures, Kandji and Camara note:

> Although promiscuity is not condoned, fulfilled sexuality is not a taboo. The only prohibitions that exist pertain to kinship relations (against incest) or to marriage (against adultery). One is free to live in cohabitation, or wait until one has one or several children before getting married. (2000, 42–43)[2]

Whether this statement is valid for the Wolof or not, it is clear that there is no mention of the practice of a virginity test among the Wolof in the numerous documents written by travel writers and missionaries, European or African, such as the Abbé Boilat and others. However, there are stories about virgins being used for sacrifice or compensation to heroes in many legends and myths. But even these stories do not clarify the difference between a virgin and a woman who has never been married, because the Wolof used the same term, *janx,* for a virgin and for a young woman who is not married. One is then tempted to say that these sacrifices were based more on maidenhood than on virginity.

It is unclear whether the Wolof adopted virginity checks from European or Arab cultures, as it appears that both practiced them at one time or another. However, most of the activities and beliefs surrounding the Wolof practice of verifying that the bride is a virgin are similar to those occurring in some contemporary Middle Eastern societies. For instance, my mother reported to me that in the past, women who were not virgins at marriage were shot by their male relatives. Writing about a bride who failed to be a virgin in traditional Moroccan society, Combs-Schilling notes:

> The groom himself does not kill her, for she is not his blood, not his responsibility, but rather hands the sullied bride over to a man whose blood she shares, her father or her brother, one of whom kills her on that very night. (Combs-Schilling 1989, 208)

This is the case in the very popular Wolof tale of Khandiou and Ndaté. On her wedding day, Khandiou, who was not a virgin, faced the possibility of being shot by her father. She confided in her best friend Ndaté, who, at night, took her place in the marital bed and saved her from death and disgrace. Because she sacrificed her honor in the name of friendship, Ndaté was given a new hymen by a spirit. While this story is more about friendship than virginity, it echoes the practice of honor killing still practiced in some Arab societies.

Another similarity with the view in many parts of the Islamic world is that female sexuality appears as very powerful, and the perception is that men's vulnerability to it can corrupt society. To protect men and society as a whole from sin and promiscuity, the female body needs to be controlled. This explains the veiling of women in many Muslim societies (Mernissi 1987, 3). Needless to say, by converting to Islam the Wolof adopted many practices of the religion and its adherents. Although the Wolof do not require women to be veiled, women are advised to cover their bodies in order not to tempt men. This ideology provides support for the tradition of genital cutting or surgery, and the sewing up of women's genitals, a practice carried out today in some Arab societies. The concept of protecting men and blaming the female for non-marital sex is a predominant pattern in contemporary Wolof culture.

Another Islamic influence lies in the word *laabaan,* which signifies "purifying" or "cleansing." In Islamic tradition, one is supposed to have a purifying bath after the sexual act, but it is not clear whether that view explains the practice. It may also be that the hymen is a symbol of innocence and that the bride is washed in order to celebrate her entrance into adulthood. Certain Wolof also refer to the ceremony as "laundry." The bride "cleans" the sheets she and her husband slept in the night before. She does not physically wash them because her mother is supposed to keep them as proof of her daughter's chastity. The symbolic cleaning is a ceremony where the groom gives a present to express his satisfaction. The bride organizes a party with her friends during which they wash some other clothes. The "cleaning" marks the bride's second step into adulthood, the first being when she menstruated for the first time. That monthly experience is also called "laundry."

I should stress that many practices associated with Islam are aspects of Arabic culture that predated the religion. In fact, in one of our interviews, my mother explained that Islam is against the publicity surrounding the virginity of the bride. In the past, the sheets were exhibited for everyone to see. Even though Islam expects both men and women to be virgins at marriage, as sex is only allowed within matrimony, the virginity test is mentioned neither in the *Qurʾān* nor in the *Hadīth*.[3]

Whether the *laabaan* ceremony is alien or not, it has been practiced for generations. Although it is vanishing today, its existence underscores the importance given to sexuality in Wolof culture.

THE *LAABAN* CEREMONY AND THE FIGHT FOR ITS SURVIVAL

The following verses are accompanied by seven drumbeats played early in the morning to let people know that a bride is a virgin:

> Mbaar
> The hyena
> Whoever does not know Mbaar
> Has heard
> Its howl
> Mbaar
> The hyena.

The drummers accompany these verses to announce the good news to the neighborhood and prepare for the *laabaan*. In many cases, the drummers already know that the bride was "given" to her husband the night before. Hence, they are ready the next morning. Wherever women are, they rush to finish their chores and head to the bride's house. Most arrive with praises and congratulations to the mother.

Laabaan is a ceremony organized by women for women. It provides the bride, her friends, and any other sexually active woman who is present with very important sexual education grounded in the culture. It can take place at the bride's parents' home or at the bride's new home the morning after she joins her husband, depending on where they sleep together for the first time. Most often, it happens at the bride's home. Because they cannot accompany their married daughter to her new home, most mothers want to be present when she goes through her first sexual experience. In many cases, the family of the bride is informed that the groom wants to "take his wife."[4] The "taking" is often permitted only when the groom has fulfilled all the clauses of the bridewealth transaction. In cases when he has not met all financial requirements, the bride's family is often hesitant to allow him to be alone with her for fear the couple may elope and not go through the ritual. This implies that the bride's family uses her virginity in order to "force" the groom to honor his financial responsibility. Otherwise, it may appear that the groom is only interested in sex.

The bride is prepared for her first sexual experience by her female family members. Men are almost never involved. The preparation for the night is led by the *baajan,* the bride's paternal aunt. She embarks on her task several days before by interrogating the bride to ascertain whether or not she is a virgin. If she is not, measures are taken by the women to fake the virginity or avoid the test.

On her nuptial night, the bride takes a ritual bath that combines Islamic and Wolof pre-Islamic practices. The young woman is bathed in herbs and waters prepared by local healers to cast away the evil eye. It is believed that virgin women are the targets of evil spirits because of their purity and innocence. While she is being bathed, some other paternal aunts make the bed. They burn incense in the room and spread a white cloth on the sheets to make sure that the stains from the hymen can be more visible. They also bless the room to make sure that their niece emerges from this experience with her head high. When all this has been done, the groom discretely enters the room to await his wife.

After the bath, the bride is dressed in a white wrap and is taken into the bedroom by the aunt, with the griotte behind her singing her praises. The aunt asks the bride to lie on her right hand and officially hands her to the groom by saying "here is your wife." After that, she leaves the room. My mother noted that in many cases, the aunt and the griotte sleep on a mat outside the room, out of concern about the outcome as well as because they are supposed to be the first to know the results of the intercourse at dawn. Early in the morning, the groom comes out and delivers the results. If the bride was a virgin, he tells the aunt that he is "happy." As soon as he says that, both the aunt and the griotte rush into the bedroom screaming and whistling, thus alerting the rest of the family and the neighborhood. They start praising the bride for meeting their expectations and honoring the family. The following words taken from one of the songs are often uttered.

You have done your share, you are innocent
The path that grandmother took,
Mother took, you have taken
May adulthood bring you luck.

Often, the groom leaves a considerable amount of money under the pillow
to signify his satisfaction. That money, called *ngegenaay*[5] (pillow), is distributed
among the griottes and the bride's "slaves."[6]

The sexual education of the bride begins at the very moment her aunt and
the griotte enter the room. She is now considered a woman and is treated as
one. The aunt asks her to sit up and spread her legs apart. The Wolof assume
that after the first sexual experience, blood remains in the woman's organ and
that if she sits up for a while, it will come out. The aunt then covers her with
the most expensive handwoven cloth while the griotte continues to sing her
praises.

The *laabaan* starts at dawn and lasts almost all day. Neighbors and friends
learn about the event from the sounds of the drums as well as from the screaming and praising by griottes. The bride's friends who are still single are also
invited to attend in order to learn from their friend's achievement. But they
are asked to cover their ears or leave when what are viewed as obscene things
are being said or discussed. They are also the pupils whom the griottes and
other women target for their lessons on sex and the importance of remaining a
virgin.

While the drums are played to announce the ceremony, the bride is given
a second bath. After that, she is dressed and brought into the bedroom where
she will lie down all day while the *laabaan* is being performed. A soup made of
lamb, vegetables, palm oil, and some medicinal herbs is then prepared for her.
In many cases the groom provides the bride with a "massage sheep." Because
the woman is supposed to be pampered for a whole week, a ram is offered by the
in-laws for her meals during that period. It is assumed that the young woman
has lost a great deal of blood. It is believed that by eating meat for a week, she
can replace that loss. She is also watched over during that week. Her paternal
aunt accompanies her everywhere she goes around the house to make sure that
she doesn't do anything that can physically harm her. For that week, she is exempt from physical chores and is forbidden to go outside the house.

She also does not sleep with her husband during that time. Because the first
night happened in the bride's home, the groom often doesn't come back until
the end of the week. He is supposed to let the bride rest from a supposedly very
exhausting first experience. Actually, his presence is a source of teasing for the
bride. Women tell her to run or hide because he is "coming after her." In cases
where he eloped with his wife, he creates much anger and invites verbal attacks

on him by the bride's family. In rural areas, women may assault him in the streets and pour water on him to express their anger. He is ridiculed because he was not man enough to face his wife's family in order to get an authorization to "take" her.

SPEAKING UP AGAINST CULTURAL CHANGE

The increasing rarity of *laabaan* ceremonies today, a phenomenon that suggests a growing lack of virgin brides, is a situation that is strongly condemned by the griottes whose songs I recorded. They use their songs to emphasize the fact that times have changed. Many women now come to marriage without being virgins. Parents then have to find ways to stain the sheets of the bride's nuptial bed with the blood of a chicken or some other animal. This is the reason why, in the following, Amy Thiam emphasizes the authenticity of the bride's hymen.

> The chicken has given me a message
> And I must deliver it.
> She says she is not afraid and she is not worried,
> She is not dead and none of her relatives is dead.

In cases when a bride was not a virgin, female family members would sometimes fake the hymen by staining the sheets with blood from a slaughtered chicken. Hence in the above song, the griotte authenticates the existence of the bride's hymen by using the metaphor of the chicken who communicates its happiness because it or its relatives did not have to die for this bride to get a hymen.

This faking of virginity and the tricks played by young couples to disguise their premarital sexual activity are the reason why most griottes have a piece of charcoal in their mouth when they perform *laabaan*. It is believed that if one sings *laabaan* when the bride has not been a virgin, one risks death or disaster for lying. Thus, the piece of charcoal is viewed as a means to protect against that possibility.

This survival move on the part of the griotte offers evidence of both the scarcity of girls who enter marriage as virgins and the griotte's concerns about the effect of modernity on the culture. Today, because many brides are not virgins and may have slept with their husbands during the dating period, couples elope right after the tying of the knot. They stay in hotels for several days and escape the test in that way. Many young people are also against the publicity surrounding their nuptial night, whether or not the bride is a virgin. This protest against the *laabaan* ceremony by younger generations of women constitutes a threat to the griottes' careers. The decline in the number of ceremonies results in reduced rewards for the griottes. For this reason, they do not hesitate to voice their concerns in their songs:

> Dear hymen, I have not seen you for a long time
> I have missed you so much.

The singer blames this shift on the intrusion of European civilization and in particular on the influence that Western education has on girls. To the extent that younger generations emulate European lifestyles and advocate women's sexual freedom, they become alienated from their traditional practices. Amy Thiam voices this concern and tries to remind young women that they can still embrace modernity without giving up the practice of remaining virgins until marriage.

> Going to school does not spoil the hymen
> Because the hymen is neither pen nor ink
> And one does not write with it.

> Going to dance parties does not spoil the hymen
> Because the hymen is neither music nor stereo
> And it is not a musical instrument that one plays with.

Amy Thiam denounces changes brought by girls' access to school and the shift in the youth lifestyle. Though she puts the blame on European civilization, she advocates resistance to change on the part of young girls and emphasizes the possibility for one to create a balance between tradition and modernity. To her, one can enjoy both without the risk of alienating the former.

Adji Diara also expresses such a view in the following song. She ridicules unmarried girls who are sexually active in the name of "modernity." In the song, *sasuman* means "sassy woman" and *kes* is an expression used when chasing a chicken.

> This is not the hymen of a *sasuman*[7]
> The *sasuman*'s hymen is in a pot
> With feathers over it
> When you say "*kes*" it flies.
> This is not the hymen of a *sasuman*.

Adji Diara employs much humor and sarcasm to depict the "modernized" woman's loss of her virginity. Instead of simply stating that "modern" girls end up losing their virginity before marriage, she offers a lengthy description of the hymen, which the listeners understand as a reference to a chicken that was sacrificed and whose blood was used to stain the sheets. In the next stanza, she implies that culturally alienated girls will instead get pregnant. In the song lyrics, *pis* is a term used for getting a baby's attention.

> You see, the *sasuman*'s hymen,
> It has legs,
> It has a belly button,
> It has ears,
> It has a mouth,
> It has hands,
> And eyes.
> They lay it in a crib
> When you say "*pis*" it smiles.
> This not the hymen of a *sasuman*!

The emphasis on the nature of the hymen communicates the griotte's and society's desire to teach abstinence to unmarried women. While a child's birth is a blessing, being pregnant while one is not married has become a source of disgrace and shame for the woman and her family, especially her mother. Ousmane Sembène portrayed this blame of the mother in his feminist film *Faat Kine*. When Kine was made pregnant by her philosophy teacher, her father tried to burn her and blamed his wife for their daughter's mischief. He later kicked both out of the home. This blame puts a great deal of pressure on mothers—hence the reason they go to great lengths to make sure that their daughters remain virgins or try to find ways to fake it when they are not. During the *laabaan* mothers are the ones whom the griottes and other women congratulate for a job well done.

> Virginity is a wrestling game
> Mothers are the cheerleaders
> Daughters play it.

SEXUAL BELIEFS AND THE SURVEILLANCE OF WOMEN'S BODIES

Because of the taboo about open discussion of sex in women's lives, the Wolof have a plethora of beliefs about anything related to sex. These beliefs are often about women and their bodies. Most of the songs in this essay seem to place more of the blame for premarital sex on women and on their bodies. Some of the songs address the inspection of unmarried women's bodies to determine whether or not they have had sexual experience. Though most of the pressure is inflicted by other women, by raising the issue of sexual experience such songs open the subject up to wider discussion. But at the same time, the foregrounding of sex here eases the minds of unmarried women who may have been having sex prior to marriage. This emphasis on controlling and spying on women's bodies is inscribed in women's awareness of the gender biases that exist in the culture. In the following stanza, Adji Diara empathizes with unmarried girls who may be facing such scrutiny.

> This song is dedicated to young girls
> Because when you are a young woman in the neighborhood
> You will hear all kinds of things.

The apparent changes that occur in women's bodies are interpreted in reference to their marital status. While the changes in married women's bodies in relation to sex are validated, those in unmarried women's bodies are questioned and given negative meanings. Girls' bodies are under constant surveillance by other women in the community. Whether they are sexually active or not is determined by physical factors such as weight gain, manner of walking, and other indicators.

> Look at the way she walks,
> She has been spoiled a long time ago.

> Look, her buttocks are so big because of men
> Don't cry,
> These are words from your enemy
> If it were your mother she would say:
> "My daughter has gained weight."

Young unmarried women are under much pressure at this stage in their lives. Their every movement is observed and evaluated. For example, some mothers listen to their daughters in the bathroom to find out whether they sound louder when they urinate. It is believed that when a woman is sexually active, her urination is louder. As Adji Diara so boldly puts it, the genital organs of unmarried women, like their voices, must be silent.

> A silent vagina,
> I prefer that to a vagina that honks like a car!

Also, because among the Wolof, as in many parts of Africa, a child belongs to everyone, older women do not hesitate to question the mother of a young girl in order to find out if she is pregnant. Other women in the community are often the first to notice the changes in her body. As a result, many girls are falsely accused of pregnancy. Because of modern medicine and access to contraceptives, many old women feel that young girls can easily get away with premarital sex.

> This girl has had an abortion
> While you have never been pregnant,
> Don't answer.

This constant surveillance of unmarried women's bodies and moves makes it difficult for them to visit a gynecologist even for routine examinations. It is assumed that women who visit gynecologists or any clinics where females are seen must be sexually active. Unmarried women who dare to enter such places are labeled as prostitutes or unruly women who are affirming their sexual promiscuity without shame. In the lyrics, P.M.I., Prevention Maternelle et Infantine, is a healthcare system for women.

> Night and day she is at the P.M.I.[8]
> While you have never been pregnant,
> Don't answer.

This pattern limits young women's movements and access to medical care by linking the places they enter to their sexual status. For example, hotels are assumed to be places where only prostitutes go, and any woman who is seen at a hotel is immediately stigmatized as "bad." This is due to the fact that most African men bring their mistresses to hotels and Western tourists in search of sexual adventure seek local women in those places. The hotel cited in the first line is well known in Dakar.

> Night and day she is at the Hotel de Paris
> While you have never known a man,
> Don't answer.

VIRGINITY: HONOR OR DISGRACE?

Because *laabaan* is a celebration of virginity, most of the songs deal with rewards received for abstaining from sex before marriage. Virgin brides are offered many presents from their husbands and in-laws. Pleased with the fact that they are the bride's first sexual partner, many men go to excess to show their satisfaction by fulfilling any fantasy a bride of her generation might have. Depending on their financial resources, some men give a stereo, a television, gold jewelry, a car, or even a house. Thus, staying a virgin becomes a means for a woman to obtain material wealth from her husband. Although this may not appear to be a very appropriate way of gaining power for women, because the bride's body is used for material gain, it can be seen as an intelligent strategy for women to manipulate men who are obsessed with being the first and only one to ever sexually possess the woman. Thus, *laabaan* songs always stress the rewards for being a virgin bride.

> Vagina, vagina, vagina
> Its name is not "vagina"
> Its name is "honor"
> Whoever spoils it does not know its value.
> A beautiful house,
> From the vagina!
> A nice car,
> From the vagina!
> A box of jewels,
> From the vagina!
> A television,
> From the vagina!
> Honoring your mother,
> From the vagina!
> Honoring your paternal aunt,
> From the vagina!
> Honoring your friends,
> From the vagina!
> Honoring yourself,
> From the vagina!

For a girl in Wolof society, being a virgin offers evidence of her good up-bringing and virtue. It is assumed that if a woman is able to remain a virgin until marriage, she will definitely be a good and faithful wife. She has proven to be very strong in front of men's temptations. However, one wonders whether the fact of abstaining from sex is empowering or detrimental to women in Wolof society. It is clearly understood that depending on the decisions women make about their genital organs, they can either obtain a wealth of material goods from their husband, or they can be subject to shame and blame from the community. The use of "prestige goods" to reward virgin brides confirms the materialism that evolved within the culture. This turns young women into "vaginas for sale," implying that their personal and intellectual qualities do not matter much in the eyes of men. The latter's eagerness to control women's bod-

ies and the society's "commercialization" of women is emphasized by the practice of giving rewards to women who are virgins at marriage. In the example
below, the price of the vagina in CFA francs is approximately U.S.$100.

> There is a vagina among vaginas
> One buys it with fifty thousand francs
> A watch and a stereo
> When you are not satisfied you're given more.

Though abstinence might be seen, then, as a good practice in contemporary
Wolof society, especially considering the threat of AIDS and other sexually
transmitted diseases, the beliefs and gender biases that surround the practice
are not so empowering for women. They echo the same materialism that cor-
rupted the old custom of bridewealth and the practice of the virginity check.

This exploitation of women's bodies is more prominent today, with the chronic
unemployment that exists among young people. To guarantee themselves a
bright future, most young women look for men who can materially take care of
them. The duplication of the common Wolof name Modou refers to Senegalese
men working abroad.

> If you hold it,
> You can get a cellular phone!
> If you hold it,
> The penis of a Modou-Modou[9] can get in there!

> If you hold it,
> You can get a visa!

> If you hold it,
> You can go the United States of America!

In modern day Senegal, there is what I call the Modou-Modou syndrome. Because many of these Senegalese migrants to France or the United States seek
what amount to mail-order brides, women remain virgins in the hope of land-
ing one of those "good catches." There is a trend for girls to marry expatriate
Senegalese men whom the people believe to be rich. The girls who dream of
joining their husbands in foreign countries are rarely aware of the difficulties
these migrants encounter abroad. This situation speaks to the problems of un-
derdevelopment and its relation to women's bodies. As pointed out in the songs,
the abstinence of women is influenced more by hopes of material well-being
than by fear of contacting sexually transmitted diseases. Clearly, the lyrics
underscore women's efforts to survive as a factor in economic underdevelop-
ment. While it is generally hard to find jobs, the chances are more limited for

women than for men. For this reason, engaging in a marriage that provides financial security is one of the few alternatives available to women.

The preference for virgins is disappearing in Senegal, but some men are still eager to be the first and only sexual partner of the woman. They still refer to the act of defloration as "opening a new can of milk." It boosts their egos and gives them a sense of ownership over the woman's body. As Holtzman and Kulish put it, "'To have a virgin' carries with it the connotations of being the first, educating, exerting control, and possessing" (1997, 8). Simone de Beauvoir argued,

> In breaking the hymen man takes possession of the feminine body more intimately than by penetration that leaves it intact; in the irreversible act of defloration he makes of that body unequivocally a passive object, he affirms his capture of it. (1949, 174)

This desire to be the only one who has sexually possessed a woman is the reason that wives are sent back to the family or beaten by the groom because the bride is not a virgin. In their frustration, some husbands take back the gifts given during the bridewealth transaction.

Another reason why women remain virgins is the pressure that exists within the marital household. Being a virgin inscribes the bride among women of virtue and is a source of respect from her husband and his family. Women believe that arriving at marriage a virgin gives them emotional security and shields them from the potential abuses of in-laws and husbands. As long as they were virgins, the in-laws should not have any reason to reproach them.

> Dear hymen,
> It is a foundation in marriage
> It is remedy.
> No matter how much you quarrel
> Your husband will not despise you
> You have given him hymen!

Women who are not virgins are chastised. Men use the women's premarital sexual activity to abuse or blackmail them should they attempt to assert their rights within the marriage. The fear of having their secrets known to everyone makes certain women accept abuse. For this reason, the songs emphasize the security and peace of mind a woman gets from being a virgin at marriage.

> You insult him,
> He will not despise you.
> You have given him hymen!

You talk back at him,
He will not despise you.
You have given him hymen!

Thus, the hymen becomes a token for married women to assert their rights. Often during quarrels a woman may point to the fact that her husband should not treat her with disrespect because she was a virgin at marriage.

You yell at him,
He will not despise you
You have given him hymen!
You fight back,
He will not despise you
you have given him hymen!

Whether virginity at marriage provides women with rights and encourages their husbands to treat them with respect is very debatable. The fact that they can claim respect only because of the decision they made about their sexual organ before marriage is disempowering and at the same time stressful. "Providing hymen" has become a security deposit that women have to give their husbands. However, women must rely on it to claim their rights within marriage. Whether it works is another issue.

GENDER BIASES ABOUT PREMARITAL SEX

Among the Wolof, premarital sex has become a dangerous act for women because they are blamed for it. Men who have sex with many women are perceived as affirming their manhood, while their unmarried female partners are seen as promiscuous. The following song performed by Adji Diara underscores that view.

I say one vagina,
Twenty circumcised penises.
You give some to the Griot,
You give some to the Laobe,
You give some to the Toucouleur,
You give some to the Manjak,[10]
You give some to the Noble,
What is left of it?
Nothing is left of it!
Contain the vaginas and have sex the legal way
Being a virgin is the in thing nowadays.

Adji represents the vagina as a consumable good and claims that if a woman has sex with several men, she eventually uses it up. The enumeration of the different types of lovers in the above song speaks to the woman's carelessness and her big sexual appetite, which again is frowned upon in females. A man's sexual appetite is viewed as normal, whereas that of a woman is abnormal. As she puts it, vaginas have to be contained. For women, sex is allowed only within marriage. Women are held responsible for non-marital sex because their sexuality is feared and they are viewed as seducers. Hence their sexuality is the one that needs to be controlled and regulated to prevent society from drifting into promiscuity and sin. This bias is very apparent in the songs. Women are themselves caught up in the idea and believe it is their duty to prevent non-marital sex.

> Leave men alone
> Men have done nothing.
> When a penis sees a vagina,
> Of course it gets hard.

Men' sexual weaknesses are thus legitimated and confirmed, while women's sexual desire is suppressed. Adji Diara composed the following song that tells the story of how a promiscuous young girl with a voracious sexual appetite literally raped a young man in front of his mother.

> She took off Pathe's jacket
> And threw it on the floor
> Pathe did not react.
> She grabbed his tie
> And threw it on the floor
> Pathe did not react.
> She took off his shirt
> And threw it on the floor
> Pathe did not react.
> She took off his glasses
> And threw them on the floor
> Pathe did not react.
> She took off his pants
> And threw them on the floor
> Pathe did not react.

The song underscores the man's innocence and his unwillingness to participate in the sexual act unless he is forced by the woman.

He said: "Mother, I want you to bear witness
You know only a man goes out to look for sex
And comes back empty-handed.
But when a woman goes out to look for sex
She definitely gets it.
She came to me."

The song positions women as sexual predators and men as the defenseless victims of the former's insatiable lust. The lyrics suggest that however strong the sexual desires of women, they, in contrast to men, are supposed to be able to control their sexual instincts. In the song below, the man reacts automatically to a light-skinned women.

Any girl who bleaches her skin really well
And enters a man's room,
He will fuck her until she is sore
And kick her butt home.

Sex is used to reward or punish women depending on their marital status. If the woman is not a wife, rough sex is employed to tame her and teach her a lesson, as indicated by the mother's response to the "victim" in the following lines.

Pathe, fuck her until she gets sore
She came to you.
Pathe, fuck her until she gets dizzy
She came to you.

If one has not paid a penny[11] for a vagina
One does not have pity on its owner!

These lyrics appear at first to be contradictory. While Adji Diara seems to say that loose women are punished with rough sex and that wives whose vaginas are paid for are treated gently during intercourse, she relegates the latter to the rank of a prostitute who also gets money for sex. However, her nuance is very clear. While the prostitute's body is temporarily possessed, that of the wife is permanently owned, at least for the duration of the marriage, and constitutes in some ways an investment for the husband. Being rough with her during sex threatens her durability as a material possession. One can deduce then that the Wolof see sex as something that can be used to reward or punish a woman. Only those who have sex within the marital institution deserve respect and gentleness, whereas those who dare to stray away from that rule are roughed up as a way of putting them in their place. Girls who are sexually active are seen as loose and deserve only disrespect and abuse from men. Those who become pregnant run the risk of having their lovers refuse paternity for the child.

In Wolof culture, mothers and aunts are the ones who handle paternity disputes in the case of pregnancy outside marriage. When a girl accuses a man of being responsible for her pregnancy, her mother and other female family members go to visit his mother. Often the family of the man questions the validity of the allegation by the young woman who, according to them, was reckless enough to have sex before marriage. Many men are advised by their mothers to refuse responsibility, because for them, a girl who engages in sex before marriage cannot be trusted to have slept with only one partner.

> Men are not stupid
> Men's mothers are not stupid.
> If a girl is serious they will marry her
> If a girl is not serious they will fuck her
> And leave her to be a burden to her mother.

The father of the man will avoid if at all possible getting involved in a paternity dispute because it is an embarrassing event. This response reflects the saying, "when a child is good, he or she belongs to everyone, but when he or she is bad, the child belongs to his or her mother alone." As in most cases, mothers are responsible for any mistakes their children make. The mothers of non-virgin brides are shunned and looked down upon. Their ways of upbringing are questioned, and even their morality is subject to scrutiny. Not being a virgin is a sign of promiscuity even if the girl has slept only once with her lover. She is compared to a prostitute who wanders around bars and offers sexual services to men in exchange for a drink or a little money. The following song illustrates in blunt terms this widespread view:

> There is a vagina among vaginas
> Only a bottle of beer
> And "fuck your mother home"
> Is its price!

This attitude puts unwed mothers in a very difficult position. Not only do they have to undergo pregnancy and its expenses alone; they must face the anger of their families and communities.

These lyrics underscore Wolof society's gender biases and its demands on women. Mothers are blamed for their daughters' mistakes and end up providing the only support for pregnant girls. Men often do not feel they have any responsibility for extramarital pregnancy. Most girls are kicked out of their homes by their fathers, who feel it is a shame to be pregnant without getting married. While they perpetuate the sexual double standards regarding nonmarital sex and the negative perception of women, these lyrics are inscribed in women's awareness of the demands of society. They emphasize men's disre-

spectful treatment of sexual partners to whom they are not married. By point-
ing to the unfair treatment of women as far as non-marital sex is concerned, the
singers underscore men's privileged position.

ABSTINENCE AS RESISTANCE

One can look at the abstinence of unmarried girls as a way of resisting men's
disrespect. Beyond the fear of being ridiculed and shamed if one were to arrive
at marriage without being a virgin, society's biases against sexually active unmarried women and men's harsh treatment of the latter are also a reason why
many young women choose to abstain from sex until marriage. Many men talk
their girlfriends into having sex and later treat them as loose and "bad" because
they are vulnerable to their sweet talk. Because of the materialism that has pre-
vailed in the culture, men utilize money to lure girls. Often, women fall into
those traps. Aware of the tricks played on women by men, the griottes compose
their lyrics to teach feminist awareness to young women. In the lyrics below,
1000 CFA francs are worth approximately U.S.$2.

> So Pathe outsmarted her.
> He played with her until she was spoiled
> And said to her:
> Go away, I have spoiled you.
> I am not going to marry you. Goodbye!
> That's what they do.
> Beware of them.
> They will promise you 10,000 CFA.
> But they will not give you 500 CFA.
> I assure you whomever they sleep with for 500 CFA.
> They will not give you 500,000 CFA.[12]
> Because if he does not have money to buy cigarettes and matches
> And his pants have holes at the bottom,
> Where is he going to get 5,000 CFA?
> Beware of these young men.

Adji Diara teaches young women how to spot honest men. Those who promise
castles and jewels but do not have enough for their own personal needs are to
be avoided. The griottes' songs serve as a call for women not to fall for men's
hypocritical claims of genuine love.

> I love you, you love me
> If I sleep with you I will marry you.

Ndeye Mareme says: she does not want that
She prefers a day of honor.

I love you, you love me
If you get pregnant I will marry you.
Ndeye Mareme says: that's not what she wants
She prefers to be a virgin.

Abstinence has become a tool of resistance against men's conniving behavior. Of course, this does not guarantee that a girl's future husband will not disrespect her if he wants to. But at least within marriage, their sexuality is validated. Standing up against a husband's abuse will be legitimate and even supported. Unmarried girls who are sexually active are deprived of the right to fight back. Their engagement in non-marital sex strips them of their right to demand respect from men.

Thus, abstinence becomes one way to avoid abuse and mistreatment. Girls who are virgins at marriage are said to have escaped men's machinations to sleep with them. Their mothers also receive praise for the abstinence of their daughters:

Tell me where you bred[13] her for her to escape men
For me to go breed there
Whoever has a daughter should bring her to you.

These lyrics reveal that women are aware of men's constant attempts to seduce girls and contradict the idea that women are the ones who initiate non-marital sex. The singer acknowledges how difficult it is for young women to stand up to men's advances. Thus, while the songs often reprimand women for their behavior as far as non-marital sex is concerned, they at the same time suggest that men do initiate non-marital sex and often are responsible for seducing girls. Girls who remain virgins until marriage are then heroines who have been able to "escape," thus confirming their strength and their unwillingness to be "toys" for men who are in search of sexual adventure.

DARING TO SPEAK ABOUT SEX

If sex is repressed—that is, condemned to prohibition, non-existence, and silence—then the mere fact that one is speaking about it has the appearance of a deliberate transgression. A person who holds forth in such language places himself or herself to a certain extent outside the reach of power; he or she upsets established law; he somehow anticipates the coming of freedom (Foucault 1976, 6).

From the evidence in the lyrics it is clear that *laabaan* songs are inscribed in this dynamic of subversion pointed out by Foucault. Beyond its celebratory function, *laabaan* becomes a place where women dare to talk about sex regardless of society's strict prohibition against such topics. The songs become a medium of transgression of cultural and religious laws and allow women to discuss the taboo of sex without fear of reprimand.

Outside the *laabaan* space, the Wolof are not atypical in their ways of approaching debates about sex. It is never discussed in public. People often use nicknames for sexual organs or anything related to them. Those who make sexual references or talk about their sex lives in public are labeled as perverts.

Laabaan then becomes a space for transgression of social order. In fact, many men think that it should be proscribed, for it perpetuates the promiscuity of women. During my research, there were many instances when the head of the household (usually the father of the bride) decided that a *laabaan* ceremony would not be held in his house although he condoned the ceremonial taking of the bride. On those occasions, women moved the ceremony to a neighbor's house. In cases where the male authority does not forbid the celebration, most male family members leave the house early in the morning. Not only is their presence a violation of women's space, but they also dread women's language during *laabaan*. When a man dares to be present, women often use him as a guinea pig in their sexually explicit demonstrations. *Laabaan* singers openly name sexual organs and the sexual act. They go into very graphic details and have a lot of fun doing so.

> I say look,
> I say girls get ready
> A lot of things are in fashion with men.
> So children get ready.
> I say the kind of lovemaking men do,
> The kind of kiss men do,
> The kind of caressing men give,
> If you are not a virgin
> What are you going to tell your mother?

Like *xaxar,* the verbal fight between co-wives that is a place where women voice their concerns about polygamy, *laabaan* provides a space for female bonding and debating on a subject that only the songs allow them to explore. Their language becomes a language of transgression and boldness. This is carried over into modern songs, where singers such as Adji Diara are most sought after because of their obscene and straightforward style. A good *laabaan* singer is the one who can say the most shocking things. The songs prompt women to drift into their sexual fantasies and explore areas that, in a regular societal setting, they dare not venture into. For example,

> There is a difference between having sex with a wife
> And having sex with a girlfriend.
> I say the way one has sex with a wife
> And the way one has sex with a girlfriend are not comparable!
> Because they are not the same!
> It is not the same!
> There is a double standard!

Here she reiterates the view expressed earlier that when men make love to their wives, they are more gentle and loving. Girlfriends are roughed up because of their assumed promiscuity, attested to by the fact that they dare to engage in sex without being married.

CONCLUSION

The rhetoric of the songs and the topics debated shows the ease and freedom of language that women enjoy within the *laabaan* space. Thus, *laabaan* as a gendered space produces an epistemological shift, allowing women to articulate their sexuality in a culture that represses sex and confines it to strict rules that are particularly violent and discriminatory toward women. In the largely Islamized Wolof society, *laabaan* performers have become agents of female resistance against religious patriarchy. Despite the culture's ongoing attempt to eliminate the performance, women like Adji Diara as well as Amy Thiam and Khady Thiam continue to have their voices heard, and in so doing, break the taboo wrapped around sex. They also offer the novice bride an opportunity to benefit from a sexual education in a socio-culturally approved format.

NOTES

1. *Neenyo* is the artisanal caste which includes griots, blacksmiths, jewelers, leatherworkers, and woodworkers. The term has evolved to refer to people who are from the sub-group of metal workers.

2. This and all other translations are by me unless otherwise indicated.

3. The *Hadīth* includes sayings of the Prophet that are not in the Qurʿān but constitute the second reference for Muslims.

4. "The taking" is meant in a sexual way without openly saying that the groom wants to have sexual intercourse with his wife.

5. It is also called *ndampaay* or *mbërënti*.

6. The word here does not mean people who are socially categorized as slaves. Rather, it refers to the bride's first cousins who are sons and daughters of her paternal aunts. Because the Wolof society is patrilineal, the children of a brother have power over those of a sister. They entertain a relationship of "master/mistress" and "servants." Any ceremony celebrating the "master/mistress" is an opportunity for the "servants" to receive gifts. They perform some domestic chores during the ceremony, and also, with griots and griottes, they are in charge of the entertainment.

7. *Sasuman* is a deformation of "sassy woman." It is Gambian slang that ended up meaning a Westernized young person, especially male.

8. P.M.I. (Prevention Maternelle et Infantine, or Maternal and Infantile Prevention) is a healthcare system put in place to help women with childbirth, contraception, sexual diseases, and anything that has to do with maternity.

9. Modou is a very common name for Wolof men. This term was created to refer to Senegalese men who are living and working abroad. They are believed to be rich and good catches. Most Senegalese girls dream of marrying one. Often, these men spend a lot of money on women. They own the most beautiful houses and drive the nicest cars when they get back from abroad.

10. The Laobe are a sub–ethnic group of the Pulaar who are woodworkers. The Toucouleur are an ethnic group in Senegal. They used to be nomads, but due to their conversion to Islam, they became sedentary. The Manjak are another ethnic group, living in the south of Senegal.

11. The payment here refers to the bridewealth, which transfers sexual rights to the husband. The girlfriend has not received bridewealth, so having sex with her is free.

12. This is in reference to what one can get for bridewealth.

13. The mother is perceived as a shepherd who must have taken good care of her children for them to turn out to be good individuals in the eyes of the society.

WORKS CITED

Boilat, David. 1984. *Esquisses Sénégalaises*. Paris: Karthala.

Combs-Schilling, E. M. 1989. *Sacred Performances: Islam, Sexuality, and Sacrifice*. New York: Columbia University Press.

De Beauvoir, Simone. 1949. *Le Deuxième Sexe*. Paris: Gallimard.

Diouf, Aminata. 2003a. Interview by Marame Gueye. 10 April. Telephone.

———. 2003b. Interview by Marame Gueye. 30 September. Kaolack, Senegal.

Foucault, Michel. 1976. *Histoire de la Sexualité*. Vol 1, *La Volonté de Savoir*. Paris: Gallimard, 1976.

Holtzman, Deanna, and Nancy Kulish. 1997. *Nevermore: The Hymen and the Loss of Virginity*. Northvale, N.J.: Jason Aronson.

Kandji, Saliou Samba Malaado, and Fatou Kine Camara. 2000. *L'Union matrimoniale dans la tradition des peuples noirs*. Paris: l'Harmattan.

Mernissi, Fatima. 1987. *Beyond the Veil: Male-Female Dynamics in a Modern Muslim Society*. Bloomington: Indiana University Press.

Niang, Adji Diara. 2003a. Interview by Marame Gueye. 9 October. Kaolack, Senegal.

———. 2003b. Private performance recorded by Marame Gueye. 26 September. Kaolack, Senegal.

Sembène, Ousmane, dir. 2000. *Faat Kine.* Video cassette. San Francisco, Calif.: California Newsreel.

Thiam, Amy, and Khady Thiam. 1998. Private performance recorded by the author. 25 November. Dakar, Senegal.

2

Jola Kanyalen *Songs from the Casamance, Senegal*

FROM "TRADITION" TO GLOBALIZATION

Kirsten Langeveld

One of the distinctive features of many Sahelian peoples is the hierarchical nature of their society, a trait that is not gender-specific. But among women, there are particular forms of hierarchy that may result from conditions emerging when a woman reaches adulthood. This is a phenomenon that may occur across the region, as in the *maani foori* rituals based on a blend of traditions of the Hausa and the Songhoy-Zarma of Niger. As Sidikou explains, women involved in *maani foori* establish a power relationship between "fat" women and "thin" women in the larger context of what she describes as a woman-centered shadow system of government (Sidikou 2001, 58–79). This form of stratification is quite different, however, from the one described in this paper. The purpose here is not to undertake a regional study of this phenomenon, but to examine more closely the procedure by which a woman's status changes among the Jola people in the Casamance region of southern Senegal.[1] The shift occurs through a ritual called *kanyalen*. Songs are a means for the woman who undergoes the *kanyalen* ritual to express her position in society.

Change in the status of an individual through ritual is a commonplace that, as Turner (1969) pointed out, is a reflection of society. Bell (1992) added that ritual is also a means to effect change. In other words, ritual does not stand apart from daily reality but belongs to it. The *kanyalen* ritual is also designed to effect change—in this case to the lives of the women who undergo it.

Other scholars have examined different dimensions of the ritual (Journet 1976; Fassin and Badji 1986; Fassin 1987; Weil 1976; Fels 1994) but not the changes that are occurring today. The focus of this paper is the lyrics of the *kanyalen* ritual and in particular the following questions: what are the dynamics of the ritual, how does this ritual change because of globalization, and how do lyrics convey the effects of globalization?

RITUALS AND SONGS

In Jola society songs are sung on various occasions, ranging from day-to-day activities to more formal rituals for a variety of purposes. Each ritual has its own songs. Broadly speaking, Jola songs often raise issues that cannot otherwise be explicitly discussed in public. Every occasion that deviates from the normal order provides an opportunity for composing a song. The lyrics are marked by metaphors, real names are inverted or replaced by pseudonyms, and words are hidden behind ambiguous exclamations such as "he he he ho ho ho." But everyone knows who is being addressed. The content of the song may have a direct influence on the listener. For example, songs that criticize a person's conduct shame the individual so that he or she will change his or her conduct or, more drastically, decide to leave the village.

Apart from these songs known to most people in a society, each sex has a repertoire of secret songs. Members of the older generations transmit the songs to the younger people during the initiation ritual in the Forest.[2] Learning the songs does not lead immediately to comprehension of the lyrics. Each generation is allowed to acquire a certain quantity of secret knowledge[3] which the elders yield up only to generations that have reached the stage of being able to guard the secrets of the Forest. In this "gerontocratic" society, the oldest generation typically exercises authority over all the secret knowledge on which its power is based (cf. Herbert 1993, 2). I place the term *gerontocratic* in quotation marks, however, because in fact the younger adult generation has an increasing say in a variety of family decisions such as migration to the cities (De Jong 2001; Mark 1985; Van der Klei 1989).

Songs are an important dimension of the *kanyalen* ritual. Every *kanyalen* group has its own repertoire that can be sung during rituals and other ceremonies. Every *anyalena,* or woman who has undergone the ritual, has her own songs that she composes mostly by herself, and they often express her fate. The lyrics she invents are, like the other songs, filled with metaphors, verbal inversions, and other devices to convey meaning through ambiguity, which, on the surface, makes the lyrics quite difficult to explain.

JOLA SOCIETY AND THE *KANYALEN* RITUAL

Before going any further into the *kanyalen* ritual, however, it is important to provide a wider cultural framework. The Jola live in the Lower Casamance, one of the most fertile areas of Senegal. The main agricultural activity in the villages is rice cultivation. In the Buluf region, where I have been conducting my fieldwork, this activity is divided between the sexes.

The Jola are organized in sex and age groups. The division of these groups starts at an early age. One of the functions of these groups is to form economic units. For example, a group of married women can be hired by someone who needs to harvest the rice crop. A sum of money is agreed on and the group works for this person. The group may also engage in other commercial activities to earn money (cf. Gerbrandy 1987). The women use the income to help other women in need—for example, an *anyalena* who is under the protection of this group.

Jola society is largely Islamic and polygamous. People live in patrilineal units in which marriage is exogamous by reference to one's own descent group but almost always endogamous within the village. In Jola society, the only way for a woman to be fully recognized as an adult is by becoming a mother within a marriage. After her first delivery, a woman is allowed to participate in rituals in the Forest of women. These spaces are different from other "forests," hence the capitalization of this particular sacred place. It is here that the most important women's secrets are guarded. The more knowledge of these secrets a woman acquires, the more authority accrues to her in the women's world.

Women become *anyalena* as a solution for particular problems, a transformation that changes their status. But not all difficulties drive a woman to undergo the ritual. For example, if a woman remains infertile, her status drops and she risks being divorced by her husband. If she is lucky, he will keep her but take on another wife. For a childless wife there is no ritual to change her condition one way or another. She must simply accept her fate.

On the other hand, women who have miscarriages or lose their children prematurely, before weaning, can participate in the *kanyalen* ritual, which represents the cultural accommodation of such unfortunate situations. Although the Jola recognize these women as "real" because they have given birth, they have to accept a role that places them outside the normal social categories.

A woman whose children die one after another prematurely, or who has children of only one sex, is believed to be the object of attack by evil forces. In response to this assault, the woman undergoes the *kanyalen* ritual and receives the status of an *anyalena,* which definitively changes her identity. She may also become an *anyalena* if her husband mistreats her. As a consequence, she will lose her authority in the society of married women. As tokens of this new identity, she will receive a new name and a special costume. From now on she has to behave like a clown. She manifests this new status by dancing, singing, and, in general, always appearing to be gay.

The *kanyalen* initiation ritual can take place inside or outside her village, but it must be in a place different from where she normally resides. She will live at this new location for about two years following her initiation. During this period she will be deprived of all the authority of a married woman. Usually, a group of women has responsibility for her. She owes obedience to this group or a person within it. She lives for these two years apart from her husband, who will not follow her to her "hiding" place. In general, it is not the woman who makes the decision to become an *anyalena,* and quite often her husband disapproves of her acquiring this new status. For example, in one case a husband threatened to call the police when another woman took his wife and initiated her as an *anyalena.* The women involved composed a song about the husband's resistance. Usually, the women of the village decide that one of their number has lost too many children and that, when the woman is pregnant again, action should be taken. The initiation ritual often takes the unfortunate woman by surprise: she is brought to the initiation site under false pretences. She has to be deceived because the status of *anyalena* is not at all attractive. One informant compared it to slavery. Indeed, one of the obligations of an *anyalena* is that she has to agree to all the demands made on her by anyone, even persons younger than herself, without exception. Obeying orders from people younger than herself is one indicator of the transformation of her status and identity. Another sign is that she is given a new first name and sometimes a new second name. The new first name is often one that is not normally given to a person but is the name of an animal, such as Dog or Pig, an institution, or a business—for example, Sotiba, a company in Dakar. Often she adopts the second name of the family that hosts her. Sometimes this leads to a change of ethnicity.

An example is a Creole woman who is an *anyalena* and is protected by a Jola family. When she sings, she uses Jola, not her own language.[4] Another mark of the identity transformation of the *anyalena* is the special costume that she has to wear during rituals and ceremonies. Her identity transformation is also expressed in her conduct. From the moment she is initiated as an *anyalena,* she has to change her behavior. At rituals she is expected to be the passage-maker, the first and last to dance. She must be provocative, break sexual taboos, and sometimes act in a childish manner. Finally, she must compose songs to be sung during rituals—a theme I will elaborate on below.[5] The following case, summarized from my field notes, illustrates the behavior of an *anyalena.*

In Sukupapaye, a ward of Ziguinchor, people had gathered in front of the house of one of my informants where an *anyalena* lived. They were in a festive mood because the ward was celebrating the visit of a high official. Around the corner the road was blocked and a square was made in which chairs were placed and a piece of tarpaulin was spread to protect the visitors from the sun. On one side a little stage was created, and loud music came from speakers in boxes. A woman with sweets passed the house of the *anyalena* and tried to sell her wares to a mother standing in front of a house accompanied by her child. The mother bought for her child a little bag of sweets made of a mixture of sugar, millet, and pounded peanuts. Happy and with a satisfied expression on his face, the child started eating, but an *anyalena*, who was standing there too, grasped the bag and took some of the candy, saying that she too was a child. To the great hilarity of other women watching the scene, the child started to cry, whereupon the *anyalena* returned the sweets to the child. Thereafter the *anyalena* started to "beg" the saleswoman to give her a bag, too, but the vendor did not give in. The *anyalena* called her insulting names such as *solima,* the term for a woman who has not undergone the ceremony of initiation that transforms girls into women. Then they both made gestures: they raised their hands and moved their thumbs up and down. Then they put their fingers in their mouths and made a clicking noise with their tongues.

According to one of my assistants, both gestures described in the above case have obscene meanings: the first gesture means that the individual "will cut your clitoris"; the second means "you make love for such a long time that it makes this clack-clack noise when you have sex and your vagina is very large." All that needs to be said here is that this kind of behavior is not that of a "normal" woman. But it is acceptable in an *anyalena,* and it is hoped that in this way the evil forces that have caused her original condition will be warded off.

After two years, if her child is still alive, the *anyalena* who has had a child can return to her husband. The homecoming ceremony is celebrated like a marriage. Although she joins her husband in his ward, the *anyalena* will never become a normal woman again: the status she accepted as the result of the *kanyalen* ritual will remain with her all her life. In other words, she sacrifices her status and her power in order to have and keep children.

To sum up, an *anyalena* has no authority, and her right to make decisions is abrogated. She is confined like a child, but, conversely, also has to act provocatively. Her emphasis on sexuality breaks sexual taboos. Her identity is shorn of the "normal" social values.

KANYALEN ENTERING THE GLOBALIZING WORLD

During my fieldwork in January and February 2003, it became clear that changes in the *kanyalen* ritual reflected the entry of women into the globalizing world. In Ziguinchor I found a discrepancy between the facts and what the participants said about the continuation of the ritual. Informants claimed that the *kanyalen* tradition was declining for religious reasons and they could hardly name any "real" *anyalena*. But at the same time I found that there are between ten to fifteen *kanyalen* groups in this city, with about forty members each. The groups operate independently of each other. In fact, the members of each share a common village of origin. The questions are, just how has their situation changed and what is the cause?

Like the Jola, the Balanta, who inhabit the same region as well as Guinea-Bissau to the south, also maintain the *kanyalen* ritual. One group of Balanta *kanyalen* from a ward of Ziguinchor entered the global economy by earning money in commercials. The women were asked by Maggi, a large food conglomerate, to act in a commercial. Maggi paid this group a large sum of money and gave them yards of yellow cloth with the word *Maggi* printed on it in red letters, similar to the logo and the colors Maggi uses for its products. The women made dresses out of the cloth and wore them during the commercial.

For several reasons this Balanta *kanyalen* group asked me for money in exchange for a performance of their songs, something that I had never experienced. They said that they needed compensation for their sad fate: like many *kunyalena* they were accused of being fools and witches who had killed their children themselves. People complained that songs of *kunyalena* were sometimes very sad. Singing them made the audience and the *kunyalena* themselves cry, so I had to pay them for it because they had endured so many hardships and their only gain, by undergoing the *kanyalen* ritual, when lucky, was a child. A second argument this *kanyalen* group in Ziguinchor advanced was that other white people had paid them. So it was clear that tourism and visits from researchers were beginning to influence the way these women responded to their position.

At the same time these Balanta *kunyalena* in an urban context were experiencing change, Jola *kunyalena* were also undergoing changes in their situation. In the example below, in the village of Thionck Essyl, I found that recently initiated *kunyalena* were given the names of characters in television soap operas instead of names with the usual negative connotations. They were given names such as Marimar, a character in a Brazilian soap opera that was very popular in Senegal.

Furthermore, if the newly initiated *anyalena* still wear the adornments required by their status, they are now beginning to look very well dressed, beautiful, and well fed. When I asked them about the change of names, they explained that this new development started in Dakar. But what I noted in Thionck Essyl was another change that went together with this new situation. As is explained above, an *anyalena* is often protected by a group of women who are responsible for her, their *anyalena*. They will do everything in their power to keep the child of the *anyalena* alive. But such a group also uses the *anyalena* as an instrument of competition and employs the songs of the *anyalena* to express the problems of this group. An example of one of these songs appears in the next section on the lyrics.

Different from what is at stake in the city of Ziguinchor, where *anyalena* act in groups and where the older women are responsible for the younger ones, on the village level, the *kanyalen* groups are less stressed. Although during rituals the *anyalena* eat together, each is individually protected by a group of non-*kanyalen* women.

I have mentioned earlier that the ceremony of the Jola *anyalena* returning to her husband is celebrated like a marriage. In the past, the *anyalena* usually received, like every bride, new kitchen utensils and new clothes. Today, each group of women now tries to give the most expensive presents to the *anyalena* who returns to her husband. For example, she receives, besides the utensils and the clothes, a wardrobe and a bed. I would explain these changes of name and competition among women as effects of a globalizing world and the market economy. The women of Thionck Essyl who are organized into groups to protect *anyalena* are, like other women, now much more mobile. They are in contact with their relatives in Dakar and the other cities, where television is becoming part of the household furniture. Even in Thionck Essyl, where some wards now have electricity, watching television is becoming a habit. At present, the women's groups of Thionck Essyl, which may include an *anyalena,* are very active at the economic level. They engage in all kinds of agricultural activities to earn money. This money is saved and often spent when there is an occasion such as a ceremony for an *anyalena* returning to her husband. The name of one of these women's groups refers to economic activity in which the women engage. The result is that the women can often earn enough money to provide for their husbands.

THE POWER OF THE LYRIC

The only source of power the *anyalena* has is her creativity in expressing her frustration about her position. But there are local variations in what she can do.

For example, she is not allowed to compose songs in every village. In Thionck Essyl and Tendouck, a nearby village, both in the Buluf region, it is the women's group that composes her songs. In other villages elsewhere in the Buluf and Fogny regions, however, an *anyalena* composes songs. Indeed, this is one of her main tasks. These songs can be sung at every ceremony and can circulate in the village. The lyrics often constitute a playful dialogue between the *anyalena* and members of the group that protects her. The themes in the songs of the *anyalena* range from criticizing her own conduct to making accusations against men. What they have in common is that they allude to the woman's fate and her powerlessness.

Having set the scene, I will give examples from ten songs. In the first the *anyalena* describes society's reaction to her fate. She notices the fact that people do not address her directly, but talk behind her back because no one will express openly the belief that it is the *anyalena*'s own fault that she has lost her children. The *anyalena* uses the song to speak openly of the hypocrisy of those who do not suffer from the same status and who therefore feel free to criticize her. In the lyrics, the *anyalena* expresses both voices, those of her critics and her own, once in the same line. *Ehheoha* conveys a sound that contributes to the euphony of a line.

> The mother ehheoha, she lost her children,
> The mother ehheoha, she lost her children,
> The mother ehheoha, she lost her children,
> When she talks people are behind her,
> People say that I am bad, that is why she has lost her children
> People talk behind my back, they do not talk face to face.
> People talk from the morning until the evening

The mother who lost her children is an *anyalena* who, like some *kunyalena*, may be accused of witchcraft and of causing the death of her own children. This is seen as a very grave accusation.

In Jola society, to call somebody lazy, as is done in the second song, is a great insult. A good Jola is a Jola who works hard, which is as true of men as it is of women. For this song an *anyalena* composed lyrics that reflect negatively upon herself. In the lyrics below, the term *ballooned* most likely refers to a man who is disgraced because he has no job, or works very little and grows fatter and fatter.

> Sotiba Badji your friends have gone to work,
> You, you say your bed is all,
> He ho he ho the ballooned.

All the women of her working group have gone to work, while the *anyalena* stayed in bed. Of course in reality she is not in bed, but this is the way she feels about herself: a lazy person who is not capable of fulfilling her main task: motherhood. In this song laziness replaces her role as a dysfunctional mother.

In the third song the *anyalena* says literally that she does not have children and in consequence possesses nothing. The implication of these conditions is that she had better leave the house. In fact she does leave the house to escape the evil spirit. But her negative self-image, conveyed in the songs, is also a ploy on her part to outwit the evil spirits.

She needs not only to leave the house, but also to go to some other place that is more distant. For example, in the song below, the singer mentions a village called Affiniam, located near Kandiou in the Buluf region. To reach the village one must cross a small river by small boat or by ferry. Although the distance between the *anyalena*'s village and Affiniam is not great, the fact that the two villages are separated by a river implies distance.

> Entré, her brothers ask, she is ill, how is she?
> She says that she does not work in the house.
> She does not have children, she does not have anything.
> One can send her with the ferry-boat to Affiniam, she can stay there
>   because she possesses nothing.
> Her mother asks also what she is doing,
> She [*the anyalena*] says that she is doing nothing because she does not have
>   anything
> She [her mother] can send her with the ferry-boat, and leave her there.

An *anyalena* is the only person in Jola society from whom boundary-crossing and abnormal behavior might be expected. Like a clown she can make fun of everyone, men as well as women. In the next song, she praises the sexual vigor of men in the Fogny region, northeast of Kandiou, because of their good habits. For example, they smoke tobacco before having sexual intercourse. She critizes men in her own village in the Buluf region because they do not have the same habits as the Fogny men. Such a criticism can be made only in a song and can never be uttered seriously in public. The women are able to make such comments in their songs because, according to Jola traditions, problems of fertility and sexuality belong to the domain of women and not to the world of men (cf. Journet 1991). Whether the *anyalena* really believes that smoking before having sexual intercourse means something is not important. In any case, she does not explain this link between smoking and sex. What the *anyalena* does stress in the song below is that men do not function well in her own village, while in the Fogny region, which has a reputation for more sexual liberty, men know how to have intercourse with women. The result of this good sexual contact will be the desired descendants.

> Men do not make love very well like there at Fogny
> Because at Fogny they use tobacco and they go to the women
> Men do not make love with the tobacco, it is at Fogny that they do that
> Men do not make love with the tobacco, it is at Fogny that they do that
> Men do not make love with the tobacco, it is at Fogny that they do that

The next three songs are by Riz N'Diaye, an *anyalena* living in Thionck Essyl. Although they were composed by the Para, the name of the group of women protecting her, the lyrics express her fate in no uncertain terms. She refused to eat for three days when she heard that she had to undergo the *kanyalen* ritual. In the first song she says clearly that she does not want to be an *anyalena*. Interestingly, the reason she gives is that she has not had many children that have died. This is another way of saying that although all of her children died, she did not have many in the first place, so she should not be required to become an *anyalena*. This song masks the difficult relationship between the *anyalena* and her hostess or protector, who is called "the mother" in the first line. She had an argument with Riz in the course of which she called the *anyalena* a hippopotamus. Riz answered that if "the mother" insulted her like this, Riz would beat "the mother" until she lost all her teeth. Riz explained this to me as follows: if you hit a dog [*the anyalena*], you yourself [the "mother"] will be the first to be bitten. According to the hostess, Riz's child had supernatural power, and the mother therefore washed the child with medicines in order to cleanse her of this power. But according to Riz's account, her hostess killed her child with these medicines. Banga, mentioned in the sixth line, is the name of a group of women. Riz tells the women to make themselves beautiful because it is time to celebrate her leaving as the result of this conflict with the mother.

> An *anyalena* who does not know the mother?
> it is a hippopotamus that you caught.
> Maman oh, I do not want the *kanyalen,*
> I do not have many children who died [so it is not necessary for me] to be
>   faced with the *kanyalen,*
> Mother oh open the door oh oh oh, the beautiful eh ohohohoheh,
> The beautiful is over there.
> Children of Banga make yourself beautiful, the time has come.
> Mother oh you have to apologize to me.

When Riz gave birth to her third child, she left her hostess and moved elsewhere in the village, all the while staying within the women's group that supervised or protected. In the second song, Riz N'Diaye expresses two concerns. The first is the conflict of authority between Riz and the group of women who are responsible for her. The second is the emerging awareness on the part of the *anyalena* that she has lost her own freedom no matter where she goes. For example, Riz attended a soccer game not far from her own ward, and thought it unnecessary to ask for permission from the women's group. The song reveals that the women responsible for her had a different view on how much freedom the *anyalena* should enjoy. At the end of the song there is a reference to the work assigned to her which she neglects to do. Limane, mentioned in the seventh line of the song, is another name for the ward Bougetir in Thionck Essyl.

> Where is the great Oulimata?
> The group Para said, NDiaye every place where we gather, we do not see her.
> They took her to keep her here,
> She goes where she wants without asking permission,
> o o o é, é o o o é, o maman o, o o o o é
> We are surprised,
> The children of Limane said, N'Diaye walks around everywhere,
> o o she does not do the cooking.

The same *anyalena*'s final song, which follows, embodies an interesting change of perspective. In the first part she adopts the view of the women who made the decision to initiate her with the aid of her maternal aunt, who is from the Sagna family. In the second part she adopts the perspective of the woman herself on her position. In the last sentence she expresses her own wish to go home. The name Fatou Badji, mentioned in the song, is the "mother" who oversees the *anyalena*. The term *consort* below is rooted in the French phrase *concertez-vous,* work together; in other words the *anyalena* should work with the members of the group.

> Mother Sagna let us lure her into a trap,
> tell her that you are taking her with you on a journey.
> Stop at Limane, we will stop her; N'Diaye a o é é.
> [change in perspective]
> I will return, o o é consort together,
> Fatou Badji made me suffer,
> It is pitiful,
> Goodbye o I return home.

The following songs are by Fouriso, an *anyalena* living in Ziguinchor who acquired this status not because her children died but because she was badly treated by her husband from the moment he married a second wife. She did not leave home, but, when problems arose, she asked the woman who had protected her to help her. This woman tried to resolve the disagreements between Fouriso and her husband, who subsequently died. Fouriso believed that the power of the amulet given to her when she became an *anyalena* caused her situation to improve. Why her situation improved because of the amulet is not explained. It may in fact be because her husband felt that he should treat her better now that everyone knew she had become an *anyalena* as a result of his ill treatment. Or maybe Fouriso has the feeling that her situation is better only because of the amulet that supports and protects her.

In any case, after the death of her husband and her move to her brother's house her situation became better than even before, it seems, because she had the amulet. When she became an *anyalena,* she followed custom, in spite of the mistreatment she suffered, by not leaving her husband during the first two years of their marriage. Because she was "only" mistreated by her husband it was not considered necessary for her to leave his house during that time. After she became a widow, she moved to her brother's house. But her status as an *anyalena* did not change. Like all *kunyalena,* she remains an *anyalena* for the rest of her life. In the meantime, her co-wife still lives with her in-laws in the house of her deceased husband. Indeed, when a widow is allowed to stay in the house of the husband after his death, this means that she has a good relationship with her in-laws, which differs, in this case, from the situation of the *anyalena.*

> Marrying in the Sagna family,
> Marrying in the Sagna family,
> When you are lazy,
> Don't marry in it,
> If you choose to marry in it,
> The pieces of dead wood,
> You carry them under coercion,
> O o o o o o o o yé Sagna o o o o o yé,
> When it is noon they eat.

Fouriso's next song illustrates her difficult relationship with her sisters-in-law. In the first and second lines the sisters-in-law tell that her that she is lazy, and that the group of which she is a member has to work without her help. In the third line of the song it is said that Fouriso does not know the Forest. This is the same insult as *solima,* the term for an unexcised girl. In other words, the *anyalena* had not even advanced to the sisterhood of women. The initiation that is meant here is the excision ritual that girls undergo between eight and twelve years old and is meant for *all* girls. It takes place in the Forest of women, a place where rituals for women take place. It is the first ritual a girl undergoes in order to become a woman. So telling a woman that she does not know the Forest means that she never reached adulthood and in fact can be considered a child. In the fourth line she expresses her wish to leave for Dakar, and in the fifth and sixth line she says that she will come back in the rainy season and will fulfill her duty.

> Who is it who works alone, it is the group who works i yo o é,
> *Fouriso you are an idiot, your sister-in-law said that you stay in the house*
> *   and just talk and eat,*
> Fouriso Badji does not know the Forest,
> All that you think of me, I am leaving for Dakar and I leave the house to
>   you,
> When the rainy season comes, you weed the bushes, I weed the bushes,
> You take your tool to work, I take my tool to work

The last song was composed by Apollo, an *anyalena* in the village of Diatock who subsequently died during childbirth. The term *efounounké* in the first line is a plant which the Jola use to cover a corpse. What the *anyalena* means is that the villagers have used up the supply of the plant for the burial of her many children. *Woyee* in the last line is an expression of sadness and pity prompted not only by the death of her children but also by the fear that those children born in the future will also die. The *brousse* is the French term for bush.

> They went into the "brousse" to search for efounounké
> But the plant was no more.
> It was no more because of Apollo
> Apollo, woyee, the children are made for efounounké.

THE SONGS OF THE ANYALENA IN THE GLOBALIZING WORLD

In Thionck Essyl, where the women's groups are strong, as seen above, the songs of the *kunyalena* are composed by the group of non-*anyalena* and not by the *anyalena* herself. This is the opposite of what occurs in other villages, where the songs of the *anyalena* constitute her only means to express her feelings about her condition. In Thionck Essyl one result of this reversal is that these women exercise a strong influence on what the *anyalena* can sing. A consequence is that some lyrics do not treat the theme of the *kanyalen* ritual at all, but focus instead, as in the example below, on problems that concern the group, such as the processing of millet, and not the worries of the *anyalena*. The song below reflects the fact that the *anyalena* must sing not about her problems, but about those of the group that oversees her activities.

> A mortar is heard in the forest,
> Who is there ? Maï Sane, Sane N'Diaye
> o o é o é this generation,
> Every year we husk the millet,
> it exhausts us,
> let us skip this year until next year.

The song above is about an *anyalena* who has the name Marimar, that of an actress in a soap opera. But there is no allusion to the *anyalena*. In this song, composed by the women's group that protects Marimar, the focus is not on Marimar. Rather, Sane, the leader of the group, is accused of giving too much work to the members.

In the next song, Marimar the *anyalena* is compared to Marimar the character in a soap opera. She explains in this song that everybody looks at her the way they look at Marimar when watching the soap opera on television.

> Listen so that I can talk to you,
> Thank you very much,
> It is time to go and watch (on television) Marimar,
> a o o o é, é o o é, é o o o é,
> That, I cannot recompense you,
> Allah will recompense you.

The comparison between Marimar the actress and Marimar the *anyalena* is extended in the next song. Like Marimar of the soap opera, Marimar the *anyalena* is called Bella because Marimar on television flees from her husband and hides under the name of Bella in another country. Finally her husband finds her. Like Bella, an *anyalena* "flees" from her husband for about two years and also changes her name to hide her original identity.

In the song, "carry on her back" means "I, Bella, did not believe that I could have a baby who stayed alive and whom I could carry on my back."

> Thioune have mercy on your mother by surviving,
> Do not worry, your mother Bella did not believe to carry on her back,
> The prayers are answered,
> Eé, éé oo é éé,
> Dabo take your flute and announce where Bella is confined,
> The Dième family is shining.

In the next song, composed by the women's group and belonging to the repertoire of Marimar, reference is made to a song by Viviane N'Dour, the wife of the brother of the famous Senegalese rock star Youssou N'Dour. There are two reasons for the reference to Viviane N'Dour. She is a very famous and glamorous rock star who represents "modern life," so the inclusion of some lyrics from her in this *kanyalen* song gives it a modern touch. The second reason is that Viviane N'Dour's lyrics criticize men opposed to the *kanyalen* ritual. It is striking that part of this song is sung in Wolof, the language that represents modern city life. In the third verse, the phrase "I will carry on my back" refers to a baby that will be carried on the back of a woman named Adièmè. In the fourth line Dième refers to the name of the family that protects Marimar.

> Adama Sadio I came to look for blessings,
> Please help me,
> I do not believe that I will carry on my back,
> The dance that is "en vogue" of Adièmè is Viviane
> [From here the lyrics shift from Jola to Wolof]
> "You men should say: 'he talks nonsense' 'I talk nonsense,'"
> Viviane let them cry,
> They are babies,
> We meet in the circle,
> Let us move !

Another token of modernity comes to the fore in the next song, which is wholly in Wolof and comments on the habits of women who, for the most part, live in the cities and use skin-lightening cosmetics. Here the singer criticizes this habit of *khèssal,* as it is called in Wolof. It is important, however, to frame this song in the complicated context of Wolof/Jola relations.

The Jola have an ambivalent relationship with the Wolof language marked by dislike and admiration. Wolof is the language of the Wolof people, who are the largest ethnic group in Senegal, while French is the lingua franca in Senegal of all peoples in the cities. The Wolof dominate not only in numbers but also in economic success. That is why other peoples admire them and at the same time look upon them with envy. This tension dates back to the period of French colonial rule. The Wolof, who originally lived in the northern part of Senegal, tended to cooperate with the French colonizers and thus to benefit from this relationship. That is also why they are still regarded with suspicion. What contributes to this view is that from the mid-1960s, after the introduction of La loi sur le domaine nationale, all ethnic groups were allowed to own land in the Casamance, the southernmost region of Senegal. So now the Wolof can also possess land in this Jola region. The result is that the prosperous Wolof from northern Senegal have become even more powerful (cf. De Jong 2001). Thus, the fact that the song is in Wolof underscores the criticism of the urban practices the lyrics describe.

The *anyalena* for whom this was composed explains that the song was originally sung by the younger generation of girls and is dedicated to her.

> Foureul Diop o, I do not want that, my sweetheart,
> I clear myself, I blacken myself, I lighten myself,
> My sweetheart tells me that it is ugly.

As indicated, despite the cultural changes listed above, the *anyalena* still dislikes her position, as is expressed in the last song, composed by the women's group but belonging to the repertoire of Marimar. Mammy Dième is the name of the woman responsible for Marimar. The women express the *anayalena*'s unhappy position for her.

> Mammy Dième what are you thinking about?
> The fatigue, mother Dième I think of,
> The fatigue, it is God who caused it.

CONCLUSION

The *kanyalen* songs play a key role in enabling society to deal with difficult situations that women encounter, such as the loss of children. The lyrics of these songs serve to mark social change by putting the afflicted women outside the status category of normal women. The woman who has become an *anyalena* appears as a means to provide greater assurance that families will have descendants and in this way safeguard society. But the result is a change that compounds the difficulties facing these unfortunate women. As seen in the lyrics above and the descriptions of *anyalena* behavior, these women must perform and sing in self-denigrating ways designed not only to express their powerlessness but also to outwit the evil spirits at the origin of the conditions from which they suffer.

But if the notion of *kanyalen* continues to survive today, it appears that the process of globalization, with the spread of Western advertising and the growing presence of television, has now affected the *anyalena*. Their roles are the same as before, but the women's groups who protect the *anyalena* now make them look beautiful and display their material success.

These two traits are new. Before, an *anyalena* had to look ugly. And displaying material success is not at all normal in Jola society. Now these women are given a new and evolving position in society. Women's groups who protect the *anyalena* now earn more money and display their material success by making their *anyalena* look beautiful and giving her many presents. The *anyalena* has become an instrument in the competition between the women's groups in the village. Contrary to participants' belief that the *kanyalen* ritual is declining, my observation is that it is maintaining its place in society and is changing its form in response to globalization. It is hard to guess where the evolution in the roles and messages of *kanyalen* songs will take those who are forced to adopt a new identity. To find answers to this question, I plan not only to examine more closely the impact of globalization but also to explore the growing role of Islam in this evolving tradition.

NOTES

1. This topic is part of my PhD thesis, "Het geheim van het masker Maskerrituelen en genderrelaties in de Casamance, Senegal" [The Secret of the Mask: Mask Rituals and Gender Relations in Casamance, Senegal] (Amsterdam: Rozenberg, 2003). This research was financed by the Netherlands Foundation for the Advancement of Tropical Research (Wotro). The fieldwork was carried out in three villages of the Casamance—Kandiou, Diatock, and Thionck Essyl—and in Ziguinchor, the capital of this region, in 1992 (four months), with intervals in 1994–1996, November 1998, and between December 1999 and January 2000. The fieldwork I conducted in Ziguinchor and Thionck Essyl between February and March of 2003 was under the auspices of the "Women's Songs from West Africa" project and was financed by funds from a Collaborative Research Grant from the United States National Endowment for the Humanities that was directed by Aissata Sidikou and Thomas Hale.

2. In the literature, the sacred forest/grove is often cited as the place where *inter alia* the initiation rituals are carried out (Thomas 1958–1959; Girard 1969; Mark 1985, 1992; De Jong 2001). I cite *the Forest,* with a capital letter, to indicate that a ritual place is meant, not every forest, and also because the Jola indicate this place as *kareng,* "forest."

3. The "secret" plays a central role in the life of the inhabitants of the Casamance. Each gender has its domain of secrets. Bellman claims that no one subject is a more suitable candidate for secrecy than any other—anything can be declared a secret—and that what makes the information valuable is the structure in which the secret is embedded (Bellman 1984). It is not *knowledge* of the secret that is important, but the prohibition on *speaking* about it.

4. Sometimes it is not only the *anyalena* who crosses the ethnic boundary but also the women who protect the *anyalena,* as in the case of a Peul woman who grew up in a Jola milieu and who assumed responsibility for protecting a Jola woman. This Jola woman speaks Peul, dresses like Peul women, participates in Peul ceremonies, and in this way has transformed her identity and become a Peul.

5. In my PhD thesis I state that an *anyalena* is a mask. To take on a new identity, the *anyalena* has laid aside all the characteristics of a "normal" woman. This new identity masks the old one. She masks the fact that she has failed as a woman; she completely hides her true identity.

WORKS CITED

Beek, W. E. A. van. 2003. De Dogon en hun toeristen. In *Dogon: Mythe en werkelijkheid in Mali,* ed. R. Bedaux and J. D. van der Waals, 196–202. Leiden: Rijksmuseum voor Volkenkunde.

———. 2007. Approaching African tourism: paradigms and paradoxes. In *African Alternatives,* ed. P. Chabal and L. Engel, 145–172. Leiden: Brill.

Bell, Catherine. 1989. Ritual, change, and changing rituals. *Worship* 63 (1): 31–41.

———. 1992. *Ritual Theory, Ritual Practice.* Oxford: Oxford University Press.

Bellman, Beryl L. 1984. *The Language of Secrecy: Symbols and Metaphors in Poro Ritual.* New Brunswick, N.J.: Rutgers University Press.

De Jong, Ferdinand. 2001. Modern secrets: The power of locality in Casamance, Senegal. PhD thesis, Universiteit van Amsterdam.

Fassin, Didier. 1987. Rituel villageois, rituels urbains: La reproduction sociale chez les femmes joola du Sénégal. *L'Homme* 104:54–75.

Fassin, Didier, and Ibrahima Badji. 1986. Ritual buffoonery: A social preventive measure against childhood mortality in Senegal. *The Lancet,* no. 8473:142–143.

Faye, Ousseynou. 1994. l'instrumentalisation de l'histoire et de l'ethnicité dans le discours séparatiste en Basse Casamance (Sénégal). *Afrika Spektrum.* 29 (1): 65–77.

Fels, Ulla. 1994. *Die Macht des Lachens.* DVD. Hamburg: SWF/ARTE.

Gerbrandy, Annemarie. 1987. Associaties van migranten in de stad Ziguinchor. In *Opstellen over vrouwen in de Basse-Casamance en Midden-Gambia,* ed. M. Jansen, J. M. van der Klei, and S. van der Valk. Amsterdam: Ready Zet Go.

Girard, Jean. 1969. *Genèse du pouvoir charismatique en Basse Casamance Sénégal.* Dakar: IFAN.

Herbert, Eugenia W. 1993. *Iron, Gender, and Power: Rituals of Transformation in African Societies.* Bloomington: Indiana University Press.

Journet, Odile. 1976. Rôles et statuts des femmes dans la société Diola (Basse Casamance). PhD thesis, Université de Lyon 2.

———. 1991. Un rituel de préservation de la descendance: Le kanyaalen joola. In *Grossesse et petite enfance en Afrique Noire et à Madagascar,* 19–39. Paris: l'Harmattan.

Langeveld, Kirsten. 1997. *Kanyalen,* eine Frauenmaske [*Kanyalen,* a womens' mask]. In *Frauen & Gesundheit—Ethnomedizinische Perspektiven,* ed. C. E. Gottschalk-Batschkus, J. Schuler, and D. Iding, 53–60. Berlin: VWB-Verlag für Wissenschaft und Bildung.

———. 2002. Gender and the *kankurang* mask: An analysis of myth and female ritual. *Mande Studies* 4:83–100.

———. 2003. Het geheim van het masker: Maskerrituelen en genderrelaties in de Casamance, Senegal [The secret of the mask: Mask rituals and gender relations in the Casamance, Senegal]. PhD thesis. Amsterdam: Rozenberg Publishers.

Mark, Peter. 1985. *A Cultural, Economic, and Religious History of the Basse Casamance Since 1500.* Stuttgart: Franz Steiner Verlag.

———. 1992. *The Wild Bull and the Sacred Forest: Form, Meaning, and Change in Senegambian Initiation Masks.* Cambridge: Cambridge University Press.

Marut, Jean-Claude. 1994a. Le dessous des cartes casamançaises: Une approche géopolitique du conflit. In *Comprendre la Casamance: chronique d'une intégration contrastée,* ed. F. G. Barbier-Wiesser, 193–211. Paris: Karthala.

———. 1994b. Guerre et paix en Casamance: Repères pour un conflit, 1990–1993. In *Comprendre la Casamance: chronique d'une intégration contrastée,* ed. F. G. Barbier-Wiesser, 213–231. Paris: Karthala.

McLaughlin, Fiona. 1997. Islam and popular music in Senegal: The emergence of a "new tradition." *Africa* 67 (4): 560–581.

Sidikou, Aissata G. 2001. *Recreating Words, Reshaping Worlds: The Verbal Art of Women from Niger, Mali and Senegal.* Trenton, N.J.: Africa World Press.

Thomas, Louis-Vincent. 1958–1959. *Les Diola: Essai d'analyse fonctionnelle sur une population de Basse-Casamance.* 2 vols. Dakar: IFAN.

Turner, Victor. 1969. *The Ritual Process.* London: Routledge and Kegan Paul.

Van der Klei, Jos M. 1989. *Trekarbeid en de Roep van het Heilige Bos: het gezag van de oudste en moderne veranderingen bij de Diola van Zuid-Senegal.* Proefschrift. Nijmegen: IKEN.

Weil, Peter. 1976. The staff of life: Food and female fertility in a West African society. *Africa* 46 (2): 182–195.

3

Azna Deities in the Songs of Taguimba Bouzou

A WINDOW ON THE VISIBLE AND INVISIBLE

Boubé Namaïwa

INTRODUCTION

Songs often provide a key to understanding the daily lives of women, but their world is not limited to the immediate concerns of child raising, meal preparation, and marriage. The system of belief that governs their society is very much a part of their worldview, and it takes shape not simply in the Islamic context, but also, at the same time, in complex networks of gods and goddesses who predate the arrival of Islam. If the contours of Islam in West Africa are familiar to scholars in African studies, the invisible world of a parallel system of belief often remains a mystery. But if, as Jewsiewicki (1987) argues, belief is social fact, the question, then, is what is the shape of that world and how does it influence daily life? The example of songs by a well-known woman from one Hausa-speaking people, the Azna of Niger, offers insights into the visible and the invisible in that world.

I propose to take up the challenge of understanding that metaphysical world by reversing the order of things, by drawing on the invisible to explain the visible. Followers of classical methods might argue that my approach is insane. They would claim that one can only explain the invisible by starting with the visible, a Cartesian approach that is no longer valid. I propose to carry out my analysis by drawing on evidence from songs sung by one of the most famous singers in Niger, Taguimba Bouzou. But before explaining just who this extraordinary woman is, it is important to frame the issue raised above in a larger context.

The French ethnographer Jean Rouch came to see this Sahelian system of belief as a form of insanity, a view that he expressed throughout his book *Religion et Magie Songhaï* (1989 [1960]). This realization was rooted in his experience of filming expatriate Songhaï disciples of Hauka spirits living in Ghana in the early 1950s for what became one of his best-known ethnographic films, *Les Maîtres Fous* (1955).

One must, in other words, be insane, or in this case possessed, to borrow a concept from Nietzsche (1990), in order to upset the existing system of values. That is precisely what I propose to undertake here—a reversal of values which might lead some to think that I, too, am insane. But following the logic of those who upset values, I am insane or not insane because I know that I am not insane. This is the condition of others who upset existing paradigms, such as Copernicus, Descartes, Galileo, Kepler, Newton, and Einstein. Thanks to their "insanity," they made fundamental contributions to the progress of understanding the world in which we live, doing so by upsetting existing systems of values.

The link inherent in this reversal is well recognized by those who understand the nature of African systems of belief. For example, Boubou Hama, the late dean of scholars in Niger, has argued that the world of the Songhaï spirits known as *gangi* is the reflection of the human world. It offers a reversed image. Rouch has described the Attakurma from the spirit world as mythic. The old Attakurma said, "As men, we have our villages we get married and we have children. As men, we eat grain, pancakes, especially bran, domestic or wild peanut and many insects" (Hama 1973, 50).

In any case, as Rouch claimed, the invisible world corresponds perfectly to the visible one. This is a phenomenon that appears in Hausa as well as Songhaï belief. Boubou Hama explained the parallelism between the invisible and the visible in his book *Le Double d'hier rencontre demain* (1973). One can grasp this invisible world thanks to what one might call magic "rings," such as those in the Platonic myth of Gyses.

Before going any farther, it is important to provide some background on the medium, the singer (or *Zabiya* in Hausa), whose songs will serve us as *anneaux,* or rings. They will allow the listener to see the village of the *gangi,* in the words of Zarmakoye Rakia, the famous diva of Tillabery, a town on the left bank of the Niger river in western Niger.

For the Hausa, that singer is Taguimba Bouzou, who came from the Aréwa region in the Dallol Mawri area of Niger, and who died in 1995. The corpus of her songs reveals not only the mastery of this well-known singer, but also how this "reversed" world in which the visible is the reflection of the invisible is part of the belief system of her listeners. In other words, the "reality" that she describes in her songs is a "reality" for her listeners that helps us to understand more deeply the complex world of Hausa-speaking peoples, in this case the Azna of Aréwa, in eastern Niger.

Adeline Masquelier (2001, 7) has emphasized the national reputation of Taguimba Bouzou in Niger, where she is called simply Taguimba. Beginning in 1984, her songs were broadcast often on the Voix du Sahel, Niger's national radio station, the only one heard throughout the country. Copied off the air by individuals and by entrepreneurs, the songs became widely available in the electronics sections of outdoor markets. Given this uncontrolled distribution of her songs, no source is cited for the excerpts presented in this study.

Her reputation, however, is not limited to Niger. She is also known to audiences in the much larger Hausa-speaking region in Nigeria, especially in the northwestern state of Kebbi. For example, in the song below she thanks the adherents of the transnational *bori* possession cult in the town of Argungu, Nigeria. She emphasizes not only the cross-border link by referring to *bori* members in Niamey, Niger, several hours by automobile to the northwest of Argungu, but also the reality that Islam and *bori* coexist in the same world of belief.

> Accika of Argungu.
> The *bori* devotees of Argungu, I thank you.
> The youngest and the oldest owe me nothing
> The *bori* devotees of Niamey, the youngest and the oldest,
> I thank the people of Niamey.
> Thank you very much!
> May Allah thank you more than me.
> You make all for me.
> May Allah protect your secrets.
> Allah protects us from disease!
> Allah, give us well-being and fulfillment.

But Taguimba was hardly the only singer who celebrated the *bori* cult in her songs. Among the others one finds Gomma Uwar Dan Garassa, Igue Maddi Maïtourou, Shatu, and Jajji Uwar Idrissa. Gomma is the one who in 1980 sang about *bori* in the ballet Mahalba (or "the bow hunters"), performed in the area of Doutchi where most of the Arewa now live, including the Azna. She was recorded for the radio in 1980, four years before Taguimba. Taguimba was heard on the radio in 1984 before appearing on national television in 1986. But after these solo performances, the three women, Taguimba, Gomma, and Igue, often sang together when they were invited at the same time to perform in *bori* ceremonies.

But Taguimba was not a singer who could induce listeners into a state of possession. It was Igué and Gomma who were most adept at this, while Taguimba became the most talented of her sisters in bringing forth by her lyrics the pride of *bori* followers. She was quicker and more skilled at integrating into her songs incidents that occurred during ceremonies while at the same time maintaining the thread linking her lyrics. She had a talent for innovation that was superior to that of the others.

How then was she able to surpass the other women? Certainly her voice was not as melodious and sharp as those of the others, with the exception of Jajji. This distinction is significant because it means that she was less able to match her voice with that of the *goge,* the Hausa and Songhaï version of the one-stringed violin, the instrument *par excellence* of *bori* music. Listeners expect a kind of harmony or correlation between the instrument and the vocal cords of the singer.

There are several reasons why she was able to overcome vocal limitations. First, in 1982 a customs agent named Moussa Maïkambou, who had a camera, filmed some performances by Taguimba. A follower of *bori,* Maïkambou advised her to go to Niamey, the capital of Niger, to perform. It was there that Mamane Garba, the director of culture in the Ministry of Culture, a man who holds a doctorate in musicology and who also sings and composes, recorded Taguimba for the national radio service, Voix du Sahel, as well as for television. Those performances launched the career of Taguimba. She did not forget to thank Garba for his help in her widely diffused song "Zatao."

> No one is superior to Mamane Garba except Allah.
> No one is superior to Mamane Garba except Allah.
> Mamane Garba heard you and he answered, Taguimba, the sister of the king.
> He took us off from a gourd [ignorance]. They took us off from a gourd. In the past our heads were deeply black in a gourd.
> Yes the great one, I greet the great one.
> May Allah permit you to become healthy.
> This is a message for you, Mamane Garba, from Taguimba. She wishes you to become healthy.
> I wish you to become healthy, Mamane Garba.
> So too all Muslims.
> May Allah protect you.
> Yes the great one, I greet the great one.
> Not only but all Muslims.
> Ubangiji-Allah, Ubangiji-Allah gives us fura [balls of millet flour]
> Allah, give us millet! Allah gives us health to eat millet!

Ubangiji-Allah the most powerful,
I invoke you, on account of the mosques of Mecca and Medina,
On account of Duna and Babay [spirits],
On account of those who benefit from those who benefit,
On account of love, on the agreement of those who agree,
Ubangiji-Allah, in Your power,
Allah, send us health. And then what health can eat.
On account of the commander of Muslims!

However, things were not always so easy for Taguimba when she first began her career. She had to face the hostility of her own family. She came from one of the Arewa families that see themselves as the most authentic of all, the Bilawa. She was the sister of the chief of one of the eight villages in the canton of Tibiri-Doutchi, a man who took pride in being from that branch of the family. Her elder brother was at one time the Sarki, or chief, of the capital of the region. The loss of this status, her *marok'i,* or griot, often pointed out, was an error caused by the Gubawa family and in particular by a leader named Maï-Aréwa.

In the song "Salamatu," the *marok'i* declares that in spite of her profession, "nevertheless she is the sister of the king of Kiada!"

Go on Taguimba sister of the king.
Taguimba mother of Mamane.

How then, asked critics, even though she could never take the lost throne, could she go against ancestral traditions by singing, an activity not normally done by people of royal origin? The spirits, it was thought at the time, could not tolerate such an error.

In addition to hostility from her family, she had to face another form of criticism from those with deep roots in the region who could not accept the idea that one of their princesses could become a singer and, worse, accept presents from those to whom, in more appropriate circumstances, she should be giving gifts. That is why in her song dedicated to Zaki Sarki, she reacts by commenting on her status as a performer who receives gifts from some and insults from others.

Today I'm called the witch,
Someone is giving me [money]
Someone is giving me [money]
Zaki of Amare, only Allah is superior to him
Another is insulting me,
Let them say, Allah is the greatest,
You [Taguimba], you never insult.
Me, I never insult.

With respect to those who insult her, she places her faith in God, and in any case, she will not stoop to insulting those who do not like what she does. She is above it all. To borrow a saying from the Sahel: the dog barks; the caravan continues on its way.

Though her repertoire was considerable, relatively little of it was recorded because of limitations on song performance time imposed by the media to meet broadcast scheduling requirements. She would have liked to record her entire repertoire, but she needed time in her songs to thank her patrons in the *bori* cult, who sought fame through her songs.

In spite of these limitations, it is important to note that she serves as a model for modern singers such as Sadou Bori, in the Akazamma orchestra of Doutchi, as well as others such as Idi Nadadaou, Dalweyzé of Ouallam, and Rakia of Tillabery. To understand the significance of Taguimba in the regional soundscape, one needs only to follow her performance during a possession ceremony, her preferred venue. During these events, she enjoyed total freedom to express herself without worrying about time limitations. Here one finds that she is more focused on the content. For her, the goal is possession, not entertainment.

Each divinity in the *bori* world has its song, or at least a song associated with it. Some have as many as four, including the families of the Doguwa, the Nabisa, and certain members of the Zanzana. With over 200 divinities, some better known than others, one can estimate that Taguimba's repertoire included at least 250 songs.

In the examples from her corpus presented here, Taguimba, like a teacher, limits herself to the best-known divinities of the Hausa and Songhaï cults, the *bori* and the *hauka*. But one could hear the majority of these songs by listening to recordings made by audience members in the Aréwa region or from the collection of the customs agent Moussa Maïkambou. The songs could be recorded also by the musicians who accompanied her and who are still playing her songs. These songs constitute in many ways a common heritage, maintained by these musicians who participate in ceremonies today as guides, somewhat like her griot.

Taguimba was not simply a singer of *bori* songs, but also a priestess of the cult. On occasion—and this is the case as well for other singers—she would assist the priest who presided over a ceremony. In other words, not just anybody can become a cult singer. It is often the human incarnations of the divinities themselves who choose who will become a singer. In the same way, not every devotee who wants to become a priest will reach this position. The divinities will decide. In fact, in the case of Taguimba, what assuaged the anger of her family was the belief that the divinities decided who would become a *bori* cult singer. It appears that Taguimba herself actually wanted to abandon this activity, especially as she began to experience the effects of ageing, but she did not succeed. In fact, she suffered so much that she sometimes fainted after performances.

Taguimba was also a talented dancer who could equal the dancers of the *bori* cult. As far as I know, only one *bori* cult member was able to match Taguimba—her sister, with whom she liked to perform as a duo. In fact, it is hard to think of Taguimba singing without dancing. This is yet another difference between her and other singers, with the exception of Jajji. In the songs presented here, each time Kassu, her *marok'i,* or male griot, salutes her, it is because she is fully involved in dancing.

When she sang, Taguimba was always accompanied by one or more violinists who also had deep knowledge of both the divinities and the sequencing of the pieces that must be played. Rouch affirms that "in addition to the message of the songs, the order in which the lyrics are sung is of great importance: the invisible world must follow a strict hierarchy. Only advanced initiates can, from the outset, speak directly to a divinity that they are calling forth. . . . But other men, in particular those involved in the ceremonies, are [also] obliged to follow this hierarchy" (1989, 97).

In this particular corpus, Taguimba was accompanied by two violinists: Tsurkay, the lead or first violin, and Gimba, the second. Two performers on calabashes served as the percussion section: Gagara and Hassan. Finally there were two calabash gourd players, Kisso and Kassu, with the latter serving also as praise singer or *marok'i.* Often, other instrumentalists joined the group, including players of the *kalangu,* the ubiquitous underarm drum. Like all other *bori* singers, as well as some traditional Hausa singers, Taguimba never performed without a *tassa,* an aluminum instrument that both amplified her voice and served as a receptacle for gifts. Some believe that this instrument enables one to intercept spells that evil people are tempted to throw at the performers. This is a common practice in possession cults. By not receiving the gifts in their own hands, but rather in the *tassa,* the singers are said to limit the risk of spells.

THE AZNA BORI PANTHEON

This, then, is the performance context for the songs. In what follows, I will examine the pantheon of *bori* divinities for the Azna people. Given the number and complexity of the divinities for the Azna and other groups in this study, I will add a chart in the appendix to show more clearly their identity and relationships.

The Azna pantheon is similar to that of the Songhaï, who live in western Niger, largely on the right bank of the Niger River. Within each people's pantheon—*bori* for the Hausa, *hauka* for the Songhaï—there tends to be a duality in the color, shape, character, quality, profession, and religion of these divinities. For example, one finds couples such as Black-White, Giant-Dwarf, Hot-Cold, Cooked-Raw, Good-Evil, Good-Wicked, and Muslim-'Pagan.' On top of these couplings, there is also a classification based on profession or lifestyle—for example, herder-farmer.

But these dualities do not reflect oppositions within the different couples. Such a concept could not exist in a world where solidarity, cohabitation, complementarity, and tolerance are the highest values.

Aiding this perspective, some divinities serve as links between families of spirits because of marriage ties, or simply because they have, by their own volition, decided to join a particular family for racial or religious reasons. This is the case, for example, with Kujji, a female member of the Doguwa family ('pagan,' masculine, or Azna) who decided to join a subgroup of the Fulbe Doguwa, with the result that her name is Bakar Bihilata, the black Fulbe. Nevertheless, she will keep all of the traits of her sisters of Azna origin, especially her thirst for human blood, a form of sorcery. The case of Zaki Sarki should also be mentioned as a link, because as a Muslim son he prefers to join the family of his "cousins" the Farfaru, white Muslims, rather than remain with his Nabisa brothers. But he is nevertheless the son of Harakoy Dicko, the spirit queen of the Niger River and mother of the Tooru spirits. Mérie is a Zanzana who is the daughter of Muslims. Gurmungna is a Tabisa (feminine for Nabisa) who was excommunicated and then founded her own family. She is at once both the sister and the mother of all the Zanzana.

The different couples relate to each other, with the families linked by marriage or by what one might call nomadism. From this perspective, there is no difference between the Azna divinities and those of Egypt, Greece, or Rome. They have their caprices, their passions, their functions, and, most notably, their *metissages,* or mixed marriages. In effect, they marry, reproduce, and die. Idrissa Diawara points out that although they possess supernatural power, spirits follow a strict hierarchy; they are divided between males and females, and they marry and reproduce, theoretically among themselves; and they are immortal (1987, 77). The great problem in counting them is that they multiply and live forever.

Here, then, the world of the spirits mirrors perfectly the world of humans; or, inversely, the world of humans is structured and organized in accordance with the laws and rules inspired by the world of the divinities.

In the Azna pantheon, there are seven major families. They are:

1. The Doguwa, or Hausa-*gangi* in Songhaï;
2. The Nabisa, or Tooru in Songhaï;

3. The Farfaru, or Gangi-kwarey in Songhaï;
4. The Zanzana, or Hargey in Songhaï;
5. The Babaku, or Gangi-bi in Songhaï;
6. The Dandagunay, or Attakurma in Songhaï;
7. The Babule, or Hauka in Songhaï.

I have listed the names of the families in Songhaï in order to show the similarities between the two pantheons. The only difference appears in the ranking
of these families. For example, the Azna rank the Doguwa first and the Nabisa
second, and the Zanzana before the Babaku. The Songhaï place the Nabisa, or
Tooru, at the top, while the Azna consider the Doguwa, or Hausa-gangi, to be
at the top.

Whenever she sang, then, Taguimba began with the Doguwa family, composed of Rankaso, Hwasa-Hwako, Sarraouniya, Zakuma, Kujji, Hajo, Dosa, Azne,
Kure, Adama, Messa, and Sama'ou, as well as many other divinities. The Songhaï reverse the order by beginning with the Babaku, or Gangi-bi, and then
the Zanzana, or Hargey. The reason that the Azna sing about the Zanzana before the Babaku is that they claim to have many hunters, and the Zanzana are
known as the spirits of hunters. Thus in a song dedicated to Mérie, a Zanzana,
Taguimba emphasized that she is a spirit of the hunters.

The Songhaï, on the other hand, start with the Babaku before continuing
with the Zanzana because in their cosmogony the Babaku originate among the
Gurmantché, a neighboring people with whom the Songhaï have had a conflictual relationship going at least all the way back to the time of Askia Mohammed, founder of the Songhaï empire in the late fifteenth century. The ruler tried
to conquer the Gurmantché but failed, as reported in the *Epic of Askia Mohammed* (Hale 1996, Johnson et al. 1997) and in the seventeenth-century Timbuktu
chronicles *Tarîkh el-Fattash* (Kâti 1981 [1913]) and *Tarîkh es-Sudan* (Es-Sa'di
1964 [1898–1900]).

With this background, let us take a closer look at some of these different
families. It would be impossible to examine all of them, not only because Taguimba did not include them all in her repertoire, but also, as Diawara argues,
because these two pantheons, Hausa and Songhaï, are to some extent open and
are constantly in the process of restructuring themselves by the admission of
new divinities (1987, 77)

The Doguwa

Very little has been written about the Doguwa. Most research on possession
cults in Niger centers on spirits in the second family because of a belief that
the Nabisa/Tooru descend from a common ancestor called Doguwa. Diawara
has taken this view, but the evidence for it is inconclusive. In reality, Doguwa

is a generic term for all the so-called hot divinities of the second family, the Nabisa/Tooru.

Doguwa, in Hausa, means "long." It is well-known among the people that all those who encounter the Doguwa, during certain hallucinations or incongruous meetings, describe them as outsized figures who are so tall that one cannot see the head. This confirms the view of this family as giants. Adeline Masquelier (2001, 7, 59, 175) has described them as local spirits who are found everywhere among the different peoples of the Aréwa region—not only the Azna, who worship the Doguwa spirits of Rankaso, Zakuma, Hwasa-Hwako, Azne, Kure, and Baka-Baka, but also among the Fulbe (who worship Kujji, Dosa, Hajo, and Adama). Other groups who live in the region include, along with the Hausa-speaking peoples and the Fulbe, the Tuareg, the Gurmantché, the Kanuri, and the Guari, a less-well-known people from the coastal region of West Africa.

The principal spirits of the Aréwa region, the Doguwa, dominate the Azna pantheon. For this reason, Taguimba began her songs by singing the praises of this family. In the lyrics, *tukudi* is a food consisting of flour of millet with spices and honey.

> A child can't compete with his elders.
> A child can't prepare *tukudi* from stone.
> Even if he prepared it he would be unable to eat its dregs.
> You are the one who takes us,
> You are the one who takes us back.

From a purely historical point of view, the juxtaposition of these diverse divinities and the ethnic groups that worship them provides the key to understanding both the relationships between these peoples and also the societies themselves. For example, each Doguwa, male or female, has its own particular role in intervening to aid or punish humans. Adama, as Taguimba says in one of her songs, is the divinity of farmers. Rankaso is the older sister of all Doguwa spirits. In this role, she protects the Azna against external threats. For this reason, Taguimba portrayed her as invincible.

> Rankaso never goes down on her knees [She is invincible];
> Only Allah can save us!
> Yes Rankaso never goes down on her knees.
> Only Allah can save us! You are the leader,
> Then *bori* devotees follow you.
> You are the leader, and then *bori* devotees follow you!
> Yes Rankaso never goes down on her knees.
> Only Allah can save us! You are the eternal.

Moreover, during wars, she takes the lead on the battlefield, with the warriors following—or, in other words, placing themselves under her protection.

As Rankaso is a spirit of war, her altar is always marked by the presence of a spear stuck in the ground. She shares this military function with her other sisters: Hwasa-Hwako; Sarraounia, the woman who was once the queen of the Azna, and best known for her resistance against the notoriously violent Voulet-Chanoine expedition across the Sahel in the nineteenth century; Baka-Baka; Kujji; Hajo; and Dosa. The reference below to the "Zabarma man" is to a person from the Zarma people, who live on the left bank of the Niger River, between the right-bank Songhaï and the Hausa farther east.

> A child without a Doguwa is vulnerable!
> Here is the thing of the chief Sumana father of Mamane!
> Dogondoutchi is dangerous for a Zabarma man!
> You telling, another telling, it is impossible!
> The black woman who leads men, by the point of a spear!

In addition to a common link with war, these women share other characteristics: they are known as sorcerers, they wear black wrappers, and they sacrifice black animals on their altars. The other Doguwa represent a range of socioprofessional categories—for example, butchers (Kure), barbers and blacksmiths (Makeriya), and herders.

The Nabisa

The Nabisa are spirits of Songhaï origin, known in their cosmogony as Tooru, the counterparts of the Doguwa. The diverse peoples of the Songhaï-speaking world—for example, the Wogo, the Kurthèye, and the Dendi—live on islands and along the banks of the Niger River from Jenné in Mali down to northern Benin. These spirits are often linked to water as well as the sky and are best known for their control of the river, as Taguimba pointed out in lyrics such as

> The husband is in the river,
> The wife is in the river, Harakoy [queen spirit of the river]
> . . . .
> only the greatest can go across a river!

The Nabisa stand at the top of the Songhaï pantheon, but are in second position among the Azna spirits, where their role is to render justice by destroying those who have committed crimes. The spirits of the Nabisa include Dandu, Zabéri, Nayanga, Harakoy Dicko, Salamatu, Maru Kiray, Mahama Surgu, Musa, Dango, Yabilan, Hausakoy, Bellah, Sadjera, and Nyabéri, a spirit who has been excommunicated from the Tooru. According to Rouch (1989, 60), the Tooru

are supposed to have come from Ourounkouma, a city in Egypt that is known
for the fact that it exists in the dark, with no sunlight. These gods are reported
to have come from Egypt to establish themselves in the forest of Gueriel in the
region of Téra, 173 kilometers northwest of Niamey. Their ancestors are Huwa
and Huwatata, who produced two children called Hagam and Urfama, sometimes known as Gingam and Gingam Falala. Hagam is viewed as the founder
of the Gangi Kwarey or Farfaru. As for Urfama, she gave birth to a single child,
Dandu Urfama, called the true father of all the Tooru. He established his home
in Bandjo in the western region of Niger.

After marriage, Dandu fathered six children, four boys and two girls: Yolo-
ga-tyindé-ga, with hair on his thigh; two girls, Nayanga Danfama and Zan-
garéna, then three boys, Kabé-ka-méné-Saru, who wipes up the river current
with his beard; Koyti-Koyti; and finally Zabéri, father of Harakoy Dicko, the
mother of the Tooru.

The goddess Harakoy Dicko reigns over the river, a position assigned to her
by her children, while they rule the sky and the elements of the universe: fire,
water, and air. Musa controls thunder as well as wind and clouds, Dango is the
god of lightning, and Hausakoy forges the axes of Dango with which he kills
his victims. Finally, Bellah controls fire.

The Farfaru

The Farfaru divinities, of Tuareg or Arab origin, largely Muslim, are known
above all to be very lazy. It is impossible to list all the members of the family
because many of them are not concerned with human affairs and thus do not
expect any worship. Those for whom there is a cult are Allarbu, Mallam Elhadji
(Alfaga, for the Songhaï), and Zaki Sarki. These are all Muslims or seeking to
become Muslims, as indicated in the frequently repeated song lyric, "Zaki is a
Muslim student."

The others in the Farfaru family simply do not appear to humans. Those
cited above, according to Adeline Masquelier (2001, 263), are very calm spirits
who teach the Qurʾān to their followers. Even during possession ceremonies,
they distinguish themselves from other spirits by their tranquility and their
wisdom, in contrast to the Babule and the Zanzana, which follow.

The Zanzana

These are divinities associated more with evil than with good. Their mother or
older sister is Gurmungna, supposed to be a daughter of Harakoy Dicko, who
wanted to rise to the sky along with her brothers. But Kiray, the oldest member
of the family, forced Harakoy Dicko to the ground, causing her to lose the use
of her legs and her ability to fly. The result was that she hops like a toad. Under

these circumstances, she decided to take refuge with her other brother, Sago, the rainbow. From that vantage, and as a consequence of her handicap, she terrorizes humans.

While the divinities of the first three families only punish people who offend them, the Zanzana are the source of all epidemics. In Hausa, Zanzana means "tremble." The term refers to the way victims of the Zanzana tremble like all people who suffer from fever. These spirits, then, incarnate evil because of the various diseases they cause. Mérie is one of them, and she is known to punish "all those who have offended her by giving them dracunculose, a fatal condition known as Guinea worm disease, the symptoms of which are wounds and stomach aches," as Taguimba points out in one of her songs. The other spirits are known to cause eye diseases and even abortions. They hate children because among these spirits, it is believed, one finds women who died in childbirth. These women, who find protection with Gurmungna, return to take revenge on humans. Thus, Mérie, Ma'inna, and Tahamu are veritable calamities. They have a great capacity to seduce people because they are either prostitutes or beautiful girls. In particular they like to seduce young men who dare to go out at night. But the seductive talents of these spirits are not limited to humans. They also seduce other divinities, causing scandals. Nicole Echard observes that in a general sense, one can see on their faces

> a budurwa, a term used to describe girls from the time their breasts begin to develop until they have given birth, even if the child is born dead. . . . Arzanzana is a woman already adult . . . who, extremely seductive, is wooed and petted by the other spirits as their favorite, though she has already contracted several marriages. Her childish, capricious, and coquettish nature causes her marital instability; she has never given birth. An analysis of the content of songs dedicated to Mérie and Ma'Inna shows clearly that they are girls who like everything that is beautiful but don't hesitate to cause trouble. They are associated with snakes whose bodies are beautiful but who also bite. And like all snakes, their natural tendency is to bite. They are also the spirits of hunters whom they help to catch game. Whoever steps beyond appropriate limits—not clearly defined—is attacked by means of seduction or disease. This is why hunters are distrustful of women who are especially beautiful, especially those who are strangers. (1991, 216)

The Babaku

The Babaku are known as "black" divinities. They represent the first inhabitants of the river region. They embarked on a losing war against the Nabisa. The result was that they had to give up their land to the victor. Other spirits not involved in the conflict, notably the Doguwa, preferred to remain in their own region, planting manioc, according to the Songhaï. In the rest of the region, the Nabisa became the masters.

These stories explain relations between peoples today and the way they see each other. The stories constitute the collective memories of the war between the Songhaï and the Gurmantché on the right bank of the Niger River in the early seventeenth century.

The spirits of Gurmantché origin have a positive relationship with other families—with the Farfaru and the Nabisa, for example, but more especially with the Doguwa. The chief of the Gurmantché spirits is Zatao, praised by Tagu-imba in her songs.

> Yes the great one, I greet the great one.
> Zatao is great.
> Yes the great one, I greet the great one

The Gurmantché are farmers and hunters who have their own system of belief. Their spirits are Bonizé, Malo, Gandey, Mossizé, Dunaba, Zuduba, and Tirsi. But little is known about them and the tendency is to fall back on better-known ones such as Dunaba and Zatao.

The Dandagunay

These are dwarf spirits, hunters of animals in the bush but also shepherds or guards for the domestic animals supposed to be part of the Doguwa world. Taguimba refers to that world in her lyrics about the unpredictable nature of one of these spirits:

> He set free all the cows of Doguwa.
> Here is a child with a purse full of money.
> Anyone who snatches it from him
> Will be struck as though an ordinary thing had happened.

The narrative below by Hama describes the first inhabitants of the region, who had to flee either because there was no more game or due to pressure from the invaders who inhabit the region today.

> Our country covered all of Africa, to the north, beyond the seas, to the cold continents that we were the first to populate. We are, then . . . the creatures of civilization that men have since developed in ways that today menace their own existence. (Hama 1973, 50)

The activities in which these dwarf spirits engage, hunting and the raising of domestic animals, reminds one of another very short people in Africa, the pygmies. For the Azna, pygmy spirits include Dan Tsatsumbé, Maman Sambo,

Dan Udé, Faraka, Janayé, and Salma. They are very much like humans, claims Boubou Hama (1973). Speaking through the character of an old Attakurma called Bi Bio, the double from the past, Hama observes:

> Our nature as spirits is similar to that of the villager. We see him, but he only sees us when we want him to do so or when, in the solitude of the bush, believing that we are safe, we cross the 'fragile barrier of the invisible' that separates us from men. In this case, we become visible to the man. But if an unusual sound is heard, we disappear instantly by taking refuge in the invisible which is . . . only a state of the universe. (Hama 1973, 61)

They thus have an advantage over humans. The Attakurma Bi Bio continues:

> We have available to us two forms of life: our own spiritual existence that is quite tangible, and yours that simply offers us the chance for access to the world of man. God has given us the power to live like them and in the same way as them. . . . In fact this is one of the advantages we have over men. (Hama 1973, 61–62)

In this case, the *bori* cult is linked to ontology. Boubou Hama observes that

> For the African, man, more than reason, is first a 'double' that surrounds the spirit where the soul lives, that conditions the essence of reason. Thus, man who lives among his equals is not only a human unit that one can count, [but] is also a double in the image of living man. After death, when this double torments the living, the Iro, priests who bury the dead, call them forth in the form of some animal. The killed double disappears from the community of the spirits of the village. The double then frees the abstract soul that cannot be detected by any of our senses. (Hama 1973, 32–33)

In possession, the idea is that humans lend their bodies to spirits because the nature of these divinities is different from that of humans.

The old Attakurma Bi Bio continues:

> You see me in flesh and blood. In reality, I am made up of neither flesh nor bones that can be reduced to ashes. I am in a material state that is invisible to villagers. My spiritual flesh does not weigh down on me the way yours does. Our bodies are not subject to the law of gravity. It is not subject to disease, only mortal accident. (Hama 1973, 50)

The Babule

The Babule are divinities produced by the encounter between the people of Niger and French colonialists. For the most part, they are caricatures of the colonial administration as seen through the most striking characters, both white and black. Their appearance is quite recent, beginning in the late 1920s: 1927 according to Idrissa Kimba (1981, 46), and 1926 according to Jean Rouch (1989, 80).

They include Istamboula, the great Muslim chief of all the Hauka, who, as a man from Istanbul, is viewed as a Turk; Gomna, the governor of the colony, in second position after Istanbul, Zénéral Malia (the "general" of the sea, whom I would simply call the admiral of the naval fleet), and King Zuzi and the king of the judges. The term *king* stems from the neighboring British colony of Nigeria or from the migration of the Songhaï to the Gold Coast, today Ghana. Others include Mayaki, "warrior" in Hausa; Komandan Mougou (as "commandant de cercle" or district officer, a man who is remembered as having ruled with great severity in the region of Filingué); Sectar, a secretary who types; Kaparan Gardi, the corporal of the guards and the assistant to Komandan Mougou, who knows how to break iron between his teeth. The most feared of these assistants is assigned the most repressive tasks in the region: Babule the blacksmith; and Fatmata Malia, the wife of the general, who has a child named Tiémogo fathered by the corporal.

Tiémogo, cited above, also knows how to dig up money hidden in the ground. He is a spoiled child who knows where his parents hide their money put aside to pay taxes. Other Babule include Kafarankot, the corporal of those who have migrated to the coast; Hanga Béri (big ears), the locomotive engineer; and Bambara Mossi, a representative of the African riflemen known generically as *tirailleurs sénégalais,* or Senegalese rifleman, who, in fact, were limited to the Senegalese only at the beginning of the colonial conquest. As the French penetrated inland, soldiers were recruited among many peoples. In this case, the *tirailleurs* in Niger are presented as Mossi from Upper Volta, now Burkina Faso, or Bambara from Mali. These "foreign" soldiers were employed by the French as *gardes cercle,* or local police, and used to terrorize people.

Others include Askandja the judge; Wasiri the executioner; Lokotor the doctor (from the French term for doctor, *le docteur*); Maimoto, the driver (from Hausa, meaning "chief of the *moto*"); Maikwano the mechanic (meaning "chief of the mechanics"); Mailamba, the surveyor or civil engineer; Dogo Malia, the giant; Maikaraga, the French colonial administrator who remains seated in his chair or hammock; and then Kafuri, the terror of the marabouts, or clerics. The women come next, such as Mouskoour; Mariama; Ramatala, a woman who has only one child; and André, a mulatto child.

Since independence in 1960, new spirits have appeared: Parsidan de la république (president of the republic), des Minis de ger (or ministers of war) and generic Minis (ministers). Next to them one finds the entire military hierarchy: Colonel, Capitaine, Lieutenant, Adjudant-chef, Adjudant, Sergent-Chef, and

Sergent. There are thirty-seven spirits in this family, but it is constantly changing. Kimba, in *Guerre et Sociétés* (1981), argues that the colonial-era spirits constitute a form of resistance to colonization, an observation made earlier by Rouch
(1989, 92n.k).

In fact, the family is much more than that. It is a call to guerilla war, as evidenced in a lyric in one of Taguimba's songs: "Tell men to go into the army."

The title of the song, "Death finds you even at home," is a call to men to go
into hiding in order to form a resistance movement. The only problem was the
lack of a leader who could channel the accumulating frustrations of the people,
who were proud, freed, and skilled in the art of war. The spirits appealed to the
men to revolt. Since the French colonials were viewed at that time as sorcerers
who sucked the blood of humans, the Babule spirits pursued and punished
them all during the night. The "kingdom" of the divinities being the night, men
are invited to do during the day what they do at night: hunt for sorcerers.

ANALYSIS OF THE PANTHEON

In the pantheon of the Azna, as well as in that of the Songhaï to the west, it is
clear that the populations are attempting to maintain their collective memory,
which suggests that there is a historic dimension that neither Rouch nor Diawara failed to see. For the latter, there are different kinds of cults:

> First, there is the cult of the spirits of the land, basically a local cult wor-
> shipped by local people. The cult of the ancestors constitutes a new layer on
> top of those of earlier generations, with the mythic ancestor serving as the
> protector of the family. Finally, there is the cult of spirits that are not rooted
> in the local region. (1987, 71)

Thus, heroes of the past are often deified and enter the mythology of the
people through other overarching divinities such as the Tooru of the Songhaï or the Doguwa of the Azna. Examples are the spirit Faran Maka Boté, the
ancestor of the Sorko of Niger; Sonni Ali Ber, the powerful Songhaï emperor
transformed into the mythic spirit of Zaberi in the Tooru family; Sarraounia
and Baura of the Azna; Harakoy Dicko, considered by some Songhaï to be their
ancestor; or Zirbine, the primary ancestor of people from the Songhaï village
of Namari-Goungou, twenty kilometers north of the town of Tillabery, on the
Niger river.

Rouch writes that in the Songhaï perception of death, "after the death of
the ancestor, his soul goes to the world of the souls, but always comes back to
visit the place of his burial in order to protect his descendants" (1989, 54). His

observation applies in particular to the djinns or spirits of whom Zirbine is the prototype in the Songhaï world. However, when the soul of the ancestor is incarnated in a stone, it then becomes one of the Tooru who responds to appeals. This is the case of Harakoy Dicko.

The Hausa of the Aréwa region believe that all of the spirits have a village that is called Konkombilo, a place of refuge when, for example, one of them refuses to free an individual even after incantations and ceremonies. The scholar of Hausa culture Graham Furniss writes that in the Katsina region of northern Nigeria, the village of the divinities is called Kangaré or Jangaré: "The spirits inhabit a parallel world called Jangare, with family groupings and hierarchies, and each has particular characteristics of speech, movement and appearance" (1996, 92). In the Songhaï world, on the other hand, people know that the Tooru have settled in a particular place after a migration that, according to Rouch, has lasted several years; their settlement is located in the former forest of Gueriel, in the Tera region northwest of Niamey. This spot has become today an important but ordinary village just like others in the Songhaï region.

Both of these pantheons, as indicated above, are in some ways a form of living memory for the people who worship the cults of the spirits. These memories, like oral epics from the region, explain migrations and the conflicts between peoples. A close analysis reveals in a broad sense the way one people views a neighboring group, both in the past and in the present. This correspondence between history and spiritual life has been observed by scholars in other parts of the world. Often, the events of the past are dramatized, just as voodoo refers audiences to the suffering of Africans in their transfer to the New World as slaves, as Guérin Montilus has shown. For him,

> It was first slavery, then the war of independence, then the establishment of a peasant society after liberation, and finally the perpetual struggle against poverty and the deficiencies of the socio-economic structures that ended up giving these members of the diaspora the chance to rediscover the rites and myths that they inherited from their ancestors and that they transformed in the New World while, at the same time, integrating new elements, the result of their encounters with other races and ethnic groups from different parts of Africa. (Montilus 1988, 50)

In his research on Brazilian candomblé, Jean Ziegler emphasized the historic dimension of and the role of collective memory played by the cult of voodoo. He concluded that

> cut from their ecological roots, dispersed by deportation and, finally, worn out by the harassment inherent in labor by slaves, dozens of African societies

have been resurrected in the Americas. To sum up, there is a search for lost unity in the possession cults and voodoo. The slave hunters, the slave traders, blessed by the church, tore apart families, separated child from mother and man from woman. For centuries, they rendered the complex fabric of warm and close human relations. (1979, 135–136)

If this diaspora voodoo is what Ziegler has described, the phenomenon of possession cults with trances in western Niger is in general quite different. What is certain, however, is that in both cases, there is a historical dimension that cannot be ignored.

The spirits that one encounters inform participants and observers about hierarchies, categories, and relations between peoples in the course of their particular histories. The Dandagunay refer to the pygmies, the Babaku to the Gurmantche, the Farfaru to the Tuareg and the Arabs, the Doguwa to the Hausa, the Babule to the European colonizers and their African collaborators. "Here again, the world of the Holley [spirits] and that of humans appear to be copies of each other's relations," argues Rouch (1989, 59). In this sense, one can say that there are forms of ideology conveyed by the pantheons—for example, domination. "This assemblage [of spirits] corresponds exactly to the world of man . . . both on the ground and in the course of historic events" (Rouch 1989, 59). In effect, in the relations between spirits in a pantheon one finds relationships of master/slave, nomads/sedentary peoples, farmers and herdspeople, life and death, nobles and craftsmen—in sum, a transposition of social relations to the supernatural level and, I am tempted to say, a kind of idealization of the psychology of social relations.

Upon a closer look at the seven great families of divinities listed, it is clear that there is a characterization and categorization marked by a social hierarchy based on conceptions that people have of their neighbors. For example, for the Songhaï a Hausa is not only a farmer, in particular a planter of manioc, but above all someone who is a miserly trader, as he appears in the spirit of Hausakoy, a god of Hausa origin whom his mother, Harakoy Dicko, conceived with a Hausa from Yauri in the Republic of Nigeria after many marriages.

One can see in the diversity and variety of these multiple marriages a search for unity among peoples in the face of a woman who does not hesitate to marry outside her community. Her goal is to have children who have different fathers but who are linked with each other by ties of blood, to the point that no son of Harakoy Dicko would dare to do anything without the presence of his other milk brothers, sons of the same mother but of different fathers.

Rouch explains that during a possession ceremony that requires a certain dispatch or speed, it is necessary that "all the Tooru always number seven, and that Harakoy, Dango, Kiray, Musa, and Hausakoy be present" (1989, 92). But there can be substitutions or transfers of spirits, adds Rouch. "At Simiri," he says, "Zabéri, who took the place of Mahama, is now replaced by Nayanga, his sister. At Niamey, Mahama is replaced by his 'brother' Sarki, but near Gaya [a town downriver from Niamey], Zabéri again finds his proper place with Mahama, but by eliminating Faran Barou" (1989, 92n.f).

For us, the numerous marriages of Harakoy Dicko reflect a search to integrate peoples. There are seven families of Holey or *bori* that are like human families with different matrimonial relations. "The divinities," writes Diawara, "are an organization that is similar to that of man of which they are almost doubles" (1987, 77). This is the same view of Rouch (1989) and Hama (1973).

CONCLUSION

The analysis of the spirit pantheon, whether that of the Hausa-speaking Azna of the Aréwa region or that of the Songhaï of the right bank of the Niger River, reveals clearly the relations between these two peoples as well as with others. They may be relations marked by conflict, as between the Songhaï and the Gurmantché, or by friendship, as with the Songhaï and the Hausa.

The *bori* and the *holey* constitute to some extent a library or an archive in which are preserved a precious document, in this case the events of French colonization, just as stories from the precolonial era have been "archived." The spirit world is a way of preserving and transmitting the major chapters of history through the figures who have influenced the past of these peoples. That is why one finds such a variety of people from different races and ethnic groups in these pantheons—in this case ranging from the Gurmantché to the Europeans, including the Fulbe, the peoples on the coast, the pygmies, the Tuareg, the Arabs, the Bambara, and the Mossi. This diversity also explains why one finds some Islamic elements in the possession cults in Niger, which, as Rouch notes, poses problems for researchers who are trying to distinguish between external and internal influences. The one feature that serves as the point of departure for analyses of this multi-dimensional phenomenon is the dynamic character of these traditions, and in particular the way that the pantheon is constantly renewed.

The Guinean author Camara Laye summed up the situation of Africans whose lives are marked by orality. He writes, "When peoples live for years and years in a state of freedom . . . it is natural that these peoples looking for their own identity, that they return to their past, and that, digging in to this past, they look intensely at the features of peoples and things that have guided their destiny" (1978, 11). For this reason, one can say that consciously or to a greater extent unconsciously, the followers of *bori,* or, in a larger sense, the peoples of Niger engaged in these kinds of traditions, are seeking their own identity in a kind of reminiscence, as Plato might say.

Another important aspect that needs to be underscored is that, like other beings, these divinities are subject not only to passions but also to action. In other words, divinities are born, grow, marry (at least some of them), reproduce, and finally die. Even if their lifespan is longer that that of the human, the divinities are not eternal. According to one tradition in Niger, the lives of the divinities are less desirable than those of humans because the spirits cannot bury their dead, but must instead be exposed to the atmosphere.

The *bori* culture includes philosophical, oral, historic, and sociopolitical dimensions. Unfortunately, few Nigeriens dare to venture into this world, just as they fear revealing their naked bodies. Nevertheless, the values of the followers of the possession cults are those that are appreciated today but that seem to be disappearing. These include, for example, generosity, solidarity, sincerity, loyalty, and respect for others and their property.

All the ancient values of the peoples of western Niger are centered in this cult. One finds evidence of similar values in peoples in central Niger who take part in these kinds of cults, including among the peoples of the regions of Tahoua, especially among the Adérawa, in the department of Maradi among the Gobirawa, and among the Katsinawa and other assimilated peoples.

When singers such as Taguimba reference these gods, either directly in lyrics or indirectly by praising the followers of these cults, she and her sister are not simply bringing to life the deepest sources of social values. The listener from another African culture, or from outside of Africa, may simply hear a long string of names and places. But for the peoples of Niger, these songs are a call to the values of the past. Even more, when these women sing, they evoke a spirit world that is in many ways the parallel of the world of the living. This spiritual world, as it comes alive in the songs and in the ceremonies of the cult, becomes a form of reality that is the template of the life of the living, rather than the reverse. Finally, one can say that the lyrics and the cults that they reference constitute a form of resistance against cultural erosion and the conquest of the country by foreign influences. The fact that these songs are sung by women, and in this case by the well-known Taguimba, underscores the public dimension of lyrics. Taguimba may appear at first as an exception to the belief that women have no voice in African societies. But the spirit world is full of women spirits, and those who sing about them best are women. It is they who provide the clearest window on the world of these spirits.

APPENDIX

Table 3.1. DOGUWA or HAUSA GANJI

Name	Gender	Ethnicity	Name	Gender	Ethnicity
1- Babay	M	Hausa	16- Baka Giwa	F	Fulani
2- Magiro	M	Hausa	17- Koré	F	Fulani
3- Duna	M	Hausa	18- Dosa	F	Fulani
4- Azne	M	Hausa	19- Sama'ou	F	Fulani
5- Mallam Alhadi	M	Hausa	20- Hajo	F	Fulani
6- Kure	M	Hausa	21- Aissa	F	Fulani
7- Mashi	M	Hausa	22- Koromniyya	F	Fulani
8- Babako	F	Hausa	23- Mai Koré	F	Fulani
9- Rankaso	F	Hausa	24- Messa	F	Fulani
10- Zakuma	F	Hausa	25- Adama	F	Fulani
11- Baka-baka	F	Hausa	26- Wankarma	F	Kanuri
12- Hwasa-Hwako	F	Hausa	27- Lady	F	Fulani
13- Maidaro (Allima)	F	Hausa	28- Karangamaw	F	Gurma
14- Karya-mai-nono	F	Hausa	29- Haggo	F	Fulani
15- Kujji	F	Fulani			

Table 3.2. DANDAGUNAY or ATTAKURMA

Name	Gender	Ethnicity
1- Maman Sambo	Male	Fulani
2- Dan Tsatsumbé	Male	Fulani
3- Dan Udé	Male	Fulani
4- Cirido	Female	Fulani
5- Janayé	Female	Fulani
6- Faraka	Male	Fulani

Table 3.3. NABISA or TOORU

Name	Gender	Ethnicity
1- Hasa + Hini	M+F	Egyptian
2- Suntanan + Mantaan	M+F	Egyptian
3- Baana + Baana Kiray	M+F	Egyptian
4- Watakari Gambo	Male	Egyptian
5- Urfama or Gingam Falala	Male	Egyptian
6- Dandu Beeri	Male	Kurumba
7- Zabéri (father of Harakoy Dikko)	Male	Songhay
8- Hala Hawa Tarakoy (mother of H. Dikko)	Female	Fulani
9- Harakoy Dicko (mother of Tooru)	Female	Songhay-Fulani
10- Maru Kirey (1st son of H. Dikko)	Male	Songhay
11- Mahama Surgu (2nd son of H. Dikko)	Male	Tuareg
12- Moussa Nyawri (3th son of H. Dikko)	Male	Gurma
13- Mande Hausakoy (4th son of H. Dikko)	Male	Hausa
14- Farambaru Koda (5th son of H. Dikko)	Androgynous	Tuareg
15- Dango (adoptive son of H. Dikko)	Male	Bariba
16- Nyabéri (daughter of H. Dikko)	Female	Djinn
17- Zirbine Sangay	Male	Djinn
18- Zaki Sarki (adoptive son of H. Dikko)	Male	Tuareg

Table 3.4. FARFARU or GANJI KOAREY (all are Tuareg)

Name	Gender
1- Hasa + Hini	M+F
2- Suntanan + Mantaan	M+F
3- Huwa + Huwatata	M+F
4- Hagam or Gingam	Male
5- Allarbu	Male
6- Alfaga	Male
7- Tahamu	Male
8- Zaki Sarki or Febana or Dawdu or Batan Balala	Male
9- Danganda or Batata	Female
10- Zakye	Male
11- Afoda	Male
12- Makoara	Male
13- Bature	Male
14- Kyagaw	Male
15- Nagari Koda	Male
16- Saware	Male
17- Guba Siki	Male
18- Maleki	Male

Table 3.5. BABAKU or GANJI BI (all are Mossi people in Burkina Faso now)

Name	Gender	Name	Gender
1- Hangu Zangu Borzangu	Male	17- Fadimata Dongayze	Female
2- Zuduba Bala	Male	18- Hawa	Female
3- Zatao	Male	19- Zambarki	Male
4- Dunaba	Male	20- Kadarinke	Male
5- Malo	Male	21- Zaagani	Male
6- Bondaru	Male	22- Ganyo	Female
7- Takun	Male	23- Hamni	Male
8- Sumana	Male	24- Singilingi	Female
9- Haudu	Male	25- Nyala Buli	Female
10- Gande	Male	26- Guba Siki	Male
11- Bonkurtu	Male	27- Maryamu	Female
12- Gamay	Male	28- Toro	Male
13- Jabyaize	Male	29- Bonizé	Male
14- Bade	Male	30- Hadjo	Female
15- Naman Kura	Male	31- Zolgu	Male
16- Gerba	Male	32- Kodyel or Ganya	Female

Table 3.6. ZANZANA or HARGAY (All are children of Djinn of Death)

Name	Gender	Name	Gender
1- Nya Beri	Female	12- Zibo	Male
2- Kokayna	Male	13- Gyinde Keri	Male
3- Sini Bana Tyare	Male	14- Kudu	Male
4- Fasigata	Male	15- Gataguru	Male
5- Fasyo	Male	16- Kumna Kumna	Male
6- Tirsi	Male	17- Bagambayze	Male
7- Tondi Kuna Malfa	Male	18- Gangani Kortu	Male
8- Hari-Hari	Male	19- Zinbi	Male
9- Masu	Male	20- Zikirya	Male
10- Masusu	Male	21- Kozob	Male
11- Bala	Male	22- Kama kama	Male

Table 3.7. BABULE or HAUKA (French colonial administration)

Name	Gender	Name	Gender
1- Istanboula, King of all Babule	Male	15- Askandia (Judge)	Male
2- Gomno (Governor)	Male	16- Wasiri (executioner)	Male
3- Zénéral (General)	Male	17- Lokotoro (doctor)	Male
4- King Zuzi (King of the Judges)	Male	18- Maimoto (chauffeur)	Male
5- Mayaki (warrior)	Male	19- Maikwano (mechanic)	Male
6- Komandan Mougou (commandant)	Male	20- Mailamba (surveyor)	Male
7- Sectar (secretary)	Male	21- Biriru (telephonist)	Male
8- Kaparan Gardi (corporal)	Male	22- Dogo Malia (giant)	Male
9- Babule (blacksmith)	Male	23- Maikaraga (the lazy one)	Male
10- Fatmata Malia (wife of Gomno)	Female	24- Kafuri	Male
11- Tiémogo (a child)	Male	25- Muskura	Female
12- Kafarankot (corporal from coast)	Male	26- Mariama	Female
13- Hanga Béri (locomotive leader)	Male	27- Ramata (a child)	Female
14- Bambara Mossi (African soldier)	Male	28- André (mulatto)	Male

WORKS CITED

Diawara, Idrissa. 1987. Les cultes de possession avec transes au Niger. In *Cahiers du CELHTO* 2 (2): 71–89.

Echard, Nicole. 1991. Gender relationships and religion: Women in the Hausa *bori* of Ader. In *Hausa Women in the Twentieth Century,* ed. Catherine Coles and Beverly Mack, 207–220. Madison: University of Wisconsin Press.

Es-Sa'di, Abderraman. 1964 [1898–1900]. *Tarîkh es-Sudan.* Trans. Octave Houdas. 2nd ed. Paris: Adrien-Maisonneuve.

Furniss, Graham. 1996. *Poetry, Prose and Popular Culture in Hausa.* Washington, D.C.: Smithsonian Institution.

Hale, Thomas A. and Nouhou Malio. 1996. *The Epic of Askia and Mohammed.* Bloomington: Indiana University Press.

Hama, Boubou. 1973. *Le double d'hier rencontre demain.* Paris: Union Générale d'Editions.

Jewsiewicki, Bogumil. 1987. African historical studies: Academic knowledge as "usable past" and radical scholarship. Paper presented at the African Studies Association meeting, Denver.

Johnson, John William, Thomas A. Hale, and Stephen Belcher, eds. 1997. *Oral Epics from Africa: Vibrant Voices from a Vast Continent.* Bloomington: Indiana University Press.

Kâti, Mahmoud. 1981 [1913]. *Tarîikh al-Fattash.* Trans. Octave Houdas and Maurice Delafosse. Paris: Maisonneuve et Larose.

Kimba, Idrissa. 1981. *Guerre et sociétés.* Etudes Nigériennes 21. Niamey: CELHTO.

Laye, Camara. 1978. *Le Maître de la Parole.* Paris: Presses Pocket.

Masquelier, Adeline. 2001. *Prayer Has Spoiled Everything: Possession, Power, and Identity in an Islamic Town of Niger.* Durham: Duke University Press.

Montilus, Guérin. 1988. *Dieux en Diaspora: Les loa Haitiens et le Vaudou du royaume d'Allada (Benin)*. Niamey: Centre de Recherches Linguistique et Historique par Tradition Orale.

Namaïwa, Boubé. 2007. Introduction à la pensée Azna. In *Lougou et Saraouniya*, by Nicole Moulin, Boubé Namaïwa, Marie-Françoise Roy, and Bori Zamo, 30–39. Laval: Tarbiyya Tatali.

Nietzsche, Friedrich. 1990. *l'Antéchrist suivi de Ecce Homo*. Paris: Gallimard.

Rouch, Jean. 1955. *Les Maîtres Fous*. Film.

———. 1989 [1960]. *La Religion et La Magie Songhay*. Brussels: Editions de l'université de Bruxelles.

Ziegler, Jean. 1979. *Le Pouvoir africain*. Paris: Seuil.

4

Initiation and Funeral Songs from the Guro of Côte d'Ivoire

Ariane Deluz

Women's songs are too often viewed by outsiders simply as a medium for passing the time while the singers are engaged in a variety of household tasks. As a French researcher living in Guro society in Côte d'Ivoire for the first time in 1958, my goal was to learn more about women's songs performed during other activities because I believed that this form of verbal art is one of the keys to understanding a society. As a female I was especially welcomed by Guro women, who have their own women's secret society distinct from that of the men. The women's society includes ceremonies centered on masks, or women who appear in a form of dress that conveys an image of the spirit world. The women gave me access to the songs they sang as part of their society's rituals and in a variety of other contexts. But as I discovered one evening, there were limits to how far I could go down the path of learning the most intimate of these songs.

An excision ceremony, part of the larger set of initiation rites for girls that are marked by a variety of songs, was scheduled to be performed one evening. Although the leader of the women's society was housing me in a sacred hut and providing me to some extent with a privileged perspective on Guro culture, it was not clear whether I should attend the ceremony later that evening. Rather than simply tell me that I could not observe this intimate and highly important event in the lives of the initiates, my host slipped a drug into my evening meal. I dozed off early and slept unusually well that night. In retrospect, and for many reasons, I am happy that she employed this subtle method to keep me from attending the ceremony.

But she and other Guro women did initiate me into the richness and complexity of songs sung for more public parts of the ceremonies marking the transition of girls to young women. For example, in the following song, the initiates are invited to dance and to undergo the excision, a small incision around the clitoris:

> *Woda a vole yu gi*
> *e nenelo*
> "We came to put seed in the *yu*
> She has to dance"

"Put seed in the *yu*" means to perform the excision rite; an equivalent is *yera sa,* or "wash the face" (Deluz 1987, 124). *Yu* is the most frequent Guro term heard during these songs because it refers to a force, in this case a hidden mask wrapped in white cloth, as well as the cult attached to this force and the dancing of this mask/force. In initiation, *yu* is also linked to the excision of young girls and their acceptance into a secret association where they learn how to master their sexual life and their fertility at puberty.

In addition to initiation songs, the women also made sure that I learned the kinds of songs that marked other important life events, such as funerals. The repertoire for these two kinds of events, however, was not closely limited to the events themselves but instead included a broad range of other kinds of songs. Many of them conveyed insults or comments on sexuality, and raised other subjects. In other words, initiation and funeral songs serve as keys to understanding both the phenomenon of songs in all of their diversity and the society that produces them. The lyrics of these songs are very short. Most songs contain only one line that is repeated in a variety of ways. I have published a few of these songs elsewhere, as indicated after the songs, but most have never appeared in print.

Together, these songs offer a window onto the complex role of women in Guro society. The lyrics reveal that Guro woman are free to say what they want within the framework of a society that has clearly defined roles for both sexes. Their freedom of expression contradicts the view of female Africans as voiceless servants in male-dominated societies.

Before turning to the lyrics, it is essential to provide a brief sketch of Guro society, because certain activities are the basis for performances of their songs.

The Guro are a Mande people on the southern fringe of that vast group of societies that trace their origins to the epic hero Sundiata Keita. For example, one finds in the Guro language words that are similar to Mande terms but that have undergone change—for example, *tre,* a word for sun in both Guro and

Malinke. But the Guro do not have a tradition of professional singers, male or female. Known in the Sahel by the more general terms *griots* and *griottes,* these singers are indicated among the Mande-speaking peoples with a variety of words—for example, *jeliw* for performers of both genders, and *jelimusolu* more specifically for females. Some elements of the *jeliw* tradition do appear to survive among the Guro, particularly the custom of providing or asking for rewards, especially during the mourning surrounding funeral ceremonies.

There is no clear explanation for the separation of the Guro from their more northerly Mande cousins such as the Malinke, the Bamana, and the Soninke. According to the traditions of the Guro, they migrated south to the center of Côte d'Ivoire two centuries ago. Today they number close to 600,000, but at the time I began my research there in 1958, census estimates for the Guro were closer to 150,000. It is difficult to determine today just how many live in their original homeland and how many have migrated to other parts of the country or the region.

They used to be warriors, farmers, hunters, weavers, and traders, but at least up to the 1980s, they focused mainly on agriculture. They have no chiefs, and political power is—or was—held by the elder men. The Guro are of patrilineal descent, which means that women and men belong to their father's family. Authority and goods are transmitted from older to younger brothers and then to sons of the older brother. When they marry, girls go to live with their husband's extended family, composed of several nuclear families whose adult men are agnates—that is, they are linked patrilineally. A young girl knows that her own marriage is a necessary condition for her younger brother's or a patrilineal cousin's marriage. Indeed, the goods given by her future husband's family to her own patrilineal lineage or family will be used to obtain a spouse for her brother or for a father's brother's son, or cousin. Consequently a lineage's daughter (*bne le e de*) is considered socially superior to a lineage's wife (*gnɛnā*).

All the conflicts concerning these women who have different status depending on whether they are single and at home ("girls"), or married and living in the family of their husbands ("wives"), are settled among themselves, not by some larger social group that might involve both men and women. The importance of handling these differences themselves appears in the lyrics to the following song by "girls" addressed to "wives."

Leno nu gulida / min e kle:
"Women have made war
why did they?"
(girls' song to wives)

The quotation marks framing these two different categories of women reflect the fact that those who are married carry a dual identity. A woman is a "girl" in her home village and a "wife" in that of her husband. She has to endure a never-ending shift back and forth between her two conflicting roles. Whenever someone of her kin has died, she visits her family and stays there, mourning with her sisters and father's sisters. Her husband has to bring new gifts (cloth and nowadays money) to her brothers, who are his brothers-in-law and wife-givers, with whom he has a polite and restrained relationship. In this way, a husband adds to the value of the bridewealth, asserts his right upon his own children, and makes his wife a more respected daughter in her own family, to which she still belongs in some way. As a wife in her husband's family, a woman is also respected and esteemed as long as she is a good worker and bears children. But should she commit adultery, the crime is considered an attack on the integrity of the earth—her husband's ancestors—and it has to be repaired by a sacrifice offered to the earth by her husband's uterine nephews, who will then insult and even "beat" her as part of their joking relationship.

All women are forbidden to be present at the rituals and the dances of the main men's cults such as *je, jo, do, gi,* and *yune yune* or even to see their masks. They are not supposed to know anything about them, and any transgression kills or is supposed to kill the culprit. In fact women chat rather freely about these cults when no man is around. Their own mask society, the *kn kne,* is recognized by the Guro, for occult reasons, to be superior to that of the males, in particular the primary one known as *je.* On the other hand, men are forbidden from knowing and seeing anything related to birth, except for the members of health services. An old man told me once, "if you are a man, to see a woman giving birth will kill you, as certainly as seeing the *j* mask will kill a woman."

Initial observations and interactions with the Guro may lead to the conclusion that men and women have strained and even hostile relationships: they openly keep apart, or they insult and even fight with each other. This tension is more apparent, claimed, and official than true. There is much evidence, especially in the songs, for a very strong hidden complementarity between the sexes as well as efficient and discreet collaboration between men and women. For example, the men's mask, *j,* nourishes his power from elements given by the feminine *kn* leader, whose name, *jau,* is a way of pronouncing *jbu,* or "mother of the *j.*" The strong antagonisms are the ones between feminine social groups such as "girls" and "wives." Moreover, these tensions exist psychologically inside every woman. It is often said that although mother and daughter openly show and feel affection toward each other, a mother is able to "bewitch" her daughter, or "eat her in witchcraft." Actually a mother is a "spouse" in the lineage where her daughter is a "girl," so that an imaginary "witchcraft" relationship between mother and daughter duplicates the social conflicts between "spouses" and "girls" within each village.

In their daily lives, women feel and act silently according to these oppositions. But they express themselves very openly during mourning ceremonies and the *kn* rituals that are sometimes linked to them. Between someone's death and burial, there may be a long lapse of time because it is necessary to collect the money needed to carry out the rituals as well as to inform the sons of the sisters of the lineage, or *yuru,* that they must return home for the ceremonies. Though the nephews in particular may reside in a distant location, they are socially obliged to come, dig the graves, and bury the corpses of the members of their maternal or grand-maternal lineage. Moreover, they ritually resist the injunctions of their uncles, complaining while doing their work and symbolically begging for money. All the invited mourning women stay in the village for at least one week after the burial.

During this time, they sing songs, some of which are supposed to tame the "double" or *lei* of the dead person, who is perceived to be still prowling in and around the village. At the same time, men perform their own rituals, but I cannot comment on them here. During all the weeks following the death, women sing, usually sitting and lying during the day and night, now and then running around the village performing the *zegli* ritual of insults between "girls" and "spouses."

When the dead person is a woman belonging to the *kn* association, a *kne* dance is performed, and initiation rites are revived in their sacred part of the savanna as well as in the village. All boys and men are then secluded in the houses. In the last thirty years *kn* rituals have very rarely been performed because no younger women are interested in the rituals, no older women responsible for the cult association have transmitted their knowledge, and there is a general disdain in Côte d'Ivoire toward "animist" cults and modes of thought.

Women performers for these funeral songs and revived initiation rites are found in several groups. For the most part they are the "spouses" in the village, and the "girls" of the village who came for the funerals. But there are also groups from maternal, grand-maternal, and marriage lineages who sometimes sing separately and at other times divide themselves between the "girls" and "spouses" groups.

Death implies desocialization and naturalization. Consequently it allows the women to express themselves with total freedom. Any accusatory or insulting song is allowed, and nobody has a right to silence the singers. So performances where sex is mentioned and mimicked meet only the silent disapproval of the participating men. Songs about sex are also sung during initiation ceremonies. In many of these songs sung for a variety of events, the man appears as the inferior of the two sexes. The lyrics of these songs offer the only medium for mothers to speak about sexuality in front of their own children.

> *Ma ka a yele e vni lo*
> *i bulu a zug gne le ki i nya:*
> "I did not see him, I have just seen him,
> your hernia is big, are you a man?"

This is an initiation song that marks the return of the girls to the village after the excision. They walk in the same way as men suffering from a hernia, with their legs apart for the first time in their lives. The Guro say that men suffering from a hernia are sexually impotent. One etymology for testicular hernia is *bu,* or pregnancy, and *lu,* or daughter; that is, "daughter of pregnancy." *Buleza,* "the man with a hernia," is also "pregnant boy," an insult so scandalous that it is almost never spoken. Songs such as this one are sung in only the most secret of places.

Some of these songs refer directly to the superior sexual power of women.

> *Kuliga, buliga*
> *We yila*
> "The penis is dry (or dead), the vagina is dry
> On salted water"

After making love a woman can know whether the man had an orgasm, but the man cannot know about the woman because he does not see her "water." This insult is directed to men who, secluded in the houses, can hear the lyrics when women sing loudly. In fact, in the following song, it is thanks to the woman's personal "force," or *yu,* that the man is able to copulate with her.

> *Vin vin kun vin vin kun*
> *Lile yule*
> "*Hin Hin* it has caught him,
> the women's *yu* did catch him"

Hin hin is the sound of a man making love to a woman. It is therefore thanks to her *yu* that he was able to make such a noise with her, or in more common terms, to fuck her so vigorously.

This freedom to say such things is linked with ambivalence. Most songs have a double meaning: what they say as well as the opposite. A song can seem to be a praise song, but in reality it is insulting or derogatory.

Since the Guro do not have a professional category of griots or *jeliw* who hold the monopoly on certain forms of singing, nearly all the women, young and old, are active singers. Some enjoy a well-earned reputation, teach other women around them, and sing with regularly invited groups. In some circumstances, usually at second funerals, two well-known singers are invited with their choir to compete. A woman named Gueiman, whose songs I have recorded, analyzed, and published (Deluz [1978] 2001), even became an eponym. I was introduced to another "Gueiman" in a remote village many years later.

At funerals, when groups of women run in and around the village, "girls" and "wives" may insult each other as a part of a cathartic *zegli* ritual (Deluz 1970, 121).

Cei ma i wi je
"Kyei, I am going to break you"

Here the "girls" are insulting the "wives." They sing this song while running through the village with a fake corpse of the "wife" for whom the funeral ceremonies are held.

This "joking speech" is extended to all spoken competitions between "wives" and "girls," ritualized or not. When they sit around the corpse, or sit after the burial around the bed where the corpse had been exposed, either the "girls" sing three songs alternately with the "wives," or one group sings during the first night and the other the following night. One solo singer, or *derevoza* (there may be several in one group), sings a song, usually one verse or two. This theme is then taken over by a second singer, or *zuoza* (there may be two or three *zuoza*). The other women answer by repeating one or two words of the song, or adding a new term, usually modulating it. Good singers repeat the theme several times with variations, and are answered by the choir. There may be slight variations in the song which inform the listeners about its significance. The same song can be performed for anywhere from several minutes to half an hour, and it is often repeated later in the night, as it is or with new variations.

With the exception of the *kene* dancing and ritual songs, which are often accompanied by calabashes, women do not play any instruments or drums. Their night performances last approximately from nine in the evening till first light. At dawn or even later, at full daylight before parting, some singers are in a possessed state, and they furiously sing songs that may vary from insults to praises.

The singers are rewarded in various ways. The family in charge of the mourning or funeral ceremonies provides food to the singers at the end of the day. For important people, these ceremonies may be duplicated one, two, and sometimes more times many years later. These second or subsequent funerals are always ostentatious and can bankrupt a family because of the high cost. Whether first or subsequent funerals, during the night the performers are offered cases of soft drinks and wine, which they distribute among themselves and consume steadily during the pauses between songs. All through the night, the hosts offer money to encourage the women to sing and to express thanks to them. Except for the children, everyone present at the singing session gives money according to the status and the relationships of the donors. Sometimes when they pronounce insulting words, singers are given money in order to shut them up. I myself usually gave an appropriate and previously agreed-upon sum at the beginning of the session, then small sums during the night. Many songs are in fact performed in order to ask for contributions, preferably of money, when women freely insult and laugh at the audience.

Although the Guro constitute a relatively small and unified people, living in several administrative units in the same region, they speak different dialects. This article is based on research conducted in areas where the Guro speak the *ma* dialect (Goitafla and part of Zuenoula prefectures) or the *yizi* dialect (part of Zuenoula and Vavoua prefectures), in the north and northwestern parts of the region they occupy. In spite of these dialectical differences, however, there is a common corpus of both funeral and *kn* songs which have been performed for decades by women not only in the central Guro region but also among adjoining peoples as the result of political, economic, and matrimonial contacts.

Since women usually marry outside their ethnic group, interesting variations emerge between the *ma* and *yizi* dialects. For example, some women's songs are based on borrowed parts of men's songs, or fragments of tales. Other songs are recent and have been composed spontaneously in documented circumstances. They are then borrowed and added to the repertoire of another group. The significance of any song can change in a new context, or even with the mood of the singers: derision can replace tragedy; insult can replace flattery. Also, women frequently trick their audience or make fun of it by proposing changed meanings: good means bad, a man means a woman, and happiness means unhappiness.

The themes of women's songs are extremely diverse. They range from death, with its personifications, to destiny, strength, the sadness of mourning, and praising or mocking the deceased and everything around him or her; there are variations in references to the *kn* cult—dance, mask, the singer, her actions, and her demands. Other themes include thanks to the singer, demands for money by the singer to the audience, contributions, thanks for gifts; songs of men's mask societies with references to epics, genealogies, proverbs, and tales; daily life and characters, animal characteristics or deeds; and finally jokes about ridiculous or silly personalities and absurd activities.

From the evidence, it is clear that songs among the Guro constitute a key medium for the participation of women in major events such as initiations and funerals and for the maintenance of cults such as the *kn,* the secret association into which I was initiated in 1958. The songs also help to define subtle relationships between the different categories of women known as "girls" and "wives." Although the focus here has been on performances at initiations and funerals, the range of songs sung by women to mark these events is quite diverse, especially those at funerals. In other words, songs at funerals are not simply funeral songs, but, in a larger sense, expressions of women on a wide range of related subjects. These songs reveal, then, that women are able to take great liberty to express themselves through the lyrics in a variety of ritual contexts. The superficial everyday separation between men and women masks an integration of both sexes in society that becomes more visible and audible in the songs sung by women.

What is not clear is the extent to which these songs are surviving today, a half-century after my initiation into the *ke* cult in 1958. When I conducted research from 1979 to 1984 with Geizou, the woman who was responsible for one of the last *kn* associations still existing in the region, the survival of this form of female group was in doubt. Fortunately, part of this disappearing tradition was documented in the film "Du village des vivants au village des morts, rituels de femmes chez les Guro" [From the villages of the living to the village of the dead: Guro women's rituals], produced by the Centre National de la Recherche Scientifique (CNRS) in Paris and Télévision Suisse Romande (TVSR) in Geneva.

WORKS CITED

Deluz, Ariane. 1970. *Organisation sociale et tradition orale: Les Guro de Côte-d'Ivoire.* Paris: Mouton.

———. [1978] 2001. Féminin nocturne. In *La Natte et le Manguier, les carnets d'Afrique de trois ethnologues,* ed. Ariane Deluz, Colette Le Cour Grandmaison, and Anne Retel-Laurentin. Paris, Éditions du Mercure de France. 187–246. Reprinted in Ariane Deluz, Colette Le Cour Grandmaison, and Anne Retel-Laurentin, *Vies et paroles de femmes africaines,* 157–206. Paris: Karthala.

———. 1987. Social and symbolic value of feminine *knè* initiation among the Guro of Ivory Coast. In *Transformations of African Marriage,* ed. D. Parkin and D. Niamwaya, 176–217. Manchester: Manchester University Press.

5

Praise Performances by Jalimusolu in the Gambia

Marloes Janson

For centuries griots have attracted the attention of scholars. However, their female colleagues, the griottes, have been largely neglected in the social sciences literature. This is true throughout the world of these performers, from Senegal eastward to Niger. The tendency to focus attention on men rather than women is all the more surprising in the Mande world because females are so conspicuous.[1] Known as *jalimusolu* among the Mandinka, the focus of this study, and *jelimusow* farther east toward the center of the Mande world in northern Guinea and southwestern Mali (for example, among the Bamana),[2] these women can be easily recognized by their flamboyant style of dressing as well as by their sharp voices, which are audible from a great distance. Their own definition of their way of singing as *wuuri,* "shouting," is very revealing of their ability to "reach" their audiences in more than one sense of the word.

Aside from the matter of just why griottes (the regional term for these performers) have attracted so little attention by researchers, more basic questions are, what is the nature of these women's roles in society, and how is their situation changing in relationship to their male counterparts? In what follows, I will present two case studies that will offer preliminary answers to these questions and also suggest further areas of research.

To understand more clearly the distinctive roles of *jalimusolu* among the Mandinka, I decided to live with them and participate in their daily activities, both domestic and professional. When I arrived in Manneh Kunda, the Mandinka village in eastern Gambia where I was going to live with these women, I met only *jalimusolu*.[3] They divided their time between traveling from event to event and spending days at the market. My initial impression, then, was that I had moved into a female-headed household. The first ceremony I attended together with the *jalimusolu* of Manneh Kunda is still fresh in my memory. When the women started to sing with their shrill voices, it seemed as if my eardrums cracked.[4] I have seen people putting their fingers in their ears when griottes in West Africa opened their mouths. Given my first experiences in the field, I was very surprised that in the literature griottes mostly appear only in footnotes, or are mentioned in passing.

Hale (1998), who devoted a chapter to griottes in his book *Griots and Griottes: Masters of Words and Music,* argues that the paucity of scholarship on these female performers is symptomatic of a male bias that marks much social science research (cf. Diawara 1989, 109–110). If griottes are mentioned, they are usually viewed by both researchers and male griots as providers of vocal backing to the men. To add insult to injury, griottes are often defined as "female griots" in Mande studies when they should be termed *jalimusolu*. Such male-biased qualifications present obstacles because they pass over the activities of griottes by taking the male as norm and starting point. If a term is defined as a general concept, there is a tendency to refer only to the male. A well-known example is the term *mankind,* in which the male refers to humanity in general. The same applies to the concept of *jali*. *Jali* itself is gender-neutral: it is the generic name for both a male and a female bard. However, *jali* is often assigned to men in the literature. In Mandinka a distinction is made between the male and the female by means of the suffix *keo* (man) or *muso* (woman). The Mandinka concept for griot is *jalikeo,* and for griotte *jalimuso* is used.

Even if one adopts the local terms, however, that is not enough. The solution is to represent griottes throughout West Africa as active people rather than as passive objects. To achieve this goal I rely on feminist anthropology, because the representation of women was the focus of pioneering work by feminist anthropologists (e.g., H. L. Moore 1988, 1994; Del Valle 1993). They reoriented accepted theories to focus on social actors and the strategies they employ in daily praxis (cf. Rosaldo and Lamphere 1974). Following their example, in my field research I studied *jalimusolu* as agents. The significance of such an approach for Mande studies is underlined by La Violette (1995, 171), who argues:

> Until Mande women are studied as social actors in their own right, rather than as passive participants in an inherited system, or in a cultural system viewed as being shaped predominantly by men, the full impact of women on Mande social structure . . . cannot be understood.

My actor-oriented approach runs counter to the widespread view among re-searchers and popularizers (e.g., Alex Haley in *Roots* [1976]) that griottes in general merely play supporting roles for their male counterparts.

What, then, do *jalimusolu* do that distinguishes them not simply from men, but in a larger sense from people in other professions and society in general? And how is their role changing vis-à-vis men? The answer lies in an analysis of the term *daaniroo*. In the literature this complex Mandinka concept is of-ten translated as "begging," a rendering that is highly problematic because of its negative Western connotations. When *jalimusolu* set out for *daaniroo,* they sing and recite the praises of their patrons or other individuals qualified as *moo kendoo,* or "good persons" (i.e., persons who are willing to reward *jalimusolu*). In return for their praises, the women are rewarded with gifts of money or goods. So, *daaniroo* can be interpreted both as praising and as a gift-exchange. During my fieldwork it emerged that *daaniroo* is a gendered activity. Although *jalikeolu* also engage in it, *jalimusolu* in particular are active praise-singers, and in most cases the activity of praise-singing is their only source of income. Talking about his mother and sisters, who are all *jalimusolu,* my research as-sistant explained, "*Daaniroo* means everything to them; it is their head, their hands, their legs." For several *jalikeolu,* on the other hand, *daaniroo* is not the primary means of subsistence because they are also engaged in wage labor.

Like Diawara (1990), who conducted fieldwork among the Soninke, another Mande people, I made a distinction between two occasions at which *jalolu* prac-tice *daaniroo*. On the first type of occasion distinguished by Diawara (1990, 88), they are invited by their patrons to perform at special events that may include naming ceremonies, initiations, and weddings. On the second type of occa-sion analyzed by Diawara (1990, 88–89), they themselves take the initiative to perform, including at the market. The *jalimusolu* with whom I worked dis-tinguished between practicing *daaniroo* during *nyaakolu,* or life-cycle rituals, and *taamang-taamang,* meaning "strolling," such as around the market. Their patrons also made a distinction between these two forms of *daaniroo*. They appreciate *daaniroo* more when it takes place at their invitation, because then *jalimusolu* can add luster to their ceremonies. The *daaniroo* practiced at the initiative of *jalimusolu* at the market is considered a financial burden by most patrons. Several emphasized that "At ceremonies *jalimusolu* work for their money, while at the market they beg for money."

To understand more clearly the nature of *daaniroo,* I observed the practice in the two different contexts described above. The evidence will come from two case studies of performances that are in many ways typical of the activities of the *jalimusolu*. The majority of the *jalimusolu* with whom I worked spent more time practicing *daaniroo* at the market than during ceremonies. For this reason, I will begin with a case study of their performance in this most public of spaces. In the second case study the performance of these women at a naming ceremony will be analyzed. In both cases I will focus on the oral genres that the *jalimusolu* adopt, how they perform, and the differences between the *daaniroo* of *jalimusolu* and *jalikeolu*.

PERFORMANCE BY *JALIMUSOLU* ON THEIR OWN INITIATIVE

Manneh Kunda, the village where I conducted most of my field research, is situated near Basse Santa Su (abbreviated to Basse), the provincial capital of the Upper River Division in eastern Gambia. In Basse there is a large market that functions every day. The location of Manneh Kunda explains the key role of *daaniroo* at the market in the lives of the *jalimusolu* from this village. The market in Basse is a convenient place for them because they are free to go there whenever they want. They can easily meet people at the market and earn a little money, because when people travel to Basse, they do not go with empty pockets.

What is of interest here is that *daaniroo* at the market is specific to the area around Basse. In the villages further removed from Basse, weekly markets (*luumoolu*) are organized. People come from far and near to purchase goods. Often the *jalimusolu* are not acquainted with these potential sources of rewards. A *jalimuso* from a village where a *luumoo* is organized weekly reported to me that "People who visit the *luumoo* do not have time for *daaniroo*. The *luumoo* cannot be compared to the market in Basse." As Basse is a small city, the *jalimusolu* are often well acquainted with the people they meet at the market, and this seems to be a precondition for practicing *daaniroo* there. By contrast, in the urban area of Kombo, the area around Banjul, the capital of the Gambia, the markets are large-scale and many-branched. The size prevents the *jalimusolu* from practicing *daaniroo*. A *jalimuso* who was born in a village near Basse but is now living in a city in Kombo said, "At the markets in Kombo people are too busy, but at the market in Basse people still have thought for us." Thus, the *jalimusolu* in villages not within walking distance of Basse have fewer possibilities to practice *daaniroo*. Consequently, they spend most of their time working their fields. Their counterparts in Kombo focus on the practice of *daaniroo* at ceremonies.

Daaniroo at the market is both a local and, quite probably, a recent phenomenon. Several middle-aged *jalimusolu* viewed it as the outcome of colonialism, a historical process that eroded the old system of patronage (cf. Schulz 2001, 73–89). In order to survive, these women had to perform at the market. The development of *daaniroo* at the market may also be related to rising economic pressure on women (e.g., Mikell 1997; Brand 2001). The *jalimusolu* with whom I worked complained that they have many "family problems" today.

The result is that they have become to a great extent responsible for feeding their households. Taking into account that most of them do not farm and that regular employment is restricted to men, these women have to generate with their own professional talents enough money to pay for food. The market is the natural place to practice *daaniroo* because food crops are sold there. The following case study of *daaniroo* at the Basse market reveals how they operate.[5]

On the morning of 21 October 1998, Gai Sakiliba, a *jalimuso* with a good voice, complained that she had no money to buy sugar for the porridge for her family's breakfast. When I asked her what she was going to do about it, she answered, "I cannot ask my husband for money to buy sugar, because he is not staying here. Therefore, I have to struggle at the market myself." What she meant was that her husband had migrated to a place where there are better job opportunities and that she has become responsible for feeding her children. Together with her sister-in-law Jonkunda Sako and her co-wife Sako Kanuteh, Gai practiced *daaniroo* at the market. There they met their male colleagues, Al Haji Ndaba Kuyateh and his brother Abdu Kuyateh, who were also practicing *daaniroo*. What follows is an account of my observations of this incident of *daaniroo*.

Early in the morning the *jalimusolu* in the compound of Kuyateh Kunda, a huge *jali* compound in the village of Manneh Kunda, woke up. First they prayed, and after praying they pounded rice for breakfast. The melodious sound of the pounding served as my alarm clock. I woke up, looked for my jerrycan to fetch water, and before walking to the village pump I made my rounds through the compound. In Gai's house I met Jonkunda, who had come to Gai to greet her.[6] When Jonkunda heard that Gai was going to the market to practice *daaniroo,* she told her that she wanted to join. They made an appointment for later in the morning at the grocery of Titjan Krubally, one of the patrons of the inhabitants of Kuyateh Kunda, in Basse.

After breakfast, Gai took a bath and dressed up. She looked magnificent in her yellow embroidered gown. After she had dressed she adorned herself with her daughters' make-up. After spraying on perfume, and putting on gold-colored earrings and a necklace, she was ready to leave. *Jalimusolu* who venture out to practice *daaniroo* are always well dressed. Gai told me, "We make our patrons happy by wearing the outfit that they have given us. Other people will admire us, and we will tell them who gave us this outfit. If we are lucky, our patrons will then give us clothes again."

Gai did not immediately go to the market. First she had to bring a bowl of porridge to her sister-in-law, who was admitted to hospital. From there on she rushed to Titjan Krubally's grocery, where Jonkunda was already waiting for her. Jonkunda, who was dressed just as finely as Gai, was not sitting alone at the shop; Al Haji Ndaba and Abdu had also gathered there to practice *daaniroo*. The *jalikeolu* always practiced *daaniroo* at Titjan Krubally's shop, which they called their "grand place," because of its central location. Al Haji Ndaba explained, "The shop is located near the big junction, so we can easily see our patrons arriving." The roads to several villages come together at this point, and therefore there is always a huge crowd in the vicinity of the shop.

Al Haji Ndaba and Abdu waited at the shop for people who would come to them to give them something. Al Haji Ndaba told me that because Basse is a small city, everybody knows that they are *jalikeolu*. Moreover, people recognize them by the way in which they dress: they usually wear a large caftan, a small cap, and leather mules with pointed toes. The *jalikeolu* greeted passersby by calling their patronymic, and several passers-by greeted them with "*jalibaa*" ("great *jali*"), while shaking hands with them. One of their patrons with the patronymic Krubally threw one *dalasi* coin, about ten cents U.S., on the mat on which they were sitting. Al Haji Ndaba told the man, "This amount is too small; you should add more money," but the patron answered, "My money is finished. You could come to my compound another time." Because Al Haji Ndaba is older than Abdu, he kept the coin. He gave it to a boy, whom he ordered to buy a kola nut for him.

After a short rest in front of the grocery, Gai and Jonkunda set out for a morning of *daaniroo*. They met Sako, who was shopping in the main street. Sako joined Gai and Jonkunda and they entered a shop where Jonkunda had noticed a customer from her native village. Jonkunda told me that this man was her patron as her parents were already acquainted with his parents. She greeted the man and introduced me to him as her apprentice. The *jalimusolu* often introduced me as their apprentice as a strategy to earn more. Most people were astonished when they discovered that a white woman was able to sing *jalimuso* songs. They usually gave me money, which I always offered to my "instructors." To prove that I was her apprentice, Jonkunda urged me to sing *Suolu wo* together with her. Jonkunda started to sing solo for her patron, because she was best acquainted with him. She gesticulated wildly, as if she wanted to reinforce her words in this way. Gai, Sako, and I joined in the chorus. The patron did not listen to our song and kept on chatting with the shopkeeper. Although he laughed when I started to sing, he tried to stop us by saying, "It is enough." However, we did not stop; we kept on singing till the man gave us a few pieces of cassava.

After singing for her patron, Jonkunda recited his praises: "Baldeh *bannaa*, Baldeh *bannaa*." Baldeh refers to the patronymic of the patron and reveals that he is of Fula origin, and *bannaa* means "rich person." Jonkunda exclaimed this praise line several times while she grasped her patron's sleeve to catch his attention. When it became clear that the man would not give more, Jonkunda stopped praising him. We strolled around the market looking for other people whom we could praise. On the road that led to the rear of the market, Sako met a man from a village near Basse. The *jalimusolu* greeted him and chatted for a while before Sako started to sing *Suolu wo*. She stood in front of the man, with her arm raised breast-high, while he looked at the ground. The women explained his position to me as follows: "Many persons feel shy when we sing for them. They are embarrassed because they cannot reward us in the same way as their ancestors did." Before the song was finished, the man gave a 10 *dalasi* note (U.S.$1.00) to Sako, who passed it on to Jonkunda. Jonkunda spat on the money before she put it in the prayer cloth that she wore around her headscarf. When I asked her why she spat on the bank note, she replied, "By doing this I beseech God to give us more."

Then we entered the covered part of the market, where everybody was busy buying and selling goods. There fewer people paid attention to us. Gai went to a woman from Basse who was having breakfast at a market stall where bread, eggs, and coffee were sold. She told this woman, "I am hungry, because I did not have breakfast this morning." Actually, she had had breakfast that morning; this was just a tactic to get something. The woman refused to give us anything and so we left. Near the car park where taxis and small vans gathered, Jonkunda met a young man from her native village. She reprimanded him because he had not invited her to attend the naming ceremony of his son. To mollify her, the man gave her a 10 *dalasi* note. Jonkunda was satisfied and started to talk in public about his good character, his accomplishments, and the deeds of his parents. She talked in a loud voice so that passers-by could hear her and would also give her something to outdo the man. Unfortunately this tactic did not have the desired effect; people ran away from her. To express her gratitude for the gift, Jonkunda prayed for the man. The man responded to her blessings with "*Amiini*" ("Amen," "may it be so"), while striking his forehead with his right hand.

Around 1 PM the *jalimusolu* complained that they were tired, and they decided to go to the market stall of an acquaintance to share their earnings. Jonkunda gave the earnings that she had kept to Gai. Sako, the oldest of the three, had selected Gai to divide up the money because she is good at arithmetic. Gai changed the notes they had earned that morning into coins and divided up the money by making three piles of it. She gave Jonkunda 6 *dalasi* and 50 *butut* (65 cents U.S.), and she kept the same amount herself, while she gave Sako 7 *dalasi*. When I asked Gai why she distributed the money in this way, she replied, "Because Sako is older than us, I should give her more to express my respect." With their earnings, the women went shopping. They spent the money on the ingredients for both the porridge to be served at breakfast and the sauce for lunch and dinner.

On the way back to the compound of Kuyateh Kunda we passed Titjan Krubally's grocery, where Al Haji Ndaba and Abdu were lying on mats. When we arrived in Kuyateh Kunda the *jalimusolu* put on other clothes. They looked less festive in their torn shirts and wraps. After the communal lunch, they spent the afternoon performing household chores and drinking tea. Al Haji Ndaba and Abdu returned to Kuyateh Kunda around dinnertime. They told me that they had spent the afternoon chatting with their patrons at Titjan Krubally's grocery. Abdu concluded, "It has not been a good day for us because we have both earned only 5 *dalasi*" (50 cents U.S.). After dinner nobody ventured out again.

From the evidence in this description of the activities of these performers at the market, the distinction between the functions of the *jalimusolu* and those of the *jalikeolu* is clearer. The men greet passers-by at the market in a dialogic fashion based on the way people normally greet each other, while the women hail their subjects by reciting or singing praises. Below is an example of how Al Haji Ndaba greeted his patron bearing the patronymic Krubally:

KUYATEH: Krubally
KRUBALLY: Kuyateh
KUYATEH: *Suumoolu lee?* [How are your people? (Literally: Where are your people?)]
KRUBALLY: *I be jee* [They are fine (Literally: They are there)]
KUYATEH: *Kori tana te* [I hope there is no trouble (with you)]
KRUBALLY: *Tana te* [No trouble (with me)]
KUYATEH: *Kayira be (i ye)* [Peace be (with you)]
KRUBALLY: *Kayira dorong* [Peace only]
KUYATEH: *I musu lee?* [How is your wife? (Literally: Where is your wife?)]
KRUBALLY: *A be jang* [She is fine. (Literally: She is here)]
KUYATEH: *I dingolu lee?* [How are your children? (Literally: Where are your children?)]
KRUBALLY: *I be jee* [They are fine. (Literally: They are there)]
KUYATEH: *Kori tana te i la* [I hope they are not in trouble]
KRUBALLY: *Tana te i la* [They are not in trouble]
KUYATEH: *I bee be kayira to?* [Are they all living in peace?]
KRUBALLY: *Kayira dorong* [Peace only]
KUYATEH: Krubally
KRUBALLY: Kuyateh

What people do in their greetings may reveal important principles governing the use of language in their culture (Bird and Shopen 1979, 91). This is very
much the case in Mande societies, where greetings are highly developed. Hoffman (2000, 21) writes that

> the simple act of greeting someone can be a reminder of that person's social
> history, for the end of a formal greeting is marked by the terse compliment of
> calling a person by the patronym, which can be understood as an abbrevia-
> tion of longer histories consisting of the names of famous persons and places
> of the clan's social history.

The Mandinka term for greeting is *kontong*. *Kontong* is derived from *kontongo,* the word for patronymic. One greets a person by first calling his or her
patronymic, which provides a clue to his or her status. The patronymic is of
great importance to a Mandinka because it is laden with heavy historical baggage. An old *jalikeo* explained, "The deeds of the ancestors are reflected in the
kontongo." Among the Mandinka there are relatively few patronymics. Each
patronymic corresponds to praise, or *jamung*. Praises are powerful since they
affect and persuade an individual by referring to the great deeds of his or her
ancestor, the first bearer of his or her patronymic. *Jalimusolu* practice *daaniroo*
at the market by reciting or singing the *jamung* of passers-by, composed of a
mixture of genealogies and formulae. Gai, Jonkunda, and Sako did not praise
all the people whom they met at the market in this way. They explained to me
that they praise only those people whom they believe will reward them when
they cry their *jamung*.

The *kontongo* of the Fula man whom the *jalimusolu* met at the market was
Baldeh, and the *jamung* with which Jonkunda praised him was "*Baldeh, bannaa*" ("Baldeh, rich person"). By praising her patron for his wealth, Jonkunda
tried to persuade him to give her something. *Jalimusolu* praise not only their
patrons' wealth, but also their achievements. The evidence here suggests that
jalimusolu practice *daaniroo* in a rather commanding way. Jonkunda grasped
her patron's sleeve to catch his attention, and she kept on praising her patron
although he asked her to stop. This may explain why Charry (2000, 95) defines
the manner in which *jalimosulu* praise as "scolding." However, the commanding tone that marks the way that the *jalimusolu* practice *daaniroo* does not always have the desired effect, because the patrons sometimes ran away from the
jalimusolu.

Praises are either recited (*saatari*) or sung (*donkili*). In the example cited
above, the *jalimusolu* sang *Suolu wo*, which means "Oh horses," for passers-by.
This is a song of praise that is well known not only locally but throughout the
Mande world. In Mande studies this song is also referred to as *Suolu kili* (or *So*

wele), "Calling the horses" (e.g., Knight 1984, 36; Durán 1995, 199; Charry 2000, 52). It was sung in the days of warfare between kingdoms to urge the warriors on to victory. It is sung today to praise any person deserving recognition for his or her achievements (Knight 1984, 13). A *jalikeo* explained the meaning of this song of praise as follows: "In the past only kings and *marabouts* had horses. When *jalimusolu* sang *Suolu wo,* one knew that an important person was arriving. Today, this song has a similar function: if *jalimusolu* see an important patron arriving, they will sing *Suolu wo.*" The informant suggests here that *Suolu wo* is a *jalimuso* song (see also Knight 1984, 36).

Because *Suolu wo* is typically sung unaccompanied by musical instruments (with the exception of the *neo,* an iron percussion rod), it is particularly suitable to be sung by *jalimusolu* at the market. Usually they start by singing this well-known song before they proceed to other songs. Below are the lyrics of the version of *Suolu wo* sung by the *jalimusolu* in this case study. They are somewhat similar to those recorded by Knight (1972, 30–31):

Suolu wo suulu Sira Makang nyanaa	Oh horses, *suulu Sira Makang nyaana*[7]
Suolu wo kele ye i fee	Oh horses, fighting is easy
I y'aa mina le i y'aa faa	You seize him, you kill him
Yammaru wo kelelaa	Oh *Yammaru* the fighter
Kele ka dii i la	You are successful in war
Suo mu janfantee ti	A horse may deceive
A karafee juloo mu janfantee ti	His bridle rope may deceive
Nungkono juloo mu janfantee ti	A harness may deceive
Kele ye i fee	Fighting is easy
I y'aa mina le i y'aa faa	You seize him, you kill him
Yammaru wo kelelaa	Oh *Yammaru* the fighter
Kele ka dii i la	You are successful in war

Suolu wo is a typical example of a song of praise. Bravery is referred to by mentioning the horses, and by referring to the skills of the fighter: he seizes his enemy and he kills him. Although a fighter runs the risk that the bridle rope and harness of his horse may break and that his horse will not obey him, which implies that a fighter falls prey to his enemies, he shows success in the war. An elderly *jalikeo* interpreted this song as a warning: "It warns patrons not to deceive their *jalolu,* like the horse deceives the fighter, otherwise their *jalolu* would kill them, like the enemy kills his opponent. But if patrons treat their *jalolu* in a respectful way, similarly to how a good fighter treats his horse, they do not have to fear deceit."

A *jalimuso* who worked for the National Council of Arts and Culture in Banjul transcribed and translated *Suolu wo* for me. She told me that songs of praise are difficult to translate because *jalimusolu* use words from different Mande languages. Creissels and Jatta (1980, 109) argue that this is a common phenomenon in the Gambia. Bamana terms, for example, often occur in the texts sung by Gambian *jalimusolu*. In this way they try to imitate their Malian colleagues, who are famous in the Gambia. A second problem in translating songs of praise is that the meaning of some archaic words has been forgotten through the years. This does not imply that these words cannot be interpreted. Griots in general are, as "masters of the word," used to re-interpret archaic elements that have become obscure (cf. Jansen 2000). In this way they can strategically adjust their oral traditions to the interests of their patrons. *Yammaru* is an example of one of those terms whose meaning is unclear.[8] It may refer to an important patron, as in phrases often sung by *jalimusolu:* "*Yammaru wo nafaa*" ("Oh *Yammaru,* the benefactor"), and "*Yammaru wo jali soolaa*" ("Oh *Yammaru,* the one who gives to *jalolu*").[9] My most senior informant, however, claimed that *Yammaru* is the foundation of *jaliyaa,* the profession of *jalolu.* He compared *jaliyaa* to a tree: "*Yammaru* is the root from which other songs stem. When *jalimusolu* start singing, they first have to sing *Yammaru wo.*" Many songs start with this expression and therefore my research assistant said, "Just as the confession that there is only one God but Allah is the first pillar of Islam, *Yammaru* is the first pillar of *jaliyaa.*"[10]

Just like the praises sung and recited by *jalimusolu,* the blessings invoked by them on their donors can be considered a strategy to encourage people to give. These blessings tend to be fairly formulaic utterances, of the sort "*Ala mu i siimaayaala*" ("May God bless you with long life"). Following the example cited above, *jalimuso* Gai explained the function of blessings as "We pray for the well-being of people to make them happy. When we meet them the next time, they will remember our blessings and give us again something."[11] From the evidence collected for this case study, it appeared that *jalimusolu* invoked blessings on their donors more often than their male counterparts.

This may be explained by the fact that *jalimusolu* are in a serious predicament vis-à-vis their religion. Islamic ethics prescribe that women should behave in a modest way, while conversely the profession of the *jalimusolu* calls for them to stand out by their behavior and dress. These women may reconcile their identity as female performers with Islamic values by punctuating their praises with blessings. Furthermore, when setting out for the market, *jalimusolu* often don the kind of headdress that is usually worn by people who have made the pilgrimage to Mecca (cf. Janson 2002b). In this case study it appeared that Jonkunda kept the money earned by practicing *daaniroo* in such a headdress. Before putting the money in her headcloth, she spat on it in order to beseech

God to give her more. Blessing is one of the most evident strategies adopted by *jalimusolu* to embed their *daaniroo* in an Islamic discourse. For *jalikeolu* this is a less urgent concern, as men are believed to be more pious than women.

It is common knowledge that across the Sahel and Savanna regions there is a particular division of tasks between griottes and griots: griottes mainly sing and griots play musical instruments and narrate oral traditions. This is also true for the Mandinka. The market context here, however, showed a different set of dynamics. Unlike the *jalimusolu*, Al Haji Ndaba and Abdu did not sing or recite the praises of passers-by; they only greeted them by calling their patronymics. Several *jalikeolu* noted that should they sing women's songs like *Suolu wo* at the market, it would damage their reputation and they would not be taken seriously. Al Haji Ndaba explained, "We do not play musical instruments or narrate at the market because there is a lot of noise there. Everybody at the market is busy selling and buying goods and so nobody has time to sit and to listen to us. For a *jalimuso* it is possible to sing at the market, because she has a louder voice. People can make time for listening to her, as the songs she sings at the market are short."

The difference in oral genres employed by men and women to praise passers-by at the market includes, then, not only the lyrics or words of their performances, but also their movement (or lack thereof). As indicated above, the *jalimusolu* strolled around the market looking for their patrons, whereas their male counterparts sat in one place, waiting for patrons to come to them. When I asked the *jalimusolu* why they did not practice *daaniroo* in the same way as the *jalikeolu,* they replied that the latter do not allow them to expose themselves to the public in front of Titjan Krubally's grocery. By practicing *daaniroo* in the same way as *jalikeolu* do, *jalimusolu* run the risk of being labeled as "wanton women."[12] In addition to strolling around, the *jalimusolu* practiced *daaniroo* collectively. To my question as to why they did not engage in *daaniroo* individually so they could keep the earnings for themselves, they replied that a married *jalimuso* venturing into the street alone is regarded as "prey to Satan."[13] Al Haji Ndaba and Abdu also practiced *daaniroo* together, but unlike the *jalimusolu* they were not obliged to do so and they could easily perform solo.

PERFORMANCES OF *JALIMUSOLU* AT THE INVITATION OF THEIR PATRONS

In the urban area of Kombo in western Gambia the population density is higher than in the area around Basse, and this explains why there are more ceremonies organized in that region. During my field research it appeared that the *jalimusolu* in Kombo, in contrast with those described above, spend most of their time practicing *daaniroo* at ceremonies. A difference between *daaniroo* at the market and at ceremonies is that those who perform at the market do so on their own initiative, whereas they are invited by their patrons to perform at ceremonies, where the *jalimusolu* are much more appreciated. However, it is important to add that not all *jalimusolu* can be invited personally to perform at ceremonies. Only those affiliated with the patrilineage of the organizer are invited, but the others are by definition welcome, if not individually invited, because a ceremony that is not attended by many *jalimusolu* is not considered complete. When many of these women are present the prestige of the organizers will rise, as this is an indication of their wealth. Another difference is that *daaniroo* at the market is specific to the area around Basse, while *daaniroo* at ceremonies is a much more common occurrence. In the previous section, I argued that the market *daaniroo* is probably a recent phenomenon. My informants suggested that *daaniroo* at ceremonies, on the other hand, is as old as the institution of *jaliyaa*.

Among those ceremonies that attract *jalolu,* whether by invitation or less formally, are gatherings to name a child, which are the most common celebrations in a Mandinka's life. Babies are born and baptized irrespective of the season, whereas initiations and weddings—the other life-cycle ceremonies at which *jalimusolu* are invited to perform—are usually celebrated in the long dry season from October to May.[14] This is a time of relative abundance with the completion of the harvest. Consequently, at this more prosperous time of year, families have enough resources to entertain their many guests. This season is also propitious for initiation because the wounds of the novices heal more quickly than during the rainy season.

The *kullio,* or head shaving, is celebrated on the eighth day after the birth of a baby. This act begins the process of naming the baby so that he or she may be integrated into society. *Jalolu* play a crucial role in the performance, which marks a change of status for the baby. *Jalimusolu* are often called upon to shave the baby's hair while *jalikeolu* publicly announce the infant's name. After the announcement, *jalimusolu* sing the newborn's praises. The lyrics of praise function as a validation of the baby's social identity.

The example of a *kullio* that I attended in Sukuta, a small Mandinka town near the city of Serrekunda, offers a clearer sense of what is entailed in these performances. Mawdo Susoo, who is regarded by many as the best *balafong* (xylophone) player of the Gambia, was invited by his patron to play this instrument during the *kullio* of his son. Mawdo asked his wives Funeh Kuyateh and Kumba Sakiliba, his brother Bamba Susoo, and his friend Musa Susoo to join him at the ceremony.

On the morning of 7 October 1998, Mawdo, Musa, and I had breakfast. We were waiting for Funeh, who was taking a bath and dressing up in preparation for her performance. Mawdo urged his wife to make haste as the rehearsal of "The Spectacular Gambian Music and Dance Troupe" would soon begin. This group had succeeded the state-sponsored National Troupe, which had been disbanded because it no longer functioned effectively. The "Spectacular Gambian Music and Dance Troupe" had been founded to promote the Roots Festival, an event organized annually for the dozens of African Americans who, in imitation of Alex Haley, author of *Roots,* visit the Gambia to look for traces of their ancestors.

Finally Funeh left her room. She was dressed in the Troupe uniform, consisting of a large blue gown with a matching wrap and headscarf. She also wore gold-colored high-heeled sandals and jewelry. In the meantime Mawdo and Musa had put on caftans and trousers made of the same cloth as Funeh's outfit. When her daughters and co-wife had admired Funeh, we took a taxi to the compound in which the rehearsal took place. All the other *jalikeolu* and *jalimusolu* who participated in the Troupe had already gathered under a mango tree. The dancers were not present; they were going to rehearse another day. The *jalikeolu* started to play their musical instruments while the *jalimusolu* sang. When the flute (*serdu;* the most widely appreciated Fula instrument) player did not keep time, a *jalimusolu* gave him instructions. She advised him to listen more carefully to the *kora* (a twenty-one-stringed harp-lute). The Troupe members performed both traditional and modern compositions. When a song was finished, the *jalikeolu* and *jalimusolu* conferred with each other on which song they were going to perform next. As the name of the Troupe suggests, the rehearsal was quite spectacular. Clearly, the most talented singers and musicians had been selected to promote the Roots Festival in the Gambia.

After a few hours the *jalimusolu* had sung themselves hoarse, and the manager closed the rehearsal. When everybody had prayed, we took a taxi back to Sukuta. After a short rest in Susoo Kunda, Mawdo asked his wives Funeh and Kumba, his elder brother Bamba, and his friend Musa to accompany him to the *kullio* organized by his patron. Mawdo's sons carried his *balafong* and two *koras* to Jula Kunda, the compound of Mawdo's patron. When we entered Jula Kunda we greeted the organizer, his relatives, and his guests, and we lined up on a mat in front of the house of Mawdo's patron. The *jalikeolu* tuned their instruments, while the *jalimusolu* were walking around the compound greeting the female guests. Mawdo started to play the *balafong,* while Musa and Bamba played their *kora*s. After a few minutes Funeh joined in. She sang *Suolu wo* while Kumba tapped the rhythm on the calabash resonator of the *kora*.[15] Later Kumba joined in the chorus, and Mawdo also sang a few lines. He encouraged his wives several times by saying, "*Toonyaa, jalimusolu*" ("You are right, *jalimusolu*").

A few men from the audience threw 5 *dalasi* notes (50 cents U.S.) on the mat on which Mawdo was playing the *balafong*, and Funeh cried their praises in order to thank them. When one man offered Funeh a 10 *dalasi* note, she danced the *lambango* to express her appreciation.[16] Only *jalimusolu* and *jalikeolu* can perform this glorious dance during which the dancer tosses the head back and sways with the arms. Normally a *jalimuso* keeps on dancing the *lambango* until her headscarf falls on the ground, which generates a lot of shouting from the audience, but in this case Funeh did not dance exuberantly as she was feeling tired and hungry. She continued singing, sitting on a plastic chair while she nursed her baby. As the organizer of the *kullio* was a Jula, a noble lineage representing a family of former traders, Funeh sang *Jula mang naa*. Then Kumba took the floor to sing *Jaliyaa*. The wife of the organizer's best friend gave Funeh a nice wrap and a 50 *dalasi* note. Funeh kept the money in her hand and she carried the folded wrap on her shoulder, so that everybody could see what she had received.

In the meantime a stereo had been set up in a corner of the compound. Youths were dancing to popular Gambian and Senegalese music. Funeh and Kumba sang with loud voices and the *jalikeolu* increased their volume, but when they could not drown out the music they ceased their efforts. A female relative of the organizer offered them a dish with rice, sauce, and meat of the goat that had been sacrificed in the morning. After lunch Funeh and Kumba entered the house of the baby's mother, who was sitting on her bed under a mosquito net with the baby in her arms.[17] Her female relatives and friends were sitting next to her. The *jalimusolu* admired the baby before they started to sing *Yee jiboo*. When the song was finished, the women gave them 5 *dalasi* notes. As she is older than Kumba, Funeh kept the money. Before the *jalimusolu* left the house, they prayed for the well-being of the baby. The women responded with "*Amiini*" ("Amen"; "may it be so").

Around 6 PM we left for Susoo Kunda, where Funeh offered the 60 *dalasi* that Kumba and she had earned that afternoon to her husband. The wrap that was offered to her by the wife of the organizer's friend was hers to keep. Mawdo added the money given to him by the organizer of the *kullio* and his guests to the amount earned by his wives. He explained to me that his patron was a "poor man," and therefore he could give him only 165 *dalasi* (U.S.$15.30).[18] Mawdo divided up the money between his wives, his brother, his friend, and himself. He did not tell me how much he gave to them, but he explained that he gave his wives a smaller amount than he gave to the *jalikeolu* because "men are the owners of money."[19] Mawdo kept the largest amount himself as he was invited by his patron to perform during the *kullio*. He tapped at his *balafong* while he said to me, "*Alhamdulillahi* [Praise be to God], this instrument has already brought in a lot."

Just as at the market, the *jalimusolu* practiced *daaniroo* at the *kullio* by singing and reciting praises. Funeh started by singing *Suolu wo*, the same song as was sung at the market. However, the text sung at the *kullio* was much longer than what was sung at the market, as there was more room for improvisation. At the market the song texts have to be short because everybody is busy buying and selling goods, whereas at the ceremonies at which *jalimusolu* are invited to perform people make time to listen more carefully to the songs. Funeh laced the standardized formulae in *Suolu wo* (see above) with her own phrases. During my fieldwork it appeared that only elder *jalimusolu* who have achieved a certain reputation as singers are able and allowed to improvise; the younger ones may only repeat the words of their older colleagues. Although both Funeh and Kumba are considered talented singers, Funeh improvised more and sang solo more often because she is older than Kumba. Moreover, she is Mawdo's first wife. Mawdo told me that he was very lucky because he had married two *ngaaraalu,* or master singers who command power and respect in performance. He claimed that when a *jalikeo* marries a good singer his prestige automatically rises.

After having sung *Suolu wo*, Funeh sang *Jula mang naa* because the organizer of the *kullio* belongs to the *Jula* lineage:

Jula mang naa	The *Jula* has not come
Jula mang naa	The *Jula* has not come
Jula a baraka	Thank you, *Jula*
Baabaa kodoo be Jula meng fee	The *Jula* who has money from overseas[20]
Jula barakamaa	The blessed *Jula*
Jula i salaamu aleyika	Peace be upon you, *Jula*
Jula mang naa	The *Jula* has not come
Jula senemaa	The genuine *Jula*
Kodi ning sanoo be Jula meng fee	The *Jula* who has money and gold
Jula a baraka	Thank you, *Jula*
Sanoo be Juloo kung to	The *Jula* is carrying gold on his head
Doo dii n ma nanbarantee	Give me some, troublemaker[21]
Keme dii n ma	Give me a hundred [*dalasi*]
Jula, Jula, Jula mang naa	*Jula, Jula,* the *Jula* has not come

Baabaa kodoo be Jula meng fee	The *Jula* who has money from overseas
Jula saramaa	The generous *Jula*
Alhamdulillahi	Praise be to God
Arabbil Alamina	Lord of the Universe
Ala Taalaa te lonna	The Almighty God is unpredictable
Jula a baraka	Thank you, *Jula*
Jula mang naa	The *Jula* has not come
Kodi ning sanoo be Jula meng fee	The *Jula* who has money and gold
I ning wuraa jaliyaa la	Good evening with *jaliyaa*
Jalimusu ning jalikeolu wo	Oh, *jalimusolu* and *jalikeolu*
Jalitigi ning jalintango	The person who has *jalolu* and the one who does not have *jalolu*
Te kaanyanna	Are not equal
Ala te lonna	God is unpredictable
Jula senemaa	The genuine *Jula*
I mang ke fara Juloo ti	You are not just a *Jula* by name
Jula a baraka	Thank you, *Jula*[22]

The recurring phrase "The *Jula* has not come" could be interpreted as a kind of challenge: by giving something to the *jalimusolu,* the *Jula* demonstrates that he is indeed present. Similarly, the phrase "You are not just a *Jula* by name" may be regarded as a challenge: by giving to the *jalimusolu,* the *Jula* shows that he is a genuine *Jula.*

The *jalimusolu* also sang *Jaliyaa,* but because of the loudness of the disco the recording of this song was inaudible. Here I can only mention that in this song it was stated that God created *jaliyaa,* or the bardic profession.[23] A patron explained this phrase as "Because God has created *jaliyaa,* we should not fool with it. If my *jalimuso* praises me and I cannot reward her, I have to tell her: 'Next time.' It is my duty to tell her that, because *jaliyaa* has been created by God. God does not like it when we run away from our *jalimusolu.*" The belief that *jaliyaa* has been created by God provides *jalimusolu* with a certain control over their patrons, as was illustrated during a performance when an elderly *jalimuso* sang "Give to the *jali.* My patron give to me. If you refuse to give to a *jali,* God would not give to you either."[24]

The song sung by Funeh and Kumba for the mother of the baby was *Yee jiboo.* In this song, which is sung at every *kullio,* the new mother—or *jiboo*—is encouraged to give something to the *jalimusolu* who have come to greet her. Here are the lyrics:

Yee jiboo i fang jansa	Oh mother of the newborn, donate yourself
Jiba kutoo i fang jansa	New mother, donate yourself

| *Yee jiboo i fang jansa* | Oh mother of the newborn, donate yourself |
| *Jiba kunandii i fang jansa* | The lucky mother of the newborn, donate yourself |

This is one of the few songs in the *jalimuso* repertoire that is restricted to a particular occasion.

What struck me was that the *jalikeolu* practiced *daaniroo* in a more active way at the *kullio* than at the market. Mawdo sang a few lines and played the *balafong,* while the other *jalikeolu* played the *kora.* However, during my field research it appeared that it is not common for *jalikeolu* to make music at ceremonies. A *jalikeo* who plays the *kora* for tourists in hotels and restaurants on the Gambian coast explained this phenomenon as follows: "Formerly, *jalikeolu* always played musical instruments during ceremonies. At the end of the ceremony the musicians had to admit that they had earned only a small amount of money. If a *jalikeo* is playing his instrument, he cannot follow his patrons to ask them for gifts. He has to remain sitting in the same place and he has to concentrate on his music. His colleagues who do not play instruments will earn a lot, because they can ask their patrons for money, but the musician will not share in their earnings. Consequently, contemporary *jalikeolu* refuse to take along their instruments when a ceremony is being organized."

Other *jalikeolu* also emphasized that the energy invested in playing musical instruments during ceremonies is not worth the earnings. One of them argued, "When we play musical instruments our patrons know that we expect a greater reward from them than when we just greet them. Most of them cannot give us much money and therefore they do not allow us to play our instruments. Why should we bother ourselves to make music if we will earn only a few *dalasi*?" Thus the fact that *jalikeolu* no longer play musical instruments on ceremonial occasions may be a sign of poverty. Many patrons prefer listening to audiotapes, as this is a cheaper form of entertainment. The majority of the *jalikeolu* with whom I worked only occasionally play musical instruments during ceremonies when the organizers have invited them to make music. In such a case they will discuss a price beforehand so that they are assured of a fixed income. Mawdo explained to me that he had felt obliged to comply with his patron's request to play *balafong* at the *kullio* of his son because they have known each other for years and term each other as "brothers." Moreover, there exists a "joking relationship" (*dankutoo*) between *jalikeolu* and *Jula* (cf. Janson 2002a, 36), and joking partners are expected to perform ritual tasks during each other's ceremonies.

In those rare cases when *jalikeolu* play musical instruments at ceremonies, they are usually accompanied by their wives' singing. However, this does not make *jalimusolu* simply vocal backing to their husbands, as is often suggested in Mande studies. Hale (1998, 218) argues that in the Mande periphery (i.e., the Gambia and the Casamance region of Senegal), *jalimusolu* tend to play supporting roles in performances. However, I observed that *jalimusolu* sometimes play a leading role. They may, for example, open a performance. Dramé and Senn-Borloz (1992, 256) claim it is the griotte who determines which tune is played. When she starts singing, the musician recognizes the song and plays the corresponding rhythm.

In the example presented in this study from the Mandinka of the Gambia, the *jalikeolu* opened the performance by playing a particular tune, but still this does not imply that *jalimusolu* are vocal backing. Each tune (*juloo*) corresponds to a song (*donkiloo*), but this is not a one-to-one relationship (cf. Charry 2000, 308–309, 323–324). An elderly *jalikeo* explained, "A talented *jalimuso* is able to sing different songs on the same tune." This suggests that a *jalimuso* is, to a certain degree, free in the choice of her songs. In this case study it appears that the *jalimusolu* had a voice in the choice of the songs sung during the rehearsal. Furthermore, a *jalimuso* gave instructions to a musician, and these are clear indications that the role of these women is not restricted to supporting *jalikeolu*. Although *jalimusolu* do not play instruments themselves, except for the *neo*, or iron percussion rod, the above example illustrated that they are capable of correcting musicians who do not keep time, as they have to tune their songs to the melodies played by the latter. Once I attended a ceremony at which the *jalikeolu* ordered the *jalimusolu* to start singing and dancing. Afterwards the *jalimusolu* called a meeting because they did not want to be treated by the *jalikeolu* in such a way.

Far from *jalimusolu* being accompanists to *jalikeolu*, the opposite seems to be true today: male musicians accompany female singers. Diawara (1997, 43), drawing on evidence from Mali, writes, "One no longer speaks of the griot and his wife, but of the woman and her instrumentalist, who may be her husband or someone else." The situation in Mali, the heartland of Mande culture, differs from that in the Gambia, but the shift that is described by Diawara also applies, to a lesser extent, to the Gambian context, as was illustrated in a speech delivered by Mawdo at another *kullio* in Sukuta. He related, "Once upon a time there lived a *jalibaa* (great griot) who taught his apprentice to play the *kora* and to sing. In time the apprentice was able to sing without his teacher. People called the attention of the *jalibaa* to inform him that his apprentice had mastered *jaliyaa*. When he heard his apprentice singing, he said that from then on his role would be superfluous." Mawdo delivered this speech when Funeh and Kumba had just finished singing at the *kullio*. By relating this story he suggested that he was only playing a supporting role; it was his wives who played the leading role in the *kullio*. After his speech, Mawdo said literally, "My role is finished now."

CONCLUSION

Although there may still be debate about the roles and performance styles of male and female griots from different parts of the Mande world, the two cases presented here from the Gambia suggest that the situations of the two genders are changing over time—at least among the Mandinka. In particular, the evidence here suggests that the most significant differences between the way Mandinka *jalimusolu* and *jalikeolu* perform *daaniroo*—the Mandinka concept for praising—emerge at the market and at life-cycle rituals.

The market calls for *jalolu* to take the initiative to perform *daaniroo*. It emerged that for the *jalimusolu* in the Basse region the market is the most convenient place to perform because they are free to go there whenever they want. Whereas *jalimusolu* sing or recite their patrons' praises at the market, their male counterparts greet their patrons by calling their patronymics. I argue that *daaniroo* at the market is probably a recent phenomenon, which could be seen as the outcome of historical changes. Since colonialism eroded the old system of patronage, *jalolu* had to search for patrons at the market. This development may also be related to rising economic pressure on women. Taking into account that most *jalimusolu* do not farm and that wage labor is in many instances restricted to men, these women have to scrape together their daily "fish money" at the market.

At ceremonies, on the other hand, *jalolu* are invited to perform *daaniroo* by their patrons, at least by those with whom they maintain a historically embedded relationship of patronage. While *jalimusolu* perform without *jalikeolu* at the market, they sometimes perform together at ceremonies. Whereas in the past *jalikeolu* always added luster to ceremonies by playing music, they nowadays believe that it is a wasted effort to drag along their instruments, since the patrons are no longer in a position to reward them accordingly. They therefore prefer to hang around at ceremonies, unless they are explicitly invited to play music. In those rare cases when *jalikeolu* are invited to play music at ceremonies, they are accompanied by their wives' singing. However, this does not make *jalimusolu* simply vocal backing to their husbands, a portrayal common in Mande studies. In some instances the *jalikeo* also sings, but the female voice is preferred by audiences.

One outcome of the differences between performance on the *jalolu*'s own initiative and by invitation is that the former is often considered not an "authentic" form of *daaniroo*. Several patrons condemned it, describing it as "begging." This explains why *jalolu* usually do not earn much when they practice *daaniroo* on their own initiative. It also explains why many people have a negative view of *jalolu,* and *jalimusolu* in particular, since they are more active in performing on their own initiative.

The most significant factor that distinguishes between the performances of *jalimusolu* and *jalikeolu* is the geography of their *daaniroo*. The *jalikeolu* hold a fixed position whereas the *jalimusolu* are mobile. The former wait or play their instruments at a strategic point till people come to them to give them something. The *jalimusolu*, on the other hand, are more outgoing in their behavior as they cry out the praises for their patrons while walking around the market or the place where the ceremony is taking place. One could thus characterize the women as dynamic and the men as static in their approach to their subjects. It remains to be seen what the long-term effects of the upsurge of a more reformist style of Islam in the Gambia will be on *jalimusolu* (Janson 2007). Will they be able to continue their *daaniroo* in public places, or will they have to search for new means of subsistence that are better negotiable with their gendered Muslim identity as pious women?

The most significant difference that emerges from the evidence presented in the two case studies recorded in this paper is that the women, rather than the men, play the dominant role. Whether this shifting dynamic between the sexes in the griot world is a regional phenomenon or applies on a larger scale remains to be determined on the basis of a wider corpus of case studies. But the evidence presented here suggests that the primary role of women in *jaliyaa* in Mali that emerged in the last few decades (Durán 1995) has now spread eastward to the Gambia. This shift calls for further research not only on Mande peoples, but also on those other cultures on the periphery of the Mande world and outside of it—for example, the Wolof to the west and the Songhaï to the east. For this reason, future studies on griots in general will need to focus more specifically on the evolving roles of griottes in society and in their relationships to their male counterparts. Since griottes seem to form a vital aspect of the Sahel and Savanna regions, they should be studied accordingly. To do justice to these women, it is high time to listen to their voices more carefully.

NOTES

1. *Mande* refers to a field of study composed of a set of culturally and linguistically related West African "ethnic groups" who live in the Gambia, Senegal, Mali, Guinea, Guinea-Bissau, and parts of Ivory Coast, Mauritania, and Burkina Faso. In this paper I focus on the Mandinka, who comprise the majority in the Gambia.

2. Each people in the vast griot region that stretches from Senegal eastward to Niger, largely within the northern and southern limits of the Sahel, has its own term for *griot*, which is a rather amorphous regional appellation of uncertain origin (Hale 1998). Following Hale's suggestion, I will use the local term for them when referring to griots in a particular context. In the case of the Mandinka studied here, it is *jali* for griots in general (pl. *jalolu*), *jalimuso* for women (pl. *jalimusolu*), and *jalikeo* (pl. *jalikeolu*) for

men. For Mande peoples further east, for example in Mali, there are slight differences in terminology (*jeli* rather than *jali,* and *jelimusow* rather than *jalimusolu*) which will not pose a problem—the major difference being the shift from *jali* to *jeli.* The goal here is greater specificity—and respect—for the language of each people. The broader terms, *griot* and *griotte,* will be limited to analyses that draw on information from more than one people.

3. This paper is based on ethnographic fieldwork that was conducted between 1996 and 2001 in the Gambia. The fieldwork has been made possible by a grant, generously furnished by the Research School CNWS of Leiden University. I would like to thank the participants in the research project "Women's Songs from West Africa," in particular Thomas Hale, Aissata Sidikou, and Jan Jansen, for their comments on an earlier version of this paper. All errors of fact and interpretation are, of course, my own. Parts of this paper have been published in Janson (2002c), with additional materials from my PhD thesis (Janson 2002a).

4. At that time I could never have expected that later I would enjoy the singing of *jalimusolu* so much that I would sometimes even be moved to tears by it.

5. See also Janson (2002a, 86–111; 2002c).

6. The first thing most people do when they wake up is to greet their neighbors. In addition to greetings, the elderly also exchange blessings.

7. My informants told me that "*Suulu Sira Makang nyaana*" is a praise line, but they were not able to translate this line. Hoffman (1998, 91) argues that this is a common phenomenon: "it is often the case that griots know how to use the phrases without being able to explain their referential meaning." Innes transcribed this line as "*Sira Makhang ngana,*" which he translates as "Mighty Sira Makhang" (1974, 63, 117 line 483ff.).

8. Another example of an archaic term in *Suolu wo* is *Makang.* Misiugin and Vydrin, who studied archaic elements in the epic of Sunjata—the most famous Mande hero—conclude that this term means "chief of hunters and/or warriors." Nowadays, the term is used only as a personal name: Sunjata is sometimes called "Sunjata Makang" (1993, 105).

9. According to Innes's informants, *Yammaru* refers to Sunjata (1974, 108 line 221). One of my informants claimed that it is not just a name, but that it means "advice." In his opinion the *jalolu* advised their master, Sunjata, when he did something wrong, but they never reprimanded him publicly. Instead of correcting him directly, they said "*Yammaru wo.*"

10. As it is often sung as an opening of songs, Jansen interprets *Yamariyo* as an exclamation in the sense of "hallelujah" (personal communication, April 1999). *Yamariyo* may be a variant of *Yammaru wo.*

11. These praises are regional rather than local. For example, Hale recorded similar forms of praise from a *jesere weyboro,* or griotte, in Niger in the short video *Griottes of the Sahel.*

12. The association between *jalimusolu* and "wanton women" is not something new. Moore, an eighteenth-century explorer, translates *Jelly moosa* (his version of what I call *jalimuso*) as "whore," whereas he defines *Jelly kea* (i.e., *jalikeo*) as "singing-man" (Moore 1738; his "List of words English and Mundingo" is cited in Charry 2000, 367).

13. Sako was shopping alone in Basse. Since her husband had migrated, and since she was his first wife, she had more freedom of movement than the other married

women in the compound of Kuyateh Kunda. However, when her husband returned to Kuyateh Kunda, he sent Sako home when he met her shopping alone at the market.

14. Funerals and other memorial ceremonies are also examples of life-cycle rituals, but in the Gambia these events are not a cause for celebration and therefore *jalimusolu* do not perform at them.

15. The tapping pattern played by a second person on the calabash of the *kora* is called *konkondiroo* (*konkon* is an onomatopoeia for "knock") (Charry 2000, 182).

16. *Lambango* also refers to the name of a song (cf. Knight 1972, 18–25). It is said to be the oldest song in the Mande repertoire, played originally on the *balafong*. It is a celebratory piece dedicated not to any single person but to the whole Kuyateh lineage (Charry 2000, 152).

17. The mother and her baby spend the seven-day period of seclusion after the delivery under a mosquito net because it is believed that this net protects the baby against witches.

18. Nevertheless, this amount is much higher than the amounts earned by *jalimusolu* and *jalikeolu* in the area around Basse.

19. Officially, men are responsible for providing for their households, but in actual fact women contribute to a large extent to the expenses of their husbands.

20. This phrase may refer to the position of *Jula* as itinerant merchants.

21. Because *jalolu* and *Jula* have a "joking relationship," they may abuse each other.

22. Unfortunately, this is not the whole text of the song. Because the stereo was producing such loud music, it was difficult to transcribe and translate the complete song text.

23. "*Ala le ka jaliyaa daa*" in Mandinka.

24. In Mandinka this phrase runs "*Jaloo n so. N batufaa n so. Ning i ye jaloo bali wo Ala si i bali.*"

WORKS CITED

Bird, C. S., and T. Shopen. 1979. Introduction: Maninka language and society. In *Languages and their Speakers,* ed. T. Shopen, 59–112. Cambridge: Winthrop.

Brand, S. 2001. *Mediating Means and Fate: A Socio-Political Analysis of Fertility and Demographic Change in Bamako, Mali.* Leiden: Brill.

Charry, E. 2000. *Mande Music: Traditional and Modern Music of the Maninka and Mandinka of Western Africa.* Chicago: University of Chicago Press.

Creissels, D., and S. Jatta. 1980. La jeunesse de Sunjata: Un fragment de l'épopée Mandinka, récité par Amadou Jeebaate. In *Recueil de littérature Manding,* ed. G. Dumestre, 108–125. Paris: Agence de Coopération Culturelle et Technique.

Del Valle, T., ed. 1993. *Gendered Anthropology.* London: Routledge.

Diawara, M. 1989. Femmes, servitude et histoire: Les traditions orales historiques des femmes de condition servile dans le royaume de Jaara (Mali) du XVe au milieu du XIXe siècle. *History in Africa* 16:71–96.

———. 1990. *La graine de la parole.* Stuttgart: Franz Steiner.

———. 1997. Mande oral popular culture revisited by the electronic media. In *Readings in African Popular Culture,* ed. K. Barber, 40–48. Bloomington: Indiana University Press; London: International African Institute; Oxford: James Curry.

Dramé, A., and A. Senn-Borloz. 1992. *Jeliya: être griot et musicien aujourd'hui.* Paris: Harmattan.

Duran, L. 1995. *Jelimusow:* The superwomen of Malian music. In *Power, Marginality, and African Oral Literature,* ed. G. Furniss and L. Gunner, 197–207. Cambridge: Cambridge University Press.

Hale, T. A. 1998. *Griots and Griottes: Masters of Words and Music.* Bloomington: Indiana University Press.

Haley, A. 1976. *Roots: The Saga of an American Family.* Garden City, N.Y.: Doubleday.

Hoffman, B. G. 1998. Secrets and lies: Context, meaning, and agency in Mande. *Cahiers d'Études africaines* 149:85–102.

———. 2000. *Griots at War: Conflict, Conciliation, and Caste in Mande.* Bloomington: Indiana University Press.

Innes, G. 1974. *Sunjata: Three Mandinka Versions.* London: School of Oriental and African Studies.

Jansen, J. 2000. *The Griot's Craft: An Essay on Oral Tradition and Diplomacy.* Hamburg: Lit Verlag.

Janson, M. 2002a. *The Best Hand Is the Hand That Always Gives: Griottes and Their Profession in Eastern Gambia.* Leiden: Research School CNWS.

———. 2002b. On the boundaries of Muslim gender ideology. *ISIM Newsletter* 11:28.

———. 2002c. Praising as a gendered activity: How *jalimusoolu* and *jalikeolu* exercise their profession in eastern Gambia. *Mande Studies* 4:65–82.

———. 2007. Appropriating Islam: The Tensions between "Traditionalists" and "Modernists" in the Gambia. *Islam et sociétés au sud du Sahara,* n.s., 1:61–79.

Knight, R. 1972. *Kora Manding: Mandinka Music of the Gambia.* Ethnodisc Recordings, ER 12102.

———. 1984. The style of Mandinka music: A study in extracting theory from practice. In *Selected Reports in Ethnomusicology, vol. 5: Studies in African Music,* ed. J. H. Kwabena Nketia and J. Cogdell Djedje, 3–66. Los Angeles: Program in Ethnomusicology, Department of Music, University of California.

La Violette, A. 1995. Women craft specialists in Jenne: The manipulation of Mande social categories. In *Status and Identity in West Africa: Nyamakalaw of Mande,* ed. D. C. Conrad and B. E. Frank, 170–181. Bloomington: Indiana University Press.

Mikell, G. 1997. Introduction to *African Feminism: The Politics of Survival in Sub-Saharan Africa,* ed. G. Mikell, 1–50. Philadelphia: University of Pennsylvania Press.

Misiugin, V. M. and V. F. Vydrin. 1993. Some archaic elements in the Manden epic tradition: The "Sunjata epic" case. *St. Petersburg Journal of African Studies* 2:98–110.

Moore, F. 1738. *Travels into the Inland Parts of Africa.* London: E. Cave.

Moore, H. L. 1988. *Feminism and Anthropology.* Cambridge: Polity.

———. 1994. *A Passion for Difference: Essays in Anthropology and Gender.* Cambridge: Polity.

Rosaldo, M. Z., and L. Lamphere, eds. 1974. *Woman, Culture, and Society.* Stanford, Calif.: Stanford University Press.

Schulz, D. E. 2001. *Perpetuating the Politics of Praise: Jeli Singers, Radios, and Political Mediation in Mali.* Studien zur Kulturkunde 118. Cologne: Rüdiger Köppe Verlag.

6

Saharan Music

ABOUT A FEMININE MODERNITY

Aline Tauzin

One of the major issues in gender relations in the Arab world today is the status of women. In Mauritania, a society governed by traditions that go back many centuries, women today are reversing some longstanding ways, especially in the areas of poetry and music. The purpose of this chapter is to document the nature and extent of those changes. Before turning to the specifics of these changes, it is essential to provide some background on a society that is not well known outside of Africa.

Mauritania is composed of two different populations: the light-skinned Moors and the dark-skinned Africans, whose roots are largely sub-Saharan. The Moors are the dominant population in Mauritania and can be defined very briefly as a nomadic group, at least until recently, living in the western part of the Sahara. They speak an Arabic dialect called Hassâniyya. They are Muslims and played an important role in the Islamization of West Africa.

Their social organization in the past has been highly stratified, with the *hassân* (in French, *guerriers,* or warriors) and *zawâya* (marabouts or religious people) at the top, and slaves at the bottom.[1] Traditionally, among the Moors, playing music and singing were, and still are, the specialty of professional men and women, keepers of the oral tradition found in the Sahel region of West Africa. In Hassâniyya the plural term for both males and females is *îggâwen*,[2] with *iggîw* for man. *Tiggîwâten* designates women, with *tiggîwît* for woman. In long poems, the *îggâwen* praised the leaders of the *hassân* tribes with a strong, shouting voice, especially before a battle or when they wanted to honor them or obtain some presents. They satirized the enemy and in so doing contributed to the competition for honor and power that marked relations between different tribes. And, of course, they provided some pleasure and entertainment for their listeners, essentially during evening sessions.

For the *zawâya,* the situation was quite different. They did not have *îggâwen* and did not even tolerate music in their milieu except that performed by women in private. As they used to say, they preferred to praise God rather than be praised by others. More deeply, the pleasure provided by music was considered by them to be a manifestation of the devil. That point refers to a long tradition among the Moors and, more widely, in Islamic dogma. The adoration of God requires from the believer the use of his mind and intellect, while music, like wine and women, leads him to a point where there is no more comprehension, a place beyond words. This incompatibility between religion and music is easy to perceive in the words naming the act of chanting the *Qurʾān:* all insist on the necessity of producing an intelligible discourse which makes God's words understandable to everyone. Religious peoples in Mauritania enjoy listening to stories that are told, and never sung, by their own blacksmiths.

So, song and music are incompatible with religion and they are also incompatible with masculinity. They belong to and lead to femininity in both Moor and Islamic traditions.[3] This place "beyond words," mentioned before, is a feminine one, as it can be seen in some tales, especially those talking about "women's trickery" and "female devils." Song is feminine because of gender definition: putting words together in order to make a poem is a man's work, while singing them belongs to musicians, or to women in the private space of the encampment. Moreover, listening to or practicing too much music may lead a young boy to be transsexual, according to Moor theory. I will be more explicit about this belief later.

But, if women can sing, they have to do it only in the circle of their relatives. They are not allowed to show themselves to foreigners because it would bring dishonor on their group.

And finally, until recently, women did not create poetry; at least, they did not let it be known (Tauzin 1989). The reason for this is that in the very peculiar gender system which exists among the Moors, women are inaccessible objects of desire. Everything is done to obtain their passivity and their impassiveness. Men do not want to confront women's feelings, hopes, or expectations, so they "force" them to be silent. And male poetry becomes a part of that kind of relationship, which can be named "courtly," wherein a man may mourn for his lost beloved who went away or who does not care about him anymore.

This outline will help to frame the phenomenon of contemporary social change. It is happening very rapidly, and, at the same time, it is meeting much resistance.

First, what was said about the *îggâwen* in terms of social role and the topic of their poetry cannot be observed any more. Today, musicians are no longer integrated members of *hassân* tribes, whose power, defined as the capacity to make war and to protect subordinates, has been weakened, first by the colonial authority, and more recently, since independence, by the *zawâya*. Most of the *îggâwen* live now in Nouakchott, Mauritania's capital, and although they know, and everybody knows, their former affiliation, they sing for the one who invites them and provides them with money or gifts, whatever his origin might be. This means that if praise songs are increasing, satire totally disappears from their corpus. Only one sign of their past link with a specific *hassân* people remains today. An *iggîw* may attend wedding festivities organized by that person's clan, without being invited, and he will receive the same amount as the hired musicians.

In the past, each performance by *îggâwen* offered a mix of seriousness and lightness. It started with long poems about war, honor, and the magnificence of the tribe and its members, sung by men, and then went on to shorter and smoother pieces, in which women were more active. Women always sang after men.

During the performance, songs were interpreted in a succession of five modes whose order could not be modified. And each mode was divided into sub-modes. The first one, *karr,* was the mode of pleasure and religious feelings.[4] The second, *vâgho,* conveyed pride and anger. It prepared listeners for war and death. The two following ones, *le-khâl* and *le-byâdh,* successively "blackness" and "whiteness," were devoted to love and sadness. And the last one, *le-btayt,* was given over to a quiet nostalgia. If I give all these details it is because today, only one of these modes has been chosen to modernize the music.

Today, women are more famous than men, and most often, they sing alone. And if there is one of them inside a wider mixed group, a kind of "diva," she performs before men. The most common form of music group includes a singing woman who generally does not pluck the *ardin,* the traditional harp played by women, a man who plays guitar but does not necessarily sing, and a third person, a man who plays the drum and who belongs to a newly observed category called *gordiganât,* or transsexuals. The word comes from the Wolof language of Senegal and literally means "man-woman." It signifies men who proclaim their femininity and denounce what they think is a biological error: a male body for a feminine identity. *Gordiganât* are not members of the musicians' group, in terms of status, but they are bound to it precisely because of their claim of femininity. Moreover, according to local theory, they have "spoiled" their male identity because of their intense involvement with music and griots during their childhood. This gives us another example of the similarity established by the Moors between femininity and music and, by the same reasoning, strengthens the hypothesis of the feminization of music in the contemporary period.

Changes in the songs themselves were introduced in the 1980s as a necessity. *Iggâwen* were obviously concerned by the evolution of Moor society and started to modernize their corpus, first by using classical Arabic instead of the local dialect. Loubâbe mint El Meïdah, Yâsîn ould Nânne, and El Alye mint ᶜEly ould El Meydâh participated in such a movement. They were expecting an opening to the Arab world and tried to achieve it through a common language. During the same period, teaching was almost completely Arabized, the classical language taking the place of French. But neither the *iggâwen* nor their audiences followed the innovators. The result was that this effort to Arabize music was abandoned.

Then a new path was created, mainly by *tiggiwâten*, professional women singers. They called it *tatawwour*, which means "change" in the dialect. It consists in choosing one musical mode, *vâgho*, the one which was associated with virility in the former musical sequence. The singers adopted this mode to perform all songs, traditional and new. This rhythm, according to the *tiggîwît*, was the most suitable for new audiences in both Arab and European societies. It is supposed to be closer to their own music than other Moor modes. At the same time, singers were looking for better comprehension of the words, and to reach this goal they tended to remove what they considered to be extraneous notes which obscured meaning.

In fact, most of the singers are now abandoning the traditional way of singing, whose intricacies are believed to be too obscure for people who are not familiar with or fond of it. The singers still know the old ways, having learned them with great effort during childhood, but they prefer not to perform in that style anymore, except in very special circumstances. Moreover, some of them want to leave tradition completely in order to create more personal compositions and to claim their membership in the world. They aspire to create a kind of music which can be played on other stages and often use the expression "world music" for what they want to do. And they tend to replace the word *iggâwen* with another one which means "artists" and does not contain any reference to their social role and status. This attitude seems to be easier for women, for several reasons.

First, Moors still want to hear traditional music for some occasions, especially praise songs during wedding feasts. Because of the weakening of endogamy, there are more marriages between tribes or clans. The result is that the demand for traditional praise songs is doubled—that is, *iggâwen* must be able to sing praises about two different groups. Each family audience wants to hear the old poems which glorify its members, their courage, and their generosity. These are men's songs. So, as the *iggîw* is required to maintain the tradition, the *tiggîwît* has the liberty to innovate. But even during the wedding festivities, except in those intense moments, people prefer a smoother, more danceable music—and dance is largely a feminine activity.

In fact, even at the very moment when a group is celebrating its continuity through the alliance of a marriage with another group, the reference to the clan, its nobility, and its honor progressively fades away behind the new notion of individual pleasure and, perhaps, of femininity. Besides, some women singers refuse to perform at weddings, arguing that they want to become free from the repetition of tradition. And when they do participate, they introduce innovation by creating new dances involving transsexuals or *gordiganât*. As they are compelled to perpetuate the tradition by the ones who pay for it and, at the same time, want new things, men singers resist pressures to modernize their corpus, expressing a kind of contempt for an evolution they call a feminine one and from which they are, in reality, left out.

This evolution can be called feminine in another way: professional women singers maintain and emphasize those elements that were theirs in the traditional corpus, and what other women were singing with them. They focus on short pieces of four lines, which were inserted, in the past, between long poems, with the intention of reviving the audience's attention. Now, quatrains become the most appreciated form of poetry. They are introduced by shorter poems of two lines, which determine the rhyme and are called *shwâr edh-dhall,* literally "poems of light." They differ from the "poems of sun," *shwâr esh-shems,* which introduce long masculine poems about courage, war, and other preoccupations defined as male by the society. Light is a synonym of femininity because of its mildness. In this system, it is opposed to the masculinity or hardness of the desert's sun. "Poems of light" are smooth and easy to sing and are composed either by griottes or by other women. Their rhymes, too, are easy, and it is not difficult to compose poems following them.

Here are some examples of the most famous "poems of light"; two old ones and two new ones:

Seyye ella âne seyye	Seyye, it is I, Seyye[5]
Hâdhi el-xâdem, hâdhi el-xâdem	This slave, this slave
Eh eh ya hâdhi el-xâdem	Eh eh ô this slave
Leyli leyli yallâli	My night, my night, ô my God
Râhu jâni mûle gerte	The peanut seller had married me[6]

| *Lâ mervûd men ilâh* | You will sneak from here |
| *Yekûn el-heylâle* | Only lâ illâha illa allâh[7] |

Concurrent with these changes, which draw on tradition, *tiggîwâten* create their own lyrics and they sing new words. To understand what is told by each of them would require the study of the entire corpus. But it is important to emphasize one point: when asking people about what they liked or what was successful in the time preceding my inquiry, I noticed that the self-praise of griots appeared frequently in the texts and was often cited. The reason for this is that today, there is much greater rivalry between *îggâwen*. In the past, these artisans of the word stayed mainly with their patrons and did not have a great deal of contact with each other. But now the tie with sponsors is looser, and the singers seek rewards from anyone. Today they say, "now, we are the *îggâwen* of everybody." The result is that they often come into conflict with each other. So fights and blows below the belt are very common, and many anecdotes are heard throughout the capital about them. Each performer tries to show his or her personal success to the audience by wearing, for the men, very expensive *boubous,* or formal flowing robes, and for woman, jewels and silk veils.

Another problem is that there is no copyright protection of their work. Tapes are recorded during feasts and concerts without any control. And duplication is made by the seller. There is no *droit d'auteur,* the French term for copyright, a notion that is new for the *îggâwen.* They have long debates about the possibility of creating an association for their own defense, but they do not succeed because of their rivalry. Such competition shows that *îggâwen* are no longer integrated into a social structure, and also that they have become individual artists.

A new space for singers was established in Nouakchott about two years ago by a *tiggîwît* named Loubaba mint El Meïdah. She defines it as a "cultural club," adding that it is the first one in town. She gave it the name of Layali Tarab, which means "Musical pleasures of the night," an evocative name for Arabic-speaking people. More recently, she opened a website[8] where one can read some details which, for my purpose, are quite interesting. For example, after having written that she belongs to one of the most famous "artistic families" of Mauritania, she explains that she has been studying traditional music since her early childhood, when she also received a religious education and went to school. Here are associated three heterogeneous elements: traditional training in music, which is expected in an *iggîw* family; religious preparation, which was not common before; and a more formal Western-style education in a school. Then, the presentation goes on with these words: "At the end of the 80's, she started her work of modernization of Mauritanian song." Further, her club is defined in these words: it is "open to all the intellectuals, poets and commercial societies, political and cultural institutions, and to everyone who is interested in music, art and culture." Of course, the choice of words and their order give some indication about the contemporary evolution of song practice and the perception a singer can have of it. One notices, too, that on the website Loubaba never uses the word *griotte,* and that she has modified her name, as some others do now, omitting *mint,* "daughter," which is the mark of filiation in traditional kinship systems. There is now a tendency to modify long family names in order to make them more understandable.

Another item strengthens the hypothesis of the feminization of song. As mentioned at the beginning, women traditionally did not compose texts of poetry and they did not sing publicly. This is no longer completely true. During the 1940s in the north of Mauritania and in the 1980s in the whole country, a new poetic form appeared, a feminine one called *tebrâᶜ.* The root of this name means, in classical Arabic, "to surpass, excel," but its use in the Hassâniyya dialect to designate this form remains unknown. A *tebrâᶜ* is composed of two lines, and most of the time, its author remains anonymous.

Tebrâᶜ probably show women's feelings and thoughts more surely than griottes' poetry. They mostly talk about love's pain, but some are less serious and give the opportunity for women to joke about men and about themselves too.

Here are some examples of sadness and powerlessness, even of desire:

O God don't kill me
  Before I see pearls to adorn myself
O God don't forget me
  And you, you know what I am waiting for

The woman implores God, first, to get married (and to wear the wedding jewels) before she dies, and second, to meet the one she is in love with. In the next poem, she complains because she loved a married man who, finally, did not choose her.

We've stopped talking about love
  Since he took back the mother of his children
The one who attacked my heart
  When he comes to see me, I turn into wool

This last expression means to lose one's identity, to grovel before somebody.

Since yesterday I know a passion
  God protect me against what is illicit

Then the criticism becomes more obvious:

> Men are *garanti*
>> You wear some and I wear some

Garanti is a French word naming a kind of cheap gilt jewelry. Applied to men, the qualifier is easy to understand.

Is the following *tebrîʿa* an answer? The two poems were sung together on the tape I had transcribed. Has it been invented by a man or by a woman? Nobody knows. If it is by a man, it could be a modern example of oral joust, *gtaʿ*, which was very common and appreciated in the past. If it is by a woman, it emphasizes their taste for mockery.

> Women are just places
>> You go inside and I go inside

Another succession of poems was made when a television series coming from Mexico was broadcast. One of the actors was, according to many Moor women, a very handsome man, so they created poems about him. The name of his character was Lucas, and if the title of the series has been forgotten, people still remember that it appeared on MBC (a Saudi TV channel broadcasting from London) in 1998. So this is the date, too, of the creation of those poems.

> Lucas has a smile
>> Which leaves the other men without any value
> Lucas if he comes to visit me
>> I cut the throat and invite my neighbors

"Cut the throat" means to organize a big party because of the importance of a visit by killing an animal in accordance with Islamic custom. The best welcome consists in offering the meat of a lamb to a visitor. Another in the same vein:

> Lucas if he comes to visit me
>> I spread out my little back flap

The flap, here, is part of the woman's veil, and the whole last line is a colloquial expression meaning "to welcome somebody cheerfully."

If one perceives some ambivalence between the expression of a lover's dream or mockery in the previous poems, now there is no more doubt. And, of course, playing with words and rhymes is also very important in this poetic practice. Women try to find the best rhymes with the funniest words or ideas, just to enjoy themselves.

> Lucas if I see him on a bicycle
>> I run and adorn myself

The mockery is increased by using a verb, in the second line, which means "to adorn oneself without keeping anything apart."

The women who compose such texts are members of the dominant groups. They belong to "high tents," to aristocratic families. As indicated earlier, they did not perform in the past because of the structure of the relationship between men and women. It was based on a courtly model, a masculine "desire's culture," similar to the expression of love in the south of France during the Middle Ages. Everything was done, in the construction of the feminine identity, to control woman's desire, which was dangerous for two reasons. First, it is because Moor society is strongly patrilineal: a man has to make sure, as a husband, that he is the father of his wife's child. So, the most shameful behavior for a woman is to give birth to an illicit child, a bastard. Such a conception is so shameful for the honor of the woman's group that it cannot be mentioned by using the precise word, which does however exist in the Hassâniyya. Moors prefer to say "she got a stomach from the desert" or "she prayed toward the north." The second reason is that women are both seductive and threatening, just as in most traditional Arab societies and more widely around the Mediterranean. The way the Moors choose to ward off the danger women represent is to avoid them and to make them inaccessible objects of male desire, and not subjects of their own. So, in order to make them passive, young girls were "force-fed" (this is a translation of the French word *gavage,* used in Mauritania). They had to drink every night a big quantity of milk. The result is that they would become fat, listless, and immobile. There was less chance that they might meet a dangerous man, dangerous for their sexual purity. And, at the same time, their impassiveness prevented them from seeking their own satisfaction and asking men for it.

In such a gender configuration, the Moors developed a love poetry which was composed by men only, a poetry in which their own fear was inverted into a distant and cruel woman's figure. And women kept silent, waiting for the men's homage.

Such a structure started to change after independence when the nomads, especially the dominant groups, settled in towns. Feminine inactivity was no longer valued, while some girls went to Western-style schools and then found employment in the growing public and private sectors. Women began to compose their own poetry or, at least, to divulge it, just as they started to get thinner. For the oldest ones, this new feminine voice was the result of a shameless modernity. In fact, women were becoming active and were becoming subjects of their own desire. Their former silence lost its meaning. The emergence of the poetic *tebrâ*^c form gave evidence of an important mutation in gender definitions.

But, if women began to talk, they could not sing their texts. These are still performed by female members of groups of professional musicians. There is an exception, a very recent one, described later. The reason for such a prohibition is that if a song is feminine, it cannot be performed before unknown people. An aristocratic woman who shows herself to a large audience dishonors her group. Tremendous debates and criticism occurred after the establishment of a theater company, probably the first one in the country, a few years ago. High-status women appeared on stage with young men. This cultural activity has slowly gained acceptance with the argument that it was a social theater, participating in the construction of a new society, a useful activity for an emerging nation which intended to abandon some of its old practices. But song is an entertainment, and it shows the singer's body acting to give some pleasure to the audience. This is quite incompatible with nobility.

So, the base of the social structure resists change. But probably not for long. Recently, a group of women became very famous. They were given the name of their village, Aïn Varbo, located in the east. Aïn Varbo is a new village, created by people who settled near the road after the severe drought of the 1970s. Nearly the entire nomadic population of Mauritania settled along that road in the last thirty years, in little towns which became bigger and bigger. These people were looking first for some help and then trying to obtain more stable incomes than what is available from animal raising. At the same time, they wanted to send their children to school. These women are members of the dominant social groups and they belong to different tribes, most of them religious ones. They started to sing together just for pleasure, then they were invited to perform at feasts, and finally, some *îggâwen* or blacksmiths, a group newly converted to music, went to their village and recorded them. These tapes are sold now in little specialized shops called *standart*. The former prohibitions are broken on two points: the intimacy of familial group, since the women belong to several tribes, and the privacy of the feminine voice, since it spreads to the outside.

And the practice of song is increasing in a more secret way, since girls share the medium with griots at the end of the wedding feasts, after the old ladies' departure. Some *tiggîwâten* even express the fear of being replaced in the public's taste by other women whose voices might be more appreciated. Today, the hereditary function does not give them any guarantee, since taste will become more and more individual and the function of the artist no longer matches its former social role. On the other hand, there is still no example of a man belonging to a dominant group who would become a singer. Resistance is much stronger on the men's side.

So what will be the future of such music? It will have only a limited influence in Mauritania and no impact outside the country. In reality, it is the Arab world which is influencing Moor society, mainly through television. Young girls only listen to Middle Eastern singers. Many of them sing in the Egyptian dialect of Arabic, which is becoming well known through TV movies. Young girls are fond of an Egyptian channel called Nîl TV, which broadcasts serials every morning, songs in the afternoon, and diverse programs in the evening. It is obviously aimed at a female audience, and has, of course, a big influence. And when they want to know more details about one of their favorite singers, the girls read a magazine whose title means "madam," *Sayyidati*.

They do not like the *îggâwen* very much now. They tend to refer to them in these terms: "They sing 'aaaaaaah' for a long while, and we don't even understand what they say." And girls bet together: the first one who finds a song which does not talk about love has won. Moor society, now, is very far from the secret of its traditional love poetry.

So the contemporary evolution leads to a feminization of song, in its practice and in its contents. *Tiggîwâten* are more famous today than their male counterparts, whom they used to follow in the past. They select in the traditional corpus the lightest and smoothest songs because it is easy for other women to compose in their mode. And they write new lyrics which are more personal, more intimate, talking about their own feelings for a man or a child, for example.

This has happened as the result of enormous changes occurring to the nomadic Moor society, from colonization to settlement in towns. Song is no longer a part of the social organization. It becomes simply entertainment, and the *îggâwen* are moving to another status, that of independent singer, each concerned by his or her own success and looking for international recognition.

Another evolution concerns women as a whole, since they started to compose their own poetry after being silent before. It shows that the gender organization I named "courtly" is lessening, even if its main orientation remains. At the opposite end, evolution is nearly nonexistent on the men's side. *Iggâwen* are still involved in the preservation and reproduction of some pieces of the traditional corpus because people expect this from them,[9] while members of the dominant social groups still abide by the prohibition against singing which applies to them. In such a social organization, strongly patrilineal, changes first affect women and are led by them. Modernity is their affair; tradition is much more the preserve of men.

NOTES

1. For a more precise description of the social structure, see Stewart (1973).
2. About the etymology of the term, see Guignard (1975, 178–179).
3. For more details, see Tauzin (2001).
4. For more details, see Guignard (1975).
5. *Seyye* is a feminine first name.
6. The woman is calling for help; she does not want the peanut seller for a husband.

7. This introduction was composed by one of the most famous contemporary singers, Dimi mint Abba. The second line is the Islamic formula of faith in God.

8. www.loubaba.mr.

9. Only men participate in broadcast programs whose subject is the traditional song.

WORKS CITED

Guignard, Michel. 1975. *Musique, honneur et plaisir au Sahara*. Paris: Geuthner.

Stewart, Charles. 1973. *Islam and Social Order in Mauritania*. Oxford: Clarendon.

Tauzin, Aline. 1989. A haute voix: Poésie féminine contemporaine en Mauritanie. *Revue du Monde musulman et de la Méditerranée* 54 (4): 178–187.

———. 2001. *Figures du féminin dans la société maure (Mauritanie)*. Paris: Karthala.

7

Songs by Wolof Women

Luciana Penna-Diaw

One of the assumptions of the wider project to which this paper contributes is that there are common features among women's songs in the vast Sahel region, in spite of the fact that there remain local differences. But can we apply the same approach to songs produced by people who speak the same language within the same region? Research on songs by Wolof women in the Cayor, Saloum, and Walo regions of Senegal suggests that the same holds true at the local level. There are common features across these three areas, but also traits that distinguish one from the other. The evidence comes from a corpus of 250 songs collected in the three regions between 2000 and 2002.

The significance of women as singers of songs and musicians in this area cannot be underestimated. The musical heritage of the Wolof is almost entirely represented by women. They sing, play instruments, and dance in several circumstances, both ritual and "profane." Some of these events allow only other women to be present, while others permit the presence of men who may be playing instruments or simply attending as spectators. In general, men play a secondary role in musical activities. They do not normally dance or sing, with the exception of some Muslim ceremonies such as initiation. But before turning to comparative analyses of the songs, it is important to situate the Wolof in the local context in order to understand more clearly the status of women.

WOLOF SOCIETY

Today, the Wolof live in Senegal and the Gambia. In Senegal they constitute 40 percent of the total population, the rest being Serer, Toucouleur, Peul, Diola, and Mandinka and other minorities. From north to south the Wolof region includes the delta of the Senegal river down to Diourbel, and from west to east it extends from the Atlantic coast to the Ferlo desert. The Wolof live in the areas of Baol, Cayor, Diolof, Ndiambour, Saloum, Walo, and the nearby islands of Cap Vert.

Historians report that in the twelfth century the Senegalese territory was divided into several kingdoms. A fraction of the Wolof population, which during the thirteenth century formed the Jolof empire (source of the term *Wolof*), reigned over the areas of Walo, Cayor, Baol, and Saloum. Toward the mid-sixteenth century these areas became independent and remained so until well into the nineteenth century when the French, who arrived in the area in the seventeenth century, completed their conquest.

The Wolof were once divided into three main socio-professional groups: the *géer,* the *ñeeño,* and the *jaam.* The *géer,* or free men, form a high-status category. With the creation of a monarchy, society divided into three branches: the nobles, the non-nobles, and the slaves.

The *ñeeño* are widely described as "gens de caste," or what might be more appropriately termed hereditary artisans specialized in particular activities. For example, one finds *tëgg* (blacksmiths), *uude* (shoemakers), *rabb* and *maabo* (weavers), *lawbe* (carpenters), and *géwél,* professional singers or musicians known regionally as griots (Diagne 1982, 66). *Géwél* play a very important role in Wolof ceremonies. Since the time of the monarchy, they have accompanied the king or *buur,* singing praises to his family to the accompaniment of a five-stringed lute known as the *xalam* in Senegal and by other terms across the Sahel. They exhort men to fight against the enemy in battle, playing the *tama* drum and singing songs of encouragement. The queen, or *lingeer,* was also accompanied by a female *géwél,* who sang songs to lull people to sleep in the evening or awaken them in the morning. Today, *géwél* still animate all the important life events and ceremonies, such as naming, initiation for females and males, and marriage. Male and female *géwél* learn from their parents, relatives, and other *géwél.* Their knowledge is transmitted from one generation to the next orally.

Finally, the *jaam* are slaves, people who were taken as prisoner in local wars, and their descendants.

Islam was introduced to the Wolof region starting in the tenth century by the Almoravides from North Africa. Today, Senegalese Islam is organized into confraternities led by marabouts. The best known of these groups are the *Qadiriyya, Tijâniyya, Layenne,* and *Murîdiyya,* the last two being typically Senegalese. *Mouridisme* is practiced above all by the Wolof.

As the Wolof shifted to Islam, they abandoned many but not all elements of their traditional system of belief. Today one finds in Wolof Islamic practices a variety of survivals of these beliefs and customs. The syncretic nature of these customs shows itself in a variety of rituals. Some Wolof still visit the marabout regularly, make sacrifices so as to obtain what they wish, and create cult objects to cast a spell over someone.

The Wolof agricultural economy provides some clues to the independence of women. Before the monarchies were established, the farming community was organized according to the principle of *lamanat:* the fields were divided and managed by the members of the same consanguineous community, including men and women (Diop 1985, 26). Even today, women have their own fields and sell the products of the harvest in the markets. A. B. Diop explains that

> le matrilignage wolof établit les liens de parenté les plus étroits: pour les Wolof, il transmet la plupart des caractères héréditaires. En d'autres termes, si quelqu'un est frappé d'une maladie, la faute en reviendra nécessairement aux membres du matrilignage. Le patrilignage a une dimension plus sociale et économique. L'héritage des droits (titres, charges, biens) suit principalement cette voie. Un enfant se trouve ainsi rattaché, biologiquement, à son matrilignage mais appartient, socialement, à son patrilignage. Pour les mêmes raisons, les Wolof reconnaissent la force des liens de la parenté utérine tout en accordant un intérêt plus important à leur parenté agnatique. (1985, 244)
>
> Wolof matrilineage establishes very close relations between relatives: for the Wolof, it transmits most of the hereditary traits. In other words, if someone falls ill, the cause will be attributed to members of the maternal line. Patrilineage has a more social and economic dimension. Inheritance of rights (titles, duties, goods) follows this line primarily. A child is thus linked biologically to the maternal line but belongs socially to the paternal line. For the same reasons, the Wolof recognize the strength of maternal ties while at the same time giving greater importance to the paternal line. [my translation]

At the time of the monarchy, the Wolof were organized in towns and villages. The towns still exist. Each area is composed of the main city, surrounded by villages. One measure of the importance of the Wolof in Senegal today may be seen in the fact that nearly 80 percent of the population speaks Wolof.

SOCIAL CIRCUMSTANCES OF MUSICAL PRACTICE

Traditional Wolof society is structured along age classes. The rituals that allow the passage from one class to the other bring together the whole community and are always accompanied by music. The music of women accompanies the various steps of Wolof life, from naming to the initiation of young boys, the tattooing of young girls, and marriage. Women do not play music for and do not participate in the ceremonies surrounding death.

However, women do not limit their relationship with music to rituals and ceremonies. They create music from ordinary household utensils such as calabashes and mortars; they sing and play during their work, to entertain their children or to have fun. Some of the circumstances that call for music no longer occur—for example, war—but given the importance of music for so many other activities in which women are involved, music continues to survive as a key component in their lives. One can only ask, however, how long this will be true, as new forms of music invade society from the outside and from within.

ORGANIZATION OF THE WOLOF MUSICAL HERITAGE

Circumstances in Which Music Is Performed

Table 7.1 below gives a clearer picture of the different kinds of rituals during which songs are sung.

In addition to initiation, tattooing, and marriage, music is performed during the introduction of co-wives into the marital home, and for invoking rain, naming children, narrating history, conducting war, praising monarchs, cheering wrestlers, and celebrating the full moon. It accompanies everyday life, including work in the fields, housework, and lullabies.

Although men may participate in female events, women have no right to participate in male events such as funerals and the initiation of boys. At women's events, generally men either are spectators or they play drums. In very few of these events do they have specific musical roles. During these female events, the griot, however, may sing laudatory songs about ancestors, compliments or praises about events or people who are there, or songs that are simply for entertainment.

With the exceptions of lullabies, of songs about other aspects of culture, and of those accompanying housework, women always sing together, whether *a cappella* or with the accompaniment of hand-clapping (*tàccu*) or with some specific instruments.

Musical Instruments

Only one instrument is used in every event: the *leket,* or calabash. It can be played by rapping the hand or striking a special bracelet against it. The water drum, or *tëmb ndox,* is often used together with the calabash. The calabash floats in a water-filled basin which may be another calabash or a large plastic container. The mortar, *gënn,* used to grind millet, can be heard during the

Table 7.1. The Musical Heritage of Wolof Women

Circumstances		Types of Songs
wrestling	lamb	taggate/màdd taasu woy u lamb
male initiation	njong	taggate/màdd woy u njong
tattooing	njam	woy u njam
co-wives go to the marital home	xaxar	taasu
the wife leaves the father's house and goes to the marital home	céyt	taggate/màdd gërëmate taasu woy u céyt
losing of virginity on nuptial night	laabaan	taggate/màdd taasu
naming	ngénte	taggate/màdd gërëmate taasu
historical	coosaan	woy u coosaan
farmwork	tool	woy u tool
fake lion game	simb	woy u simb
invocation of rain	baaw-naan	woy u baaw-naan
songs for the sovereign	lingeer ak buur	taggate/màdd woy u lingeer/buur
housework	liggéey	woy u liggéey wou u mbëggeel
full moon	ngonaal	wou u mbëggeel taasu
lullaby	naxtal	woy u naxtal

xaxar ritual when the co-wives enter the marital home. There are also more recent instruments: a metal basin, *ndab,* and the *ngalandu,* an iron vessel that replaces or joins the *leket* or calabash. Drums of different types are only played by men. The *tama* is placed under one's armpit. The player presses on the *tama* strings, covered at the two extremities with reptile skin, while the drum is beaten by a curved drumstick to vary the tone. The *tama* is played in almost all the rituals. The Wolof regard it as the most ancient membranophone. There is also a set of *sabar* drums of a cylindrical shape, with only one leather head, played with a stick called the *galañ.*

Types of Songs
Tàggaate (praises) are present in seven circumstances: wrestling, initiation, departure of the bride from her father's house to go to the marital home, nuptial night, naming, praises to the monarchs, and the fake lion game.

Gërëmaaet (acknowledgments) are also played when the bride departs for the marital home as well as during naming ceremonies. Female *géwél* are in charge of playing *tàggaate* and *gërëmaate.* The phrasing of the songs is often in a declamatory mode punctuated by or alternating with lute and drum music. *Tàggaate* and *gërëmaate* songs are different because of the words: in *tàggaate,* the *géwél* relates the chronology and sings the praises to the persons concerned, while the *gërëmaate* regards only the person for whom they are played, male or female. *Woy* songs are sung in the following circumstances: wrestling, initiation, tattooing, departure for the husband's house, the game of fake lion, invocation of rain, fieldwork, housework, lullabies, the full moon, war, and praises for the ruler as seen in the table below. Each circumstance corresponds to a specific group of *woy,* except for housework, an activity that is marked by both *woy u liggéey* (songs of work) and *woy u mbëggeel* (songs of love). The love songs are also found in another form called *taasu,* or songs of amusement associated with the full moon.

Taasu are present in five circumstances: wrestling matches, the wedding night, the arrival of co-wives in the marital home, naming, and, as indicated above, the full moon. Each circumstance calls for a specific *taasu* containing words linked to the context. These are different from the more general *taasu* that have no tie to an event and are therefore called itinerant because they may be sung in a variety of circumstances.

Like other forms of African music, that of the Wolof women is grounded in two principles: repetition and variation of the same material (Arom 1985, 58). In general Wolof songs are divided between a soloist (*debbe*) and a choir (*awu*), according to two forms: one antiphonal (solo a / choir a), the other responsorial (solo a / choir b).

Table 7.2

SONG GENRES		CAYOR		SALOUM		WALO	
		Griotte	Non-griotte	Griotte	Non-griotte	Griotte	Non-griotte
Circumcision	*Njong*	X	X	X	X	X	X
Farmwork	*Tool*		X		X		X
Praises	*Taggate* *Madda*	X		X X		X	
Acknowledgments	*Geremate*	X		X		X	
Historical	*Coosaan*	X		X		X	
Lullaby	*Naxtal*		X		X		X
Invocation of rain	*Baaw-naan*		X		X		X
Love	*Mbëgeel*		X		X		X
Full moon	*Ngoonal*	X	X	X			
Housework	*Liggéey*		X		X		X
Marriage	*Céyt*	X	X*	X		X	X*
Wrestling	*Lamb*	X	X*	X			X*
Tattooing	*Njam*	X	X*	X		X	X*
Naming	*Ngénte*	X	X*	X		X	X*
Amusement	*Taasu*	X	X*	X	X*	X	X*
Fake lion game	*Simb*	X	X*	X		X	X*
Party	*Xaware* *Ndaga*	X		X X		X	

The songs are primarily monodic, although sometimes one hears short plurivocal passages. Melodies are based upon bitonic, tetratonic, pentatonic, and hexatonic ranges. The entertainment pieces known as *taasu* are *recto tono;* that is, they remain on the same note. Voices are mainly situated within a low register. Often the singers produce a series of "youyous" or ululations.

In table 7.2, one can see the distribution of songs by region. The three geographically distinct areas, Cayor, Saloum, and Walo, have many common features.

X* indicates songs played by both professional (*géwél*) and non-professional singers.

The second column presents the distribution of musical repertoires between professional singers, or *géwél,* and non-professional singers in the Cayor, Saloum, and Walo regions. In these three regions, praises, acknowledgments, historical songs, and party songs are sung by female *géwél*. Lullabies and songs performed during housework and fieldwork as well as for the invocation of rain and for romantic occasions are not necessarily played or sung by a *géwél*. Initiation songs can be played or sung by both géwél and non-géwél women, depending on the circumstances.

A noticeable and inexplicable generic distinction between the regions is the absence of full moon songs in the Walo region. In the Cayor and Saloum regions, this repertoire is sung by both *géwél* and non-*géwél* women. In Cayor and Walo regions, wrestling, naming, marriage, tattooing, and fake lion songs are played by both professional and non-professional singers. In the past, only female *géwél* played and sang on these occasions.

Today, Wolof society is changing. Tasks traditionally specific to *géwél* are now fulfilled by non-*géwél*. One result is that music is affected. But this phenomenon varies by region. Traditional social roles and activities are maintained more in the Saloum region than in the others. For example, repertoires of praises (*màdd*) and party songs (*ndaga*) are specific to Saloum. Legends are played by both professional and non-professional singers. The female *géwél* always sing and lead ceremonies and non-professional singers accompany them (chorus, musical instruments).

The texts of the songs talk about the pain of tattooing, the monarch's genealogy, the strength and skill of wrestlers, the members of a family, the wedding night, love, religion, and the hard work in the fields. Wolof lyrics can include Serer, Pular, or Arabic words. Lyrics are flexible and adaptable according to the events and the people listening: songs can therefore be longer or shorter, especially in praises (*tàggaate*). The appendix offers a small sample of what is without doubt a corpus of thousands of songs by women.

CONCLUSION

From the evidence available one can draw several conclusions. First, between the Wolof regions studied, there are clearly strong regional similarities in the circumstances in which songs are sung. Moreover, the same melodies can occur in different events. Aside from these regional similarities, however, there are numerous differences. For example, in the region of Saloum the marriage, naming, wrestling, tattooing, and fake lion game songs are played or sung only by female *géwél,* which does not occur in the Cayor and Walo regions, where these repertoires are now played by non-*géwél* as well. Furthermore, party (*ndaga*) and praise (*màdd*) songs are specific to the Saloum region.

In the regional context, then, one can conclude that at the local level these similarities and differences constitute a microcosm of the much larger Sahelian picture. At every level, we must be alert to these differences and similarities. Like the pattern in a large handwoven West African blanket, they constitute a mosaic with its subtle variations. How these local features stand out and intermesh with those of neighboring peoples—in this case the Serer, the Diola, Toucouleur, Mandinka, etc.—should be the object of further research on the music of West Africa.

APPENDIX

Seyna, did you lose something?

(song for amusement)

Seyna, did you lose something?
Kodou Fall, did you lose something?
Adj Fall, did you lose something?
This kid does not have self restraint
He is daring
He loses also his cattle
Kodou, did you lose something?

Kine Fall, did you lose something?
Taye, did you lose something?
Fatou Diop, did you lose something?
Soda Gueye, did you lose something?
My son, did you lose something?
Our traditional songs, you have to sing them
And . . .
To have rotten luck
My boy, did you lose something?

If you still miss me, my dear

(love song)

If you still miss me, my dear
If you still miss me
Come, I take you away

Raseck Balla Ndiaye
Ndiape Ndiaye's darling
Come, I take you away

Here is Ibrahima Diaw
Mrs. Diaw's darling
Come to greet me

Ibrahima is far from here
Mrs. Diaw's darling
You have to be nice

You are Mari Yves Ndiaye, your mother
Mrs. Diaw's darling
Come to greet me

You, if you still miss me
Take the moon as a point of reference
We can not love two persons at once
Mrs. Diaw's darling
Come to greet me

You, if you still miss me
You, Dieynaba your darling
Come to greet me

Eye way! Mrs. Diaw
Dieynaba your darling
Come to greet me

Seynaba Lo is your daughter
Mrs. Diaw's friend
Come to greet me

Mrs. Diaw
We cannot love two persons at once
And wedding is not a game
Come to greet me
Maseck Souleye Ndiaye

You, if you still miss me
Take the moon as a point of reference
It is far

Here is Louise Diagne
Ibrahima's mother
Come to greet me

It is the daughter who inherits her mother
That is the tradition
And it is clear

Khady is far away
You Ramata Sow
Come to greet me

You Kalidou Ndiaye
It is the daughter who inherits her mother
This is the truth

Her mind is far
Mrs Diaw's darling
Come to greet me

Maréme is far from here
Here is Ibrahima Diaw
This is the truth

Here is Ibrahima Diaw
Mrs Diaw's darling
Come to greet me

Way! Maréme is far from here
Ibrahima is far from here
That is true

Here is Ibrahima Diaw
Mrs Diaw's darling
Come to greet me

Yandé the Wrestler

(wrestling song)

Yandé wrestler
Fighter you are the one who will win
Yandé wrestler
Wrestler you are the one who will win

Yandé wrestler
The best might win
Yandé wrestler
Wrestler you are the one who will win

Baaw-naan

(rain dance)

Ritual songs and dances to call the rain
We are going to organize ritual songs and dances
Likaba Djali

Ritual songs and dances to call the rain
We are going to organize ritual songs and dances
God give us the rain
Likaba Djali

God give us the rain
Ngokhi ngokh

WORKS CITED

Arom, S. 1985. *Polyphonies et polyrythmies instrumentales d'Afrique Centrale*. 2 vols. Paris: SELAF.
Diagne, Y. 1982. L'Ordre de la tradition et les pouvoirs de la paroles chez les Wolof du Sénégal. PhD Diss., Ecole des Hautes Etudes en Sciences Sociales, Paris.
Diop, Abdoulaye-Bara. 1981. *La Société wolof: tradition et changement: Les systèmes d'inégalité et de domination*. Paris: Karthala.
———. 1985. *La famille wolof*. Paris: Karthala.
Diouf, Jean-Léopold. 2003. *Dictionnaire wolof-français et français-wolof*. Paris: Karthala.
Magassouba, Moriba. 1985. *L'Islam au Sénégal: Demain les mollahs*. Paris: Karthala.

8

A Heroic Performance by Siramori Diabaté in Mali

Brahima Camara and Jan Jansen

THE DEBATE

Jelikèw (male griots) and *jelimusow* (female griots, or griottes) have many roles in the West African societies in which they practice their profession. There are some differences in what they do, however. For example, *jelimusow* do not normally play the same instruments as *jelikèw*. In the Mande world, *jelikèw* play stringed instruments while *jelimusow* sing songs and strike the *karignan* (or *nege* [Bambara] or *neoo* [Mandinka], which means "iron"), a notched narrow metal tube held in one hand while the other rhythmically scrapes it with a thin metal rod (see Charry 2000, 87). But one of the most widely studied functions of these performers is the narration of epics.

In the 1990s, Hale (1994) and Sidikou (2001) raised the question as to whether women are totally excluded from narrating epics. We feel that any answer to this important issue[1] will be framed by four analytical dimensions:

1. However "epic" is defined,[2] this definition is always based on performances by men, thus implicitly taking men as a standard for the genre.[3]

2. Local terms for "epic" may analytically conflict with the general definitions that have been inspired by the Eurasian literary corpus.

3. Local terms for "epic" may be context-related rather than text-related. This argument can be illustrated as follows. The *jeliw* ("griots," male and female) of Kela—an important "school of oral tradition" famous for its version of the Sunjata epic, which narrates the foundation of the medieval Mali Empire—have a term for their "epic"[4] which they might use for a localized

performance rather than for the text that is recited during that performance. Well-orchestrated recitations of Sunjata's history are a *Mansa Jigin* ("The Genealogy of the Kings") if the performance includes a chorus song (with the title *Dibi kèlen*) and takes place in their own village (Kela) or in Kangaba, the location of the Kamabolon sanctuary, where the Kela *jeliw* are supposed to perform the *Mansa Jigin* every seven years during a five-day ceremony.[5] If this recitation of Sunjata's history does not meet these two criteria, people won't call it a *Mansa Jigin,* but—for instance—"laudable words" or "stories about ancestors." On other occasions they might give a quite similar performance, but then classify it as much less prestigious, for instance as "praising names" (*matogoliw*). A major indication of the status difference between these performances is the fact that recordings of non–*Mansa Jigin* performances are allowed, while it is strictly forbidden to record *Mansa Jigin* performances.[6]

4. The mode of performance may be relevant. Durán (in Hale 1994, 80) witnessed a *jelimuso* singing an epic, and we feel that, at least among Mande peoples, it might be impossible to consider a sung narrative as an epic since sung words are valued and appreciated differently from those that are recited. Sung words are less prestigious, since (alleged) errors are never the point of discussion; although a serious affair, they are considered to be entertaining and to create feelings of harmony and unity.[7]

Jelikèw themselves have claimed that only they recount epics, while *jelimusow* seem to add songs to the performance. Using a case study of the illustrious *jelimuso* Siramori Diabaté (c. 1930–1989) from Kela and focusing on her relatively well-documented life and works, we wonder if the lines between the sexes can be drawn so strictly. Asking whether Siramori Diabaté could and would perform epics might enable scholars to draw a more nuanced portrait of the *jelimuso*'s craft.

SIRAMORI DIABATÉ, LIFE AND DOCUMENTS

In Mali, Siramori Diabaté is considered one of the most celebrated female artists of the twentieth century. Being born to the famous Diabaté *jeli* family from Kela gave her the opportunity to grow up in a setting in which she could fully develop her musical and verbal talents. The traditional material of Kela's *jeliw* consists of praise songs for the heroes who once founded society, which is called Mande or Manding. These heroes are the ancestors of the present-day population, nowadays labeled an ethnic group called the Maninka or Malinké. The praise songs are part of a wider narrative about the foundation of Mande, a narrative widely known as the Sunjata epic, which has been told in large parts of the West African Sudan for centuries.[8] The Kela *jeliw* have held, certainly for decades, but probably for centuries, a prestigious position in the area south of Bamako as the performers of the authoritative version of the Sunjata epic (Jansen 1998). Although they seldom perform the epic in public, they systematically organize rehearsals of it, in particular in the months before a septennial ceremony in the Kamabolon sanctuary. Moreover, the men responsible for reciting the epic also organize their private rehearsals. Siramori must have attended both the private and public rehearsals very often.

Siramori was a talented artist capable of memorizing the complex praise songs, as well as a keen performer; she was able then to relate the large and complex corpus of praise lines to the needs and desires of her audience. Therefore, purely mnemotechnically, she must have been able to comprehend superbly the Sunjata epic: she had the right talents in the right setting.

Siramori Diabaté's vocal talents became apparent when she was very young. In the choruses that performed traditional praise songs she was given a featured role, as we can hear from recordings made in 1949.[9] But she quickly became a solo singer. Her fame spread with her interpretation of the song "Sara,"[10] an amusing account of an "emancipated" woman who, against the will of her family, manages to marry the partner of her choice.

In her personal life, Siramori Diabaté fused Sara's emancipated example with the traditional ideal of marriage.[11] She herself married balafon player Nankoman Kouyate (d. 1998), but she did not accept the regional tradition of patrilocality by settling in the village of her husband's family. Instead she settled, with her husband, in the historic town of Kangaba, an alleged former capital of the medieval Mali Empire, five kilometers from her native village of Kela. Siramori Diabaté often stayed for prolonged periods in Mali's capital, Bamako, one hundred kilometers from Kela, but she did not buy a house there as her daughter, the *jelimuso* Sanungwè Kouyate, did later. Siramori took advantage of the changing conditions in Malian society. After World War II the French constructed roads and bridges that connected Kangaba to Bamako. Thanks to the increasing availability of cars and trucks, she was able to work in the rapidly growing city of Bamako, where the new political and economic elite lived, while maintaining close ties both to her roots in Kela and to her domestic base in Kangaba.[12]

Siramori's life and work have been fairly well documented, in particular compared with other artists of her era. In addition to commercial recordings based on radio appearances and a few short articles in local media, there is a commercially available audio cassette with an interview (*Sorofè* n.d.) and an ethnographer's attempt to systematically collect and translate her repertoire.[13]

Given these extraordinary conditions for research, Siramori Diabaté is probably the only *jelimuso* who offers us the opportunity to make an "educated guess" about the question of whether women perform epics in the Mande world.

Our answer to this is reluctant, probably even confusing, since Siramori's case raises more questions than it answers. However, these questions may deepen our understanding of the complex relationships between gender, knowledge, genres, and cultural style. In the next section we will present a song by Siramori in which she refers frequently to heroic ancestors who feature in the Sunjata epic. This is followed by a section in which her text is analyzed.

A HEROIC PERFORMANCE BY SIRAMORI: THE HUNTERS' SONG "GWÈDÈ"

"Gwèdè" is a song in praise of the hunter, an archetypal hero in Mali.[14] It is therefore not surprising that Siramori relates praise for the hunter to acts by the ancestors who founded Mande: almost any hero can be pictured as a hunter (cf. B. Camara 1998, section 1.5 in particular). Siramori starts her rendering of "Gwèdè" with "general" references to hunting, an activity that takes place at night. Hence the hunter is compared to an owl. Siramori elaborates also on the hunting of hippopotamuses in the river and on the Somono fishermen who hunt the giant Nile perch (*capitaine* in West African French). The hunter is a Simbon, a brave hunter. At the end of the song she turns to scenes we know from the Sunjata epic:

> This melody is dedicated to the hunter heroes
> Aaa, the hunter hero hasn't arrived
> The cat that passes one single time
> Has sown terror at sunrise
> 5   Long time ago
> This melody was dedicated to the hunter heroes
> Aaa, the hunter hero hasn't arrived
> The owl from the mountain of Kanjan hasn't arrived
> I'll tell you the person who slays and pushes the wild animals is feared
> 10   Long time ago
> Not all people know how to dance to the melody of the *janjo*[15]
> The hunter hero from the mountain of Kanjan isn't there
> Jankina, the hunter hero isn't afraid
> The owls have brought antelope horns
> 15   The owls have brought them
> The owls have brought horns of Buffon antelopes

The owls have brought them
The owls have brought horns of koba antelopes
Really, he isn't afraid, Jankina, the hunter hero
20   Aaa, aaa, aaa the bird of the days of the past
Peace and hail for you
Be patient, followers of Muhammad
Isn't it that some people sleep
While others are awake
25   You compare the Brave
Well, there is a big difference among the Brave
Isn't it, eh, eh, eh, life!
Are there many hunter heroes in one's life?
The hunter heroes have become scarce
30   Aaa, to which hunter hero do I refer?
Owl—for you the wilderness
Kunkunba and Bantanba
Nyani-nyani and Kanbasiga
Kayirumajikiso
35   Namitè, namijokola[16]
Isn't it true that some brave are more courageous than others
Aaa, you are a hunter hero
Bebe Jigi is a hunter who loves the bow
Aaa really numerous are the hunter heroes
40   Traveling salesmen[17] who walk the entire night, hail to your efforts
Traveling salesmen who walk the entire day, hail to your numerous efforts
Do you know to which hunter hero I refer?
Hunter heroes of the waters, hail, too, to your efforts
Jèbè is the small tip of the pirogue
45   Jèbè is the large tip of the pirogue
Jèbè is the small tip of the first *juba*
Jèbè is the large tip of the huge *juba*
Children of the Somono[18] women, where are you, hunter heroes?
Look at Muntaka Kamara!
50   Fasinè Sokore, Alama Sokore, Kasumu Sokore
Aaa, aaa I recall the hunter hero
Eee, eee, the owl-son of Bintu
Is there in the bush far away
Naman really is a hunter hero who loves the bow
55   Spouses of Somono women, where did the *kolon* spend the night?
Spouses of Somono women, where did the *kolon* spend the night?

Aaa, owl-son of Bintu, where did the *kolon* spend the night
Owl-son of Bintu, where did the Nile perches spend the night
Aaa, the great traveling salesmen . . . Allah
60　Isn't it so that
Naren Makan Jata in his identity of Sirifiya Makan Konate[19] has arrived
He who glances through the big and the small brushwood
I apologize
Really, brave men have become scarce
65　It is really difficult to know Mande
Mande is here
The spinning well
The well you talk about
Which some people call "the spinning well"
70　In that well one won't drop a blind person
But only the few people from Mande who can see[20]
Certain people know Sunsun, but don't know Manko[21]
Certain people know Manko, but don't know Sunsun
Aaa, powerful traveling salesmen, the hunter hero hasn't gone to sleep
75　One day, Sirifiya Makan Konate convoked the brave
Rise up, rise up, please, braves of Mande
That each of you will demonstrate his capacities
That after this day this country, Mande won't be without real men
This being said, Konè from Kasawura, Konè drinker of large quantities of water
80　Sirifiya Makan Konate descends from the Konè[22]
This being said, the ancestor of the Kamara
Wana Faran Kamara from Sibi
Wana Faran Kamara from Tabun
Wana Faran Kamara from Nyènkèma
85　If you cut his arm in the morning
Watch how it recovers
An arrow killed Kaman the Tall
And sorcerers gave Kaman the final blow
As a hunter like lightning
90　Kaman the Tall drew his sword from the sheath that hangs on his hips
And transfixed the Mande hill,
Thus creating the arch of entrance and exit of Kaman the Tall[23]
That is the way the *jeliw* tell it
Where have Tiramakan and Kankejan gone!
95　He said: "Rise up! Brave men of Mande, if you don't rise up,
The buffalo will soon exterminate Mande[24]

Every day it makes three victims
Brave men of Mande, rise up!"
Fakoli, the son of Koman Kòdòma, the killer of enemies, rose up
100   Fakoli with the big head, Fakoli with the big mouth
Koli[25] with the big umbilical, Koli without umbilical
He marched, marched, and marched
Oh! It is not easy to see the buffalo
Yes, powerful traveling salesman, it is difficult to see the buffalo of Mande
105   Who was also called to appear?
Soma Dòbi, the ancestor of the Konate
The horn of an ourebi antelope kills someone
That object will kill its owner in Mande
The horn of a "cephalophe" kills someone
110   That object will kill its owner in Mande
Sirifiya Makan Konate said uh, uh
It really isn't easy to see this buffalo
Sirifiya Makan Konate ordered to call Tiramakan
The servant who digs his own tomb as well as his master's[26]
115   The black dog without horns, the son of Nakana
If you don't rise up, Tiramakan
The buffalo with soon exterminate Mande
It makes three victims a day
Tiramakan and Kankejan rose up
120   He went to see Siriman Kanda Ture
[And] Manjan Berete from Tonbondò
"Siriman Kanda Ture, do help me
Tonbondò Manjan Berete, you must help me to beat this buffalo
Because many brave men from Mande have left to chase it in vain"
125   The first and last Koranic scholar of Mande
He did a magic spell on the wings of a partridge that he sent to fly away
Then he said to Tiramakan, rise up, you will beat the buffalo
Searching for the buffalo, you will meet
Two old ladies collecting wood—don't you ever pass them, Tiramakan
130   Tiramakan, the king of behind the river, took his quiver and his bow
And said that he would go after the buffalo
Arriving at the crossroads, the crossing of the roads,
He saw two old ladies gathering wood
"Hello, grandmothers," he yelled
135   "Why do you greet us, Tiramakan, we don't work for you"
"I greet you, because you are comparable to my mother"

He went into the bush and collected two piles of wood
That he deposited on the crossroads, the crossing of the roads
"Grandmothers, come and take this wood
140 And return to your house, because you are tired
You suffer under the sun"
Tiramakan, you have become . . .
You are a little, provoking child
Tiramakan, you have become . . .
145 You are a bellicose man
You are in search of the buffalo
That makes three victims everyday
Tiramakan, I am this buffalo, it is not easy to see me
Tiramakan, what you want (is this):
150 I will give myself to you, servant who digs his own tomb as well as his master's
You, dog-without-horns, son of Nakana[27]
I will give myself to you
And it will be remembered in your praise song from here to the afterlife
If you look for the buffalo, go and look in the big woods at the lake
155 When you see the buffalo, one eye is golden
When you see the buffalo, one eye is silver
Tiramakan, when you see the buffalo, if you don't fear
You, servant who digs his own tomb as well as his master's
If you beat the buffalo
160 It will be remembered in my praise song from here to the afterlife
Tiramakan and Kankejan, king of behind the river
I will give myself to you
Tiramakan took his quiver and bow and started to march
He saw the buffalo
165 Which had one eye golden
He saw the buffalo
Which had one eye silver
He bent, like a reaping-hook, a reaping-hook to cut to the *nèrè* tree in Mande
He mustered his strength in such a way . . .
170 And his hand produced evil, the celestial drum
Tiramakan bet the buffalo
Tukuru and Kasinè, Kasinè and Kasinèsa
Sèlèn Fabore, Danka Fabure
Makanta the Black and Makanta the White
175 Dog-without-horns, son of Nakana[28]
You bet the buffalo to make this part of your praise song

You, king of behind the river
Tiramakan bet the buffalo and the *jeliw* of Mande say [since then]
That Tiramakan and Kankejan should be glorified
180 That the quiver and the bow will be given to Tiramakan
Tiramakan, he is the servant who digs his own tomb
Aaa, the lance may refuse, but Tiramakan doesn't fear
Tiramakan, the servant who digs his own tomb
To Tiramakan has been given the call for war
185 Tiramakan, the servant who digs his own tomb
Hail to your efforts, hail to your efforts, Tiramakan and Kankejan
Hail to your efforts, hail to your efforts
Muke Musa and Muke Dantuman, hail to your efforts
Aaa, Tiramakan and Kankejan didn't fear
190 The servant who digs his own tomb as well as his master's
This melody has been dedicated to Tiramakan and Kankejan
Soriyo, aaa, dimè
The horse isn't insidious, but the reins are insidious
The horse isn't insidious, but the [inaudible] is insidious
195 The servant who digs his own tomb as well as his master's
Do . . . Show the gunpowder publicly, so Tiramakan will come out
Tiramakan, the servant who digs his own tomb
Aaa, the lance may refuse, but Tiramakan isn't afraid
Tiramakan, the servant who digs his own tomb

TEXT ANALYSIS: SIRAMORI DIABATÉ AND THE SUNJATA EPIC

In this song Siramori tells the story of the buffalo of Do, whose death was a prerequisite for establishing the marriage between Sunjata's parents. This hunting story is a widely known theme from the Sunjata epic, definitely among the *jeliw* with whom Siramori grew up in Kela (cf. Belcher 1999, 95, nos. 26 and 27). She follows many descriptions and expressions which can be found in the Kela recordings of the Sunjata epic, which illustrates and demonstrates that she was a keen listener.

However, her lyrics also challenge what one expects on the basis of the published Kela versions of the Sunjata epic. First, the killing of the buffalo is always attributed not to Tiramakan, but to his ancestors/predecessors Danmansa Wulani and Danmansa Wulantanba, after having met one old woman (and not two). Moreover, the theme of the Qurʾānic scholars and the partridge is a theme that is particular to the Kela version of the Sunjata epic (see Jansen 2000 for an explanation; see Jansen 2010 for a video recording). In Kela it is told in relation to Sunjata's clash with his antagonist, the sorcerer-blacksmith-king

Sumaoro Kante. It has never been recorded in relation to the Traore, neither to Sunjata's "servant" Tiramakan nor to the hunter twins who killed Do's buffalo.

A *jeli,* male or female, may have the literary freedom to replace one Traore ancestor with another.[29] Indeed, in the context of a hunters' song of praise such a transformation is definitely acceptable. What strikes us is that Siramori also "confused" other male antagonists, by deviating from the Kela standard when rendering her story of the Qurʾānic scholars and the partridge.

What is happening here? First, it must be noted that these transformations are not mere coincidental mistakes. They appear again in a text recorded by Jansen in March 1989 in Kangaba, a few days before he was about to return home. At the end of his fieldwork period in Kangaba, Siramori invited him to a voluntary (i.e., without any financial remuneration) recording. While usually accompanied by her son, the guitar player Sidiki Kouyate, she now invited Jansen to her room, and recited (instead of the usual singing!) to him the following text (taken from Jansen's unpublished MA thesis from 1989; translation slightly edited by Cemako Kanté, Institut des Sciences Humaines, Bamako).

Si tu vois les griots parler de Sumaoro Kante, l'exploit qu'il a fait, c'est pourquoi les griots crient son nom. Sumaoro était le premier roi du Mande; il fut le premier à gouverner le Mande.[30] C'est pourquoi on parle beaucoup de lui. Sumaoro n'a pas blagué au Mande, lorsque Sumaoro venait au Mande. Les gens avaient peur de lui; ils avaient peur tellement, qu'ils ne pouvaient pas parler. 'Ne parlons pas avec nos bouches. Sinon, Sumaoro va nous punir,' se disaient-ils. Sa royauté avait atteint son paroxysme; on ne peut pas parler de la sévérité du pouvoir de Sumaoro. Sumaoro était un vrai homme, l'homme qui attrape les hommes. On déclame sa *fasa* grâce à son titre. C'est après le pouvoir de Sumaoro que Sunjata a pris le pouvoir. Makan Konate de Sirifiya.[31] Lui aussi prit le pouvoir avec force et puissance. Makan Sunjata aussi n'a pas blagué; il a gouverné sur le Mande. Il fit entrer les gens et les fit sortir comme des troupeaux. Ça c'est Makan Sunjata: qui quête dans la petite et grande touffe. Simbo a régné et a disparu. Si tu entends parler de Tiramakan. De Tiramakan par les griots du Mande. Celui-ci aussi a fait des exploits. Il a tué le buffle du Mande. Je l'ai la dit dans la chanson. Tiramakang et Kankedjan, Tukuru et Kasine, Kasine et Kasinesa, Fabure de Selen, Fabare de Danga, Magatafin et Magatagwè, fils de Nakana, porteur de dix cornes de chien noir.[32] Il était brave. Il avait un couteau à double tranchant. C'est lui qui a tué le buffle. Pour cela il a consulté Maganjan Berete à Tomono qui a travaillé pour lui pour battre le buffle.[33] Il tua ce buffle et donna sa queue au roi du Mande à Dakadjala. Tiramakan a accompli des exploits. Après lui, il y eut le grand griot de Julafondo du nom de Madisilla.[34] C'est lui qui est venu après Makan Sunjata. A ce Madisilla de Julafondo on disait: 'Torifo et

Sambuya, l'épervier qui abat son maître, débris de mil en miniature, gros débris de mil, gros arbres aux grosses feuilles. Clairière de Warakatamba où siègent les abeilles qui tuent facilement les hommes. Il alla s'installer dans cette clairière durant dix jours et est retourné en bonne santé.'[35] Madisilla était de la grande famille de Diawara de Julafondo.

Although she speaks of only one buffalo here, the recurring "repositioning" of Tiramakan[36] and Tomono Maganjan Berete strikes the reader's eye. Siramori must have known "better," but she walked an alternative path. Siramori deviated from the epic she must have learned by heart. But did she create a form of heroic narrative that transgresses all academic classifications so far?[37] Or was this an indirect critique of the central position attributed to men in the Sunjata epic and thus Maninka society, thereby voicing a "feminist" perspective? We may never know, but we do know and feel that Siramori's rendering of "Gwèdè" is a heroic performance that supports Hale and Sidikou's call for more research on griottes if we ever want to understand the craft of these performers in all its rich panoply of color.

NOTES

1. We would like to thank the editors for their stimulating comments and the anonymous reviewer for a valuable critique of the validity of our arguments in the first draft of this paper.

2. We have adopted Stephen Belcher's definition (Belcher 1999, viii): "[An epic] evokes monuments of the written literary tradition, a larger-than-life scale of narrative that may be tinged with divine inspiration. . . . Implicit in the term 'oral epic' is the notion of a certain similarity of materials within the Eurasian literary corpus."

3. Janson (2002) raises this analytical problem regarding the study of *jelimusow* in general. This analytical problem seems hard to avoid, since the same author uses it in opposition to Sidikou's claim (2001) that women recite epics: Janson (2004) argues that Sidikou's evidence is rather scarce and that the alleged epic does not meet generally accepted criteria, although he adds that he agrees with Sidikou that "theory on epic is male-centered and needs to be redefined" (2004, 82).

4. *Mansa Jigin,* which means literally the "Genealogy of the Kings."

5. For an overview of the literature on this ceremony, and details of the 1997 rehearsals and performance, see Jansen (2001b).

6. For an elaborate description of the variations in Sunjata performances, see Jansen (1999).

7. This explains why *jeliw* often add to their praise songs the proverbial comment *Tulon tè sèbèn faga* (literally "Play doesn't kill serious [issues]"—or in local French, "l'amusement ne tue pas le sérieux").

8. For a collection that covers the wide range of scholarly research on the Sunjata epic, see Austen (1999).

9. There are some songs by Siramori in the

historic collection of several dozen songs recorded in Mali and Guinea by Arthur S. Alberts in 1949, now housed at the Archives of Traditional Music (ATM) at Indiana University. Alberts recorded some of the most renowned musicians of their time, including the family of Sidi Djeli Dioubate of Kankan, Guinea, the creators of the musical event Mamaya, and the family of Kayra Sekou Koita and Siramori Diabaté of Kela, Mali, the subject of this article. Alberts's recordings from all over West Africa were released on a series of LPs and a recent CD. . . . A version of Kayra (Kahira) from Kissidougou, Guinea, with two koras and a guitar, as well as excerpts from the Kela Diabaté performances, were issued in 1954. . . . Alberts recorded three pieces in all of the Kela griots on 2 May, 1949 in Bamako (according to his notes). 'Sara,' one of the three pieces, is known as the signature song of Siramori Diabaté. Although the artists were unidentified on the recordings, the Kela Diabaté family of griots were readily identified in the 1990s when Eric Charry began inquiries (Camara, Charry, and Jansen 2002, 300–301).

10. See also Jansen (1996), Diabaté (2002), and Bird (1997). According to Bird, in his contribution to Johnson, Hale, and Belcher's 1997 anthology of epics in Africa, "Sara" bears many of the traits of an epic.

11. In the official media, Siramori claimed that her favorite song was "Nanyuman," a song with a more "traditional" view on marriage; it is an appeal to women to ensure their marriage endures. If they did not, the country would fail to prosper. Siramori also publicly criticized strategies by modern artists: on the audio cassette *Sorofè* (n.d.) she complains that these singers are too money-minded and lack love of their fatherland. She remarked that these singers sing praises without knowing if a person really deserves such adulation, and argued (sarcastically): "If you praise someone as sitting on a horse, and you have never seen him sitting on a horse, you insult the horse [*i bè sò labin*]."

12. See also Jansen (1996). Siramori's prestigious position and her achievements are well expressed—although slightly exaggerated and mystified—in *World Music: The Rough Guide. Africa, Europe and the Middle East, Volume 1,* whose author writes about her: "probably the most respected of all the jelimusolu was the late Sira Mory Diabaté (Kasse Mady's aunt) from Kela, an imposing, nearly blind woman with a moving alto voice, and composer of several famous songs such as 'Bani' and 'Sara.' Unlike many of today's jelimusolu her voice is low-pitched and leisurely, her lyrics more moralistic than praising. . . . Sira Mory had uncompromising principles: she was favoured by President Modibo Keita but neglected by his successor, Moussa Traoré, because she did not sing praise songs for him" (Broughton, Ellingham, and Trillo 1999, 550). To this we would add that "Sara" was probably not composed by her—it was already a "traditional" by the end of the 1940s—but Siramori did make the song popular. Moreover, in April 1989 Siramori told Jansen, during a chance meeting in Bamako, that she performed for Moussa Traoré on a regular basis.

13. Jan Jansen made field recordings with Siramori during his MA research between December 1988 and April 1989. This was a few months before her unexpected death in December 1989. The field recordings have been issued, together with two 1974 record-

ings of Siramori by John W. Johnson, on CD (Diabaté 2002), and four classical praise songs from this collection are accessible on the internet through the Verba Africana project at http://www.hum2.1eidenuniv.nl/verba-africana/malinke-fr/b-songs.htm (last accessed 24 March 2012).

14. For two differing analyses of the cultural and social importance of hunters, see B. Camara (2008) and Jansen (2008).

15. A classical song/melody popular among hunters; it is a great honor if the *janjo* is played for them.

16. Standardized praise lines for people bearing the patronymics Kouyate (*jeliw*) and Kante (blacksmiths).

17. Tentative translation of *Kalajula Sangoyi,* which is a greeting formula of praise for a bearer of the Diabaté patronymic.

18. Ethnic group of fishermen with whom the Maninka have long cohabited.

19. Both names are synonyms for Sunjata, the legendary founder of society in the Maninka worldview.

20. For an extensive comment on Mande society as the metaphorical spinning well, see Jansen (2001a).

21. Probably references to the tree species *sunsun*—an indigenous tree—and the mango tree, which was introduced into Mali in the first half of the twentieth century.

22. Sunjata's mother Sogolon Kéjugu was a Konè.

23. Standardized praise for the Ka.

24. A reference to the killing of Do's buffalo by an ancestor of the Traore, which was a prerequisite for arranging a marriage between Sunjata's parents. This is a common theme in text editions of the Sunjata epic collected in the second half of the twentieth century (see Belcher 1989, 94–95). For a discussion of this theme, see below.

25. "Koli" indicates Fakoli, the ancestor of several Maninka clans, bearers of the same patronymic.

26. A reference to a story about Tiramakan, the ancestor of the Traore, who compels Sunjata to give a particular military task to him, Tiramakan, by threatening to bury himself if Sunjata refuses.

27. Greeting formula of praise for a Traore.

28. Praise lines for a Traore.

29. A point made by an anonymous reviewer of this paper.

30. The image of Sumaoro Kante as a great Mande king is, according to Kaba (2001, 31n20), typical for the Kangaba region.

31. Honorary title for Sunjata.

32. Praise lines for Tiramakan Traore in particular and for the Traore and Diabaté in general.

33. Again a man is "repositioned": in the Kela tradition "Maganjan Berete de Tomono" is a marabout who was among the group that traveled to Nema in search of Sunjata after he and his family had fled into exile.

34. Siramori liked to mention this ancestor of the Diawara *jeliw:* she "composed" a song about him which she had performed previously (see Diabaté 2002) and which was also performed by her daughter Sanungwè Kouyate on her first commercial cassette, in the early 1990s.

35. Praise lines for the Diawara (either of noble or *jeliw* origin) in the Kela tradition.

36. Therefore, it is "logical" for Siramori, who put much emphasis on Tiramakan Traore in her interpretation of "Gwèdè," to conclude her performance with a "Tiramakan fasa," a praise song for Tiramakan; at the end of the song her son Sidiki Kouyate, who accompanied her on guitar, changes the melody he plays and starts the "Tiramakan fasa."

37. An idea inspired by Karim Traoré (Traoré 2000), who suggests that there are many more literary genres among the Maninka than scholars generally opt for in their genre analyses.

WORKS CITED

Austen, R. A., ed. 1999. *In Search of Sunjata: The Mande Oral Epic as History, Literature, and Performance.* Bloomington: Indiana University Press.

Belcher, S. P. 1999. *Epic Traditions of Africa.* Bloomington: Indiana University Press.

Bird, C. S. 1997. The epic of Sara—Narrated by Sira Mori Jabaté. In *Oral Epics from Africa: Vibrant Voices from a Vast Continent,* ed. J. W. Johnson, T. A. Hale, and S. Belcher, 114–123. Bloomington: Indiana University Press.

Broughton, Simon, Mark Ellingham, and Richard Trillo. 1999. *World Music: The Rough Guide. Africa, Europe and the Middle East, Volume 1.* London: Rough Guides.

Camara, B. 1998. *Jägerliteratur in Manden: Gattungs- und Übersetzungsprobleme afrikanischer Oralliteratur am Beispiel von Baala Jinba Jakites Epos Bilakoro Mari, Teil 1.* Bayreuth: Edition Schultz und Stellmacher.

———. 2008. The hunter in the Mande imagination. *Mande Studies* 10:121–132.

Camara, S., E. Charry, and J. Jansen. 2002. The Mande praise song Kayra (Peace): Mande global perspectives. *Metamorphoses* 10 (1): 300–320.

Charry, Eric. 2000. *Traditional and Modern Music of the Maninka and Mandinka of Western Africa.* Chicago: University of Chicago Press.

Diabaté, Siramori. 2002. *Siramori Diabaté: Griot Music from Mali No. 3.* Leiden: PAN Records 2104.

Hale, T. A. 1994. Griottes: Female voices from West Africa. *Research in African Literatures* 25 (3): 71–91.

Jansen, J. 1996. "Elle connaît tout le Mande": A tribute to the griotte Siramori Diabaté. *Research in African Literatures* 27 (4): 180–197.

———. 1998. Hot issues: The 1997 Kamabolon ceremony in Kangaba (Mali). *International Journal of African Historical Studies* 31 (2): 253–278.

———. 1999. An ethnography of the epic of *Sunjata* in Kela. In *In Search of Sunjata: The Mande Oral Epic as History, Literature, and Performance,* ed. R. A. Austen, 297–312. Bloomington: Indiana University Press.

———. 2000. Masking Sunjata: A hermeneutical critique. *History in Africa* 27:131–141.

———. 2001a. *Épopée, Histoire, Société: le cas de Soundjata: Mali et Guinée.* Paris: Karthala.

———. 2001b. The Sunjata epic: The ultimate version. *Research in African Literatures* 32 (1): 14–46.

———. 2008. From guild to Rotary: Hunters' associations and Mali's search for a civil society. *International Review of Social History* 53:249–270.

——, ed. 2010. *Mali: l'Épopée de Soundjata: Verba Africana 3.* Leiden: Faculty of Humanities, Leiden University. http://www.hum2.1eidenuniv.nl/verba-africana /malinke-fr/.

Janson, Marloes. 2002. *The Best Hand Is the Hand That Always Gives: Griottes and Their Profession in Eastern Gambia.* Leiden: CNWS.

——. 2004. The narration of the Sunjata epic as a gendered activity. In *Epic Adventures: Heroic Narrative in the Oral Performance Traditions of Four Continents,* ed. J. Jansen and H. Maier, 81–88. Hamburg: LIT Verlag.

Kaba, L. 2001. Almami Samori Touré within the West African imperial tradition. *Mande Studies* 3:15–34.

Sidikou, Aissata G. 2001. *Recreating Words, Reshaping Worlds: The Verbal Art of Women from Niger, Mali and Senegal.* Trenton: Africa World Press.

Sorofè. n.d. *No. 9: Siramori jansa (k. 2043).* Bamako: Editions Jamana.

Traoré, K. 2000. *Le jeu et le sérieux: Essai d'anthropologie littéraire sur la poésie épique des chasseurs du Mande (Afrique de l'Ouest).* Cologne: Rüdiger Koppe Verlag.

9 ⎯ ⟨⟩

Women's Tattooing Songs from Kajoor, Senegal

George Joseph

One of the most common vocal genres across the diverse cultures of the Sahel is the tattooing song, sung while a woman undergoes the painful experience of having her face, lips, or gums inscribed in various ways with a thorn or a needle. Wolof *woyu njam,* or tattooing songs, are meant to accompany the process of tattooing the mouth with bundles of thorns and a black dye made of burnt peanuts and clay. The result is a blackening not only of the lips but also surrounding areas, notably the chin. The gums are also dyed black in a way that sets off more strikingly the whiteness of the teeth.

One might assume that this form of body art, created in an intimate space, reflects exclusively feminine values. In fact, when asked, women do assert that the only purpose of tattooing is to heighten the beauty of an individual. But on closer examination, it appears that tattooing and the songs women sing to accompany the person undergoing the process are more deeply embedded in a wider range of social values that go far beyond the concern for beauty. What, then, are these values, how do the singers interpret them to listeners, and what is the wider significance of tattooing and the songs that mark what is becoming a tradition no longer practiced by many women? By analyzing here a corpus of songs that I have collected since 1973 in the area of what was once the Wolof kingdom of Kajoor, I will offer some preliminary answers to these questions.

Kajoor covers the area that extends roughly along the Senegalese coast between Dakar and Saint-Louis, and constitutes the westernmost region of the vast Mande culture. Kajoor has a recognizably Mande-type social structure based on three classes: those people who were once of captive origin, *ñeeño;* artisans such as goldsmiths, shoemakers, and *gewal* ("wordsmiths"); and finally *geer*, or aristocrats, a group that includes warrior nobility.[1] Griots or *gewal* inherit their charge and are attached by birth to a noble family, whose traditions they keep.[2]

Although women played an important role in the traditional society of Kajoor, they were and remain, nevertheless, clearly subordinate. For example, the ruler of Kajoor, the damel, had to descend from a male line of Falls and one of seven female lines, the most important of which was Guedj, but the damel was always a man.[3] Furthermore, there are women as well as men *gewal* and the lines between their repertories are blurred. Men *gewal* sometimes teach their wives and daughters what is normally intended for their sons.[4] The lyrics analyzed in this study are, however, limited entirely to the world of women. No male *gewal* would ever sing a tattooing song. In spite of this separation, however, tattooing songs reveal that even this most intimately female experience is charged with metaphors drawn from a masculine value system.

For this project, I recorded nine tattooing songs as well as interviews with the singers in spring 2002 with partial support from the National Endowment for the Humanities–funded Women's Songs from West Africa project and the help of A. Badara Sissokho of the Senegalese Ministry of Culture as well as Mamadou Guèye, a technical assistant at Institut Fondamental d'Afrique Noire. We recorded, translated, and transcribed both the songs and the follow-up interviews in which the singers answered questions about the meaning of the songs as well as of tattooing itself. The women we worked with came from distinguished *gewal* families responsible for important historical traditions in three communities of political significance in Kajoor: Batal, Ndatt, and Xandaŋ.

As a practice, this kind of tattooing seems largely though not entirely of the past. Some of the women we recorded knew songs but were not themselves tattooed. In one case a woman we spoke to was tattooed but could not sing songs. Only some of the women knew how to tattoo.

All of the women we interviewed said that the main purpose of *njam*, or tattooing, is beauty, but as is often the case, beauty here turns out to be much more than skin deep and connotes moral character and the medical values of good health.[5] For example, Marème Mbaye of Xandaŋ describes the significance of tattooing as a healthy kind of beauty. Her references to the beauty of tattooing glide inevitably toward moral connotations of courage, respectability, and good living, even though at times she and others say that tattooing is "only for beauty" (*rafetal dozz*). She told us, for example, that tattooing

> is only for beauty. It is for nothing else. It is only to make someone beautiful. If you are not tattooed, they say that you are not beautiful. Like the rice that one has just eaten that does not have enough tomato sauce.[6]

Elsewhere she also claims that tattooing is for the purpose of being beautiful in ways that seem to concentrate on the surface aspects of appearance:

> If your gums make for a good smile, you know that you are beautiful. Your teeth are clean. Your gums are black. But red gums and teeth are not beautiful. It is good to have big eyes.[7]

But in the following passage, we see that this visible beauty for Marème Mbaye connotes a moral value of "respectability" (*baax*):

> When you were not tattooed, our age group did not consider you to belong to respectable people [*duñu la boole ci ñu baax ña*]. They said of the woman that her only flaw was tomato. That is why everyone in our age group was tattooed.
>
> Now, they no longer get tattooed.

This kind of beauty also implies a simple kind of personal cleanliness as opposed to today's piling-on of skin-lightening creams.

> Now they seek to lighten the skin of their bodies. As for us, we did not know about body creams. We did not put creams on; we did not do anything, only tattooing, and washing our bodies vigorously.[8]

For Marème Mbaye, the beauty of tattooing also has health consequences. She explained that one of the purposes of tattooing was

> perhaps to purge bad blood. It also made teeth solid. Did you see that gums were tattooed to the point of cutting the nerves? Tattooing is the soap of the mouth. It makes teeth solid and blackens gums, and makes the vision clear, and makes the head lighter, especially when you have a headache.[9]

Adja Macoumba Mbaye of Ndatt suddenly shifts to the moral value of the beauty resulting from tattooing in the following passage after saying that it was done just for beauty:

> It was just to be beautiful that people wanted to do it; because when you had your gums tattooed black, everyone liked it when you laughed, everyone was happy. Her gums are black and her teeth white. If you do not get tattooed, your gums are red. When you laugh, people make fun of you and say, "She is afraid."[10]

This beauty, therefore, implies the courage it takes to undergo the painful process of thorn pricking. According to Adja Macoumba Mbaye,

> if you are courageous, you lie down and they tattoo you. You do not flee; you do not move; you do not shudder; you do nothing. You do not move.

Your mother sings for you and recites genealogies. They sing for you and give money for you.[11]

Fali Mbaye of Batal also emphasizes the moral courage necessary in the following description of the tattooing session:

To she who was brave, tattooing was something else. You have to be brave. You have to have the courage to be tattooed. If you inherit courage, when you are tattooed, it does not get to you. They beat the drums for you. They dance. They sing for you, they dance. They kill a sheep for you. They dance.[12]

Since any woman who undergoes *njam* without flinching or fleeing is marked for the rest of her life as belonging not only to the beautiful, but also to the respectable (*ñit ku baax*) and the brave (*ñit ku am fit, ñeme*), *njam* possesses many of the characteristics of a female initiation parallel to male circumcision—called *njong*—where resistance to pain literally separates the men from the boys. Parallelism, however, does not mean equivalence.

Women's songs for both *njam* and *njong* fall under the same musical category in that they use similar instruments, rhythms, tones, and combinations of solo and chorus (Penna 2000, 34), but the category also includes songs women sing (1) to inspire men going off to war (*xare*), (2) to encourage a bride about to leave her parents and move to her husband's home (*ceyt*), and (3) to honor royal princesses (*woyu lingeer*). None of these three represents the kind of once-in-a-lifetime experience implied by *njam* and *njong*. Songs for war and royal princesses may be sung on many occasions in a person's life. Although a *ceyt* is presumably a once-in-a-lifetime occasion, it can occur again if a widowed or divorced woman remarries. Thus, one can only say that this musical category is used for important occasions in a person's life, but one cannot say that the occasions all have same significance.

There is another similarity between *njam* and *njong* that is just a coincidence. The technical term *lakk,* which literally means "burnt," is used to refer to the end of both tattooing and circumcision. In the case of circumcision, one says, "The boys burnt [it] down yesterday" (*xale yi lakk nañu démb*), meaning that they have burnt down the circumcision house (Fal et al. 1990, 115). Fatou Mbaye of Ndatt uses the same term to refer to the end of tattooing. She says, "*Bés ba nga xam ne ca nga lake, say moroom yépp ñów toog.*" ("On the last day of tattooing, your friends all come to sit down.") But here, *lakk* or "burnt" probably refers to the blackness of the lips, chin, and gums, since no reference is ever made to burning down the place where tattooing took place.

The most significant difference between tattooing and circumcision is the fact that tattooing seems to be a matter of free choice. There is no set time of life when it is required; women decide to do it when they want and to some extent where and how they want. For example, Fali Mbaye of Batal explains that she got tattooed because she saw a beautiful woman in Pekesse:

> I saw her tattoos. At that moment in the evening we were coming into Pekesse. She was very beautiful. I had a friend, Gandiol-Gandiol, who said to me, "Fali Mbaye, with your lightness, get tattooed." I said, "Me, I'll get tattooed." Then we went to the village of a tattooer who is named Barka Mbaye. Early that morning, I got up and went with my housemate, who is called Meysa Dior Fall. We went and I said, "I will bow down first." I bowed down. They tattooed me until my lips swelled. When my mother was there, there was no problem. They tattooed me, they sang for me, my mother took out *pagnes* [two-meter lengths of cloth that serve as wrap-around skirts] to give away, people danced, everyone made a circle around me. The beauty of tattooing alone was the reason I did it.[13]

Fali Mbaye's friend followed suit in a way that recalls the conformity dictated by fashion rather than the requirements of initiation.

> Everyone said, "Today we are going to be tattooed." Everyone got tattooed. Some went to Laobés. Some went to *gewals*. Tattooing started spreading everywhere. Today children do not have the courage to be tattooed. They do not even like it. They are white people.[14]

Marème Mbaye of Xandaŋ had a different kind of ceremony. She was tattooed alone in her room with just her mother and her grandmother without any singing.

In contrast to the statements about tattooing, the song lyrics do not refer to beauty, but rather they evoke the courage a woman must draw on to resist the pain of the tattoo and stay still. As the tattooer pricks her thorns in a woman's lips and gums, the singer soothes the ears with the encouraging words of song. In other words, tattooing songs function as an anesthetic. On a purely material level, the songs, which are extremely repetitive, have a hypnotic quality. For example, Fali Mbaye of Batal and her chorus repeat, "*Nduuti ee / Nduuti ari oo, / Ndokk yàlla*," with only slight variations for ten stanzas. The meaning of *Nduuti* is not clear. It seems to be a Peulh word that the *gewal* themselves did not understand, a problem that appears also in longer texts such as epics. For the next thirty-four stanzas the singers repeat hypnotically:

Doo daw,	You do not flee,
Doo jaab,	You do not run away,
Doo rocci	You do not take flight,
Maamoo jambaar nga aa.	Mame, you are a heroine.

At the same time there is a symbolic structure, which gives meaning to the pain by situating it for the most part, but not entirely, in a patriarchal vocabulary of war. By symbolic structure, I have in mind the birthing song that Levi-Strauss analyzes in his *Anthropologie Structurale*. In his chapter entitled "Efficacité symbolique," Levi-Strauss describes the way in which a traditional Cuna healer (the Cuna are a people living in Panama) helps a woman through a difficult labor by narrating a story in which her pain and difficulties are given meaning (1958, 205–226). The Cuna narrative functions very much like the Freudian narrative, which releases a patient from his or her symptoms. This narrative, however, instead of coming from an individual past, is the property of the entire society. As Lévi-Strauss puts it, "La cure consisterait donc à rendre pensable une situation donnée d'abord en termes affectifs: et acceptables pour l'esprit, des douleurs que le corps se refuse à tolérer" (1958, 217).

In the case of tattooing it is not a question of a cure and there is not a complete narrative, but pain is made bearable nevertheless by a symbolic order suggested by bits of narrative elements and genealogies. Tattooing songs are lyric poems that elliptically allude to the fuller narratives of epics and history. It is impossible in this short study to do justice to the richness of these songs. I shall outline only a few aspects as illustrate a symbolic order.

The songs themselves imply a narrative. Some are sung at the beginning of the ceremony, some during the ceremony, and some afterwards. To mark the beginning of the ceremony, Adja Macoumba Mbaye sings a song, the first lines of which are as follows:

Jun-juŋ rëkk na,	The drum has sounded.
Garmi day waaj	The princess is getting ready.
Juŋ-juŋ rëkk na	The drum has sounded.
Nogay waaj naa.	Nogaye has gotten ready.

In the following song, the singer Yacine Ngom marks the beginning of a tattooing ceremony with an Islamized comparison of tattooing and the learning experience of a Qurʾānic school pupil.

A !Bisimilaay oo,	In the name of God the merciful
Dongo dal na baa,	The student began to read the first letter
Bsimilaay	In the name of God the Merciful.

Fali Mbaye's song "Nduuti oo, Nduuti ari oo, Ndokk Yàlla" is sung after the lips finish swelling.

The songs allude to two larger structures, war narratives and genealogies, to make pain bearable. I shall take as my example for the rest of this paper Fali Mbaye's "Nduuti oo," for Xadijatu Gote Mbaye.[15] Through the genealogies, one recalls Xadijatu Gote Mbaye's male and female relatives, but the courage that makes Xadijatu "worthy" of the family is described in terms that come from the male narratives of war. In other words, this anesthetic of pain is based on a patriarchal esthetics of courage. No mention is made of a specifically female courage such as that to be shown during childbirth. Marème Guèye told me that her mother used to say, "How can you expect to bear children if you cannot bear the pain of tattooing?" But no mention of childbearing is made in the songs I have recorded.

Fali Mbaye's refrain, "*Doo daw, Doo jaab, Doo rocci, Maamoo jambaar nga aa*" ("You do not flee, You do not run away, You do not take flight, Mame, you are a hero"), which begins in stanza 11, alludes to the *gewal*'s position on the front lines of battle to remind "Mame" that she has "inherited" the courage of the male *gewal* from which she is descended. Here is how Fali Mbaye explains it:

> "You do not flee, you do not run away," means someone who is courageous. When there was a battle, their grandparents, the *gewals,* were on the front lines. In war the *gewals* were on the front lines; the nobles came afterwards. So before a noble was killed a *gewal* was killed first. If you do not see a *gewal* fall, then a noble will not fall. The battle continues. That is the meaning of "You do not flee, you do not run away, you inherited courage." We are *gewals* but courageous. When they went to war, also our grandparents alone could go with their nobles to fight. They fought, and fought and fought. If a *gewal* did not fall with his horse, the noble did not fall. If a noble fell with his horse, the *gewal* says, "You will not leave without me. Do not leave me here." That is the meaning of "You do not flee, you do not run away, you do not take flight." *Rocci* is to run fast without stopping.[16]

The inherited courage that a woman is given the chance to show during tattooing is thus for the most part a patriarchal one. To call her *jambar,* which the *Dictionnaire wolof* defines as "homme brave, courageux," is to say that she has inherited male courage. Now one can say that *jambar* is used figuratively here, like using the male pronoun in English to refer to both male and female, but later on in the song, the full meaning becomes clear. In stanza 35 Fali Mbaye sings, "*Cëy sama sët bee góor la*" ("Hey my granddaughter is like a man.").

From this limited sample it is clear that the lyrics of the songs function as an anesthetic of pain to validate a woman's resistance in terms of male courage in times of war. Thus the esthetics of beauty that results from tattooing rests on a patriarchal system of value that extends its reach even into this intimately feminine practice. The songs quiet a woman's pain without voicing what is specific to her potential for bravery—that it may be seen, for example, while giving birth. Given the ubiquity of tattooing songs across the Sahel, the examples described here call for a wider study to see if masculine values are common to the many other diverse peoples of the region.

NOTES

1. For a discussion of griots and the caste system see Camara (1992, 75–99) and Diop (1981, 59–71). For the term *wordsmith,* see Hale (1998, 114).

2. For a discussion of the role of griots in Mande culture see Hale (1998).

3. For the role of the female lines (*garmi*) in the royal succession see Diouf (1990, 56).

4. For a discussion of the pedagogy of the *gewal* see Joseph (1998, 21–23).

5. For a discussion of this double function of fashion discourse to denote an object and connotatively open it to the world, see Barthes (1981, 277–278).

6. Xanaa rafetal doŋŋ, du baax du dara, Rafetal doŋŋ. Boo jamuwul Ñu ne rafetoo, mel ne ceebi bi ñu doon lekk léegi te kenn defu ci tamaate.

7. Bu sa siiñ neexee ree, nga xam ne rafet nga, sa bëñ set na, sam siiñ ñuul na. Waaye siiñ mu xonq, bëñ yu xonq, taar du fa am. Waaye bu bëñ weexee, siiñ ñuul, taar am. Nga am bët baax na.

8. Ñoo ngi wut lu ñu xollee seen yaram yi. Ñun xamuñu woon ag diw. Ñun duñu diwu, duñu def dara, jamu rekk, ragg suñu yaram yi.

9. Xanaa génne deret ji. Dana daral bëñ bi. Gis nga sama ciiñ mi dama ko jam ba siddit yi dagg. Njam mooy saabu gémmiñ. Mooy daral bëñ, di ñuulal siiñ, di leeral bët, di woyafal bopp, bopp buy metti.

10. Pur taar rekk moo daan tax ñu daan ko def. Ndax boo jamee sa siiñ ba mu ñuul, boo ree, ñépp kontaan ni: Siiñam ma dafa ñuul ay bëñam weex. Bu ko defee doo jamu nag sam siiñ xonq coy, foo ree, dañu lay reetaan ni kii dafa ragal.

11. Xanaa kiy jamu, nga ñeme, nga tëdd ñu di la jam. Doo daw, doo yëngu, doo raf, doo def dara. Dangay gore rekk. Sa yaay di la woy, di la tagg, Di la kañ, ñu di la mayeel xaalis.

12. Ku amu fit dëgg moom, njam li moom day nuru sax leneen. Dangay amu fit. Dangay ñeme njam. Boo donnee ñeme ak doo ëf bët, booy jamu doo ko yëg. Ñu di la tëggal, nit ñiy fecc. Ñu la woy nit ñiy fecc. Ñu reyal la xar nit ñiy fecc.

13. Ma séen njamam li. Booba Peekees, guddi la ñu ko daan duggu. Mu rafet lool. Ma am sama xaritu Ganjóol-Ganjóol ñu ni ma: Faali Mbaay sa xeesaay bi jamul waay. Ma ne man de dinaa jamu. Daldi dem dëkk jamkat buñu wax Mbarka Mbaay. Ma xëy sëpp samay tànk ànd ak sama moroom mi ci kër gi ku ñuy wax Maysa Joor Faal. Ñu ànd ma ne ko man sëgg naa. Man su ma jëkkula sëgg rekk man sama yaay dina ma tere. Ma daldi sëgg ñu di ma jam, di ma jam ba tuñ mi fuddu. Nga xam bu sama yaay ñówee duñu ko yeggale. Ñu dima jam dima woy, sama ndey di génne sér yi di maye, nit yi di fecc, ñépp yéew ma. Rafetaayu njam rekk moo taxoon ma def ko.

14. Ñépp ne tey lañuy jamu ñun. Ñépp di jamu nag. Ñii dem ci lawbe yi, ñii dem ci géwal yi. Njam yi ne gànñ nag. Tey nag juddu yi ñemewuñu njam. Bëgguñu ko sax. Ay tubaab lañu.

15. Recorded in Batal on 2 March 2002.

16. Doo daw, doo jaab li mu tekki, mooy donn ñeme. Bu ñu masaan di xare, seen maam ñoom géwal yii ñuy woy tey mooy jiitu, ca xare ba mooy jiitu, géer ña topp ca. Balaa géer ña daanu, géwal daa daanu ca kanamam. Boo gisul géwal bu daanu, géer ga du daanu. Ñuy xare rekk. Mooy doo daw, doo jaab, dafa donn ñeme, donn ab bër. Ndax géwal lañu waaye ñun dañoo ñeme. Ba ñuy xare it seen maam rekk mënoon àndak seen géer ñuy xare. Di xare rekk. Di xare rekk. Bu ab géwal daanuwul rekk ak ug fas rekk, géer gi du daanu. Bu géer gi daadoo ak ug fas nag, géwal bi dafa naan ko doo ma raw. Doo ma fi ba. Mooy doo daw, doo jaab, doo rocci maamoo. Rocci maamoo mooy dangay daw rekk.

WORKS CITED

Barthes, Roland. 1981. *Système de la Mode.* Paris: Seuil.

Camara, Sory. 1992. *Gens de la parole.* Paris: Karthala.

Diop, Abdoulaye-Bara. 1981. *La Société wolof: Tradition et changement: les systèmes d'inegalité et de domination.* Paris: Karthala.

Diouf, Mamadou. 1990. *Le Kajoor au xixe siècle: Pouvoir ceddo et conquête colonial.* Paris: Karthala.

Fal, Aram, Rosine Santos, and Jean Léonce Doneux. 1990. *Dictionnaire wolof-français, suivi d'un index français-wolof.* Paris: Karthala.

Hale, Thomas A. 1998. *Griots and Griottes: Masters of Words and Music.* Bloomington: Indiana University Press.

Joseph, George. 1998. La Pédagogie des griots. *Diagonales: Le Revue de la Francophonie linguistique, culturelle, éducative* 47 (August): 21–23.

Lévi-Strauss, Claude. 1958. *Anthropologie structurale.* Paris: Plon.

Penna, Luciana. 2000. Chants des femmes wolof du Senegal: le repertoire feminine des villages de Meke, Risso et Batal. Diplome d'Etudes Appliquées, Ecole des Hautes Etudes en Sciences Sociales.

10

Drummed Poems by Songhay-Zarma Women of Niger

Fatima Mounkaïla

INTRODUCTION

In the preface to his book *L'Essence du verbe* (1988), a collection of sayings by Songhay-Zarma women, the late Boubou Hama, one of the most respected and knowledgeable analysts of African traditions in Niger, observed that the knot that always hangs at the end of the ribbon or belt around a woman's cotton wrapper was both the place of gestation and the site of maturation for the well-turned words that they often recited. But in a society that places high value on restraint and the concept of shame for anything related to the expression of intimate thoughts, one finds that oral art—for example, sayings, mottos, songs, and stories—offers the only medium for people, and especially women, to openly compose and express feelings. These may include love, admiration, disdain, or exasperation toward people in their entourage—sons, daughters, families, clans, co-wives, and other adversaries who are part of their world. Even when they are not the original composers of the words that they speak or sing, women transmit their views as part of the education that they provide for their children. The texts convey in polished form the values that these women contribute at the privileged sites of female expression. There, women compose and declaim poems called *zamu* as well as drummed mottos or sayings which convey in short, concentrated form the ideals of their society.

These *zamu* poems, voiced and drummed, allow the women to praise and formulate portraits of individuals or groups through the medium of names that the subjects share with other, often more famous, people. Thus, these women poets draw on an unlimited repertory that they can use to link a son, a daughter, or a brother to the local leader, the winner of a sports competition, or someone else who incarnates the ideals of their society.

As a form of "inside" poetry expressed in private spaces limited to mothers, grandmothers, sisters, and friends, the poem conveys the shape of individual success in the domestic context. When it takes the form of "outside" poetry performed in public spaces, one hears women singing songs about political figures as well as champion farmers and athletes who incarnate individual perfection. That is how *zamu,* or poems about names declaimed by Songhay-Zarma women in their courtyards or as an accompaniment to their dances at "tam-tam" parties, contribute to the shaping of heroes representing the social ideal.

The corpus that will serve as evidence for the analysis here comes from three sources: *Les Zamu ou poèmes sur les noms* (Bisilliat and Laya 1972); recordings by the Nigerien Committee for the Women Writing Africa project (Sutherland-Addy and Diaw 2005); and a selection of dance texts from the collection recorded by Aïssa Ganda Mahamadou (2003) for her master's thesis. Together, the texts are remarkable not simply because of the spontaneous character of the performances but also because of the way the women choose their subjects and prepare listeners to adhere to ideals that are also conveyed by the much longer oral epics heard on the radio or at a variety of events—weddings, naming ceremonies, and installations of chiefs.

Not everyone can be an epic hero or heroine such as Mamar Kassai, the well-documented Songhay ruler known as Askia Mohammed, who governed from 1493 to 1528, Issa Korombe, the nineteenth-century warrior known as Wangunya, or mother of the science of war, or even Fatoumata Bi Dâni, the nineteenth-century Fulbe heroine who stood up to the bravest warriors of her time in the Macina region of present-day Mali. But the recitation of these poems about names in the courtyards of homes or in the drumming party space makes everyone dream that he or she can be one of these famous figures, and perhaps even surpass their deeds!

But the values transmitted in these poems are often seen as obsolete or at least no longer appropriate in the economic, social, and political circumstances of today. The behavior of these historic figures may seem totally irrational for those who see things in more "practical" terms when framed in the context of modern Nigerien life. How, then, can one explain the fact that the values conveyed in these texts live on today? How is it that at the same time that the epic, the primary vehicle for those values, appears to be dying out, *zamu* or drummed poems are flourishing and being heard in new spaces for new audiences? In order to attempt to answer these questions, I will first analyze the form and content of two series of poems which evoke, each in its own space, the values that continue to inspire people far more than is realized by individuals and groups. Then, in a second section, I will analyze the *mode d'action* of these *zamu* with the goal of understanding the role of a genre that is doubly marginalized, first as non-professional texts and second as verbal forms by women.

THE CORPUS

The samples for this study will be examined in two groups based on the space where they are performed and the social focus—the individual, or poetry from inside; or a group, poetry for outside. Rather than relegate the poems to an appendix, I have put them in each of the two sections as a group so that they can be read before the analysis. Translators and performers will be indicated where this information is available.

Zamu Poems about Names: Poetry of Inside or from under the Apatame

The kitchen and the *apatame de repos,* a shaded spot in the family compound, are privileged spaces for the performance of songs about names composed and recomposed by Songhay-Zarma women. These are very brief texts, sung or declaimed, that are rhymed. The line length is marked by the breath of the reciter, with assonance or rhymes marking the prosody. Except where noted, all transcriptions and translations are mine. There are ten sample *zamu* in this section.

1. Biba
Biba, wife of Moussa Bibata
Bibata do not force me to curse
She does not offer to share pieces of meat that can cause the heart to suffer

The singer explains that among the young women who, in their sharing of meat, give me the best pieces, there is Biba, the wife of Moussa, who gives me large pieces. On the other hand, there are those who give me only small pieces. When I glance at this food, I push the plate back with disdain, for there are offers that are made only to upset your heart. They prevent you from swearing that you have received nothing, while you have received so little!

2. Dâri
I dreamed last night
That Dâri de Tchiga was advising me
Dagni, mother of Oummou, warned me that
These hairdos that you know how to style on [women's] heads
Avoid doing them on the heads of spouses who are not well loved
For those done on the heads of women who are not well loved
Devalue mine.

I then replied
Two persons suit me:
The younger sister of Koungo, Safi the dark-skinned
Safi, whose scars on her cheeks make her look so good
She is among those who dine with princes
And Gatti the daughter of the teacher
Who wears a zeffa-style wrapper
She, too, can dine with princes.

Sung by Oumougna de Dantchandou
Transcribed and translated by Fatima Mounkaïla

3. Hamsatou
Hamsatou, the mother of Maygounia
Wife of the father of Dalaïzé
Accept my congratulations, Hamsatou
The wishes of adversaries will have no effect on you
For, given the innate good fortune that you have been able to grasp,
No adversary has yet the eyes
To be able to pursue and hide it.

Hamsatou, the mother of Hammadou,
Mother of Hassane and mother of Maygounia
The ridge beam of the neighborhood on the side of the hill
It is while waiting for a day like today
That a Zarma girl must eat her millet bran.
So that her gullet saves her from shame
It is my courage that shields her from shame
Blooming gourd stalk of the master of the Sudan
The white administrator cannot throw me into prison
As for the *cadi* [Islamic judge] who is a man of justice
His just rulings cannot cause me any wrong
The village exciser cannot get mad at me

Hamsatou from Tchôta
Who knows how to say gentle and pleasant words
Who offers princely words
She tells me: Dagni, the mother of Oummou
This activity of hair dresser that you do
Stop doing it for ill-loved wives
Because an ill-loved wife will devalue my coiffure
Stingy people should keep from
Thinking of coming to you, mother of Oummou

Narrated by Oumougna de Dantchandou
Transcribed and translated by Fatima Mounkaïla

4. Hassane
Hassane the twin, producer of white manioc
The twin is never happy with a little porridge
He demands an entire calabash full
So that the ladle floats freely in it.

Hassane the twin, producer of white manioc
Bearer of a saber, a spear, and a shield
Came to the village
Followed in his entourage *malikata* and *kambari* [weapons]
The girl, seeing him, cried out that he had come for her.
Seeing him, the mother says that he has come for her!
With his manner of dragging his *malikata* and *kambari*.

Hassane the twin
Is inheritor of the elephant [large family]
Hassane is not satisfied with a little porridge
He demands that the calabash be full
Hassane Nouna the twin, a model of a farmer
Hassane Nouna does not have to beg a mother
Whether she likes it or not
He will marry her daughter
Hassane does take the spouse for a stroll around the village
Hassane does not pick up sand to throw on the spouse
He does not say haya! Now there's just the two of us, woman
Hassane Nouna is not an ant of a husband
The ant husband inflicts suffering
Hassane Nouna is not a couscous pot husband
Who takes into the street the image of his wife
Hassane doesn't say to her haya, now there is just the two of us, woman
What you are looking for, I'm ready too.
The willing son, owner of a handsome stallion
The son who does not forget his mother when
He goes to Gourounsi country
It is a large home with a large porch
That he builds for her.
He brings back caftans and caftans,
and *barâze* [blue indigo] wrappers
This is what this obliging son does for his mother

Child of a hyena among Zarma children
When you focus your eyes on a man, he collapses
When a man takes aim at you, he produces dust.
Hassane the young producer of white manioc
He who has the siiriya tree, he is bent down

The prestigious chief of the town of Say
The discussion starts, and quarrels start
The mother says, He came for me
The daughter says, He came for me
Prestigious chief of Say
They both quarrel over my child.

(Bisilliat and Laya 1972, 122)

5. Hawwa
Tchaguio said move ahead!
The Songhoy daughter said move ahead!
The donkey refused to raise his hoof
Hawwa got off and sat down on the ground.

(Bisilliat and Laya 1972, 67)

6. Kadiijatu
Kadiijatu Kadi Gôro
Kadi wife of the judge
Wife of judge Souley
Kadi is neither tall nor small
Kadi does not look like the little hyena
She is not a woman of the size of a camel
She is not too slender
She is also not too tall

Kadiijatu Kadi Gôro
The one who has five bundles of millet for supper
The one who has ten bundles of millet for supper
The one who does not have enough millet for supper
Go implore Gôro
So that Gôro will add some to what she has

(Bisilliat and Laya 1972, 72–73)

7. Mariyama
Gambina Gambinaare mother of Yansambou
The face adorned with decorations from Dandi, Gambina,

Gambina with sixty husbands
And seventy suitors
Some on the bed
Some on the ground

Gambinaare mother of Yansambou
Mother of fonio [small millet]
Mother of fonio, Gambi
Mother of Bella Keyna, Gambi
Gambinaare mother of Yansambou
Look over the fence and throw something at the stranger
Misfortune, the stranger will cause harm
It is Gambina who throws something on the stranger
Misfortune, the stranger will cause harm

Gambu Garbu Gambina
Gambina the beautiful

Sister of Seydou, Gambina
Sister of Iliyasu, Gambina
Sister of Dogoolu, Gambina
Sister of Jerizé, Gambina

You who keep moving objects from place to place
In order to say Give me my little calabash
Your throat is black like vitex berries
Your belly is like a well-stocked pond

Gambinaare Gambina
Gambi said that she mocks the malicious
Because a malicious person is no more than an earthworm
That one must crush with the foot.

(Bisilliat and Laya 1972, 74–77)

8. Salaamatou
Salaamatou Ummu Daado, mother of Dawsana
May the gates of paradise open for Oummou
Salaamatou is the foam around the rock
It is there that she finds that dawn appears
Koogi with her husband, the chief of Taabuutou,
Said people of Saaga Fondo, bearers of misfortune
You who claim that the older sister of Ayya is Koogi

Koogi does not dry up because of a pretty girl
Koogi welcomes her guest
Even if she does not know him
She prepares porridge for him
Even if she has not farmed the smallest plot of land
She will place porridge in front of him
Koogi does not dry up because of a pretty girl

The elder sister of Ayya said
That even princes who wear print fabric
And whose red sandals spend the morning under the bed
Princes whose teeth are stained by kola nuts
Even those who cannot prevent themselves from spending the evening in
    town
Even less the unfortunate one who borrows his caftan and his pants
And whose horse that he mounts is borrowed.

Salaamatu Ummu Daado
Saley beautiful like melted butter

Salaamatou whose curdled milk gives much butter
Salaamatou, take it and put it into your mouth
May your cheeks be filled
Salaamatou, churn so that there will be much and that each one may have
    some

(Bisilliat and Laya 1972, 82–85)

9. Zainabou
Zainabou is fire
Fire cannot be held in the hand!
Zainabou is hot pepper;
And hot pepper cannot be held, pinched between the teeth!
You are the brew of *lolo*
Your equal cannot dare to fall on you.
She crouches down to aim at your ankles
For the pepper corns cannot be chewed
Zongo, native of Tilli, has made a big gamble
She made a big gamble and obtained gold
She obtained the best silver
Having carried off the heart of the canton of Famaye
That is all fine, my daughter Zainabou

That you have swum in prosperity and offered me some of it
You are still a brew of *lôlo,* Zainabou!

Text narrated by Oumougna de Dantchando
Transcribed and translated by Fatima Mounkaïla

10. Wonkoy Zibbo
When the sun sets and dark falls
It is the hour for Galadima to make his rounds
Whoever sees him stop before his home
While he prepares to do an evil deed
Must implore Birgui and seek his pardon
Before the father of Sâdi is informed of it
If the father of Sâdi discovers it, the offender will be soaked
Without a drop of rain falling from the clouds

Father of Sâdi, master of a pinto horse
Whose sharp eyes grab your throat
All the more so when he is holding a whip
Father of Sâdi, master of a pinto horse
Your ancestor bests the other ancestors
Your father himself has recast the fathers
It is now your term to flatten the sons!
May the audience implore God to pardon me
For having called the canton chief by his given name

Narrated by Oumougna de Dantchandou
Transcribed and translated by Fatima Mounkaïla

Drummed Poems: Poetry for the Outside and about the Social Ideal

Texts from the dance arena appear in the form of dialogues between the dancers or between the dancers and the orchestra, especially at the dance parties. There, the singer celebrates the subject's beauty, birth, and successes as well as the social values conveyed to the entire audience as the result of the repetition of poems on names. Before the recent development of modern means of communication, the dance arena was the best place to build a reputation, offering the base for a public relations campaign in the best and worst senses of the expression. Good citizenship and identification with the community were taught here in what amounts in some ways to a sociology class. Here, one hears about alliances, antagonisms, and conflicts among people in the society. Nobody is upset over the truths that emerge during this spectacle because each person enjoys the opportunity to respond as long as he or she can advance appropriate arguments to support a particular view. Here the audience listens to oratorical combat that often involves the settling of scores—all to the rhythm of the drum and the dance step. The participants advertise themselves or others as well as cite contracts, pacts, and differences between people and groups. While in the preceding series the songs were organized in alphabetical order, this second series follows a thematic structure which goes from portraits of individuals to their relations with other members of society and their place in it.

11. Mother of horses
She speaks, a smile on her lips, the mother of the horses
The elephant, great silo, in the heart of the forest
In the absence of the mother of the horses on the trail
The fillies cannot celebrate all by themselves

Without question, beauty exists
Daughter of Bibata, Hâwa
Sister of Yayé, Hâwa
Sister of Karimou, Hâwa
It is in Dosso that Hâwa lives
Hâwa who places horse upon horse

Call forth, for me, the one who speaks while smiling
Call forth, for me, the spouse of Daouda
Biba, the producer of caftans
Biba, the producer of wrappers
It is in Dosso that Biba lives

In Darey, I encountered a mother who raises horses
It is Fati, who speaks with a smile on her lips
Call forth for me the girl from Bakasso
For Fati is, she also, a mother who raises horses

I call loudly the mother who raises horses
At Koygourou, I encountered a mother who raises horses
I name the girl the chief of the village.

Call the mothers horse raisers
I'm the one who speaks, a smile on my lips
Mother producer that I am, mother of horses, I am
Without wheat bran which I've eaten much of
Wheat bran and water that I've drunk in quantity
Without cream of millet that I've used much of
One could not have cursed me, mother who raises horses.

Transcribed by Aïssa Ganda Mahamadou
Translated Diouldé Laya and Fatima Mounkaïla

12. The Champion
The one who enters to great fanfare does she have an equal?
Watch out, watch out, pay attention to yourself
One must fear the woman who has the title of emir
The male cobra is not the equal of so and so
The striking viper is not the equal of so and so
Watch out, fear the female emir

One must fear the woman who has the title of emir
The stone pedestal is not the equal of so and so
Even if she is mistaken, nobody will mention the mistake
For lightning will strike anyone who dares to do it
The buffalo-toad is not the equal of so and so
When one sees her coming, one steps out of the way
If not, the woman emir will crush you

Transcribed by Aïssa Ganda Mahamadou
Translated by Aïssa Ganda Mahamadou and Fatima Mounkaïla

13. The Short One
The short one has entered the dance arena
Thick and round like the shadow of the detarium tree.
The short one endowed with a wide pedestal
A large bust and a broad base

The tree trunk that has stayed in the water
Is a tree trunk that cannot get up
That a single person cannot raise
Anyone who tries
Will tear apart his sternum

Breadfruit and ficus don't grow just anywhere
They grow in the houses that chance has chosen
They grow in the courtyards of royal houses.

Transcribed by Aïssa Ganda Mahamadou
Translation by Diouldé Laya and Fatima Mounkaïla

14. The Arched One
The drum of the arched one has sounded
It is the graceful girl who has arched her body
From the back to the front

The arched one says that the Bella woman is not a Tuareg woman
Except Tassala, the Bella girl
She arches from the back to the front

The drum for the arched one sounds
The arched one who thrusts out
She thrusts out from the back
She thrusts out from the front

The Bella is not a Tuareg
Millet contains oil
But the silly woman will not discover it.
Leaving this year to encounter the next
I'm not speaking of the end of the current harvest
May it please Dieu that I be arched
The way the millet stalk bends
In that way, the arched one will arch

15. Crowned with Love
Crowned with love, and with loved crowned
Is the young woman stuffed with heavy soup
Happy is the young woman filled with millet with milk
Is happy
Whoever is loved by her father-in-law
Is happy.
Whoever is loved by the siblings
Is happy.
Is happy the one who with the goodness of her parents
Sees added the kindness of her husband
Crowned with love, with love crowned
My daughter is happy

Transcribed by Aïssa Ganda Mahamadou
Translated by Diouldé Laya and Fatima Mounkaïla

16. Sondo
The mothers are calm
The beautiful woman has spared them of gossip
She spared them of the nasty gossip from the market
She spared them of the tattle around the well
Karma can sleep, Boubon can sleep
And Tondibia sleeps in peace
What village never sleeps.

Congratulations, the beautiful one has triumphed
Nyâlé is beautiful and her disposition is beautiful
Carry her on the back
May she be lulled on the back
The vagabond girl cannot have this honor
The light-footed girl cannot have this honor
No kind of bicycle
Has carried my daughter
No kind of motorbike
Has taken her
It is the wrapper of Zaria or of Zirikilema
That will serve to carry Nyâlé the beautiful on the back
Carry her on the back
Lull her on the back
Whoever carries on the back will not have carried shame
Whoever married her has not fallen into a hole
That will serve to lull Nyâlé the beautiful on the back

Transcription and translation by Aïssa Ganda Mahamadou

17. Do as you like
I who do as I like
This tune doesn't resonate for unloved women
Ah! say together that one must be sorry for the unloved woman
Also for the miserly young woman
An unloved woman

Me, I do as I like
This tune does not resonate for unloved women
The same is true for the curt young woman
An unloved woman
The young woman with misty eyes
An unloved woman

Ah! say together that one must be sorry for the unloved woman!

Transcribed by Aïssa Ganda Mahamadou
Translated by Aïssa Ganda Mahamadou and Fatima Mounkaïla

18. Shame to Detractors
The detractors are mistaken
Whoever has the skill, will know how to do it
The detractors are mistaken

Whoever has good [to say] is rich
Slander can do nothing against the taste of honey
Slander cannot take away the whiteness of milk
The detractors are mistaken
The children of those who possess are rich
The detractors are mistaken
Whoever has the skill will know how to use it
The razor makes a mistake
The whiskers regrow
The ax is in its hiding place
The combretum plant will regrow
The chicken is wrong to boast
The threshing ground cannot be without grain
But when the little wading bird hatches
The grasshopper stops parading around
Shame to detractors
Shame on detractors!
They are only vermin
Honte aux détracteurs!
Ils ne sont que de la vermine
That must be crushed under the foot.

Transcription by Aïssa Ganda Mahamadou
Translation by Aïssa Ganda Mahamadou, Diouldé Laya, and Fatima Mounkaïla

19.
The water is cold
I would like to take a bath
But the water is too cold
I would like to take a bath
But people are here
Whoever is skinny does not take a bath
As long as there are people around
Whoever has a prominent backbone will not take a bath
As long as there are people around
Whoever has a coccyx with a tail will not take a bath
As long as people are around

Text spoken by Aligna de Boye Bangou
Transcribed and translated by Fatima Mounkaïla

20. Flour of Bitterness
Shard of pottery from the former site of the village
Natural branches of the doum palm
Whoever is sick ends up cured
Unless he dies from it.
Flour of khaya [medicinal tree bark] I am the flour of bitterness
That the young girl does not dare sip
Flour of khaya, flour of bitterness
I am the wild grass that grows near the houses
That the young girl does not dare to taste.

Transcribed by Aïssa Ganda Mahamadou
Translated by Fatima Mounkaïla

21. The Song of the Singleton
The chorus:
May God allow that one may outclass certain peers
And permit one to outclass them really well!

The group of brothers:
See the group of singletons arrive
They don't arrive in a military truck
Like those who come as aggressors
They arrive in the truck for good works
They arrive via the truck that carries good things
By an airplane with a white nose
With a hundred cars and one hundred cargo trucks
All of them loaded with print cloth with white piping

The chorus:
May God enable one to outclass certain peers
And permit one to outclass them really well

The group of half-brothers:
Blood brother, my brother with the golden head!
May a blood brother fall into a well
And that a singleton fall in too.
We'll see which one of the two comes out
It is the blood brother who will escape from it
While the singleton remains in the well
For if a singleton falls into a well
Who will cry about him, who will lament about him
Who will go look for rope

To haul the unfortunate one out of the well.
Who will run around the well
Crying about the death of the child of his father
The only remaining witness at the edge of the well
Will be the little gourd, with the rope around its neck

The chorus:
May God enable one to outclass some peers
And permit one to outclass them really well

The group of brothers:
The blood brothers are only bark of the pilostigma [medicinal tree]
That peel off the trunk in parallel strips
Unworried that they are of reciprocal well-being
That one doesn't discover parents except in cases of conflict
Because we brandish our axes against the others
Because we each brandish our machetes against the others
While their idiot of a father remains seated.

The chorus:
May God enable one to outclass certain equals
And permit one to outclass them really well!

The group of half-brothers:
If we brandish our axes at others
If we brandish our machetes at others
It is preferable, in the absence of a half-brother
The absence of a half-brother is a lack to fill
If my half-brother goes down to Gulf of Guinea
He brings me back cloth from the coast of Guinea
I receive shoes from the gulf
That the children of witches cannot have
Daughters of women with the head tied with little knotted strings
Women keeping all kinds of powders in little pouches
Women who wear necklaces of amulets

The chorus:
May God enable one to outclass certain equals
And permit one to outclass them really well!

The group of brothers:
When our blood brothers go to the coast of the Gulf of Guinea
And if the singleton goes there too

The blood brother earns only a few francs
While the singleton earns millions
It is this one that the blood brother will steal
In order to transform it into wrappers for his sisters

The chorus:
May God enable one to outclass certain equals
And permit one to outclass them really well!

The group of half-brothers:
On the occasion of the marriage of our half-brother
The siblings arrive in comfortable cars
That they do not drive on bush roads
The half-brothers swim in happiness
On the occasion of their beautiful and grand wedding
Where the singleton does not dare step

The chorus:
May God enable one to surpass certain peers
And outclass them really well!

The group of brothers:
The assembled group of half-brothers
Is never worried about the happiness of the other brothers
Whose parentage doesn't come into play except in conflicts
In which they battle each other as wild dogs
One of them grabbing the axe of his father
One of them grabbing the machete of his father
To go after the co-wife of his mother
To kill the co-wife of his mother
While their male donkey watches them

The chorus:
May God enable one to outclass certain equals
And permit one to outclass them really well!

The group of half-brothers:
If some of us brandish our axes
If some of us brandish our machetes
It is preferable to the solitary state
Of the singleton, alone and solitary
Like earrings at 25 francs [5 cents]
Singleton, with the head of frog

With a head of a dog, a head of a scorpion
Wearing around the neck a black amulet

May God enable one to outclass certain equals
And permit one to outclass them really well!

The group of half-brothers:
My mother doesn't have to share her 25-franc salt
Nor does she have to share the hot pepper purchased for 25 francs
She doesn't have to share some *soumbala*
That she has to share spice from the market
My father is neither dead nor gone on a trip
He can remarry when it pleases him.

May God enable one to outclass certain equals
And permit one to outclass them really well!

The group of half-brothers:
His search for a spouse has lasted too long
That your father dies during his endless quest
That my mother doesn't have to share her 25-franc salt
That she have to share the hot pepper bought home
That she have to share some *soumbala*
That she have to share her supply of spice
Is preferable to the situation of a singleton
My mother does not kneel at the feet of the marabouts
My mother does not go to the dens of the seers

May God enable one to outclass certain equals
And permit one to outclass them really well!

The group of brothers:
It is always better to be alone than always in conflicts
The half-brothers have been the laughter of the village
Ever since Jattou wore their batteries out,
By throwing his mother-in-law with judo moves
At my arrival at his house, Dodo was in tears
Crying that nothing was right in the village
Don't pretend that the village is troubled
Rather, say that nothing is right in your own compound
Dodo, I've warned you for a long time
That polygamy is not a way of life
And if it hadn't been for the arrival of Kaydiya the elder

And of Hamsa who came running down the hill
Kaydiya the younger would have been killed
She would have been drawn and quartered

Text narrated by a group of young girls from the village of Nazey
Transcription by Boubé Saley Bali
Translated by Diouldé Laya and Fatima Mounkaïla

22. In the style of the weavers
Weaver, daughter of weavers
Of the weaver who protects people from shame
Of the weaver who protects people from many kinds of shame
Without us people would reveal their shameful parts
Without us people could not do their prayers
Let us give thanks to the sorghum stalk
That supplies the weavers with its suppleness
Authorizing him to prevail

23. The four battles of Dosso
The patrimony is the heritage
It is there in the refrain of Dosso
The power is the heritage
There were only two trees left, the sediya and the ficus
The Muslim cleric and his prayer skin
On that Thursday battle of Dosso
Where the sabers were everywhere, unsheathed
Without stopping they climbed over the ramparts
And the Zermakoye, who had not moved

Courage is heritage
Strength is distributed depending on the houses
The prince and the subject do not war
Because such a conflict destroys the reputation of the prince
Grandson of Kossom and Sâdi
Great grandson of Lawzo
Awta, the father of el-Hadj
Awta, the father of Kimba
Awta, the father of Marâfa
Awta, the father of Seyni the elder
Awta, the father of Seyni the younger
Handsome horses, one finds them at Dosso
Beautiful women, one finds them at Dosso

The full gourd makes no noise
For the power rules at Dosso

Transcription by Aïssa Ganda Mahamadou
Translation by Aïssa Ganda Mahamadou and Fatima Mounkaïla

24. The harvester of heads
Put the heads in a pile, Mayaki
We are under your protection during the battles
Don't cut me down, don't kill me Mayaki
I am your servant, Mayaki
Who takes your water to drink
In the city of Hamdallahi, there is a Mayaki
In the city of Damana, there is a Mayaki
In the city of Loga, here is a Mayaki
At Dosso also, there is a Mayaki
Don't cut me down, don't kill me Mayaki
What are your orders, Mayaki
Master of red and black horses.

Transcription and translation by Aïssa Ganda Mahamadou

ANALYSIS OF THE *ZAMU*

Songhay-Zarma literature, and especially epics about nineteenth-century leaders, portray two kinds of conflicts: first, between religious chiefs from different regional movements; second, between traditional chiefs who defend the powers that they feel are disappearing to the benefit of the first group. The opposition to the advance of Islamic values that are sometimes incompletely integrated is reflected in the *zamu,* which portray, in the words of Jean Rouch, this network of basic structures that the events and the places have linked, and whose traces, even the oldest, are still deep and respected (1989, 20).

For example, audiences admire and respect the heroes portrayed in the Zarma version of the politico-religious conflict between Boubé Ardo Galo and El Hadj Umaru Futiyu/El Hadj Omar narrated by the griot Djâdo Sékou (Bornand 1995) as well as the *Geste de Zabarkane* told in the form of a creation and migration myth (Mounkaïla 1989). These epics clearly reveal the opposition between Islamic and pre-Islamic values.

In the *Epic of Boubé Ardo Galo,* based on the life of the nineteenth-century figure El Hadj Omar, who dies in the narrative, the sympathy of the narrator for the loser of the conflict is evident. He is a symbol of the traditional system of beliefs that is no longer in style, but he remains constantly present in the epic, which belongs to the cycle of the path, epics devoted to heroes of jihads (Kesteloot and Dieng 1997, 360).

Boubé Ardo Galo, the hero of this epic, sees himself as one who will say his Islamic prayers, a communal act and therefore good, but cannot accept the prostration that is required. Muslim Zarma listeners to a radio broadcast of the epic narrated by Djâdo Sékou and Karimou Sâga sense the discomfort that the character feels:

> However, the fact of coming
> To clasp hands over both ears and of genuflecting
> To the point that the air in the anus
> To come out of the mouth
> He cannot see
> Anything more shameful for a noble.

On the other hand, the *Geste de Zabarkâne* reveals a rather complex relationship to Islam for the Zarma. Prior to the adoption of Islam, they were forced to migrate to the left bank of the Niger as the result of differences with peoples farther to the west. The Zarma, Islamized rather late, accept into their system of beliefs Mecca and the saints of Islam because of the omnipresence of the religion. But this outward respect is contested by many elements in the narrative, beginning with the Arabic character Zabarkâne, a little-known companion of the Prophet. But strangely enough, the myth foregrounds him even though he is Arab only in name. If the narrative affirms that the hero knew and frequented the first Muslim community in history, it adds that he converted to the religion on his own terms, since it is to his horse that he announces his allegiance to the Prophet.

> He asked
> That he be presented to the Messenger of God
> To whom one made one's submission
> He is the one who is seated there, he was informed
> Zabarkâne halted his horse and said
> That he, too, would submit himself to the Prophet

Finally, the *zamu* Alarba, marked by Islam, conveys in two verses the same type of refusal to submit entirely, without conditions.

> Yes, Alarba!
> The stick that does not pronounce invocations
> That does not say invocations, unless standing on one foot. (Bisilliat and
> Laya 1972, 51)

Alarba chooses the provocative words and gestures used by Boubé Ardo Galo, the epic hero who resists, who becomes the enemy to kill. But the poems about names convey other historic and social indicators. They present themselves as vestiges of the era of noble warriors.

Vestiges of the Era of Noble Warriors

One finds in the *zamu* references to precolonial historical narratives. These *zamu* call forth numerous figures from the second half of the nineteenth century, a time that saw the emergence of the *wangari*—warrior chiefs seeking to overthrow chieftaincies established earlier that had become weakened by internal dissension, various jihads, and constant raids (Gado 1980). If it is true that the original *zamu* of these noble warriors were not specifically composed by women, these singers were inspired by the earlier versions. Rather than cite the original name of the hero, they adopt instead the name earned as the result of war. Instead of naming a son Issa, they choose Korombeyzé [the Son of Korombé], whose *zamu* is:

> The hot soup of *potasse*
> The son of Korombé, Modi said he would not see the day!
> I did not say that he would not see the day, he said,
> But as soon as he sees the day, the *nasse* will spend the day on his head
> The husband will not know where to find his wife
> The wife will not know where to find her husband (Gado 1976, devise III)

Women participate in drumming sessions when they think that they can claim the most slender family tie with one of these predators of the nineteenth century who caused such political disorder. Part of the problem is, as Gado notes, that if the colonial armies were able to overcome the local peoples because of superior firepower, their mission was facilitated by the weaknesses of the traditional rulers. Today, however, the women ignore this inconvenient truth about the past. They demand to dance all the warrior hymns that include the repertory of drummed mottos from the Songhay-Zarma region of Niger. These hymns include "Mayaki, harvester of heads," "The Lance Throwing Sons of Toranthé," "The Gôlés descendants of death," and "The four battles that established power in Dosso."

The new powers that emerged from the colonial occupation and the independence that followed it have taken over to a large extent in the dance arenas. Moreover, the holders of power do not hesitate to force or distort the historical facts in order to construct genealogies linking them to the figures of the precolonial era, who, in the process, gain even more prestige. It is as if the valorization and legitimizing of new powers resulting from voting today depend to a large extent on the revalorizing and relegitimating of heroes of the past.

The superior social status legitimized by the past or the present constitutes, in effect, the ideal that calls forth all the names that are sung, and the poems dedicated to them (under the *apatame* of repose that is in the dance area of the drum session where one celebrates first political power).

Political Power

Masculine and feminine figures in these songs are presented on all sides with power. Aysata, Amsatou, and Domme, feminine figures, are each one:

> Mother and wife of a chief
> Who gave birth to a chief
> And whom a chief engendered (Bisilliat and Laya 1972, 55)

They are mothers, wives, or daughters of chiefs whose legitimacy was acquired somewhere on the winding path of history—ancient or modern. Whatever the case, surrounded and protected by powers as they are, nothing nasty can happen to such characters, who inspire fear and respect. A Nigerien woman offered an example in which she praised herself.

> Daughter of a colonel
> Wife of a colonel
> Sister of a colonel
> For whom the gun opens and closes the market

This claim that the author makes with pride shows clearly that the gun has become, at some point in the minds of the population, a more common image.

On their side, masculine characters are presented by bards as having political, economic, and financial power. These figures take on the virtues of princes of yesteryear. But these traits must come not only from heredity but also from deeds. They must be rooted in the past, while, at the same time, emerging from the world today. For if the innate attributes of birth and strength confer power, the man must also be portrayed by bards, professional and non-professional, as having bravery, endurance, wealth, generosity, discretion, and self-control. The hero acts and the person praising him describes his virtues.

> When the gourd is full, it does not tip
> The gourd that is half full, its contents stir
> The child of Louré, Dommo
> Dommo, the wife of Idda
> Mother of the chief, wife of the chief
> Who has given birth to a chief, and which a chief has fathered.
> Power does not have to be proclaimed
> Stroll around with elegance and dignity

A clay pot sitting on the ground
Net enclosing a loaded basket (Bisilliat and Laya 1972, 95)

In the next poem, the narrator reminds listeners that the man with merit has no need to praise himself. The narrator declares that the subject's merit depends on divine election that nothing can upset. The challengers, who are the patrilineal brothers, the gossipers, and other adversaries of all kinds, waste their time in vain opposition to such a great man.

The detractors are mistaken
Whoever has the art will know how to do it
The detractors are mistaken
Whoever has the attributes is rich.
Gossip can do nothing against the taste of honey
Gossip cannot take the white out of milk

The next text accompanies dance steps. The lyrics offer support to the legitimate power of a man that is nourished solely by his reputation. Fame is more often more powerful than the original act. For example, many epic heroes terrorized their enemies simply by mentioning their own exploits, as in this passage from the epic of Boubé Ardo Galo.

This griot who was going forth to face his enemies to tell them of his exploits
Boubé Ardo Galo treats the enemy in this fashion
He does this
He does that
He does like this
Thus, the enemies become afraid
The lucky ones, especially the most aware of them
Become afraid and flee in order to survive (Bornand 1995, 31)

And may the recalcitrants take heed! is the subtext of this next text, composed specially by a women for her relative, the ruler of his state.

When the sun sets, and the shadows arrive
The hour when Galadima makes his rounds
Whoever sees him halt in front of his place
While he is doing something wrong
Must implore Birgui and ask for his pardon
Before the father of Sâdi hears about it
For if the father of Sâdi happens to hear about it
The wrongdoer will be soaked
Without a drop of water
Falling from the clouds (see text 10 above, "Wonkoy Zibbo")

Economic Power

But one must remind listeners that power is a fire that one must constantly feed. One who wants to keep it going must not be afraid to allow it to consume his own possessions. That is why wealth and power are required in order to maintain one's social standing through the redistribution of wealth. This was in fact the regulating principle imposed on all those who held political power. They had to agree to be both a bank and a dump. In other words, those who agree to give and receive cannot be upset by ingratitude and even insults from the beneficiaries. One expects that the prince adhere to his own scruples and that he know how to receive in order to redistribute to others.

A chief who is worthy of holding traditional African power cannot, in effect, die rich. What he leaves to his descendants and to his successor is only an official residence, a bed, and the many good works related to his position. Referring to the precolonial era, before the colonial administration chose Zarma chiefs for artificially created cantons and provinces, Zarma bard Tombokoye chides hoarders who think only of accumulating their own fortunes. Poems on names remind listeners of the need to distribute wealth in order to maintain the equilibrium of society. They also refer to more recent generations of bourgeois compradors who attempt to legitimize their own status.

> Kadijatu Kadi Gôro
> Who has five ears of millet for dinner
> Who has ten ears of millet for dinner
> The woman who does not have enough millet for dinner
> May she implore Gôro
> Until Gôro adds to what she has (see text 6 above, "Kadijatu")

The essence of economic success is therefore not to be sitting on a fortune, but to be the one through whose hands the fortune passes. The rich man must be able to offer millet, animals, beautiful clothes, and, above all, the cash that today allows access to everything mentioned above. In spite of good sense and the contemporary situation of want in the country, socio-religious ceremonies in Niger today are marked by gestures of great generosity from people moved by these songs, even though the values articulated in the lyrics may be old and out of date.

> Garaw ga no
> Samba ga no

These two lines mean

> Borrow to give
> And take in order to give

These verses are an echo of the mottos of the Maiga, originally Songhay princes from the dynasty of the Sonni, before Askia Mohammed came to power in 1493. The griots remind the subjects of their duty to give with generosity what belongs to them and even to assume the right to give what belongs to others if necessary to satisfy the obligation to redistribute wealth. Goods, in this context, offer the guarantee of their reproduction by a people that, as in most Sahelien societies, requires that the more one gives, the more one receives from providence, a providence that is always sensitive to the songs of thanks by those who benefit from these acts of generosity. In any case, more than by their contents, it is by their form that the *zamu* impact those who are their subjects, as will be seen in the analysis that follows.

FORM OF *ZAMU* AND DRUMMED SAYINGS

For the listeners, *zamu* on names and drummed sayings are permeated with the political, economic, and social history of the society. But the similarities between the two genres are not limited to analogies based on content. Another reason for linking them is that they are both sung or chanted in performances that lend themselves to the poetic form. The rhythm punctuated by assonance and rhymes that one finds in each genre is heard by foreign listeners as poetic. Here is how Jeanne Bisilliat describes her discovery of the genre:

> By chance—something that plays a major role in ethnographic field work—I was seated next to a woman who was reciting words rhythmically while her ten-year-old son was returning to the family compound with a load of deadwood on his head. The mother praised his name, she told me, to thank him for his work. (Bisilliat and Laya 1972, 7)

Jean Derive says the same thing when referring to how different audiences, Japanese, Greek, or African, hear the rhythm of the verses in epics (Derive 2002, 102). One finds numerous analogues between the composition and style of the two genres, epic and *zamu*—the first long, the second short.

Like many epics in West Africa, the *zamu* often bear the name of the figure who is being celebrated. Even when the reference is to clans, these are given with a generic name which serves to call forth individual members of the group. Character and lyrics are mixed when it is a question of domestic texts, spoken in the courtyards of a home. It is the same for drummed sayings, poetry outside the home, which includes both the ancestor and the clan.

For example, the motto of "The Si" celebrates those descended from the Sonni dynasty of the Songhay empire; "Maiga" is sung for those who are connected to that of the Askias; and "Torance-izo" is related to the son of a man from Tekrour. The reference to Tekrour, located in the area of Senegal, Mauritania, and Mali, is important to the history of Niger because it is the home of griots who fled the disintegrating Ghana empire. "Korombeyze"/ "Issa Korombé" celebrates the warrior who fought against Peul hegemony over the Zarma in the nineteenth century, and who with his name dominated the Gole people.

The motto of "Mamar Kassai," the Songhay name for Askia Mohammed, shapes many of the poems and dances about ancestors linked to him. This focus on the person who represents an entire clan or people evokes all the typical praises that identify the individual with the ancestor. The cries of encouragement prompted by *zamu* about Wonkoy Zibbo or Hamsatou, from domestic or "inside" poetry, transcend the home space when the poetry is performed outside the home.

The first part of the *zamu* sets the scene in which the person is presented. His qualities are rooted in space and time. At the same time, they are valorized by kinship as well as political, social, and economic standing. Feminine *zamu* emphasize those qualities that are admired in the Zarma woman: beauty as well as possession of an abundance of millet, butter, and milk. A woman who is not a mother is compared to a dead branch or a pond without fish.

These portraits teach us, for example, that the woman who is named Kadijatou does not display the broken back of the fleeing hyena and that she is not a woman who is built like a camel. She is described for us as a woman with infinite, even prodigal generosity (Bisilliat and Laya 1972, 15).

Male *zamu* feature physical harmony, power, and wealth. The last two are inseparable in the minds of the Zarma, and are more important than ephemeral physical beauty, whether male or female. A man does not need to be physically handsome if he possesses power, wealth, and those qualities that allow him to survive and prosper. He is labeled as a good husband, a good son, and good neighbor.

On the other hand, the mother-in-law, granted many privileges because of her beauty, does not want to be known only for her power because

> Meeri si wayboro sara
> Ada no ga na a hanse

Or

> Ugliness does not devalue a woman
> Her value is based on her moral qualities

Thus, the composition of *zamu* texts always presents this binary structure that juxtaposes physical and moral portraits, but always gives preference to the second. Even qualities acquired by merit, such as wealth, are subordinate to the preservation of the moral.

Duura ka s haawi gaaray ya dwu gusam no

Or

> Good luck does not protect one from shame, it is nothing more than a pile
> of chaff (Tombokoye Tessa, Zarma bard)

Shame in society is the stain that isolates the individual and forces him into
exile, a form of social suicide. In sum, the *zamu*/saying appears as a call to solidarity and to integration in a society marked by precariousness and where one
knows that no one can survive alone without the help of others.

THE INTEGRATION OF THE INDIVIDUAL

The past and present of a region allow one to find the bearer of a name that
serves as a model and an inspiration for mothers, grandmothers, and great
aunts to compose their *zamu* with many variations on the same name. And as
one cannot imagine how reality can always coincide with dreams, one assumes
that the poets have the power to distort the canonical model. It is therefore the
re-creation of the text that allows one to proceed to modifications and to the
pragmatic management of the *zamu* to be composed, and to make it serve in
a given situation. This re-creation is a process of adaptation in time and space
and a function of the purpose of the composer. This is one of the reasons why
the repertory offers not only exceptional portraits marked by many superla-
tives, but also some that are quite ordinary, such as the *zamu* titled "Nyaale/
The Little Woman" (Bisilliat and Laya 1972, 103). Here it becomes apparent that
the heroine, who is quite small, would be placed in danger if she had to possess more qualities than those mentioned in order to make up for her physical
handicap. For if it is not desirable that a woman have the shape of a camel,
the arched body remains nevertheless a requisite for feminine beauty. It is her
large size that produces the curves and carefully proportioned *minceurs* that
constitute beauty for the Zarma woman. But since not everybody can have
everything, the saying encourages short women who could not, in such a context, earn the prized label of most beautiful woman, to valorize what she has
received from nature and from men.

Taasu gaase go Nyaale bande
Taasu tuwey go Nyaale bande
Nyaale kuturmey
Birjihaynikucum
Sako dunguri
Gaasu taka nda gondi gaa naa se

A sinda biri
Da Ko o baaya gaa
Deene ga di

Or

The calabashes full of millet paste are behind Nyaale
The ladles of millet paste are behind Nyaale
Nyaale the little woman
The beautiful millet with short stalks
The bean seed
The form of the calabash and the body of the snake, that's what she has
She has no bones
Si Ko o has gone beyond this stage
The tongue will grab her (Bisilliat and Laya 1972, 103)

In the same way, the particular drum rhythm for short women accompanies songs that praise them for their numerous qualities.

Dense and round the shadow of the detarium tree
The short woman who has a large bottom
That the trees around her surpass in height
But who possesses, above all, the most beautiful shade

In any case, the modification can also be made in the reverse direction when the ideal is seen as insufficiently merited and valorized. That is the case in the *zamu* dedicated to those named Hassan (Bisilliat and Laya 1972, 123). It offers the model or ideal for the happy Zarma man in a village who is a good husband and good son, virtues that have become more important since migration and other forms of departure have made some of them forget that they have left behind their old mothers and spouses. This *zamu* allows one to see clearly in its structure the different thematic levels that each one of the composers has given to the poem in its ideal form.

THE DANCE ARENAS: A PLACE OF INSERTION FOR GROUPS

The texts from the dance arenas that are performed on the occasion of dances attracting a large crowd sing of archetypes rather than of individuals. In contrast with the songs heard in the interior or domestic space, these songs focus on common names and titles that symbolize the values inherent to them. The song of the singleton that presents factions ready to confront each other offers an example.

Hymns to Beauty

In these public spaces, one also heard drummed hymns to beauty at the gatherings that used to be organized to celebrate the moment when women came out of seclusion from fattening periods (in the Songhay-Zarma region, the most beautiful women are fat). This was a tradition that occurred after the harvest. There was a great show of both clothing style and beauty. The master of ceremonies was the *waymonzon,* or elected chief of the well-nourished woman of the village or group of villages. The competition opened with the distribution of specially prepared pieces of braised chicken. Each young woman received, in good humor, the piece that characterized her the best, whether it had lots of flesh or was in an angular shape. On a chosen day, the dance began with the "Komkom-no-a-ci" tune or "She is smooth," played for those who had become more beautiful. There was a different tune to criticize the thin ones who, in spite of great efforts, could not become fat. After that, those who had managed to become fat paraded around the arena. In any case, if the fat ones remained the queens of the dance arena on this occasion, those who remained thinner were also at the celebration and benefitted from the right to respond to the attacks of their fat counterparts. And while the thin ones displayed their graceful necks, the short ones were also free to enter into the arena to show off their qualities.

Benefits of Birth and Personal Merit

The benefits of birth and personal merit also contribute to a network of solidarity. One never rejects one's own in Africa, just as the guinea hen cannot reject the mosaic of its plumage. Together, the dancers emphasize their birth and the social status that it conveys. They brag about having relatives who are well off and of having a rich husband. If one is not the sole wife and the only one in the heart of one's husband, one will brag about her position as *mowa* (in Hausa) or *waykwaaso* (in Songhay-Zarma)—that is, as the preferred wife in a polygynous situation. Women are the sources of many stories and fables on this theme. Moreover, in a society where marriage does not produce in sociological terms any change in identity, women will also valorize whatever group to which their parents belong, such as professional groups (blacksmiths, griots, weavers, etc.) or social classes (in particular, nobles, soldiers, marabouts, or artisans). One sees, then, that the dance arena serves for all kinds of oratorical jousts where, whether one is beautiful or not, rich or not, well born or not, it is essential to have a poem ready to chant. A protagonist goes to these balls in order to respond to any verbal aggression against her, her clan, or, today, her political party. It is no surprise also that these gatherings offer co-wives an ideal occasion to pursue their own domestic duels.

The Dance Arena as Media Space

Before the development and expansion of modern media, the dance arena was the best place to make or break the reputation of a man, a family, or a faction because it was animated by women. In this space, a well-turned *zamu* may create the equivalent of a media buzz, in the good and bad senses of the expression. It would be, as in the Hausa adage, to have one's wrapper ripped off in the middle of the market. People from surrounding villages who come in the morning to these weekly gatherings will at the end of the day leave and go in all directions, carrying the news of the day. The dance arena as a space for a great drumming session is, in this sense, an extremely interesting space, because what happens there is disseminated to a large number of people, not only those who attend, but those who hear about it from the participants.

CONCLUSION

Raphaël N'Diaye (1987), speaking of Serer women of Senegal, calls these dance arenas spaces for female discourse because they serve both to disseminate information and also to regulate social tensions In the texts presented here as well as in many others that could not be included for lack of space, it is clear that the women who have, in principal, no authority over speech manage to offer their views on all of the aspects of life, individual and social. They do so in a variety of domestic and public spaces, from the kitchen to the dance arena. If, as indicated by N'Diaye, these theaters of female discourse allow one to shine by the creativity of one's inspiration, the beauty and the depth of one's ideas, and the harmony of one's voice, they do so in ways that are eminently subversive because they often upset the existing social order. The marabouts who today are the keepers of social values in Sahelian villages are not mistaken in the importance of these locales when they issue decrees to suppress activities at these dangerous places. By using the mortar blows as a means of expression, the women assume for themselves the right to determine and to contest social labels. They put themselves in the position of organizing society according to their own views and present themselves as holders of the power to "speak" inside and outside. In this sense, one can say that those who hold the power of speech, in both traditional and contemporary Africa, have themselves a strong grasp of power.

WORKS CITED

Bâ Konaré, Adame. 1993. *Dictionnaire des femmes du Mali*. Bamako: Jamana.
Bisilliat, Jeanne, and Diouldé Laya. 1972. *Les zamu ou poèmes sur les noms*. Niamey: Centre Nigérien de Recherches en Sciences Humaines et Techniques.

Bornand, Sandra. 1995. De l'idéologie dans l'Epopée de Bubu Ardo Galo: analyse d'une épopée songhay-zarma (Niger). Licence Diss., University of Lausanne.

———. 2005. *Le discours du griot généologiste chez les Zarma du Niger.* Paris: Karthala.

Derive, Jean. 2002. *L'Epopée: unité et diversité du genre.* Paris: Kathala.

Diarra, Fatoumata-Agnès. 1970. *Femmes africaines en devenir: Les femmes zarma du Niger.* Paris: Anthropos.

Gado, Boubé Alpha. 1976. Le Zarmatarey, voyages de migrations, formations de provinces historiques, avènement des Wangari. Mémoire de maîtrise, Université de Paris VII.

———. 1980. *Le Zarmaterey: Contribution à l'histoire des populations d'entre Niger et Dallol Mawri.* Etudes nigériennes no. 45. Niamey: Institut de Recherches en Sciences Humaines.

Hama, Boubou. 1988. *L'Essence du verbe.* Niamey: Centre d'Etudes Linguistiques et Historiques par Tradition Orale.

Kesteloot, Lilyan, and Bassirou Dieng. 1997. *Les Epopées d'Afrique noire.* Paris: Karthala.

Mahamadou, Aïssa Ganda. 2003. Poésie de l'aire songhay-zarma: les devises tambourinées. Master's thesis, Abdou Moumouni University of Niamey.

Mounkaïla, Fatima. 1989. *Le mythe et l'histoire dans la geste de Zabarkane.* Niamey: Centre d'Etudes Linguistique et Historique par Tradition Orale.

———. 2001. Femmes et politique au Niger: Présence et présentation. In *Niger: Etat et Démocratie,* ed. Idrissa Kimba, 83–101. Paris: l'Harmattan.

N'Diaye, Raphaël. 1987. Chants-poèmes sereer. *Présence africaine,* no. 141:83–101.

Rouch, Jean. 1989. *La religion et la magie Songhay.* Bruxelles: Université de Bruxelles.

Soumaila, Hammadou, dit Bonta, Moussa Hamidou, and Diouldé Laya. 1998. *Traditions des Songhay de Téra.* Paris: Karthala.

Sutherland-Addy, Esi, and Aminata Diaw. 2005. *Women Writing Africa: West Africa and the Sahel.* Vol. 2 of The Women Writing Africa Project. New York: Feminist Press.

11

Space, Language, and Identity in the Palm Tree

Aissata G. Sidikou

One of the common themes of African literature written in European languages is the emphasis on identity in works that appeared both before and during the national era. But too often one gets the impression that concerns about identity were solely the product of the contact between Africa and the West, especially during the last half-century. But listeners to the oral art of West Africa cannot miss the same issue, whether the performance is an epic about the creation of an empire or a song about raising children. What is distinctive about these performances, especially those by women, is the recurrence of the themes of space and language as contributors to the formation of identity. This observation prompts several questions: how do women portray these themes, what do they mean for both the artist and the audience, and how do their concerns relate to African literature in written form?

A short answer for the theme of space is that it can convey a sense of belonging to a specific community, a sentiment that appears in all forms of African literature, oral and written. But this site of unity can also serve as a source for a code of signs, verbal and non-verbal, that force women to comply with the dominant norms—again, no matter the medium. There is much more, however, to the complex roles of language and space in the creation of identity in women's songs. In the analysis below of an exemplary song, published in French by Couloubaly (1990) and in English in my book, *Recreating Words, Reshaping Worlds: The Verbal Art of Women from Niger, Mali and Senegal* (2001), I offer some preliminary answers to the questions raised above. Two factors contributed to the decision to choose this particular song: the economical and rather direct concern about identity, and the themes of space and language that one finds in the powerful lyrics.

> To the native country
> To the native country I have been
> The native country has not welcomed me

> To the maternal country
> To the maternal country I have been
> The maternal country has not welcomed me

> To the conjugal household
> To the conjugal household I have been
> The conjugal household has not welcomed me

> The palm tree
> I have become a palm tree
> Tree with no bark.

(Couloubaly 1990, 35; Sidikou 2001, 33–34)

The song was sung by a woman caught in an extremely difficult situation because of the rejection she experienced after she refused to remain in a marriage. One of many songs on this theme that one finds across the Sahel, this one conveys the variety of contradictions that surround and determine women's being and status in West African societies. There is evidence for it in many of the songs about marriage in the volume *Women's Voices from West Africa* (Sidikou and Hale 2011) as well as in some of the papers in this volume.

In "The Palm Tree" one finds three kinds of space—paternal, or societal; maternal, or domestic; and conjugal, or foreign. Within each the singer implies that there are also three different languages. She speaks the languages of the different spaces—that of her father, the literal representative of patriarchal society, that of her mother, who, like most women socialized in that system, accepts its values, and, finally, that of her husband, the new authority figure in her life at a different location. All three categories define her as a woman. But at the same time they can be interpreted as spaces that oppress her, spaces from which she wishes she could escape because all are dominated by the spirit of patriarchy. Fleeing from them presents an enormous problem: there may be no place for a woman to go. The search, then, for a comfortable space can be an endless and often fruitless quest.

These spaces are unwelcoming to the young woman not just because of the individuals—father, mother, and husband—but more deeply because of the confining and controlling atmosphere that permeates the environment. As she becomes more aware of the atmosphere of these spaces, a sensitivity that is heightened by the move to the husband's home, the woman realizes that confinement and control will be her lot for the rest of her life.

> The palm tree
> I have become a palm tree
> Tree with no bark

With no protest or apparent anger in the words, but simply an overwhelming feeling of sadness, she sings of her distress in an environment where no one seems to want to listen, and where the norm appears to be silence in the face of the harsh realities facing many women. The metaphor of the "tree with no bark" conveys the singer's sense that she lacks any protection against what she sees as the negative patriarchal forces of society. The bareness of the tree reflects the bareness of the woman's body, a condition that diminishes her identity formation. The metaphor echoes the reality in many African societies that the only people who wander naked are those who suffer from mental derangement.

The image of the palm tree evokes other qualities that convey her sense of discomfort. Whatever the species, in the Sahel the palm often stands alone in its own space. It does not often appear as part of a thick and impenetrable forest. This comparative isolation describes the situation of the singer. Another feature of palm trees of different species that relates to the condition of a woman in an ambiguous condition is the split of the trunks. For some of these species, there are several trunks growing out of the ground at the base. The doum palm typically divides halfway up the trunk, and then these two branches divide again, a metaphor for the condition of the woman who starts out on one path, growing up in her family, and then undergoes a separation within her own identity as a result of her shifts to new spaces. Unlike other more familiar trees, such as the acacia or the gao, whose branches divide constantly to create the image from a distance of a mass of foliage, the divisions described above of the doum palm are stark, with no other branches issuing from these divided parts of the trunk. The isolation and the splits of the doum palm serve as symbols for the sense of separation within the self that is described by the singer—what one might term alienation. She must be daughter of her parents, wife of her husband, and, above all, submissive woman to the wider patriarchal values of her "native country." But the singer goes against her own instincts as she tries, without success, to divide her self up in order to adapt to the different vectors of patriarchy.

The fact that the palm in the metaphor has no bark leaves it more open to borers and other insects that will eventually weaken and destroy it. The singer too has no "bark." She has no way of responding to what she sees as the refusal of protection on the part of the people in her life. Hers is not an unusual experience, as other songs using different metaphors reveal. See, for example, the song about the girl who prefers to be boiled in porridge rather than submit to an arranged marriage, recorded by Aissata Niandou and included in Sidikou and Hale (2011, 38).

The metaphor of the tree here, however, has limits. As with the baobab tree that has so many positive connotations in African societies, the new shoots and fruits of the palm are edible. Its leaves are used to weave mats, hats, baskets, and a variety of other useful items. But these positive attributes do not diminish, in any case, the negative aspects of the singer's desperate identification with the most visible features of the palm tree.

Compressed in this short song are travels and experiences that enlarge the space of the singer, but also open to her the confines of her new world. In the first lines after the palm tree metaphor, the listeners hear a reference to "the native country," the singer's own land. It is not clear that she has traveled around the country, but she has come to know at an early age that the values of her own family are consonant with those of her patriarchal society. One of those is that a woman, old or young, married or not, requires an authority to oversee her existence, especially as she passes from the home of her parents to that of her husband and even to that of a son if she has one who can meet her needs as she ages.

In the sequence of spaces conveyed by the lyrics of the song, the conjugal home ultimately defines the identity of the woman because it provides the arena where she will be obliged to exemplify society's idea of feminine success— obedience to her husband, fertility, childcare, and contributions to the maintenance of the family through agriculture or sales of goods she produces. The values, implied or explicit, that permeate this space will govern her life until she dies.

One might expect the maternal space of the home to be a refuge, a source of maternal comfort. This is not simply because of the concern of the mother about her child, as is evident in so many songs about childcare, but also because in some African societies maternal uncles never reject under any circumstances the child of their sister. But in the song, it appears that the singer has lost the support of her mother, an icon of security, and can no longer communicate with her.

Throughout her development as an individual, the identity of the woman is formed according to that of the "other," who could be a man or older women or women from the male lineage who enjoy authority based on their age or status as siblings. It is only when the singer tries to define herself by rejecting the sources of her troubles that she realizes her only choices are to comply or rebel. The singer's expression of sentiments that everyone recognizes but few dare to utter constitutes a desperate attempt to engage society in order to improve her own situation and, by extension, the condition of all women. But because the only language available to her comes from the system in which she lives, her effort to effect change is doomed to failure. There is no tool available to the singer that would enable her to break out and claim agency for herself.

The use of the pronoun *I* might suggest a way out. It conveys the notion of individual authority and identity, emphasized by her identification with the palm tree, especially the ubiquitous doum palm whose divided shape reflects her split condition. The subject is forced out of the collective *us* which suggests a sense of unity, but unfortunately unity in recognition of the values of patriarchy. The *I* transforms her into a subject capable of producing her own text or speech because she does not want to accept the dominant discourse about women. But the *I* is left bare because in this society it is the community that controls attention. The text is not a confession but rather a testimonial, an unveiling of the singer's uncertainty. At the same time, the pronoun *I* becomes subversive because it transgresses and disrupts an existing order founded on the notion of *us*.

The crisis of identity conveyed by the song about the woman who suffers from such a devastating sense of alienation is no different from what one finds in much longer narratives in European languages by African writers, both during the colonial era and up to the present, for men as well as for women. When women emerged on the literary scene in the 1980s, the same story played out. In *Le baobab fou* (1984) by Ken Bugul, a fictionalized autobiography, the author also identifies with a tree whose condition reflects her own difficult situation as she seeks escape in Europe but discovers only drugs and prostitution. She speaks of being

> No longer able to recognize among one's own people the true bonds that used to shape and could guide destinies. That aura of serenity and of being accepted surely was a necessity. I had played a character too long: a woman, a Black woman, who had for a long time believed in her ancestors the Gauls, and who, unrecognized, had blamed everything on a childhood not lived, on colonization, on the separation from the father and the mother. (Bugul 1984 [1991])

In *Riwan ou le chemin du sable* (Bugul 1999), another novel with a significant autobiographical dimension, the narrator returns home and finally finds a sense of self by, paradoxically, voluntarily accepting patriarchy in what turns out to be only a fleeting solution to her crisis of identity. She becomes the twenty-seventh wife of a spiritual leader who has a large family of many co-wives.

At bottom there is no difference between the anguish expressed in the short song in the oral medium and the equally unhappy experience expressed in the novel. In each case, the narrator's itinerary leads to a similar sense of alienation. But women are not the only ones who suffer from identity problems. Readers of African literature are familiar with the inner conflict endured by the protagonist of *L'aventure ambiguë,* a semi-autobiographical and highly philosophical account by Cheikh Hamidou Kane (1961). The young man's move from the Islamic values of his people in Senegal to a European society dominated by Christian beliefs leads to a crisis of identity with a tragic outcome. In a more recent work, Joseph, the protagonist of *L'Impasse* (1996) by Daniel Biyaoula, suffers an identity problem triggered initially by a name given to him by his mother that causes great discomfort as a result of the discrimination he experiences in France because of his race and origin.

> Wherever you go, you have the feeling of not being in your place. You feel like a nonentity! That is what happened to me. Badly loved, rather, not loved at all, unwanted, that was how I was at home, in my family. (Biyaoula 1996, 181; my translation)

The singer of the song analyzed in this study as well as the protagonists of these novels all suffer from marginalization, exclusion, and incomprehension. They are extremely unhappy because of the structures and mechanisms of their societies at different times and in different spaces. In each case, the narrator arrives at some form of self-understanding as the result of questions directed at the values of society.

Space and language in these novels offer keys to understanding the nature of the problems that affect the identity of the protagonist. The evidence from "The Palm Tree" and the novels cited above suggests the need to erase the barriers that divide verbal art into two seemingly unrelated media—the oral and the written. The vast majority of scholarship on African literature today is focused on works written in European languages. But if we want to reframe that literature as a more fully representative whole, then songs, now on the most distant margin of African literature, need to be brought into the center. "The Palm Tree" is just one example. If one examines the numerous songs in the anthology *Women's Voices from West Africa* (2011), it will become apparent that the singers of the lyrics have much to say to the narrators in the novels—and vice versa. Above all, both media offer to enrich our understanding of African literature as a vast area of inquiry with a long history.

WORKS CITED

Biyaoula, Daniel. 1996. *L'Impasse.* Paris: Présence Africaine.
Bugul, Ken. 1984 [1991]. *Le baobab fou.* Dakar: Nouvelles Editions Africaines. Published in English as *The Abandoned Baobab,* trans. Marjolijn de Jager. New York: Lawrence Hill.
———. 1999. *Riwan ou le chemin du sable.* Paris: Présence Africaine.

Couloubaly, Pascal Baba F. 1990. *Une société rurale bambara à travers des chants de femmes.* Dakar: IFAN.

Kane, Cheikh Hamidou. 1961. *L'aventure ambiguë.* Paris: Juillard. Published in English as *Ambiguous Adventure.* Trans. Katherine Woods. London: Heinemann, 1972.

Sidikou, Aissata. 2001. *Recreating Words, Reshaping Worlds: The Verbal Art of Women from Niger, Mali and Senegal.* Trenton, N.J.: Africa World Press.

Sidikou, Aissata and Thomas A. Hale, eds. 2011. *Women's Voices from West Africa: An Anthology of Songs from the Sahel.* Bloomington: Indiana University Press.

12

Bambara Women's Songs in Southern Mali

Bah Diakité

In many cultures, songs are seen primarily as entertainment. The form appears more important than the message. But on closer examination, it is clear that one can learn as much about a people from songs as one can from any other source. But the question is, what kind of information is embedded in such ephemeral verbal forms? What, for example, can one learn about women who sing songs as they go about their daily tasks?

In Mali, the songs from Bambara women in the south enable one to learn about their hopes, their wounds, their anger, their fear, and their needs—not only in the present but also in the context of the past—in other words, their lived experiences in the larger context of their society. The purpose here is to discover the range of those feelings and how they are expressed in song.

SCOPE OF THIS STUDY

The region that is the focus of this study is the frontier zone in southern Mali near the border with Côte d'Ivoire, and in particular the prefecture of Kolondiéba. It is a fairly large region, covering about 9,000 square kilometers, divided into 12 rural communes that include 203 villages and hamlets. In Kolondiéba live groups of Bambara who are, to some extent, so bound to their own traditions that local economic development has suffered. It is a situation marked by cultural and linguistic withdrawal from the larger Malian society, which is evolving rapidly as the result of Western influence. Such intrusions from the outside world as do occur come largely from Côte d'Ivoire to the south.

This is an area that is not very high on the list of concerns for the government in Bamako in part because of its difficult accessibility. In many ways the region is more closely linked with the economy of Côte d'Ivoire, a country that attracts many young migrants from Mali. The wealth of Ivoirians in comparison with their neighbors to the north stems historically from greater resources, a longer tradition of economic development, and the access that country has had to a wide range of imported goods from Europe.

Women in the largely agricultural region of Kolondiéba not only suffer from the challenges of life in a torrid climate but also suffer considerably from the patriarchal and gerontocratic structure of the society. They are the first to awaken in the morning in order to carry out their many tasks—cooking, farming, collecting and bringing home firewood, picking karite nuts in the bush, and raising children. Under these circumstances, it is easy to understand why a woman often becomes impatient for her husband to add a co-wife to the family, a change that, under less demanding circumstances, would not likely be welcomed by a spouse in a monogamous marriage.

In this region, as in many other parts of the Sahel, the long-standing presence of Islam is increasing. Nevertheless, the historical resistance of the Bamana to the religion has not disappeared. Many people have remained faithful to some of their ancestral traditions, and in particular to a large white well for which the main town of Kolondiéba is named: *kolon* ("well"); *dié* ("white"); *ba* ("great"). To this day, people make weekly offerings of kola nuts, chickens, and sheep.

That community is also viewed as what one might term a "folk scandal" because women, in contrast to what one often finds in other areas, have assumed a much more significant role than men in musical activities, not only vocal but also instrumental. In the region of Kolondiéba, women have developed a large repertory of performances involving songs, dancing, and instruments. These diverse musical activities are linked to their numerous occupations. In their songs, they also seek to communicate the values of the past. The results are songs considered to be high art capable of eliciting a powerful response in listeners (Diakité 1997a).

THE CORPUS

The corpus of songs analyzed here comes from two sources. The first set is from recordings I made of women in Kolondiéba and in the surrounding region in January and February 2003. The second was selected from a collection of songs of women pounding karite nuts that was preserved at the National Museum in Bamako. They were recorded in a Bambara region north of Kolondiéba.

The richness of songs by women in the larger region, Kolondiéba and the area to the north, stems in large part from the link with their many tasks. In fact, women have been composing and singing songs for centuries while working in the fields, pounding grain and nuts, and spinning cotton. They also sing and dance to express their joy at naming, initiation, and wedding ceremonies, as well as their sorrows at divorces and funerals.

These songs derive their names both from the function to which they are related and, in many cases, from the instruments that are involved. The most important categories of songs are those of the *guita,* the *ya* (or *boyi*), the *bari* (or *didadid*), and *nkuren,* all forms of music that are rooted in their own particular instrument of the traditional orchestra. In the analysis that follows, I will focus on songs typically related to a particular activity, circumstance, social group, or age group. These songs convey the anger, the fears, the needs, and the aspirations of the singers and their audiences (Diakité 1997b).

The *guita* songs occur during a ceremony that focuses on the social and economic activity of women as they evolve from adolescence, known as *nyè-yèlèbeli,* meaning "the one whose eyes are not yet opened," to maturity and old age. One example appears in the song "*Dununkan n bolo*" ("I've got a drumming word for you") where the older women initiate their younger sisters into the life experiences ahead of them—a life of hard domestic work that is full of interpersonal challenges. The newly married woman is trained in how to behave correctly in her responsibilities to her husband and to her in-laws. She is advised to maintain self-control during conversations after meals when women from the same compound come together to gossip and talk about the events of the day. The newly married woman is advised to just listen and to talk only with those in her age group. It is during these sessions with women from the entire compound that jealousy and conflict can sometimes emerge, sentiments that lead to divorce, with a newly arrived wife sometimes ending up as the victim of accusations. The following song offers an example of these feelings.

I've Got a Drumming Word

Singer:
1   I have got a drumming word for you.
2   Yes, I've got a drumming word
3   I've got a drumming word
4   I've got a drumming word for Hawa

Chorus:
5   We've got a drumming word
6   Yes, We've got a drumming word

7   We've got a drumming word
8   We've got a drumming word for Hawa.

Singer:
9   When she who is a novice [or innocent] will have to leave
10   I've got a drumming word for her
11   When they start the after-meal chats
12   Do not meddle with it.
13   When you do interfere
14   You'll hear old women say:
15   The girl hasn't even come out of her eggshell yet
16   She bears malice to old persons
17   Here is your message dear junior.

Chorus:
18   We've got a drumming word
19   Yes, we've got a drumming word
20   We've got a drumming word
21   We've got a drumming word for Hawa

Singer:
22   When you go to the field to pound millet
23   When they start millet-pounding chats
24   Do not meddle with those chats.
25   When you do interfere
26   You'll hear old women say:
27   The little girl hasn't even come out of her shell yet
28   She bears malice to old persons

Chorus:
29   We've got a drumming word
30   Yes, We've got a drumming word
31   We've got a drumming word
32   We've got a drumming word for Hawa.

Singer:
33   When you go to your husband's
34   When passing by old men
35   Talking on wooden *gwala*
36   Don't meddle with the talks on it.
37   For their malicious *kôrôti-bôriw* are dangerous
38   Old men's *kôrôti* do not tolerate
39   When women start fetching water from the well

40   When they start to chat on the way to the river,
41   Do not meddle with it.
42   When you do interfere
43   You'll hear old women say:
44   The little girl hasn't even come out of her shell yet
45   She is bearing malice to old men.
46   Oh dear, that was the drum for Hawa

Chorus:
47   We've got a drumming word
48   Yes, we've got a drumming word
49   We've got a drumming word
50   We've got a drumming word for Hawa.

Singer:
51   My greeting to Hawa
52   My greeting to Titian-Npènè
53   My greeting to Niankoro Yamou
54   I am only a beginner [in singing]
55   I haven't even grown feathers yet
56   That is the drum for you, dear junior!

One other important aspect touched by women's song is *kôsira,* or the path to the river, pond, or well followed by groups of women to fetch water. It is a place for conversations, advice, and the sharing among close friends of sensitive information. But it can also become a dangerous place when some women take the opportunity to slander or to take revenge against others. The trail linking the village to a source of water is, then, a particularly important pathway for Bambara women. Unfortunately it is also a space that is disappearing because of projects initiated by the government in cooperation with foreign development partners to provide cleaner and safer water. The goal is to install water pumps in the middle of a village in order to provide water that is cleaner and much easier to obtain. But that central source of purer drinking water is sometimes abandoned by women for the lower-quality water at the end of the path on which they walk. That time away from the village on the path to a source of water requires more physical effort, but the daily trek allows them an opportunity to escape from the male-dominated village environment. For the women, that world includes dangerous men who deploy evil spells or poisons known as *kôrôti-bôriw* to attack other people.

"*I mana wa le*" ("When you will go") is another very typical song of advice for younger women. To understand it, one must be aware of the village social environment, in particular the central space, or *fèrè,* a public place where cultural ceremonies are held—for example, to ask the spirits for protection, peace, and unity in the village. Gatherings of members of age groups which link their members for life no matter how far away they may go are also held there. Given the significance of the space for so many purposes, it is not surprising that one hears many references to it in songs.

When You Will Go

Singer:

1   When you go, when you go to your household
2   Do not stick to unmarried life, instead get married

Chorus:

3   When you go, when you go to your household
4   Do not stick to unmarried life, instead get married

Singer:

5   When she goes
6   When she goes for marriage
7   She's got to forget unmarried life and rather long for married life
8   There, she has already gone to an arranged marriage for her parents' sake
9   There is no more to say.
10   That's the end of youthful talk.
11   Crying is useless
12   Young girls, endless tears can't do anything about it.
13   It's no use to be lying down all the time
14   Yes, there's nothing more to say.
15   The hoe is put aside [abandoned]
16   The hoe of youth is put aside
17   The weekly party is also given up.
18   Yes, young girls, the fair in Kolondiéba is over now
19   Time for marriage has come.
20   Do not insult your father-in-law when you get there
21   My dear junior, do not insult your dear mother-in-law
22   Words are of no use about that.
23   Ended, your gossiping in the public place, young girls.
24   Here is the day for marriage
25   Drop the baggage of youth and pick up that of marriage.

Chorus:

26   When you arrive at your new household
27   Forget about unmarried life and focus on marriage

Singer:

28   Forget about unmarried life and go for marriage

Once a girl is married, she must then adopt behavior that is appropriate for her situation within the larger family of her husband. The song *"Nden Ki kuma"* ("Don't speak, my daughter") focuses on the virtue of silence. The same song informs listeners about some of the tools of the women's environment. For example, the *wugu,* a stone used to grind karite nuts, is mentioned as well as the tools employed for the making of *karite,* or shea butter, one of the most important sources of income for the women of the village. In the lyrics, these tools and the karite nuts provide the means for the women to buy clothing and jewelry.

Don't Speak, My Daughter

Singer:

1   There, she is going to the marriage arranged by her parents
2   Don't speak, daughter

Chorus:

3   Don't speak, daughter
4   Don't speak, daughter

Singer:

5   Do not insult him there dear
6   Do not insult your husband there,
7   I say, do not speak, daughter
8   Do not insult them there,
9   Do not insult your husband's younger brothers and sisters there
10   Do not speak, daughter
11   Take good care of him there
12   Take good care of your dear husband.
13   Bear not malice to me
14   Go and take care of her
15   Go and take care of your mother-in-law
16   Dear friends, bear not malice to me
17   For whom have we left
18   The karite nut grinding stone
19   Bear not malice to me
20   For whom have we taken it.
21   For whom have we taken the millet pounding mortar.
22   Bear not malice to me

23   For whom have we taken it.
24   Everybody knows for whom we are fetching water from the big tap.
25   Bear not malice to me.

Chorus:
26   Don't speak, daughter
27   Don't speak, daughter

Singer:
28   We're going to advise them
29   We're going to advise young girls
30   You'll go, dear friends, to the marriage arranged by her parents
31   Bear not malice to me, dear friends.

Chorus
32   Don't speak, daughter
33   Don't speak, daughter

The song "To decline fresh water" is an anxious appeal by elders to girls who refuse to accept deeply rooted traditions such as arranged marriage, a custom common in many parts of Africa. For the Bambara, it is widely believed that a marriage arranged by parents is blessed and can never fail, neither from internal conflict nor from the impact of social changes from outside the home, viewed as the most common causes of early divorce between young couples. These arranged marriages are also seen as a means to give to all society's members, including the handicapped, the right and the possibility to benefit from the kind of happy married life they wouldn't be able to obtain on their own. For these reasons, young girls are asked not to refuse marriage to a suitor proposed by parents because that is supposed to be the destiny of all parties concerned. The following song illustrates the importance of these marriages through the metaphor of fresh water. But the singers undercut the positive nature of this liquid symbol by implying that marrying someone one really likes is a question of luck and should not be expected by every girl.

To Decline Fresh Water

Singer:
1   Refuse water, my relative refuses fresh water
2   Oh yes, young girls refuse fresh water

Chorus:
3   She refuses water, my relative refuses fresh water
4   Oh yes, young girls refuse fresh water

Singer:

5	Stay, stay in the marriage your parents arranged for you
6	But they say that you refuse water in spite of my request!
7	It is an honor
8	A young girl's marriage arranged by parents.
9	Refuse not fresh water; one can't be lucky in everything
10	In this world, all is not luck
11	The conversation on the way to the river says so
12	I tell you that marriage is arranged by parents
13	Refuse not fresh water, one can't be lucky in everything
14	Refuse not fresh water, for one can't be lucky in everything
15	I tell you that marriage arranged by parents is honor
16	Refuse not fresh water at my request

Chorus:

17	She refuses water, my relative refuses fresh water
18	Oh yes, young girls refuse fresh water

Singer:

19	We came down here just to chat
20	Refuse not fresh water
21	Man can't refuse his destiny, and a person can't be lucky in everything

Chorus:

22	She refuses water, my relative refuses fresh water
23	Oh yes, young girls refuse fresh water

The theme of destiny appears not only in songs about marriage, but also in a variety of others about orphans, the sick, the childless, widows, and aged people. The purpose is to attract the attention of society to these people whose lives have been marked by an unfortunate destiny.

Another category in the Bambara women's musical repertory is linked to *ya* or *boyi,* songs that exalt good deeds, work, and honor. The lyrics glorify and ennoble women, often when they are heading out to the fields. The purpose is to inspire them as they work together on group projects such as sharing the task of clearing or sowing each member's field. These are songs that are gender-specific, but are sung by both women and men in their own groups. The goal is to muster strength and courage by recalling heroines or heroes from the past. Turning to the past helps the individual face the future.

The lyrics in the song "The women's bara is being played in my hands" condemns women who think that "being a woman is a curse" by replying that "such women, even if they were men, wouldn't take any challenge."

The Women's Bara Is Being Played in My Hands

Singer:

1   Listen, listen to the sound I have,

2   I have here the women's bara sound,

Chorus:

3   Listen to the sound I have, I have a sound.

4   I have a sound of the women's bara

Singer:

5   Listen to my bara, listen to my bara.

6   I have the bara with which women come to the rescue of men.

Chorus:

7   Listen to the sound I have, I have a sound.

8   I have a sound of the women's bara

Singer:

9   Listen to my bara, listen to my bara.

10   Listen to me, playing the bara that women inherited from their father

Chorus:

11   Listen to the sound I have, I have a sound.

12   I have a sound of the women's bara

Singer:

13   Listen to my bara, listen to me, playing my bara.

14   I'm playing the women's working bara

Chorus:

15   Listen to the sound I have, I have a sound.

16   I have a sound of the women's bara

Singer:

17   Eh, seeing a wild cock is the real sign of misfortune

18   Let's live our life, because no one is going to live endlessly in this world!

19   Can't you see that I have the bara?

20   Yes, I'm playing the bara, I'm playing it.

21   Kouloukoutou Nianan is a dangerous fetish

22   The real child of a rabbit will never be born with short ears!

23   Can't you hear the sound of bara?

24   When women cry

25   When the lazy women cry all the time,

26   Pretending that being woman is a curse

27   In reality, being woman has never been a curse
28   The curse is being lazy in an extended family
29   The curse is being good-for-nothing.
30   The curse is laziness.
31   Such a woman, even if she were a man, would never take up a challenge.
32   Let all of us be aware that being a woman is not a curse

Chorus:
33   Listen to the sound I have, I have a sound.
34   I have a sound of the women's bara

The *ya* or *boyi* refers both to the traditional orchestra and to the genre that congratulates men and women, famous and great, those whose deeds and celebrity mark them for posterity. Their achievements, embodying the Bambara ideal of noble human qualities, are sung to educate the future generation of girls (Diakité 1997b).

Bambara society has placed the child at the top of all treasures that a man and a woman produce. The loss, lack, or extended absence of a child has an enormous impact on the family. The significance of a child appears in lyrics such as "the light of the family," "set of jewelry for a woman," and "the reason for marriage." Although praises for the child are heard in all of the women's repertoires, songs about children are sung mainly in the *ya* genre because of the importance of children. The song "The childless old man," with its images and hyperbole, illustrates many of these concerns about children.

The Childless Old Man

Singer:
1   The day the childless old man dies
2   The childless old man will be like a stump of firewood

Chorus:
3   The day the childless old man dies,
4   He will be like a stump of firewood.
5   Oh, the childless old man
6   Yes, being childless is so hard!
7   Jokala, the little singing bird, will be the announcer of that death.
8   Yes child, the childless old man has a very hard situation.
9   Ayyena will replace the bull of the death sacrifice.
10   Oh, childbirth is a problem, a real problem!
11   The turtledove will be weeping in the place of the childless parent who is
        supposed to weep.

12   Child, the childless old man, that's a difficult situation.
13   Jokala, the singing bird, will be alone to take care of you
14   It's so hard to be alone,
15   Yes, my brothers, it's very hard to stay alone.
16   Being old and childless is an awful situation.
17   The white heron will be your shroud, oh my parents,
18   The childless old man, a difficult situation!
19   The day the childless old man dies,

Chorus:
20   He is like a burning log

Singer:
21   The day the childless old man dies,
22   The childless old man is a burning log.

The songs presented here are just a small sample of those sung by women to address particular concerns. The actual corpus is much larger, and include songs about many other problems facing women. They include the departure of young men to seek work in Côte d'Ivoire, illness, healing, and death. In a society that suffers from a high rate of infant mortality and epidemics, without easy access to modern medical facilities, women often rely on spirits or, in the case of Muslims, Allah, for protection of the family. One often hears songs praising spirits who inhabit different sites of worship and divination. In case of death, there are songs that convey solidarity with the bereaved so that he or she is not alone in a misfortune that is part of the human condition. In sum, the songs of *guita* are both a psychological preparation for the hard passage for a woman from youth to womanhood and a helping hand toward adults suffering under the heavy burdens of life.

The songs examined here enable women to express their concerns about the difficult aspects of Bambara life in a region that is to some extent isolated from the currents of contemporary society. The songs also enable them to engage collectively in meeting everyday challenges, from farming under difficult conditions to arranged marriages. Above all, these songs offer a valued medium for individual and collective expression in a society in which men dominate the public space. The songs and the places where they are sung, from the path to the river to the central space, provide a privileged medium for these women. In the songs, they not only express their concerns, but emphasize the virtues of women. The songs strengthen them, glorify them, and create models for future generations. Finally, they also enable women to educate, in the broadest sense of the term, the younger generation.

The question is just how long these women will be able to maintain both the values expressed in the lyrics, such as hard work, and the songs themselves. How long will it be before young women refuse entirely to accept arranged marriages? How long will it be before the younger women cast aside these didactic songs in favor of more popular Western music? *Nkuren* songs, performed by a solo singer accompanied by the *nkuren* instrument, focused on two subjects, advice for wrongdoers and the disappointments encountered in love, but these are disappearing. Another genre that is disappearing is the rich repertory of songs by old women performed when they are spinning cotton, an activity replaced by the wide distribution of industrially woven cloth. The same could be said for agriculture. Will the songs by teams of men and women who go out to work in the fields disappear with the introduction of plows and tractors?

The salvaging of these songs through recording and preservation in archives is a temporary means of saving the cultural heritage of a people. In the long term, however, the small number of researchers in the field can hardly stem the diverse impacts of the rising tide of globalization. The songs presented here offer a variety of insights into the way women have asserted their presence in society. It is likely that the situations and roles of women in the future will change, but the songs that enable them to survive and flourish today will be replaced by new forms of expression about the different aspects of life that are now appearing on the horizon.

WORKS CITED

Diakité, Bah. 1997a. Lire dans notre patrimoine oral pour mieux voir et transcender les limites de notre école formelle ou Réflexions autour de l'ouvrage de Madame Annik Thoyer: "Récits épiques des chasseurs Bamanan du Mali." *Etudes maliennes,* no. 51:30–33.

———. 1997b. Traditional music and dance of Mali. In *The Spirit's Dance in Africa: Evolution, Transformation and Continuity in Sub-Sahara,* ed. Esther A. Dagan, 136–139. Westmount, Québec: Galérie AMRAD African Arts Publications.

13

Patriarchy in Songs and Poetry by Zarma Women

Aissata Niandou

Those unfamiliar with women's songs from the Sahel may be surprised at first by the subversive nature of the lyrics, as evidenced in songs recorded by many other researchers. Zarma society is not an exception to that trend, with women functioning within their own subculture. In their songs, as well as in other forms, they raise their voices against what they see as the unfair constraints of patriarchy that dominate Zarma society. But their songs raise a basic question: can they, in their verbal art, divest themselves of the patriarchal values that permeate not only their society, but also their own language and the deeper values that it conveys?

In this study, I will examine examples from a corpus of twenty-five poem-songs sung by Zarma women that are, on the surface, quite subversive of patriarchal values. But a close study of the poem-songs will offer evidence for a more nuanced view of the subversion conveyed by these poem-songs, and may suggest the need for new analyses of women's songs from other peoples in the Sahel.

Before going any further, however, it is important to provide both context and parameters for this study. As Finnegan points out, songs, like other categories of verbal art in Africa, do not "fit neatly into the familiar categories of literate cultures" (Finnegan 1976, 1). This is why I prefer to use the compound word *poem-song*, because it better conveys the diversity of the lyrics I shall analyze. Some of the songs are recited as incantations, others are sung with musical accompaniment, while one also finds those that are performed without music. These songs constitute a dynamic verbal art form which, unlike written genres, functions to a large extent as a regulator of society. Sorgho (1984) explains that cette régulation s'exerce dans le domaine moral . . . , dans le code de conduite sociale, dans la pédagogie qui est une didactique de la transmission du savoir, et même dans les domaines tels que la politique au sens platonicien du terme. [This regulation works in the moral domain . . . , in the social behavior code, in pedagogy which is a means for conveying knowledge, and even in domains such as politics in the Platonian sense.] (70–71, my translation)

As Finnegan points out, "several dimensions, not necessarily valid in writing, are significant in the analysis of these works: the performing dimension, and the personal aspect, room for improvisation that might change the rendition of the work" (1976, 7).

The songs presented here will be analyzed on two levels. First, evidence from a corpus of songs will reveal the subversive nature of the lyrics. Second, the songs will be reexamined at a deeper level to determine to what extent the same lyrics convey the values of patriarchy that permeate Zarma society.

The first set of poem-songs deals with contemporary concerns such as marriage, arranged marriage, the right of the woman to choose her life partner, and polygyny. Although these themes are important today, they are deeply rooted in Zarma society—as well as in cultures across the Sahel—and are not the result of recent influences from the West.

The first poem-song comes from a teenage bride pounding millet on a rainy season day.

Korsal wate annasara	The white man of the rainy season
No ka ci somno gollo	Is last year's millet stalks
Din na ceeri humburora	You break them in the mortar
A man nan ka gombol	They only bend
Din na dooru mo a kay beene	You take them out of the mortar
Ka ce kogandi	They stand on their straight legs
Waayi Inna da Baaba	Oh Mommy and Daddy
Kan man nan ay ma beeri	Who did not wait till I'm grown
Waayi Baaba Kan na	Oh Daddy
Zambar waykindigu ta	Who took 75.000 CFA [U.S.$150]
Ba kan a na ta mo	Though he took them
Manci hala a na nwa no	He never spent them
Li saayo da li boogo	He had to buy the yellow and green bed
Da fatilla kwaray	A white lamp
To ima dan doodo mo	And for good measure
Ga ne mo nyum yan bidayze	Even a wash-up gourd

This is the cry of a twelve- to fourteen-year-old girl who finds it too hard to prepare the food for a large family of in-laws with whom she now lives as a new bride. In Zarma rural areas, having such a responsibility means working long hours at the difficult task of turning the millet stalks into porridge for lunch, and millet paste and gravy for dinner. The bride's eventual acceptance depends on her physical strength in a society where there are no machines to help her. The woman has to work from dawn till nine or ten in the evening. This is why the singer of this poem-song denounces her parents, who married her off too early, with her father taking the "bride-price" and spending it on his own needs and those of his wives. The bed, the lamp, and the gourd will go with the bride to her husband's house, hence the purchase of these items. This is a voice against "mariages précoces" for girls, who must attempt to integrate themselves into a family of strangers with whom they may not get along well. In this case there is no female bonding, and she, unlike the other women, ends up working alone with no one to share the burden.

Another aspect of culture that this set of poem-songs deals with is polygny, as we see in the following lyrics:

Sappu ga Sambu	What a quick wedding
Wondekoy hiijayo	The already married man's wedding
Da nin sambu	The way he carries you
Danga da sin jiisi	Seems as if he'll never
Gangani beeri	Set you on the floor
Noa ga to ga ni faara	But he'd look for a hard ground
Kin te calle calle	To break you to pieces
Kin te casay	To make with you
A min te hamni baano	A thin flour without
Ba leesa si	The slightest grain.

The criticism here does not fit the widespread view of critics that rural women easily accept polygyny while only the literate, urban women in the Sahel denounce it. For example, some critics find fault with the main character in Mariama Bâ's *Une si longue lettre,* an urban school teacher who suffers from both the consequences of polygyny and abandonment by her first husband. Her reaction to the situation is viewed as an example of the negative influence of Western feminism (Sidikou 2001, 16). The same issue appears in *The Still Born* by the Nigerian author Zaynab Alkali.

What is even more surprising is that the critics even attack the authors through the characters, as if they are the characters they produce. Sometimes African women critics themselves are influenced by the rhetoric of the African male critics who feel uncomfortable with women's writing. The critic Aissata Sidikou, in her discussion of the theme of the right of the individual woman to choose, writes in her book *Recreating Words, Reshaping Worlds* that "Bâ's portrayal of the main characters in *Une si longue lettre,* Ramatoulaye and Aïssata, two middle-class women, does not reflect the condition of rural Senegalese, South African or North African women" (Sidikou 2001, 16). Of course it does not; but this does not make the book unrealistic and less relevant. Who is the author who can write about the experience of African women as a universal and monolithic phenomenon?

The following two poem-songs offer evidence that a woman can be illiterate and be against polygyny, just as one can find women educated in Western-style schools who are not against polygyny. This is the kind of poem-song young girls produce at gatherings to celebrate social events, in particular weddings. The singer criticizes the behavior of many polygamous men who treat their bride very well right after the wedding but soon change their behavior. The song constitutes a very strong public warning to the woman who might be approached by married men eager to ask for her hand.

In the second and third poem-songs, the performer declares that she'd rather die than marry an already married man. Here the message needs no comment.

Hala da wondekoy ka cay sintina	If I were to marry a married man
Ay nya may tuti	Let my mother push me
Ay ma kan taljira	In some boiling porridge,
Ay nya may tuti	Let my mother push me
Ay ma kan taljira	In some boiling porridge
Hala taljo ga faw	Before the porridge gets done,
Kulay mo ga nin	I'll be well cooked too.

The third poem-song echoes the second:

Ay yeeriye riye	*Ay yeeriye riye*
Hala wondekoy	If the married man
Ka ci fondo	Were a path
Ay si fondo gana	I would not take the path
Subu nay ga taaru	I'd rather cross the weeds
Ay yeeriye riye	*Ay yeeriye riye*
Hala wondekoy	If the married man
Ka ci zaara	Were a wrapper
Koonu nay ga dira	I'd rather walk naked
Zankay ma haaru	For children to laugh.

Young women also raise their voices against arranged marriage. Even if in many African cultures the family is more important than the individual, people have always claimed this right to choose even in the most closely bound groups.

The point here is not that the individual's desires should be more important than those of the family, but that the clash between the individual and society does happen as part of the dynamic nature of culture: people conform, but they also subvert cultural norms.

The poem-song that follows illustrates this theme of choice. The reference in the song to Côte d'Ivoire is to men who migrate to that country in search of work, and who thus abandon their families at home in Niger.

Arwusu kanna boro zalay	The interesting marriage
Hiijay no ga kaanu	Is to be with he who has dated you
Wokan manna boro zalay	The man who has not
Seeja kala ibayi	The bastard cares only about himself
Seeja kala ibayi	The bastard cares only about himself
Kala modabay zinayze	The bastard will ignore your needs
Kan koy Yamma	Whoever goes to *Yamma* [Côte d'Ivoire]
Kulu ma ci ay nya Yamma yan se	Should tell auntie *Yamma*
Ay nay hawru kurba no	I just made my millet paste
Follay yan tunay bon	When I became possessed
Ay na kuso boogo	I broke the cooking pot
Ay na kusu goobo za ga leelaw	threw the cooking ladle
Ay nay kambewo sooro	I hit my husband
Dan gay kurnye soote	With a left-hand whip
Ce fa ceeri	He got one leg broken
Kambe fa ceeri	He got one arm broken
A go dima bon	He is in bed
Hay kulu sa tunandi	Nothing will heal him
Kala hari dungonda leesa	But hot porridge
Hari dungonda leesa	Hot porridge
Wala kuubu soorize hinza	And a three-strand whip
Day na walwal	I'll hit him hard
Ay ma te kuubora curayze	And disappear in the woods like a bird
Day na walwal	I'll hit him hard
Ama ne way Inna da Baaba	He'd call his mommy and daddy
Way Inna da Baaba	Was it mommy and daddy
See no ni na Maddu Tuku	Who told you to provoke Maddu.

This poem-song is about a young girl who is forced to marry a man she does not like, even though she has a boyfriend who is courting her. In the song, the young woman rebels against forced marriage by fighting to free herself from the man. She goes as far as beating her husband and suggesting that in a moment of rage, when she is possessed by a spirit, she might pour hot porridge on him. Since according to the norms of the society a woman must not raise a hand against her husband, the woman has to be possessed to do such a deed. It could be a fake possession. It could also be genuine, as some spirits fight whoever ill-treats their host, whether the person is a husband, or even a mother or father.

The five songs presented above suggest a strong subversive streak in the verbal art of women. The singers appear to have no fear of expressing their concerns about the values of society as these affect them. But despite this subversive aspect, women's verbal art carries signs of patriarchy, as will be seen in the second part of this study.

The most striking patriarchal sign in the next set of poem-songs is the recurrent theme of rivalry between women. It is reflected in many relationships between women:

Mother-in-law vs. bride
Sister-in-law vs. bride
Thin women vs. plump women
Senior wives vs. late-comers (second, third, and fourth wives).
Good looking vs. ugly
"good" bride vs. "bad" bride
tall vs. short

If we consider the recurrent rivalry between women in these selections, and if we think about how this rivalry is so present and real in women's interactions, one is bound to assume that it has to do with the way women are socialized. Many women wonder why a woman almost always sees in another woman a rival, even when there is no apparent reason for this rivalry.

For example, in the first poem-song plump women are set up against thin women, with the underlying message that plump means good, and thin means bad. In a society where being fat is a criterion of beauty, thin women appear as misfits and undesirable. And it is fat women who produce discriminatory poems about thin women. The patriarchal aspect of this is that women like to be plump because men like fat women, as many of their stories and jokes reveal. Of course when one asks women's groups that organize a fat women's festival why they want to be fat, some might answer, because they like it too. But this reason always comes after the first one, which is to make the husband happy. Also, the physical appearance of the woman is supposed to reflect how her husband is a hard worker and how he takes care of his wife or wives. If the woman is thin it implies that the man does not produce a good harvest. If she is fat it means the husband is a successful farmer and that he is not stingy, because the wife manages the food supply and the meals the way she likes, with the result that she gains weight.

The following poem-songs show how plump women make fun of skinny ones. The tone is always humorous and the woman being attacked is not supposed to be angry or react defensively.

Satara kanga doobu han	The woman who drinks millet bran
Da ga fun dayobon	On her way from the well
Mate no a ga te gaka	How does she walk
Ya ciine no a ga te gaka	Here is how she walks
Banda kulu ga zingino	Her buttocks shake
Satara kansi doobu han	The woman who does not drink millet bran
Da ga fun dayobon	On her way from the well
Mate no a ga te gaka	How does she walk
Nyay nyay no a ga te kaka	She goes nyay nyay
Ya wala gangi yoo ize	like a baby giraffe.

The singer matches the lyrics by imitating the walk of a plump woman coming back from the well, as well as that of the skinny woman.

In the next poem-song, the proud and fat woman challenges other women to look like her:

He wa kobayse	Clap your hands
Ay go ka	I'm coming
He wa kobayse	Clap your hands
Ay go ka	I'm coming
Bakay go ka	Though I do not see
Ay manday wadde	My equal (among you).

In the third poem-song, which follows, the speaker goes as far as insulting and cursing skinny women. This shows how hard plump women are on skinny women. They can insult them or even do mean or wicked things to them. For example, the Queen of the Fat Women might declare a skinny woman the slave of another woman, a fat one of course. This means that every day the skinny woman should do certain chores for the fat woman before doing her own housework.

Minkiriu	(expression for thinness)
Ga maati maatize yan	(descriptive of thinness)
Hando kan ga djaje	This coming month
Way faabo ga ye	Thin women will go back

Inga nya ra	To their mother's wombs
Irkoyse	For God's sake
Ima way faabay sambu	Take these thin women
Di ma konday beene	Bring them all the way up the sky
Di ma kambe ka iga yanay	Let them fall on the ground.

The fourth piece is a "conflictual duo" in which a plump and a skinny woman attack each other verbally. Such a poem can be very long as each woman uses her imagination to attack the other.

Gawo nya kooga	The dry gao tree
Kan fun Zarmaganda	That came from Zarmaganda
A go ga kay karaw	It is "standing" completely dry
Dinga karkaray	With its ethnic facial scars

In the first part of this poem, we hear the voice of the first wife, who is plump. She attacks the second wife indirectly through the metaphor of the gao tree. Thus, just like the tree, the second wife is said to be tall and dry (i.e., fleshless). The ethnic scarification mentioned is evidence that she is talking about her co-wife.

Gawo nya kooga	It is the very dry gao tree
Day gin kom ni kurnyc	That snatched your husband
Kala ni goro ga he	You had to sit and cry.

Here it is the second wife who answers back by claiming that although she is a gao tree, she has managed to snatch the husband from the plump first wife.

The fifth is a personal praise-poem produced by a small plump woman. In this piece she praises her own physical qualities. At the same time, she criticizes and makes fun of women whom she describes as her antithesis.

Tintirmay fantu bi	The tiny nice shade of the *fantu* tree
Gazera kante daaba	The short woman with a large base
A bi kaani gandase	It is because of its nice shade
No koyo na windi	That the owner put a fence around it
Tintirmay fantu bi	The tiny nice shade of the *fantu* tree
Gazera doogo deesi	The short woman, the tall woman
Man ci doogay kulu ga ay bara	I am not addressing all tall women
Dogo safa bon kayay	I'm talking about small-headed tall women.

By calling herself a *fantu* tree shade the praise singer claims that she is highly valuable for her husband, who is the owner of the *fantu* tree. This is the reason why the latter has made a fence to protect the tree (herself). Thus, her husband protects her the same way the farmer/owner of the *fantu* tree protects his tree.

Through this type of poem-song women themselves foster the rivalry between women. They invest much energy in these conflicts, as seen in the lyrics. These differences become more acute when women live as co-wives. In fact, there is a special type of poem-song that co-wives produce to fight each other verbally. Most of the time, they are produced to the rhythm of the pestle while women pound millet. For example, in this short poem-song one can easily guess that the singer/narrator is a late-comer:

Wonde beeray	"Senior" wives
Barma cilayze yan	The key to the silo
Wande kaynay	"Junior" wives
Mooto cilayze yan	The key to the car.

The senior wife incarnates the key to the silo and supervises the preparation of food for the family while the late-comer, possessor of the key, has the use of the car, and by extension, access to the husband. This reflects the fact that many polygamous men travel to Côte d'Ivoire with the late-comer in order to find work while the senior wife stays home. This is the case in the next poem-song.

Having heard the news that she and her husband will be leaving for Côte d'Ivoire, the second wife composes a mocking poem while pounding millet.

Balkissa Boboy	Balkissa Boboy
Ya go ga koy	Is leaving
Kamba ma haaru	Whoever wants can laugh
Kamba ma he	Whoever wants can cry
Kamba ma mudun te Bontoboy	If (s)he wants, (s)he can make
	A turban out of a pair of trousers
Kamba ma tonko ta kaliso	If (s)he wants, (s)he can use
	Hot pepper to make his/her underwear
Kamba ma hauru hiina butara	If (s)he wants, (s)he can
	Cook in a plastic pot
Buta ma manne, hauro ma ton	Let both the pot and the food burn.

But unfortunately for this second wife, the husband has heard how she is making fun of her co-wife, and he changes his mind about her departure. He decides to go with the senior wife to punish the second wife. Then the latter continues as follows:

Djamila walle wale wale	Djamila *walle wale wale*
Djamila saamo go ga koy	The dummy Djamila is going

Din koy saamatara cabe	If you go and show your stupidity
Nodin kan nyasi baabasi	Over there without your mother and father
Kala imin samba bido bido	You'll be sent [back home] like
Bido kan haari si ba ara	A waterless empty gourd
Din koy gin hauru tara dake	If you go and cook your tasteless food
Barzo go daaro kambe ga	The whip is under the bed.
Ay wace ga saamo	My co-wife/rival is stupid
Bina ga bi	And wicked
Ay wace binaya tondi no	Her heart is a stone
Ay wace binaya tondi no	Her heart is a stone
Karo ma bare nday wace yan	I wish the car crashes with her.

And the senior wife answers:

Zamayne ay wace	Because I said
Ay go ga koy	I'm going
Saama da izay kulu go ga he	The dummy and her kids are crying
Acaka nin	The aceke [Ivoirian dish] is done
Dundu kuso dake	The yam is being cooked
Inday maygida tu no ay ga ka	I am cooking for Maygida [the husband] and myself
Saama go gawo nyanywo cire	The stupid woman is under the gao tree
Saama na dambu tara	She's cooking her untasty food
Ji si romaji si ara	With no oil and no seasoning

These are short pieces that also work as "conflictual duos" in which the two wives fight verbally. They even insult each other. The husband is partly responsible for this, as it is his unfairness that makes the two women look down on each other and even fight. In most polygamous households the women are continually in conflict, each one struggling to be the favorite wife. Some men do not like this, while others take advantage of the situation. We see that the woman who is taking the trip with the husband is proud to show that her life would be better than that of her co-wife. Once in Côte d'Ivoire, she would cook Ivoirian dishes while the co-wife will cook bland, tasteless food as she says. The wife who is not going with the husband claims that the senior wife cannot cook well and urges the husband to beat her if she is not successful. This is the acceptance of wife-beating, which many people in the culture think can be justified.

Apart from the rivalry between co-wives, there is also competition between the bride and her mother-in-law. Here it is the conflict between two powerless people who find themselves at the bottom of the ladder of power, each one trying to gain some small control in a system that denies them power.

In the following poem-song the bride is fighting her mother-in-law:

Ay si hin izenya yanje	I cannot afford fighting a mother of many children
Nya ma ka nya kayna ma ka	The mother comes, her sister comes
Baaba kayna ma tun ga dake	The father's sister comes
I goga faafe soli ga kayga	They are all dangling their breast on me
Ha zogop*Zogop*	
Ha zoppaway*Zoppaway*	[onomatopoeic words that convey the movement of the old woman's breasts]

Also, in their role as regulators of the society, women support and perpetuate some sexist aspects of their culture. We have already seen how in the first part, a young bride denounces the hard work she has to do. But, despite that, the same subculture teaches young women to accept hardship as their lot. To be a woman means to be able to bear hardship without complaining, as seen in the poem-song above. This is why in the following poem-song, a young bride who complains about pounding a large quantity of millet is mocked:

Buffu baabu dadi	Worthless fat woman
Gaham beeri kan si goy bay	A fat body that knows no hard work
Saama ga duru, a ga heeni heeni	The stupid pounds and complains
A go mo buffu babu dadi.	Though she is fat, she's worthless.

These poems and songs are not atypical. They reflect the fact that patriarchal values such as rivalry or competition in the negative sense, which in Zarma is appropriately called *baba-ize-tarey*, literally "father-child-ness," permeates society. Thus, women are not exempt from it and quite often they are the ones who foster this value. The other value or counter-value, *nya-ize-tarey*, or "mother-child-ness," conveys the concept of cooperation, often viewed as a more feminine value. But women tend not to foster it much. Men and women incarnate both values to varying degrees, a phenomenon richly illustrated in the autobiographical narrative *L'Enfant noir* by Camara Laye as well as in many other texts.

In the case of the women depicted in these songs, one finds the more patriarchal and competitive spirit of *baba-ize-tarey*, normally associated with male children of different mothers but the same father, rising to the surface in somewhat negative ways among the singers. On one level, these women are protesting against the long-standing traditions marking a patriarchal and polygynous society. But on another level, among themselves, they incarnate the same "patriarchal" ways rooted in ancient values. They compete among themselves in a manner that echoes the competitiveness and conflict that marks relations between men. The oral epics of the past, as well as chronicles written in Arabic, report on the murderous results of these conflicts as princes who are the issue of the same father but of different mothers compete for the leadership of a society.

Even though women do raise their voices against what they see as unfair aspects of their culture, they unconsciously adopt patriarchal male values not only to convey their responses to male domination, as seen in the poem-songs about unwanted marriages, but also in their relations with each other. In this way, older women who are the preservers of traditions are the ones who socialize younger women to follow the "right path" set by tradition. In these poem-songs, subversion in the sub-culture of women is subverted by the adoption of values absorbed from the wider, male-dominated culture.

The messages conveyed in the poem-songs presented here appear also in those of other societies in the Sahel. The question is whether the same phenomenon occurs—subversion subverted by languages, behaviors, and adherence to patriarchal values. Further research on this little-studied subject by other scholars may reveal a pattern across the region.

NOTE

Poem-songs were recorded from a group of girls in Fandou, 10 January 2003, and in Deytagui, 20 January 2003, on the entertainment ground, the public space for the amusement of the youth. It is the place where girls and young men meet, sing, dance, and test each others' knowledge of verbal art such as riddles and proverbs.

I conducted an interview with older women in Deytagui, 20 January 2003. Deytagui is a small village in the Canton of Tondikandia, department of Filingué, in Tillabery Region, Niger Republic. I also conducted an interview with Zali, a woman from the village of Nazai in the Canton of Simiri.

WORKS CITED

Finnegan, Ruth. 1976. *Oral Literature in Africa*. Oxford: Oxford University Press.

Sidikou, Aïssata G. 2001. *Recreating Words, Reshaping Words: The Verbal Art of Women from Niger, Mali, and Senegal*. Trenton, N.J.: Africa World Press.

Sorgho, Germain J. 1984. La Tradition orale africaine face au défi de l'écriture: fossilisation forcée ou mutation nécessaire. In *La Tradition orale, source de la littérature contemporaine en Afrique*. Dakar: Les Nouvelles Éditions Africaines.

14

Muslim Hausa Women's Songs

Beverly B. Mack

The study of songs by Hausa women in northern Nigeria raises a major question for Western scholars. Since these performers both sing and compose poetry in writing, where is the line between the two genres, vocal and written? For Hausa listeners, there is no line between them as the two forms exist in a porous continuum of performance and communication. This study offers perspectives on the wide-ranging platform of Hausa performance communication through analysis of Hausa women's song and poetry,[1] both of which are marked by the Islamic influence that is integral to all aspects of Hausa culture.

Part of the problem for the researcher is Hausa terminology for the two genres. *Waƙa* (pl. *waƙoƙi,*) is the Hausa term for a broad range of works from poetry to declamation, all of which is normally sung or chanted. The term is not readily translated, but comprises a range of meanings in English from song to written verse. To the Hausa, however, it is all "song." Thus the plural term *waƙoƙi* is used here to refer collectively to both orally composed and written songs. The songs themselves are as varied in style and theme as the circumstances in which they are performed, and their content is gauged to the situation in which they are delivered. They are sung at naming ceremonies, at wedding celebrations, in praise of important people, as commentary on social behavior, as announcements of changes in social practices, as work songs, and as mnemonic teaching aids. That they occur in such a wide range of social situations is testimony to the genre's pervasive role in Hausa culture. The works analyzed here are popular pieces by contemporary Hausa women who use *waƙoƙi* as entertainment that is alternately didactic, informative, ritual-oriented, paced to domestic tasks, and celebratory.

The fact that each of these singers is an observant Muslim woman shapes the ways in which they use language. Even orally composed songs like ritual music for the spirit possession cult (*bori*), naming and wedding celebrations, and praise songs demonstrate in their language or style a foundation in a Muslim cultural context. In the written works, their relationship to Islamic literary contexts is evident in poetic features that echo patterns found in the Qur³ān and other spiritually focused sources. For this reason, the examination of oral and written Hausa Muslim women's songs in this study will rely not only on the messages of the lyrics, but also on literary techniques such as satire, irony, and metaphor as well as on non-verbal performances styles, patterning, and repetition. Islam provides essential keys to understanding the meanings of the songs.

In the Hausa language many forms of musical and literary expression are described by the term *waka*. The two closely related types of *wakoki—wakar baki* (oral) and *wakar rubutu* (written)—are quite similar. Sometimes they are indistinguishable, except by being categorized as *waka* I and *waka* II. Dalhatu Muhammad (1977, 9–14) notes the differences between these two classes of *wakoki* by men, but for women's *wakoki* the differences do not apply in the same way.[2]

The term "orality" refers to aesthetic works that are communicated through the spoken word. Traditional studies of both Arabic and Hausa poetics differentiate between the presumably non-Islamic oral performance and the more conservative written works, but of course the two cannot be separated entirely in any context, since they exist symbiotically in the culture. All art forms in a culture necessarily relate to one another because they serve to define the same context. To some degree, all Hausa poetry is oral, because both written and oral works are chanted, or sung in public performance.

The origins of written poetry are found in song and music. The root of the Arabic term for song, *nashiid,* means the raising of the voice, as well as referring to the work itself; the Arab adage "Song is the measure for poetry" (Adonis 1990, 15) indicates that song traditionally was the means of measuring rhyme and meter. "Meters are the foundations of melodies, and poems set the standard for stringed instruments."[3] Poetry's synonymity with recitation and song is evident in fourteenth-century historian Ibn Khaldun's observation:

> In the early period singing was a part of the art of literature, because it depended on poetry, being the setting of poetry to music. The literary and intellectual elite of the Abbasid state occupied themselves with it, intent on acquiring a knowledge of the styles and genres of poetry. (Cited in Adonis 1990, 15–16)

At the same time, oral recitation has long been the basis for Islamic education. "Oral instruction was the rule not only in the teaching of hadith, but also in other sciences and arts" (Schimmel 1994, 130). Oral poetic recitation is well integrated into Islamic life. Among the Hausa, written and oral works share common ground in their oral delivery. The oral poetic performances described here are at once decried and lauded by audiences who revel in the bawdiness of the works.

ORAL SONGS

Oral Hausa songs are not written, but only delivered extemporaneously. These pieces are not completely ephemeral, however, for they follow established patterns of the genre that may be studied almost as readily as one of the written poems. Repeated performances of extemporaneous orally composed songs on the same topic indicate that a poet's repertoire consists of many interchangeable patterns. Thus there is an established form for oral songs as there is for written ones.

The categories of public and private, royal and non-royal, constitute performance situations that often overlap. Female artists are not restricted to performance for certain occasions, but commonly move from one to another. For example, a woman who performs for a private audience of women during a naming ceremony might also perform in public for a mixed university audience. One who performs in the palace might also perform in the privacy of the women's quarters (in Hausa, *cikin gida;* in Arabic, *harem*) of a home in town. Oral poets perform by invitation only, unlike itinerant beggars who shout praises in public, hoping to collect money. A woman who is normally accompanied by an all-male chorus must sing without male accompaniment when she performs in the privacy of a home's *cikin gida,* because this area is off-limits to men who are not part of the household. These settings exclusive to women are the arenas for songs by women performers.

Many of the recordings I taped for this study were performed in a harem, with an audience restricted to the women of the household and their female friends, relatives, and guests. The recordings were made during wedding and naming celebrations, and during non-celebratory events, when music and song were purely for entertainment. Other recordings—especially those of professional women singers—were dubbed from local radio, television, and ministry tapes.[4] These recordings, often broadcast on local media, regularly are heard and enjoyed by the public, and especially by women in seclusion who model their own songs on them.[5]

WRITTEN SONGS

Written songs are usually delivered orally, though they may also be printed in local newspapers. They are more often transmitted over the radio and performed live, and thus, they remain identified as songs, regardless of their mode of composition. The more conservative written works are also delivered orally, not just passed around in published form. Indeed, it is in the oral recitation of a written work that authorship and credibility can be confirmed. Authorship often is woven into the end of the piece, but is confirmed in its recitation by a scholar who knows the work and can verify its authenticity, correcting it to conform to its authentic state. Oral recitation is the correct means of presenting written works.

Literacy has been a part of Hausa culture for many centuries, since the advent of Islam in the region. Hausa traders and peripatetic scholars with Arabic literacy as early as the sixteenth century told stories and were the subjects of stories, wrote letters and made lists for a paying illiterate public, and perpetuated oral traditions about Arab origins of early settlers in Hausaland. Fifteenth-century King Muhammad Rumfa's innovations in Kano's royal court are remembered to this day in oral histories in verse. He is renowned in oral traditions as "the Arab King, of wide sway!" (Palmer 1967, 111–112). Hausa oral traditions are replete with literate characters whose scholarly acumen often functions as the magic that can resolve the tale's dilemma. Thus, Arabic literacy has been known about in the region for at least four centuries, even if it has been the privilege of only a minority of the population. Those who cannot read and write surely can talk. The medium of communication is Hausa, but Islamic precepts and Arabic language are integral to the analysis.

Hausa is the *lingua franca* of the region, and even those who actively promoted Islam and its preference for Arabic have acknowledged the importance of using a commonly understood language. In the nineteenth century the Fodiyo clan produced a proliferation of written narrative and poetry, much of it dealing with theological and political perspectives on the Sokoto jihad. Some of it, however, covered issues of common concern, like morality, practical aspects of conversion, social order in a reformed Islamic state, and women's roles in society. Nana Asma'u recognized the oral nature of Hausa culture, so she wrote the works she felt should reach the people at large in Hausa instead of her first language, Fulfulde: the Qur'ān, *Sufi Women,* and *Be Sure of God's Truth.* In terms of content, religious concerns were integral to the curriculum, but not its sole focus. On the contrary, contemporary concerns had to be part of the resocialization process that confirmed the jihad's success in Nigeria. It was not enough to tell people about God; they also needed to be instructed how to pray, what to wear and eat, how to conduct themselves, and how to think about their history. The oral dissemination of these verses was central to the resocialization of jihad battle refugees, and instrumental in reforming Islam in Hausa culture. In writing these documents originally in Hausa, Nana Asma'u rendered them immediately available to the masses, most of whom were not literate and spoke only Hausa. These works were meant to be committed to memory by both the itinerant (*Yan Taru*) teachers, and then their students, young women in seclusion in their homes. Singing these works constituted the lesson plan, and served as a lesson that students could integrate into their own experience, even without writing it down. In both oral and written works repetition is a central mnemonic device that depends on metaphoric transformation to save it from becoming boring. Schimmel discusses poetic repetition in high Islamic poetry as involving the circumambulation of a central idea, focusing attention on it from all directions, just as the pilgrim in Mecca devotes her focus to the Kaaba. Using a repeated rhyming word or phrase (*radif*), the poet "tries to approach the Divine from all possible new angles to give at least a faint idea of His greatness" (1994, 115). This technique would be at least implicitly familiar to Muslims familiar with the Qur'ān and poetic expression related to it.

SINGERS, MUSICIANS, AND POETS

Studies of poetry and song in Hausa culture have focused on poets, male praise singers, popular singers, and musicians (Ames and King 1971; Daba 1981; Furniss 1996; Muhammad 1977; Smith 1965), but none has profiled just women singers. Praise singers have been described as praise shouters, or "masters of begging" (*maroƙa,* pl.), as often as they are called "masters of song" (*mawaƙa,* pl.) because they rely on the patronage of their subjects for their income. The praise singer's low social status has been the subject of studies that emphasize singers' high income and powerful capacity for social influence, even in the face of their low social standing. They are often considered to be non-professionals. However, the social status of a poet is quite high in relation to that of singers and musicians, perhaps because literacy and the pursuit of knowledge are so highly esteemed in an Islamic culture. Despite the existence of a rich variety of popular song that defines contemporary Hausa culture, most scholarly works have focused narrowly on the extremes of the continuum: there seems to be only ephemeral praise song or written poetry. In fact, the complex array of Hausa singers and songs defies simple description. Each form of musical artistry overlaps with many others, and each singer influences and is influenced by others in his or her performance.

The singer is less likely than the poet to see his or her performance in print unless someone records and transcribes those works, as is the case here. But contemporary music is popular throughout the culture, and its form depends upon its function. Singers mix words and music, performing with or without accompaniment, touring the region for performances, and sometimes cutting records or recording songs for radio and television broadcast. Hausa musicians never perform on the streets, or without invitation, but always for specific events to which they have been invited as paid performers. Among the women in this category, some have female choruses or bands, with whom they can perform either for public, mixed audiences or in private, exclusively female settings. On the other hand, female singers who have male bands must perform without accompaniment for private women's events. In a royal setting, the emir has his own royal musicians, men whose job it is to perform only for him, for special occasions throughout the year.

Performers in the category of praise singer function as public relations people promoting specific patrons, which they accomplish by shouting praise epithets without musical accompaniment. A praise singer's status depends on the patron served and the material produced, both of which affect audience perception of the role. Female praise singers perform only in the royal setting, because it would be unseemly for an adult woman to be wandering around the city, seeking money on the streets. Royal settings may provide the most richly compensated and most restrictive venue for the delivery of praise epithets, which in this setting serve to announce the arrival of the emir in procession, and confirm his position by reminding the audience of his accomplishments, lineage, and affiliations. Since the royal praise singer is attached to the royal house, it is rare that he or she will perform for other patrons, although exceptions sometimes are made, as in Maizargadi's case, discussed below.

Other public praise singers (*mawaka,* pl.) for wealthy patrons act as freelance artists, performing for various individuals on special occasions. Their purpose is to confirm the high status of the patron, and the quality of their praise determines the compensation the patron gives them.[6] Imitating this form, others known as beggar-singers (*maroka,* masc.; *marokiya,* fem.) hang about the streets, shouting praise epithets for whomever they see whose attire and/or entourage indicates ability to pay. These shouters of praise epithets are poorly regarded in society as having little skill, perhaps by virtue of their not having honed their craft sufficiently to succeed in performing for higher-status patrons. Beyond the confines of the palace, these praise singers and beggars are only men.

The female counterpart of the *mawaka* (masc., sing.) is the *mawakiya,* or more specifically, *zabiya* (pl. *zabiyoyi*). A *zabiya* performs for the emir, and lives near the palace so that she may be summoned whenever she is needed. The term *zabiya* has been said to come from the word for guinea fowl because the woman's ululations are said to sound like the bird's shrill cry.[7] But the royal *zabiya* does not ululate; the *marokiya* who accompanies her does. Palace women make adamant distinctions between those who shout praises and those who ululate, explaining that the work of the *marokiya* is different from that of the *zabiya,* and less complicated. They merely "speak praise epithets when the Emir passes by, they say 'Tread softly' ['*Takawa a hankali*']" and ululate. The *zabiya* proves herself to be a professional singer by the skill of her performance. Women in the harem recognized Maizargadi's work as that of an accomplished artist because of her ability to sustain running narrative replete with both epithets and historical allusions.[8] The royal *zabiya* may also receive a royal title, thus raising her status above that of the *marokiya*.[9] Thus the *zabiya* is felt to hold a higher social status than the *marokiya*.[10]

Royal male musicians have been discussed in several studies.[11] They are "in constant attendance at the palace, and announce the arrival of the distinguished visitors . . . by trumpet fanfares, drumming and [praise]shouting. They also salute the king . . . nightly during the annual feast of Ramadan" (Smith 1965, 31). These male musicians[12] perform for the Emir in public and private gatherings of other men, but only their female counterpart, the royal *zabiya,* is allowed to accompany the Emir all the way into the *harem,* the heart of the palace, the women's quarters.

METAPHOR

Among the Hausa, poetic creative capability is judged by one's facility with metaphor, the juxtaposition of disparate images to establish an effect unanticipated by either of those images alone. The more complex a metaphor is, the better it is judged to be. Any network of interrelated visions inspires, more readily than an intellectual response, an emotional response that is difficult to describe, as linguistic spareness fosters a fecundity of aesthetic appreciation. The combination of images in metaphoric technique creates far more than the sum of those parts. Not only does a good metaphor require a plethora of related images, but also those images should be distinct, even weirdly unrelated. Indeed, the more distinct the images compared, "the stranger the image appears and the more delight it arouses in the soul" (Adonis 1990, 46). Metaphor has been described as the "magic" through which poetical speech gives a multiplicity of meanings in a simple form. Good metaphor depends on distance from cliché and readily understood simile. A comparison of strangely juxtaposed images challenges and pleases the listener, whose imaginative appreciation of the contrast is at odds with her intellectual understanding. Determining the quality of good poetry is an imprecise science: "meaning in poetry . . . is like the pearl in a shell . . . Not every thought will lead to the discovery of what it contains, nor every idea be permitted to reach it; not everyone will succeed in splitting open the shell, thereby becoming one of the people of knowledge" (al-Jurjani in Adonis 1990, 47–48). The effort to understand is what underlies the process of appreciation; as Hausa poet Hajiya Mai Duala said, "Crack the shell if you would know the color of the nut" (*Song for the Emir of Ningi,* 1. 7). Knowing what is at its essence requires effort.[13]

The complexity required of effective metaphor is intensified when dealing with material from another culture; literal meaning can be quantified and translated, but figurative meaning must be intuited. Puns and jokes work by the same technique, which is why one cannot laugh unless one is sufficiently literate in the joke's "cultural language" to understand the common ground between the disparate images that creates a synthesis of differences: "extreme convergence in extreme divergence."[14] Indeed, metaphoric expression defines the audience, unifying them in a mutual understanding of the performer's symbolic allusions, and creating a community of the informed. The Hausa poets who rely on metaphoric language in their works appeal to their audiences to interpret what is implied by the metaphors inherent in the figures of speech they use. The use of metaphor involves "the capacity to form or acknowledge a (progressively more select) community, and thereby to establish an intimacy between the teller and the hearer" (Cohen 1980, 7). The mutual acknowledgment of a metaphor signals a bond between audience and performer. Whether alluding to the unspeakable or the sacred, the poem's multiple meanings are understood by a community of individuals who share a common culture. Thus, the cross-cultural poetic analysis that characterizes this study is a means of examining Hausa culture at its deepest levels.

ISLAM AND POETRY

Islamic influence affects the lives of both the literate and the illiterate. The Hausa/Fulani women of northern Nigeria are Muslim, a fact that determines their values, ambitions, and opportunities in ways distinct from the contexts of non-Muslim women. The measure of Islamic influence is little understood in Western cultures at the beginning of the second millennium; at this point in history the non-Muslim world is conditioned to expect that Muslim women's lives are restricted by religious tenets that constrain their circumstances. The Hausa Muslim women of this study work through their social system to achieve what they want, just as Western women negotiate demands on their social roles. The Muslim women among whom I lived and whose literary works I recorded for three years in northern Nigeria are typical of middle-class, moderately educated women in the region. They and their artistry are not exceptions to the social order, but are representative of women in their culture.

Hausa Muslim women's daily life is affected by the importance of the sacred word. From the moment that a child's name and a Muslim prayer of welcome are whispered in her ear just after birth, the word of God is meant to have profound meaning for every individual. Children begin the practice of formal prayer five times a day as early as age three or four, even if only in imitation of adults. The ritual of praying five times a day is arguably the most important of a Muslim's five obligations,[15] and it is through these daily prayers that an individual's attitude toward her relationship to God is felt to be shaped. The Prophet Muhammad understood that belief could not be legislated, but habits could be instilled; through the habit of prayer five times a day, a Muslim lives in constant remembrance of God.[16]

Just as oral songs and written poems overlap in style and form, so too their themes are often contingent. Among the Hausa the song traditionally has been an instrument of political and religious advocacy.[17] Written poems by Hausa women fulfill the same traditional function; political life in Nigeria is active, and Islamic traditions render literature that reflects religious concerns. Many of the themes central to the oral compositions offer critical, frequently satiric commentary, while the written works represent Islamic didacticism.

A blend of traditional and Western philosophies is evident in the predominant themes of these works. Founded on the Islamic orientation characteristic of Hausa literature, these poems comment primarily on the acquisition of knowledge, community solidarity, and historical accounts. Each of these concerns is of an Islamic orientation by virtue of its being related to religious obligation. First, as discussed earlier, literacy is necessary for studying the Qur'ān, and thus important to one's salvation. Second, community solidarity is founded on a sense of brotherhood among people, specifically manifested in northern Nigeria by association with religious brotherhoods.[18] Third, historical accounts, especially genealogies, but also narratives of contemporary political issues and the individuals involved in them, reinforce the hierarchy of authority which until very recently has been closely linked to the Islamic religious community. While the oral works critique the commingling of traditional and Western values, the pervasive intention of the written works is the promotion of a sense of progressive development to benefit both individual and state.[19]

The orally composed works, like the written, are sprinkled with opening invocations to God ("Let us begin in the name of God the Almighty, the Merciful") and invocations for God's aid. But in accordance with Hausa praise song tradition they also exhibit varying degrees of criticism—from good-natured critiques to biting satire. When they are part of spirit possession cult (*bori*) performance, the orally composed songs juxtapose reference to God with reference to spirits and requests for money; such simultaneous expression of the sacred and the irreverent occurs in performances of oral songs outside the *bori* environment as well. Opportunities for oral song performance cover the widest possible range of Hausa social experience, from the most exclusively private situation to a public setting with a general audience. These songs can be made to suit any social setting as the composer tailors her material to the individuals and the particular situation. The content of the oral performance, therefore, will describe the subject and situation for which it is created. The degree to which it is satiric reflects the relative levity or solemnity of the occasion, and the relative status of the performer and patron. The more solemn or important the occasion, the more subdued the performance. Those who perform in circumstances at the extreme top and bottom of the social hierarchy (as in a royal setting, and for *bori*, respectively) are accomplished musicians whose ability is well established. They provide the aesthetic model for other, newer artists who perform in public in less noteworthy circumstances. The content of works by consummate performers and novices may differ in quality, but not in intention, for the aim is always to praise and criticize one's subject with as many diverse epithets as one can. While written works more often include narrative accounts set in poetic style, oral performances are usually comprised of laudatory and critical description of their subjects. They are most readily employed for entertaining at purely celebratory events, or as historical accounts of leaders or events that have occurred in the past.

The topics treated in the written works in this study are for the most part relevant to the secular world, and gauged toward practical concerns. The acquisition of knowledge is discussed in these works in many varieties, and each work itself constitutes a lesson plan on a particular topic. Some of them advocate the unified effort of a community of the faithful, while other works are important as historical or political accounts. They include works such as a catalogue of the city wards in Kano, an account of the Biafran war, and memorials to fallen political leaders. While these topics are clearly secular in nature, they are set in traditional literary form, and are embellished with phrases that reflect traditional Islamic trust in God's will.

WESTERN AND TRADITIONAL INFLUENCES

Hausa women's poems reflect the cultural context in which they are produced, so they are replete with allusions to traditional and Western values that are

often in conflict with one another. But just as Hausa performing artists derive
a modern form by mingling stylistic features of oral and written poems, so
a familiar admixture of traditional and Western influences is evident in the
content of these works, reflecting the complexity of daily life in Kano. Features
of metaphoric language discussed earlier are set in structures of inherited and
adopted social attitudes that distinguish the predominantly contextual nature
of these works.

Both oral and written works contain images of material modernization in
northern Nigeria. Conservative written poems describe material culture in a
framework that praises the "progressive" nature of some Western influences
(driving cars, universal primary education, the children's hospital, the benefit
of a census) and the detriments the West has brought to traditional Hausa society (drugs, indecent attire). The least reverent—primarily the oral songs—
criticize most freely the social conflicts created by such influence, their praise
of attendant economic benefits notwithstanding. They are also critical of traditional mores. Pervasive among these various treatments of diverse themes and
images, however, is the common concern of women interpreting social situations in regard to their own changing roles in Hausa society.

EDUCATION

Attitudes toward the acquisition of knowledge—whether abstract or concrete,
philosophical or practical—are evident in both written and oral works. With
its long history of Islamic literacy, northern Nigeria has fostered for centuries
the education of young boys in local Qurʾānic schools (*makaranta allo*), where
they are taught fundamental literacy skills through the medium of religious instruction. Women of religious or wealthy families are given the opportunity to
share such education, though they are taught for fewer years. The education of
women has long taken second place to the education of men in society.[20] Theoretically, intellectual development parallels religious awareness as one learns
through literacy to understand more fully God's message: "He has revealed to
you the Qurʾān. Some of its verses are precise . . . and others are ambiguous"
(Sura 18:54–55). The Prophet Muhammad advised that seeking knowledge is a
religious duty; a famous *hadith* recommends, "Seek ye knowledge, even unto
China."[21] Active promotion of intellectual development has always been at the
heart of Islamic ideology, from the inception of Islam. However, since patriarchy took hold as the predominant social order in the world during the same
historical period in which Islam unfolded, the result has been that education
is denied to women in many polities that became Islamic. When women feel
moved to justify their ambition to acquire education, they look to Qurʾānic

sources, where gender equity is expected, even though it did not unfold as outlined by divine mandate.[22]

In northern Nigeria a traditional system of Islamic education was in place in the seventeenth and eighteenth centuries. In the nineteenth century jihad leader Shehu Usman ɗan Fodiyo overtly supported the education of women. He advocated the obligation of men to facilitate the education of their wives and daughters, remembering that the Prophet said a man who educates his daughter will receive twice the heavenly reward of a man who educates only his sons. The Shehu's attitude was exemplified by his prolific scholar-daughter Nana Asmaʾu, whose renown as an intellectual and educator of both men and women spread throughout West Africa. Her example is not unique. Her sister Maryam took over from Asmaʾu in the training of women teachers (*yan taru*), and another woman, Tamodî, took over from Maryam in the training of women, a tradition which continues in Sokoto to the present. When the British colonized Nigeria in the late nineteenth century, Islamic schools still included women scholars.[23] The Western educational systems introduced by the British at the beginning of the twentieth century, however, served the needs of men, not women, following the pattern established in Britain. Even as the British schools appeared to serve the needs of young men, they were eschewed by many, and perceived as a threat to traditional educational systems and a signal of the breakdown of traditional mores in society. Western education in Nigeria in the late twentieth century has been viewed alternately as a vehicle for corruption and debasement of traditional values, and as a means toward progressive development. The coexistence of such conflicting attitudes is not surprising; either stance may be supported by various interpretations of passages of the Qurʾān. Ambiguity like that found in the Qurʾān occurs in other written literature as well.

The "war on ignorance" (*Yaki da Jahilci*) is the name of a movement that originated around 1950 when leaders of the Northern Region realized that years of northern resistance to the kind of Christian missionary primary and secondary schools that had proliferated in the south had resulted in an economic disadvantage to northerners. Their lack of English literacy meant that they were not able to fill new jobs being created with the establishment of British banks and other foreign businesses. Suddenly British-educated southern Nigerians, many of them Christians, were flooding into the north for employment opportunities. As the British prepared to leave Nigeria just prior to independence in 1960, it became clear that those with literacy in English would not only have jobs in the commercial sectors, but would also be the ones to qualify for government positions in the new independent polity that was about to unfold. Realizing their disadvantaged position, northern leaders began a regional program to educate in the north, an effort whose aim was as much to bolster their own party's popularity as to fulfill more altruistic goals. Both the government and individuals participated in promoting the cause of literacy. Sa'adu Zungur, one of the first poets writing on secular topics to be published widely, began at this time to write on the need for Western education among the Hausa (Hofstad 1971, 28).[24] In 1963, the sardauna of Sokoto, Ahmadu Bello, initiated a "*jihad* against ignorance" organized by a committee of northern men who strove to foster unity among northerners along religious lines (Paden 1973, 184). Bello, who was the premier of the north, promoted a government based on Islam. His political endeavors were coupled with a public campaign against illiteracy, which was couched in terms of religious obligation. Local government campaigns for self-awareness, self-improvement, and appropriate participation in public endeavors began under his influence and spread throughout the north. The program fostered adult literacy classes, health and nutrition courses, instruction in social services,[25] and later, in January 1974, the promotion of free primary education. Hauwa Gwaram and Hajiya Yar Shehu were young adults during this period, and the influence of these campaigns is evident in their poetry, many of which were written in support of these programs. Several songs treat these issues from a perspective of fulfilling one's religious obligation through the acquisition of knowledge, a concept that becomes clear with the realization of Bello's role as a spiritual as well as political leader in the north.

A severe but highly dramatic portrayal of the dangers of ignorance is narrated in Hauwa Gwaram's *Song for the War on Ignorance* (circa 1974). Nomau, the main character of the work, represents the stereotype of the uneducated farmer, whose life is fraught with difficulty because he cannot read, write, or calculate simple money transactions. His ignorance invites abuse by others, who wish to take advantage of him, and in that way he inadvertently encourages their participation in evil. He is cheated by traders on the street, robbed by gamblers, and exploited by those who (inaccurately) write his messages for him. Nomau takes the wrong road, both literally and figuratively. Following a lengthy catalogue of his misdeeds, Hauwa Gwaram summarizes: "He took a road one shouldn't, and was arrested / He brought it all on himself by not fighting ignorance" (v. 24). Fighting ignorance is like jihad in its true meaning, the struggle against negative impulses, and the effort to perfect oneself. This obligation of jihad as a personal struggle for perfection is incumbent upon every Muslim, and so, by extension, Nomau's is a religious failure. This would be very clear to Muslims in the region. The metaphor of taking the wrong road is also closely connected to religious obligation, for a Muslim is obligated to follow the *sunna,* or the example of the life of Muhammad. *Sunna* also is understood to mean "path" or "way," so the implication is clear to Gwaram's audience. The metaphor also implies that the need for worldly knowledge parallels the need for religious knowledge; both ensure success. Gwaram criticizes Nomau for not having sought religious knowledge: "May God protect us from failing to seek advice from religious men / Do you hear? Such is the failure to fight ignorance" (v. 26).[26] She is addressing a woman in this verse; "*kin ji?*" is "Do you hear?" with the "you" in feminine form.

Nomau's ignorance is connected to his lack of piety, for he ignored the opportunity to acquire literacy skills in a Qurʾānic school, just as he failed to pursue other opportunities for self-improvement. Primary schools and adult education classes offer paths away from ignorance, too:

45　　Adults and children, we are called to class,
　　　So we can understand everything and live without ignorance.
46　　Children should go to primary classes and seek education,
　　　Adults should go to classes too, in the war on ignorance.[27]

Nomau ignores all forms of education, and his unhappiness is the consequence of failing to strive actively to acquire knowledge. In this poem Hauwa Gwaram emphasizes the need to acquire knowledge by any of many possible means, thus satisfying one's moral obligation. She compares Nomau's blind ignorance to that of his ancestors, who suffered from lack of opportunities for education:

In times of ignorance [before Islam] people wouldn't admit to
Sickness, because of ignorance.
They ground together potash, herbs, and bark,
To spread all over their bodies, because of ignorance.[28]

Nomau's refusal to pursue any of his several opportunities for education constitutes a moral failure on his part, for he has not progressed beyond the situation of his ancestors. Early in the work Gwaram has warned: "You know about taking up the rope of knowledge, and ignoring it, / Everyone who leaves wisdom [aside] endures bad fortune" (v. 4).[29] But Nomau eschews the "rope of knowledge" which could be his lifeline to salvation and upward mobility. Ignorance, like sin, Gwaram implies, is a poison that debilitates Nomau and ruins his life: "Stop and listen, ignorance is filth. / The damage it does and that of a snake are no different" (v. 50). The "war on ignorance" movement established by the government to promote Nigeria's progressive development in the 1960s assigned to each citizen a responsibility to improve his own situation. When Nomau makes no progress in his own life because of failing to pursue the advocated means toward upward mobility, he is compounding his lack of piety with social irresponsibility. He is simultaneously a sinner and a bad citizen.

This poem always inspires great amusement, increasing disbelief at the subject's unfathomable stupidity, and finally much head-shaking. Its popularity may be based on its portrayal of a character that may safely be ridiculed by everyone who hears the work. Nomau is a stereotype through which Hauwa Gwaram hopes to put forth her message without blatantly advocating the concept of self-help. Those who join in condemning Nomau's habits are transforming a negative role model into a positive one by disapproving of those habits. Thus the critical nature of the work, in which the audience takes an active part by expressing disapproval, is executed to positive ends—the revelation of the path to moral righteousness through the acquisition of knowledge.

In thematic contrast, Maimuna Choge's Bayero University Hausa Conference performance (1980) provides a platform for satiric rebuttal to Hauwa Gwaram's highly moralistic views on education. Choge's praise of Western university education is belied by the bawdy execution and irreverent import of such praise. Her performance opens with a brief doxology praising God, followed by praise to *Inna*. While *Inna* is a common term for mother, it is also a name for the principal figure of the pre-Islamic *bori* spirit-possession cult (Nicolas 1975, 151–152).[30] Thus, Choge's arrangement begins with the irreverent juxtaposition of both God and non-Islamic possession cult goddesses, setting the tone for her performance. Throughout the evening, Choge maintains a running parallel of reverent and irreverent references, juxtaposing contrastive images of many types through her work, addressing the audience indirectly by invoking God to grant them money. The patron pays the praise singer, yet God is the universal patron whose generosity provides everyone with what is needed to live. Implying such a parallel between the human patron and God is an irreverent suggestion to begin with; the sacrilegious tone it represents is reinforced by the repetition of the exhortation, "May God grant us money!" recurring nearly as a leitmotif in the work.

Choge expresses ambivalence toward the merits of Western culture. She is being paid to praise the university students at this conference, which she does at great length, commenting on their prospects for material gain, high status, and professional incomes. She here extends praise to an extreme, saying, "All those who do not hold the pen do useless work" (1. 47). Choge suggests by her commentary that there is no better-paying or higher-status job in Nigeria than a white-collar one. Then she turns to the subject of professionalism in general, reminding the audience of her own relatively exclusive position; her own material accoutrements rival those of the educated elite. Thus, Choge's second perspective is a direct contradiction of the first, transforming her previous comment on the value of education into satire.

Finally she is explicit, stating her position relative to that of an educated individual: "And for a long time he has held the pen; for a long time I have been well off" (1. 75). The two professions represent the highest and lowest on the social scale, but Choge's point is that there is little difference between the two. They both involve sufficient economic gain, which is expressed in the acquisition of material wealth. Here is none of Hauwa Gwaram's altruistic belief in the virtues of acquiring knowledge for the inherent betterment of an individual's character. Choge finds neither spiritual nor moral virtue in the acquisition of an education. Instead she draws a parallel between the educated professionals and the performer of orally composed songs; each type of performer, she implies, is in his or her profession primarily for economic gain and its attendant status.

The audience's response to Choge's performance indicates that they delight in her irreverent imagery and behavior. When she shakes her body provocatively, they shower her with whistles and shouts of approvals. Although nearly all members of the audience are involved in academia, they understand Choge's remarks about economic gain. She can say what respectable, scholarly individuals cannot: that an altruistic approach to one's work is a fine preoccupation, but it will not feed one's family. These audience members sincerely believe in the social benefits inherent in education, but like scholars everywhere they are fortunate to be among an elite that can benefit from a loftier and less physically stressful livelihood than most individuals must pursue. They understand that, and accept from Choge criticism of their profession that they prefer not to voice themselves. Choge delights them with risqué humor, satiric commentary, and provocative behavior, but under it all there lies a truth that her audience recognizes and must accept. Their rising status is an indication of progress only as it represents their economic gain. It is not necessarily the pursuit of knowledge for moral salvation, as advocated by Hauwa Gwaram.

EDUCATING WOMEN THROUGH POETRY

Several of Hauwa Gwaram's poems were written as teaching aids when she worked for the Kano state government, teaching adult education courses on nutrition and childcare for women in the 1960s. In *Song for the Course at the Children's Hospital and for Public Involvement* Gwaram advises women on food preparation and water sterilization, personal hygiene, and household responsibilities (verses 8, 15, 16, 26–30). She appeals to women directly to help educate themselves by attending a clinic on public health and maternity care (vv. 2–5). Advising women to bring their friends to classes, she urges them to trust in Western medicine and the efficacy of regular medical check-ups at the clinic (vv. 18–20, 35, 39–40).

From one perspective, Hauwa Gwaram's participation in this adult education program seems indicative of her explicit approval of these forms of Western intervention in traditional society. At the same time, however, her attitude, her activity, and her writing all reflect the nineteenth-century example of Nana Asmaʾu, whose activist role in educating women on the same topics was also accomplished through the use of poetry. Although both Hauwa Gwaram and Hajiya Yar Shehu consistently cited Nana Asmaʾu as their role model ("Why should I need permission from a man to write poetry? Nana Asmaʾu didn't!"), the idea of women educating other women has long been current in Hausa culture. The works produced by these two contemporary poets share the same concerns evidenced in Asmaʾu's works. Such parallels are not coincidental, but testify to the underlying presumption in Hausa culture that the pursuit of knowledge is required of all individuals. This perspective surely is connected to the rights guaranteed to women by Islam, and, more importantly, women's awareness of those rights, which cannot be denied.

Hauwa Gwaram's participation in the adult education program is indicative of her explicit approval of attitudes about women's discreet comportment, for women did not have to meet publicly for these classes; the meeting place itself was secluded from men, and women needed their husbands' permission to attend. Ultimately, however, attendance at these classes ensured for Kano women—and especially for Hauwa Gwaram herself—a greater freedom in the name of a morally upright pursuit, the value of which could not be questioned by devout, reasonable Muslim men.

Hausa women maintain independent incomes by cooking snacks or making craft items that their children sell for them on the streets or in the market. Traditionally they were the spinners for huge commercial cloth markets. In this way a woman in seclusion may participate in the market economy without violating her social obligation to remain in the home. Obligation to seclusion is incumbent upon upper-class urban women who are not white-collar professionals. In Kano there are many examples of highly educated professional women who serve in jobs in the public sector without being expected to be secluded in the home. Women are attorneys, doctors, broadcasters, journalists, and educators in public schools. In addition, huge numbers of rural women work in the fields, go to market, fetch water, and gather wood, among other activities in public. Some of the classes offered to women included craft classes to establish or improve their skills, while others dealt with literacy skills to ensure against their being cheated in trading (vv. 36–38, 41–43).

Hauwa Gwaram advocates women's acquisition of skills associated with Western education systems, and she encourages women's participation in the endeavor to educate other women. What Gwaram suggests—the progressive development of each individual's skills—can benefit the state as well as the individual by raising income level and standard of living, thus buttressing the nation's economy. Every suggestion, however, is made within the context of Islamic philosophy. The jobs and skills women are encouraged to acquire are all domestic, in keeping with traditional Islamic tenets specifying a woman's prime responsibility to her family and home.

Binta Katsina's oral composition *Song for the Women of Nigeria* echoes on one level Hauwa Gwaram's plea for "progressive" behavior. On another level it is anarchistic. She expresses a belief in the potential professional equality between Nigerian men and women, encouraging women to teach, to do clerical work, to work for the government. She assures women that what is traditionally "men's work" can also be their own, advocating that women pilot airplanes, drive vehicles, and run machines (ll. 300, 344, 358, 360). The skills required for these jobs are literacy skills that are best acquired at public schools outside the home rather than the skills learned in traditional Qurʾānic classes or at home. Her song clarifies the need for Nigerian women in the public work force, and supports the desirability of literacy among women. In these respects it is expressive of a "progressive" approach to economic and educational matters.

Attendance at secondary schools requires that women travel outside the home, a situation that presents a two-fold problem between traditional Hausa men and women. First, the Hausa woman who is secluded in the home would have to relinquish seclusion, a sign of high social and economic status, to attend classes, and later, to work outside the home. This is a situation that could constitute a loss of social standing for both husband and wife. This dilemma can be solved very easily by the use of hijab, the "full veil" that assures respectability for the woman who moves about in public. The second part of the problem is one faced by many young Hausa couples that have tried to become more "Western" by circumventing the first dilemma with the rationale that pursuit of a higher degree constitutes a sign of higher social status in itself. While this reasoning mitigates the first concern, a new potential problem is created in regard to women's fulfillment of their religious obligations to oversee the domestic sphere, although most families at this level can afford to hire domestic help. A woman who is preoccupied with her profession cannot fulfill her religious obligation to her family and home. Binta Katsina's song, purportedly commissioned by a national government eager to get women into the work force, advocates what may be a progressive new role for many Nigerian women, but in the context of Islamic Hausa culture, it deviates so thoroughly from what is considered acceptable that it may as easily be considered criticism of Western feminism as imitative of it.[31]

One of the beneficial legacies of Western influence on educational systems among the Hausa is the concern engendered for the establishment of primary school systems sufficient to educate all children. The consensus among Hausa people is that such education is beneficial to all, though they may disagree on the importance of university or post-primary (secondary, technical, teacher-training) education for young women. The concept of universal primary education is not without its problems. It can seriously damage the economic welfare of a lower-class family in several ways. First, the children who attend classes during the day have less time to help with household chores, selling market items, and running errands. Second, *free* universal primary education has not yet been instituted; parents must pay school fees, buy books, supplies, and school uniforms, and provide lunches or money for midday meals.[32] The first problem could be dealt with more willingly were the economic burdens reduced by the institution of free primary schools, the subject of Hauwa Gwaram's poem, *Song for the Institution of Free Primary Education.*

Appealing to individuals of all walks of life, Hauwa Gwaram seeks to foster a sense of solidarity on this issue (vv. 2–13). The length of her catalogue emphasizes the magnitude of her appeal; no one is omitted in what she hopes will be a unified effort for the benefit of all. As is common with such lists, the penultimate and final citations are magnified by their positions; in them, Hauwa Gwaram speaks of women's roles in the effort toward free primary education, and finally, like every devout Muslim, she leaves the matter in God's hands:

> Prior to this [time] few women were teachers;
> Well now we will try to make some improvements.
> May God give us the power to achieve our hearts' desires,
> And see teachers who give universal primary education. (vv. 17 18)

Hauwa Gwaram's explanation of women's roles is made important to begin with by its strategic and emphatic placement near the end of the list, but it is further enhanced by this juxtaposition to stanza eighteen's line, "May God give us the power to achieve our hearts' desires." Implicit in this line arrangement is the wish to promote women's active participation in the teaching profession.

COMMUNITY SOLIDARITY

Hauwa Gwaram's *Song of Self-Help and Community Work* conveys a sense of community responsibility and nationalism. She begins with the smaller unit, expanding her range of imagery to cover areas outside the immediate neighborhood, outside the town, and finally extending the view to include the nation itself. She comments on the benefits of improved living conditions—proper waste collection, insect eradication, and road repair (vv. 19, 20, 22, 47, 48)—emphasizing the positive results of such organized efforts to improve the environment. Gwaram fosters an awareness of one's neighbors and their contributions to the group effort to improve living conditions in the area, repeating the phrase, "They help themselves through community work." The unspoken follow-up to this is, "and so can you," bearing the implication of an individual's responsibility to his neighbors. Employing the catalogue technique, Gwaram expands her imagery, mentioning all 126 wards of Kano's Old City sector, and extending her verbal map to include areas in metropolitan Kano and in outlying rural areas beyond Kano's geographic limits. Implicit in such wide-scale geographic narration is the impression that community work can benefit all groups, not just those in the urban areas. The sense of community solidarity guaranteed by Islamic brotherhoods is thus expanded to a feeling of unity on a broader scale.

In regard to women's roles in such an effort, Hauwa Gwaram specifies the function of adult literacy and craft courses as an important aspect of community work. Women teach and learn through these classes, which are sponsored by the community itself. Ultimately they are for the benefit of that community:

Well, here is our cause, women, we are making efforts
We've striven mightily and we are continuing with community work
We teach occupations to women, so they can all do some work;
Literacy too, through community work (vv. 61 and 65)

Hauwa Gwaram's emphasis on the need for a unified effort among both men and women signifies a new perspective on women's roles in regard to public activity. The strict traditionalists advocate the seclusion of women in their homes, while Gwaram's commentary suggests that Kano women may extend their circles of influence to those outside the home. She maintains a conservative perspective, however, by restricting to domestically related skills the kind of work women are encouraged to pursue as part of the community effort.

Both Hauwa Gwaram and Hajiya Yar Shehu advocate the acquisition of knowledge on a community scale through cooperation in the nation's census effort. In songs on the 1972 national census, they try to dispel suspicions about being counted for tax purposes. Explaining that the purpose of the census ultimately is to benefit the people themselves, Gwaram warns them that mistrust on their part is founded on ignorance: "All who refuse to count / Because of taxes are foolish" (v. 12). Hajiya Yar Shehu points out that those who refuse to participate are no better than the trickster figure of Hausa narratives, the spider Gizo, discussed earlier:

Oh, God, the Wise, Your wisdom suffices.
Make us understand so that we may explain the truth,
8   Lest we fall into the bad ways of the loose-mouthed Gizo,

Who, when he couldn't hear something, just shouted louder. ("Song of
the Census," vv. 7–8)

Such association of humans with animals is derogatory—only an animal is ex-
cused from being informed on social issues and from behaving with discretion.
Association with Gizo the trickster, however, carries a doubly serious accusation, for Gizo is more than an animal lacking reason. He is an animal who,
having acquired some human attributes, misuses those potentially redeeming
qualities to abuse and destroy those around him. Gizo's concerns are for his
own welfare, not for the betterment of his associations. His lack of generosity is
as well established as his ignorance, and thus the two qualities are related. Gizo
is the prototypical irresponsible citizen.

Those who are responsible for counting individuals in the Kano area owe
a great debt of social responsibility to the people they count. Their accuracy
is deemed a direct reflection of the sincerity of their nationalistic feelings, as
is the cooperation of those they count. Hajiya Yar Shehu's admonition to listeners to count every individual, regardless of age, sex, or health, emphasizes
that failure to do so signals a failure of citizenship. An individual has a moral
obligation to participate in the government's acquisition of this specific information that will eventually benefit all citizens by guaranteeing the equitable
division of funds, and ultimately contribute to the nation's progressive development (vv. 30, 31).

An accurate count depends on the counters' literacy skills and the cooperation of the populace. Among individuals of both these groups the success of the
effort is contingent on a clear understanding of the purpose of the count and
a fervent sense of responsibility toward the government. Dispelling ignorance
on a local and ultimately on a national scale is the mandate of every citizen,
whether she is being counted or doing the counting. Each one is in part responsible for the success of a united effort. This attitude also reflects the Muslim's
obligation to the community at large, the *umma*. By appealing for cooperation
on the basis of it being good for the community, Hajiya Yar Shehu cannot help
but imply that it is in part a religious obligation to cooperate as well.

Like the poems on the census, Hauwa Gwaram's *Song of Preparing to Drive
on the Right* and *Song of the Naira and Kobo, the New Currency of Nigeria* inform the public of nationwide policy changes. The first poem concerns the
change from left- to right-hand driving, while the second is an explanation of
the change from British currency to Nigeria's own monetary system. Each of
these poems serves several purposes: informing the public, couching the news
in religious as well as public policy terms, and celebrating implicitly the feel-

ing of nationalism that flourished with Nigerian independence from Britain in 1960.

In *Song of Preparing to Drive on the Right* repeated invocations to God comprise over half the work's content. Gwaram's repetitions of God's laws are paralleled by her repetitions of the authorities' laws of the road, creating a relationship between the importance of following God's laws in life, and the necessity of obeying the government's laws on the road. This poem, whose purpose is to describe the major changes in public transport, draws upon an assumption of an individual's obligation to God to inspire a comparably strong obligation to the state, making one's responsibility as a citizen concomitant with one's responsibility as a member of the Islamic congregation. Knowing the laws of the road facilitates one's own safety and the safety of those in and around the vehicle. But as is the case with Islamic law, knowledge of the laws is ineffective without implementation.

Hauwa Gwaram's poem on Nigeria's new currency was written to inform the public of the change of monetary systems which occurred in 1973. She states that the purpose of the work is to inform everyone, rich and poor, urban and rural, Muslim and non-Muslim, about the new currency (vv. 5, 28, 29, 40, 41). Describing the legal tender, Hauwa Gwaram reminds Nigerians of their country's rich resources, which are depicted on the coins and bills (vv. 4, 15–17, 21, 23, 25, 27). The exportation of palm oil, groundnuts, cocoa, cotton, and petroleum oil is Nigeria's own form of material tender in the world market, from which is culled the income for import trade. The government crest appears on all currency (vv. 8, 23), and the coins no longer have the center hole that was characteristic of British colonial currency. These are completely Nigerian coins, made and distributed by an independent Nigerian government, and guaranteed by that government (vv. 7, 8, 23).

Implicit in all these poems on social change is the belief that the literate person is best able to participate in the progressive development of the nation. In urban areas billboards advising people to drive carefully and advocating health care often accompany advertisements for commercial products. People who read these billboards and those who can read the newspapers can be best informed of social changes like those conveyed in these poems. In fact, poems are often used in advertising, as short jingles tout the best attributes of products. Certain nation-building projects such as the census and currency changes are successfully implemented only with the aid of literate participants. While the written poems in the previous section of this chapter advocate blatantly the acquisition of literacy skills, these poems demonstrate implicitly the manner in which such skills contribute to the fulfillment of individuals' responsibilities as good citizens, and the importance of each citizen's contribution to a community effort which is ultimately for the benefit of the nation as a whole.

HISTORY

Written and oral poetry has been more than a vehicle for the static recording of historic events throughout the last half of the twentieth century in Nigeria. Independence from British colonial rule in 1960, the establishment of a civilian government, a coup and military takeover, a three-year civil war, assassinations of political leaders, and the country's democratic elections in 1979 all have been described in popular poetry. Furthermore, poetry has been important as a political instrument in the struggle, focusing public attention on certain political positions and influencing the public's attitudes.

The most dramatic moments of the twentieth century in Nigeria involved the deaths of noted and beloved figures Alhaji Sir Abubakar Tafawa Balewa and Alhaji Ahmadu Bello, the sardauna of Sokoto, in 1966. They are commemorated in ta'aziya poetry, the genre that expresses condolences. This traditional form of expression of bereavement for the deceased involves praising the subject's finer attributes; this is commonly the poetic style used by Hausa poets to honor fallen political figures. Hauwa Gwaram's Song of Condolences for Tafawa Balewa and the Sardauna of Sokoto describes Alahji Sir Tafawa Balewa, a northerner who was federal prime minister, and Alhaji Ahmadu Bello, sardauna of Sokoto and premier of the Northern Region, both beloved northerners who were murdered in the coup of 1966. Her poem explains their roles as victims of the political upheaval of the period. She mentions them together with former emir of Kano Muhammadu Sanusi, deposed in 1963 by Ahmadu Bello (v. 13), and describes Ahmadu Bello's efforts to unite the north by traveling to "Kacako...Gwaram, Sumaila...Dutse...Birnin Kudu" (vv. 24–25) to ameliorate the unrest of the time. Subsequent stanzas relate that Ahmadu Bello's advice to his people was always to follow the tenets of Islam (vv. 26–32), an intention made clear by the previous discussion of his efforts to institute the war on ignorance movement in the north. Major Hassan and General Yakubu Gowon were active in the 1966 counter-coup, against secessionist Biafra, after General Aguyi Ironsi was overthrown. Hauwa Gwaram describes these events (vv. 41, 43), as well as the installation of Alhaji Ado Bayero as the new emir of Kano, and the leadership of Alhaji Audu Bako as the Kano State governor (vv. 47, 53).

Hajiya Yar Shehu's Song for Alhaji Sir Ahmadu Bello, Sardauna of Sokoto gives a far more extensive account of Ahmadu Bello's travels (vv. 32–40), which some believe served the solidarity of the north by better informing the sardauna of the state of Islamic affairs throughout the rest of the world (see Paden 1973, 189 and passim). Hajiya Yar Shehu's work more closely resembles oral praise songs in its inclusion of praise epithets such as "The king of truth" and "bull elephant . . . father of the north" (vv. 10, 41). Ahmadu Bello's role as the leader of Islam in northern Nigeria—the pillar of the north—is legitimized by repeated references to his lineage, a technique also common to oral praise songs. He is linked to Fatima Zahara, the Prophet's wife (v. 6), and to Shehu Usman dan Fodiyo, leader of the region's nineteenth-century jihad (v. 8). Ahmadu Bello's connection to Mohammadu Atiku, Fodiyo's full brother, caliph (1838–1842), and a nineteenth-century sultan of Sokoto (v. 16), strengthens his connection to a family with a significant role in the region's governance.

Another condolence poem (*ta'aziya*) praises Murtala Muhammad, who took over after Lieutenant Colonel Gowan was ousted in 1975. Muhammad himself was assassinated in 1976. The condolence poem Hauwa Gwaram wrote for him is brief, but in it she describes some of Muhammad's accomplishments (vv. 18–21), appeals to God to forgive and welcome Muhammad (v. 11), and implores all people to bear their bereavement with the fortitude that is expected of devout Muslims (vv. 11–13).

Hauwa Gwaram's and Hajiya Yar Shehu's poems draw direct links between religious and political authority in the north. Indeed, the confluence of traditional and Western values is involved in a complex way in the integration of religious and political history in Kano. Since Usman dan Fodiyo's nineteenth-century jihad, Islamic ideology has been integral to the emir's policy, and to regional governmental policy in the north. While Kano was never strictly a theocracy, the tendencies toward such policy made it logical that oral and written works function to promote theocratic ideology. The feeling continued through the end of the twentieth century, as these poems indicate. In March 1981, the idea of an Islamic state was expressed by Alhaji Sir Abubakar, then sultan of Sokoto, who said: "In Islam there is no distinction between religious and political leaders because Islam, being a way of life, governs the day to day activities of its followers."[33] The 1981 riots had their basis in disagreement about the role of orthodox Islam in Kano, and the early years of the twenty-first century have indicated a rise in fundamentalist sympathies in the region.[34] It is a disagreement that continues, as religious issues remain pertinent to politics in the region.

Every Kano leader since the nineteenth-century jihad has been a Fulani emir, whose authority is affirmed through Islam.[35] *Song for the Fulani Emirs* is a traditional poem originally transmitted orally but written down and revised by several authors. As Hauwa Gwaram explains in a preface to her version of the work:

Well, this poem is about the Fulani emirs, and it is written by me, Hauwa
Gwaram. That is, I heard it from Alhaji dan Amu, the [former] Imam of
Kano, who composed it in Arabic. As for me, I went to visit Sidiya, a wife of
the [former] Emir of Kano, Alhaji Inuwa. We read it together. We studied
until we mastered the song. She said she got it from the head wife in the white
compound. That's it . . . I too said that she gave it to me. I went to ask at the
house of Alhaji dan Amu for permission [to work with it], and I wrote it in
Roman script, in order to study it in that form. I have added Emir Sanusi,
Emir Inuwa, and Emir Ado Bayero because it was originally written before
they took office. And in recent times we had Emir Abdullahi too. So. Let us
begin in the name of God . . . [36]

Reworking and revising another author's work is common in Arabic poetry, and the tradition continues in Kano. Like the songs recounting new urban
development in Kano, the *Song for Fulani Emirs* contains narrative segments
that explain emirs' contributions to the city: the mosques, hospitals, schools,
and libraries built, and the technological advances made (vv. 55–56). Hauwa
Gwaram's description of Alhaji Ado Bayero, current emir of Kano, is also com-
plimentary (vv. 89–90). But he is most thoroughly described in relation to
Abdullahi, his father, and Hauwa Gwaram compares the two repeatedly (vv.
84–88, 91–93).

In Hauwa Gwaram's version of this work the entire line of Fulani succession
to emirateship in Kano since 1806 is recounted. The work is a king list, and a
partial genealogy, since there are familial connections between several emirs.
Hauwa Gwaram's version represents a transitional song style: it is a written
composition that includes description and praise of the development of Western technology under recent emirs, but it is also a composition in the oral song
style, resembling royal praise song performance by women praise singers (in
Hausa, *zabiyoyi*) in the emir's court.

Hauwa Gwaram's *Song for the Fulani Emirs* includes all thirteen emirs of
Kano cited in order, with only a few inaccurate lengths of reign.[37] Her tendency
to describe through narrative marks Hauwa Gwaram's version as typical of
written poems in Hausa. She also includes, however, several epithets that are
common to oral praise songs. For instance, she refers to Dabo and Abbas as
"brave warrior" (*sadauki*); Abbas is also known as "the lion" (*usudu*).

Royal women praise singers like Maizargadi naturally refrain from criticizing their patrons. Instead, their praise songs express loyalty to the traditional
Hausa leader just as lavishly as the written poems. The form those praises take,
however, is different, involving less narrative explanation than in the written
poems. They consist of a lengthy catalogue of praise epithets (in Hausa, *kirari*),

which constitute by their number and variety a multifaceted perspective on the subject of the work. Praise epithets are considered here as direct reflections of support for whichever current Hausa leader is the patron of the performer. Maizargadi's *Song for Alhaji Ado Bayero, Emir of Kano* describes Emir Ado Bayero's wealth (ll. 47, 69, 70–71, 74), but Maizargadi proclaims his wealth for another purpose than mere blandishment. By recounting his possessions, inheritances, and distribution of gifts, she binds the concept of wealth to the obligation incumbent upon every devout Muslim to distribute that wealth (and she hopes some will come her way). Charity (in Arabic, *zakat*) is a pillar of Islam that requires the recognition that all wealth and fortune come from God, and therefore is not to be hoarded, but shared willingly. Maizargadi expresses appreciation for the emir's magnanimity: "You gave me a gift, and it was not a loan" (1. 82). The emir is depicted as a patron, the leader and protector of Kano, with praise epithets that are reserved for him alone (ll. 15, 17, 62). His foresight in helping his people to deal with changes resultant from greater contact with the West is implicit in references to his capable leadership abilities.

The most often-repeated message in this work, however, is the right to inheritance enjoyed by Alhaji Ado Bayero. This is not a technical right, as a council of kingmakers selects emirs; succession by a son does not happen automatically, and many vie for the position. Alhaji Ado Bayero's father, Alhaji Abdullahi Bayero, was the tenth emir of Kano, who enjoyed a long (twenty-seven-year) reign, and was well liked by his people. Alhaji Ado Bayero is not the only one of Alhaji Abdullahi's sons to reign after him, but Maizargadi reminds the audience of Alhaji Ado Bayero's personal link with authority. She refers repeatedly to Alhaji Ado Bayero as his father's son (vv. 66–67), perhaps feeling she must reinforce his right to the position. In a passage of consecutive lines Maizargadi repeats a list of groups over which he has control through inheritance, attesting to Ado's having "inherited the house" of each one. (ll. 69–71).[38]

Maizargadi's song is typical of her other performances. She combines praise for many aspects of her patron's character—wealth, generosity, concern for modernization, attention to people's welfare, family relations. By juxtaposing images of the emir's inherent right to authority and his individually achieved capabilities, Maizargadi conveys a sense of his total competence, of Ado Bayero's unquestioned suitability for the position as the emir of Kano.

Because oral songs reflect in content the occasion of their composition, they are historical documents by virtue of recounting the names and relations of people present for the celebration. When Hauwa Mai Duala, a praise singer from Ningi and an old friend of Maizargadi's, visited Kano for the naming ceremony of one of Maizargadi's grandchildren, she performed a song for the women who attended the celebration. The song reflected the makeup of the audience and the occasion, as well as being representative of the kind of royal praise song that is generally associated with performances inside the palace. A guest in Kano, Mai Duala expresses her appreciation for the hospitality extended to her in the town by praising Kan Emir Alhaji Ado Bayero. Simultaneously she praises her own patron, the emir of Ningi, Garba Inusa. But shortly after her opening doxology to God (1. 1) and brief reference to Alhaji Garba Inusa (11. 2, 3, 10), Mai Duala launches into a catalogue of the women known by or related to those present at the ceremony, or somehow connected to the emir of Kano. Since this naming ceremony is the place for women to gather, women are the focus of the work.

In the first hundred lines, Hauwa Mai Duala establishes the groups to which she refers—the women of the palace communities in Kano and Ningi. She cites a sister of the emir of Kano (11. 18–22, 60, 62), the emir of Kano's new daughter (11. 44–45), and one of his wives (11. 95, 96, 98), as well as her own friend, Maizargadi (11. 128, 135, 158, 163), and Maizargadi's friend, Binta Baturiya (11. 87–89, 115–120).[39] Women of the Ningi palace community are mentioned in relation to the Ningi emir's royal status; he is identified as the descendent of various women (11. 36, 37). Throughout the work Hauwa Mai Duala repeats allusions to women of the Kano and Ningi palaces, and to emirs of Kano and Ningi. Clearly this is a song by and for women.

Meanwhile, Hauwa Mai Duala has introduced another important figure in Nigerian news, [former] President Shehu Shagari, just seven months in office at the time of her performance (11. 150–151). In addition to the highest-titled individual in the nation, Hauwa Mai Duala cites several individuals by their royal titles: attendant to the emir (*barde*), ruler (*mai gari*), royal mat spreader to the emir (*dan kilishi*), senior son of the emir (*ciroma*), and senior son or brother of the emir (*galadima*). Quotidian epithets are also part of Hauwa Mai Duala's song, and many of them refer to women. *Mai Babban Dakin Kano* (literally "head of the big house") refers to the emir's mother, visited often by the royal woman praise singer Maizargadi, Mai Duala's friend. *Uwa mai bene* ("rightful mother of the second storey") alludes to the head wife, who sometimes enjoys the privilege of sharing the upper-storey room with her husband. A woman called Rekiya shares the same status; she is described as "Rekiya *mai sauwa* [*soro*]," which has much the same meaning as *mai bene*.

The predominant imagery of Hauwa Mai Duala's song reflects directly the environment in which the work is performed. Though the song is primarily an expression of allegiance to those male political and community leaders named, Hauwa Mai Duala's performance is set among women in an exclusively female-occupied setting, the inner compound. Her constant repetition of praise for women is expressive of a woman's milieu; this song is not appropriate to a mixed public audience, but is geared to the private portion of a naming ceremony in which women celebrate separately from men. Hauwa Mai Duala's performance is simultaneously a declaration of political loyalties and an expression of the network of women who are the individuals of Hauwa Mai Duala's most immediate concern.

CONCLUSION

Praise songs and poems composed by contemporary Hausa women reflect a pervasive concern for literacy and for social and religious obligations of devout Muslims, especially women. The works express an obligation toward and participation in the urban community that is manifested in the teaching of local self-improvement projects sponsored by government policies: "war on ignorance" (*yaƙi da jahilci*), "free primary education" (*ilmi kyauta*), "association," "community" (*jama'a*), "community work" (*aikin gaiya*). Free primary education, known as Universal Primary Education, or U.P.E., was announced in Sokoto by General Gowon in January 1975, and *Aikin Gaiya* was familiar in colonial days as a way of getting roads built.[40] The works often address social problems such as drug abuse, or social changes such as new driving laws and currency changes. They report historically significant events including the civil war, census reporting, and the establishment of local mosques, clinics, and parks (such as the Kano zoo), and they name the principal figures in those events. Songs—especially those performed for spirit possession cult (*bori*) events—are always performed for the sake of entertainment, and yet most are also blatantly didactic. Their quality is judged not solely on technical grounds, but also in regard to the information they convey. Like beautiful pottery that is also functional, these songs are pleasing to the ear, as well as useful in their didacticism.[41] For a song to be popular in Hausa culture, it must have message as well as melody.

These are not feminist tracts, but the existence of these songs speaks for the changing roles of women in Hausa culture. These songs are testimony to Hausa women's awareness of social and political events and personages, though only the extemporaneous, itinerant performers are free enough to be critical of those institutions. What oral works share with the written ones is the intention to transmit information to all members of Hausa society, whether women or men, urban or rural, professional or non-professional. In Hausa culture oral performances are indigenous theater that fulfills a multiplicity of needs for education, entertainment, and the communication of news about current events. The "forces that have molded" northern Nigerian culture have been refined and transformed into new social standards that affect current perspectives. These women's songs and poems represent such varied perspectives on contemporary culture; considered together they contribute to a portrayal of culture in transition.

From the evidence presented here, it is clear that Hausa women's verbal art cannot be classified according to the medium in which it is composed or transmitted—oral or written. Of greater importance than the medium, however, are the insights these lyrics offer into Hausa women's perspectives on traditional and Western education, on the regulation of mores and values, and on the maintenance through *wakoki* of certain historical and political perspectives.

Although this study can offer only a preliminary insight into such a complex art form, the evidence is indicative of the views of women's artistic voices, whose impact has not fully been recognized in the areas of education, politics, and social history among the Hausa. To ignore the social function of these literary works is to deny their purpose in Hausa culture; to ignore women's perspectives on these issues is to hear only half the sound of contemporary Hausa voices.

NOTES

1. The reader is referred to my book, *Muslim Women Sing: Hausa Popular Song* (2004), which contains an MP3-format CD at the back, allowing readers to listen to the complete performances of all the songs discussed in it. This chapter was completed before the publication of that book, so all that is in it is discussed in deeper context in the book, with the exception that the book contains only English translations in print, with Hausa versions of the works in audio format on the MP3 CD.

2. The details of these classifications are discussed at greater length in Mack (2004, 33).

3. See al-Marzubani's *al-Muwashshah*, p. 39, and Ibn Rashiq's *al-ʿUmda fi Mahasin al-Shiʾr wa Adabihi wa Naqdihi* (Cairo, 1934, vol. 1, pp. 9, 15), both cited in Adonis (1990, 14–15).

4. These are not analyzed here but are included in my tape collection, housed in the Archives of Traditional Music at Indiana University. In several cases they are the same songs that I recorded in public performances.

5. For instance, a Radio and TV Programmes column in the 16 July 1979 *New Nigerian* newspaper lists these programs for Kaduna Radio on that day: "1:30 Music while you work; 2:00 *Kawa zuwa kawa* [Friend to friend]; 2:45 *Lafiyar uwar jiki* ["Health is the mother of the body"].

6. Jean Boyd reports that she saw new "millionaires" tossing out money and bestowing Mercedes cars on praise singers during the 1970s, when oil profits flowed and revenue was misappropriated into private accounts. Personal communication with author, circa 1995.

7. The female praise singer is "known as *zabiya* [lit. guinea fowl] from the shrill ululating sound which it is her function to let out at odd moments, such as during the

king's address to his assembled subjects after Sallah" (Smith 1965, 31). Her ululation is not delivered randomly, but for the express purpose of emphasizing the action of the moment.

8. Other researchers have reported that certain women of the palace community in Kano have discounted the work of all *zabiyoyi* as "meaningless" (Muhammad 1977, 9–12), as they are anxious not to be associated with entertainers, characteristically individuals of low status. Although these women do in fact enjoy performances by *zabiyoyi,* they are unwilling to admit to such interest. Among certain female artists the social stigma attached to *maroka* and *zabiyoyi* makes them resist being included in these categories. I find this puzzling, since the harem women I knew well were very accepting of the royal court praise singer, a woman appointed to the position by the emir. Furthermore, one needs to question the origin of social stigmas; do they depend on a gendered reading of who is valued in society?

9. Royal male musicians sometimes are "turbaned" as an indication of honorary status. Women are not turbaned. Whether this is because a woman is assumed not to be able to bear a turban, or due to other reasons, bears investigation.

10. Personal communication with women of the emir's palace, during fieldwork, 1980.

11. Besmer (1983); Ames and King (1971).

12. There are exceptions: in 1980 a few were women who were performing in the place of their fathers, who had trained them because there were no boys in the family to carry on the role.

13. Schimmel (1994, 131–132) refers to a Turkish medieval poet's mystical verse in volving a paradox of Ultimate Truth as hidden inside a nutshell: "the attempt to attain reality or truth is often likened to the hard work that is needed to break a nut before one can enjoy the sweet, wholesome kernel."

14. This and the spirit of the paragraph are from Adonis's discussion in *An Introduction to Arab Poetics* (1990) and his citations of Al-Jurjani's ideas in *Dalaʿil al-Iʿjaz* (Cairo, 1969) and *Asar al-Balagha* (Cairo, 1959).

15. In addition to daily prayers (in Arabic, *salat*), the other obligations of Islam include declaration of faith (*shahada,* Ar.), charity (*zakat,* Ar.,), fasting at Ramadan (*sawm,* Ar.), and pilgrimage to Mecca if one is able (*hajj,* Ar.).

16. These obligatory prayers consist of the process of preparatory cleansing (ablutions of the extremities and orifices by rinsing with clean water), physical stance in three varying positions (standing, bowing, prostration), and the recitation of specific chapters of the Qurʾān as one moves from position to position. Some prayers are set; some are supererogatory.

17. See also Ames and King (1971, 151–152) for discussion on this topic in other cultures' poetry. Also see Paden (1973).

18. Women's associations, which flourished in the last three decades of the twentieth century, were also known in the nineteenth century, especially in the example of the *Yan Taru* teachers trained by Nana Asmaʾu. Men's brotherhoods such as the Tijaniyya and Qadiriyya had their origins as religious affiliations, but moved actively into political operations in the twentieth century. Women's participation in these brotherhoods has rarely been acknowledged (see Sule and Starratt 1991). Other exclusively women's organizations have been oriented toward education and social services. It should not be

argued that there are no women in brotherhood, or women's organizations to parallel men's religious organizations, but only that women's activities have not been recognized as men's have been.

19. I appreciate Allan Christelow's thoughtful comments in a discussion of Hausa *wakoki* in relation to politics and religion in the Kano area (Madison, Wisconsin, August 1981).

20. There are certain historical exceptions to this standard. Nana Asma'u, for example, educated cadres of women in the nineteenth century who then educated other, secluded women in their homes. Many scholars point out that women have little opportunity to study extensively, or to become legitimate *malamai* themselves: "Les ecoles coranique lui sont practiquement fermees et la qualite de *malam* lui est refusee" (Nicolas 1975, 205). Louis Brenner's recent study of Islamic education in West Africa, said to constitute "decades of research," barely acknowledges that women exist in society, much less includes them in the study (2001). But this work, like Boyd and Mack (1997) and Mack and Boyd (2000), attempts to redress the perception that women are uninvolved in education.

21. This is discussed in Schimmel (1994, 134). She notes that religious knowledge is what should be sought.

22. Contemporary Muslim women increasingly rely on Qur'ānic sources to justify their autonomy in education and personal human rights issues. See especially Mernissi (1991) and Ahmed (1992).

23. Jean Boyd notes that Malam Junaidu in Sokoto was trained by a woman scholar, and that Jean Trevor reported that in 1934 women scholars were common to the region. Personal communication with author, circa 1995.

24. Also, Mu'azu Hadeja was one of the first published poets to write on social and religious themes around the same time.

25. Urban and rural adult education programs were popular when I lived in Kano 1979–1982. I visited many of them.

26. *Allah tsare mu rashin fatawa ga malami / To kin ji aikin rashin yakida jahilci.*

27. 45 *Manya da yara ana neman mu je mu aji, / Mu fahinci komai mu zauna babu jahilci.* 46 *Yara su je su furamare gun bidar ilmi, / Manya su je su ajin yaki da jahilci.*

28. Line 5: *Ya zamo ku baiwa malamai, / Du tambayarsu, ku bar fusata.* Line 6: *Ku tsaya ku ga sunanku har, / Sunan iyali, sun rubuta.*

29. *Ku san rikon igiyar ilmi ku san ta bari, / Kowa ya bar ilmi ya sha wulakanci.*

30. *Iya* and *Inna* are cited as heads of the *bori* spirit possession cult.

31. Those who enjoyed this song most thoroughly and displayed greatest interest in its revolutionary news were, as might be expected, the younger generation of university students. Even they, however, pointed out the difficulty of carrying out such radical role changes. Women who try seriously to follow the spirit of Binta Katsina's song find the difficulty of juggling domestic responsibilities and professional pursuits is nearly insurmountable, even with domestic help. And the calumny incurred for abandoning those domestic responsibilities is even worse. This is the classic double bind known to women in the West.

32. According to Jean Boyd there is great concern about standards in schools, and therefore a great recent increase in the number of privately funded schools that charge high fees. People are concerned about pass rates, which tend to be low universally. Personal communication with author, circa 1995.

33. Datelines Africa column in *West Africa,* 23 March 1981, 652.

34. The Yan Izala movement caused tremendous controversy in the 1970s and 1980s. Fundamentalist sympathies have continued to rise since the 1990s.

35. Prior to the nineteenth-century jihad, Kano's kings were known by the Hausa term, *sarki.* Since the jihad, they have been called emirs, from the Arabic *amir,* and overtly representative of Islam in the region. The separation of religious beliefs from politics is a recent development whose philosophical basis is not yet fully accepted in northern Nigeria.

36. "To, wannan waƙa ita ce ta sarakunan Filani daga gare ni Hauwa Gwaram. Wato, ai na jinta Alhaji ɗan Amu liman Kano shi ne ya yi ta da Arabiya. Ni kuma na je wa gurun Sidiya matar Sarkin Kano Alhaji Inuwa. Muna yin karatu. Na bincika sai muka same ta. Ta ce a gurun ꜥuwan soro ta ƙarba ꜥuwan soro ta faren gida. Shi ne . . . ni kuma na ce ta ba ni. Na je na tambayo izo mai gurun Alhaji ɗan Amu na rubuta ta da boko dalilin da na karanta ke nan. Ammma da Sarkin Kano Sanusi da Sarkin Kano Inuwa da Ado ni ce na faɗi lokacinsu domin tun da lokacin da ba a yi su ba aka yi wannan waƙa. A zamanin Sarkin Kano Abdullahi. To, Bismillahi arrahmani arrahim . . ." Personal communication, Kano, Nigeria, 1979.

37. For example, instead of 26 years, she says that former Kano Emir Dabo ruled for 23 years, Mamman Tukur for 1 year instead of 2, Abdullahi II for 26 years instead of 27, and Sanusi for 9 instead of 10.

38. These are the houses of Famda, Takai, Dorayi. I assume she is referring to the fact that the emir is understood to be the main landholder of the entire city of Kano, and that he "rents" places out to families for large periods of time—one hundred years or so.

39. Binta, "the European woman," is the name by which I was known in Kano.

40. I am grateful to Jean Boyd for these details.

41. Nasr (1987, 67) discusses the inextricable relation between function and beauty in the original meaning of the Persian term for "art" (*sanꜥat*).

WORKS CITED

Adonis. 1990. *An Introduction to Arab Poetics.* London: Saqi Books.

Ahmed, Leila. 1992. *Women and Gender in Islam: Historical Roots of a Modern Debate.* New Haven, Conn.: Yale University Press.

Ames, David, and Anthony V. King. 1971. *Glossary of Hausa Music and Its Social Context.* Evanston, Illinois: Northwestern University Press.

Besmer, Fremont. 1983. *Horses, Musicians, and Gods: The Hausa Cult of Possession-Trance.* South Hadley, Mass.: Bergin and Garvey.

Boyd, Jean, and Beverly Mack. 1997. *The Collected Works of Nana Asmaꜥu, bint Shehu Usman ɗan Fodiyo 1793–1864.* East Lansing: Michigan State University Press.

Brenner, Louis. 2001. *Controlling Knowledge: Religion, Power, and Schooling in a West African Muslim Society.* Bloomington: Indiana University Press.

Cohen, Ted. 1980. Metaphor and the cultivation of intimacy. In *On Metaphor,* ed. Sheldon Sacks, 1–10. Chicago: University of Chicago Press.

Daba, Habib Ahmed. 1981. The case of 'Dan Maraya Jos: A Hausa poet. In *Oral Poetry in Nigeria,* ed. U. N. Abalogu, G. Ashiwaju, and R. Amadi-Tshiwala, 209–229. Lagos: *Nigeria Magazine.*

Furniss, Graham. 1996. *Poetry, Prose and Popular Culture in Hausa.* Edinburgh: Edinburgh University Press.

Hofstad, David. 1971. Changing a colonial image—Poet singers and a dynamic newspaper feed northern Nigeria's political awareness. *Africa Report,* October, 28–31.

Mack, Beverly. 2004. *Muslim Women Sing: Hausa Popular Song.* Bloomington: Indiana University Press.

Mack, Beverly, and Jean Boyd. 2000. *One Woman's Jihad: Nana Asmaʾu, Scholar and Scribe.* Bloomington: Indiana University Press.

Mernissi, Fatima. 1991. *The Veil and the Male Elite: A Feminist Interpretation of Women's Rights in Islam.* Reading, Mass.: Addison-Wesley.

Muhammad, Dalhatu. 1977. Individual Talent in the Hausa Poetic Tradition: A Study of Aƙilu Aliyu and His Art. Ph.D. Diss., University of London.

Nasr, Seyyed Hossein. 1987. *Islamic Art and Spirituality.* Albany: State University of New York Press.

Nicolas, Guy. 1975. *Dynamique sociale et appréhension du monde au sein d'une société hausa.* Paris: Institute d'Ethnologie.

Paden, John. 1973. *Religion and Political Culture in Kano.* Berkeley: University of California Press.

Palmer, Sir Herbert Richmond. 1967. *Sudanese Memoirs: Being Mainly Translations of a Number of Arabic Manuscripts Relating to the Central and Western Sudan.* London: Frank Cass. (Orig. pub. 3 vols., Lagos, 1928).

Schimmel, Annemarie. 1994. *Deciphering the Signs of God: A Phenomenological Approach to Islam.* Albany: State University of New York Press.

Smith, Michael G. 1965. The Hausa of northern Nigeria. In *Peoples of Africa,* ed. James L. Gibbs, Jr., 121–155. New York: Holt, Rinehart and Winston.

Sule, Balarabe B. M., and Priscilla E. Starratt. 1991. Islamic leadership positions for women in contemporary Kano society. In *Hausa Women in the Twentieth Century,* ed. Catherine Coles and Beverly Mack, 29–49. Madison: University of Wisconsin Press.

15 ⟶♋

Lamentation and Politics in a Sahelian Song

Thomas A. Hale

Researchers in a variety of disciplines who have recorded songs by women from West Africa are now providing evidence for this most widespread but also most ephemeral form of expression by women. The research leads to several questions. Is there any way of documenting the existence and the roles of women singers in the pre-independence era? Did they have a public voice? If so, what were women doing and saying with their songs?

In the introduction to the collection of songs published in *Women's Voices from West Africa* (2011), Aissata G. Sidikou and I included a history of the genre that began with the lyrics of an Egyptian love song dating to 1300 BCE. Since that period, it is difficult to find references to women singers, let along lyrics, although in the Sahel one finds mention of them in the fourteenth century. The North African traveler Ibn Battuta described singers at the court of Mansa Suleyman, ruler of the Mali empire, in 1352–1353 (Hamdun and King 1975). But in the history that followed, though there are numerous references to singers, one encounters no lyrics until 1918. Below is a summary of sources described in more detail in the introduction to *Women's Voices from West Africa*.

In the *Tarîkh el-Fettâch* (Kâti 1913) and the *Tarîkh es-Soudan* (es-Sa'di 1964 [1898–1900]), long narratives composed in Arabic by scribes in Timbuktu in the sixteenth and seventeenth centuries, there are a few brief descriptions of women singing during the time of the Songhay empire in the fifteenth and sixteenth centuries. As is the case with the performers for Suleyman Mansa in 1352, women are cited as performing at the court of rulers of the Songhay empire.

This image of women as performers for important audiences and major events appears in the account of Michel Jajolet de La Courbe, who was the local director of the Compagnie du Sénégal in the late seventeenth and early eighteenth centuries. He describes a performance for him by a *tiggiwit*, or Moor griotte, but even though he comments on the style of her singing, he is not able to transcribe and translate the lyrics sung in Hassâniya Arabic. He also describes Wolof women singing to mark the end of Ramadan, but again there are no lyrics (La Courbe 1913).

A century later, in 1784–1785, a French naval officer named De Lajaille (1802) witnessed griottes singing to celebrate evidence of the virginity of a newly-wed woman. At the same time, Lamiral (1789), a former slave trader, described the dances of women, but does not mention the message of their songs. In the early-nineteenth-century narratives of a French army engineer named Silvestre Golberry (1808) we do learn about griottes as historians, but not about the subject of their songs. The traveler Anne Raffenel included a sketch of a griotte in a volume of drawings published in 1846. Three decades later, a photographer assigned to an expedition heading into the interior of the Sahel in what is known today as Mali took a photo of the wife of an interpreter and her griotte (Hale 1998). These references, verbal and visual, are all interesting because they tell us about the functions of these women and also about their social status, but none of the reporters had the means or the interest to record, transcribe, and translate songs.

Not long after the turn of the twentieth century, however, a song published in 1918 offers an example of verbal art by a woman that is significant for several reasons. First, it is the earliest song in print by a woman that we have been able to find. Second, in its lyrics one finds both a lamentation, a genre that is common to women, and sharp criticism of two leaders for the way they carried out one of their most important roles in society, that of defending their people. Men are frequent subjects of songs by women, but the context is often courtship, marriage, some other aspect of domestic life, or praise for the achievements of heroes. Third, the song offers an excellent example of intergenerational solidarity. Although this tradition is not rare, in assembling the collection of songs that appeared in *Women's Voices from West Africa* we came across many that expressed conflict between young women and their elders. Often, the dispute was over marriage—whether or not one should become a second wife, marry an older man, or flee the home of abusive in-laws. In this song, however, it is a group of young women, the chorus, that promises to support the singer who, without a son, fears that she will end her years in poverty and solitude. Finally, the song was recorded and published not for ethnographic reasons, but to show that the leaders of the revolt did not enjoy local support for their decision to fight the French. This last aspect emerges clearly when one looks more closely at the collector and the political context.

Jules Brévié, a colonial administrator in 1915 in what was then known as the Soudan, today's Mali, would later become governor of Niger (1922) and governor-general for all of French West Africa (1930–1936). He was known for his interest in collecting oral traditions from West Africa. In 1935, he sent a circular to administrators who served under him to persuade them of the importance of verbal art. He wanted them to collect material from oral sources that would help the French to understand better the people they subjugated. The goal was to make the colonial mission more effective (Hale 1998, 222).

In 1915, while visiting the Beledougou region, Brévié heard about a lamentation composed and sung by a woman named D'Namba Kouloubali in the village of Massantola. An interpreter most likely carried out the transcription and the initial translation of the song, with Brévié polishing the French before publishing both the original Bamana version and the translation, along with notes and commentary, in Dakar in 1918.

Under the modest title "A propos d'une chanson bambara," or "A propos of a Bamana song," Brévié reported that the singer sang about her grief over the death of her only son in a battle between French-led forces and two local leaders in the region. He explained that in February 1915, there was an insurrection in Beledougou. The leaders were two canton chiefs, Diossé of Koumi and Samba of Massantola. They had attempted to launch a revolt nearly two decades earlier, in 1898, when the French were still in the process of conquering peoples further south around the city of Sikasso.

On the surface, it appeared that the two chiefs were simply trying to take advantage of French weakness at a particular juncture in the history of colonialism. France's military resources were stretched to the limit during World War I and there was little manpower remaining to send to the front. For this reason, the French government was beginning to recruit Africans to help defend France against the Germans. According to Conklin, insurrections occurred east of Bamako in 1915 because of French recruiting of young men to defend France in World War I.

> In May 1915, the canton chiefs . . . collectively refused to give up a single tirailleur [rifleman]. They then stopped the mails, executed the local circle guards, and retreated armed to a village, where they awaited the French. Within three weeks they were defeated. (Conklin 148)

But Conklin then goes on to explain that subsequent analyses of the outbreak revealed deeper roots. The policy of direct rule had been imposed recently by the French on the region of Beledougou in spite of resistance by local chiefs. The reason for their reaction was that direct rule diminished the power of chiefs and increased that of local French administrators. The rebellion against the draft was part of a more widespread reaction to French colonialism.

According to Brévié, after the rebels suffered a defeat at Zambougou and were forced to retreat at Ouolodo, they then took refuge in the fortress at Koumi. At the end of a difficult siege that cost the French-led forces heavy casualties, a column commanded by an officer named Caillet forced its way into the village. But, says Brévié, "Diossé, faithful to the traditions of Bamana chiefs, blew himself up with his best soldiers and some members of his family rather than survive the disaster that he had caused. Samba, less energetic, fled and tried to regroup with new forces." Brévié explained that this failed revolt traumatized the local Bamana population, which had counted on a quick victory against the French (1918, 217–222; my translation). The revolt is described in French colonial accounts as a major victory. For the people of Beledougou, the defeat was a tragic event in the history of the region. Today, in their songs, women still remind listeners of the conflict.

In the lyrics below from 1915, one hears three voices: the grieving mother, Diossé, and a chorus of young women.

> The old woman:
> Diossé lost the men uselessly.
> Where did you leave your men?
> Where did you leave your warriors?
>
> Diossé:
> Leave me alone. I tried to get out of this difficult situation.
> Go ask the whites.
> Go ask their soldiers.
> Go look at the edge of the dry swamp.
>
> The old woman:
> Diossé didn't flee, but he lost his reputation.
> Samba fled, the whites are brave.
> Samba was afraid.
> Samba of Massantola is not a man!
>
> The sisters:
> Samba and Diossé unleashed a war for no reason.
> They had our elders killed uselessly.
>
> The old woman:
> I no longer have a son, I will have nothing more to eat.
> I will have no more clothing . . . and I am old.

The sisters:
Old woman, don't cry.
We'll marry, will nourish you.
Don't cry, we'll watch out for you.
Let go of Samba and Diossé, they are evildoers.[1]

The singer criticizes the leaders' judgment and their masculinity in a way that, to outsiders, may seem rather atypical. But it reflects a boldness that one finds in other songs by women that we have included in *Women's Voices from West Africa,* especially those in which they warn men that they can do a better job, whether in wrestling or in governing.

Brévié offered several interpretations of the song. On one level the French administrator was evidently quite happy to discover a song that cast blame on African rulers rather than on the French conquerors. He would not have de-voted so much time to it, going so far as to publish the lyrics, if he did not see a benefit for the colonial mission. As if to justify his interest in the song, however, he also included in his comments an evaluation from a formal perspective. For example, he distinguished the structure and tone of the song from griot narra-tives and compared it instead to ancient Greek texts. He argued that griot texts are more narrative or documentary, like stories, fables, or tales, "mimed with a debauchery of gestures, deafening cries, and instrumental noises that are more or less melodious. The psychological and human side never appears." Here, he says, referring to this song, the human side is the essential trait of the lyrics.

Brévié as literary critic goes on to argue that the song is in a genre that he qualifies as much more evolved—his term—than all other lyrical manifesta-tions of the African genius—in part because of the role of the chorus. This feature, he argues, contrasts with griot narratives where the chorus does not respond but simply follows the narrative, serving as a transition between epi-sodes. By his high praise for the song, he appears to want to emphasize the message that these African leaders were worthless and that they did great harm to their people.

Leaving aside the political, generic, and stylistic elements evoked or implied by Brévié's analysis, it is clear that the lamentation constitutes an unusual ex-ample not only of lyrics that convey multiple messages, but also of how verbal art can be co-opted to serve other goals. As we frame this song in the context of the other references cited earlier, several themes emerge that echo the research reported by other scholars. First, women do exercise a public voice. While men may hold political authority, women express their power in a wide variety of songs. Finally, that power often comes from collective activity that involves both professional and non-professional women singers. What are needed now are deeper analyses of the complex nature of that power.

NOTE

1. Brévié (1918, 217–222; my translation from the French); I thank Kassim Koné, who comes from this region, for verifying the French translation of the original Bamana and for confirming the significance of the revolt today in the collective memory of the region's people.

WORKS CITED

Brévié, Jules. 1918. A propos d'une chanson bambara. In *Annuaire et mémoires du Comité d'Etudes Historiques et Scientifiques de l'Afrique Occidentale Française, 1917,* 217–222. Gorée: Imprimerie du Gouvernment Géneral.

Conklin, Alice. 1997. *A Mission to Civilize: The Republican Idea of Empire in France and West Africa, 1895–1930.* Stanford, Calif.: Stanford University Press.

De Lajaille. 1802. *Voyage au Sénégal pendant les années 1784 et 1785, d'après les mémoires De Lajaille, ancien officier de la Marine française; Contenant des recherches sur la Géographie, la Navigation et le Commerce de la côte occidentale d'Afrique, depuis le cap Blanc jusqu'à la rivière de Serralione [sic]; avec des notes sur la situation de cette partie de l'Afrique jusqu'en l'an x (1801 et 1802) par P. Labarthe.* Paris: Dentu.

es-Sa'di, Abderrahman ben Abdallah ben 'Imran ben 'Amir. 1964 [1898–1900]. *Tarîkh es-Soudan.* Trans. Octave Houdas. Paris: Ecole des Langues Orientales Vivantes. 2nd ed., Paris: Adrien-Maisonneuve.

Golberry, Silvestre Meinrad Xavier. 1808. *Fragmens [sic] d'un voyage en Afrique pendant les années 1785, 1786 et 1787, dans les Contrées occidentales de ce continent, comprises entre le cap Blanc de Barbarie, par 20 degrés, 47 minutes, et le cap de Palmes, par 4 degrés, 30 minutes latitude boréale.* Published in English as *Travels in Africa,* trans. William Mudford. London.

Hale, Thomas A. 1998. *Griots and Griottes: Masters of Words and Music.* Bloomington: Indiana University Press.

Hamdun, Said, and Noel King. 1975. *Ibn Battuta in Black Africa.* London: Rex Collings.

Kâti, Mahmoud. 1913. *Tarîkh el-Fettâch ou chronique du chercheur pour servir à l'histoire des villes, des armies et des principaux personnages du Tekrour.* Trans. Octave Houdas and Maurice Delafosse. Paris: Leroux.

La Courbe, Michel Jajolet de. 1913. *Premier voyage du Sieur de La Courbe fait à la Coste d'Afrique en 1685.* Ed. Pierre Cultru. Paris: Champion.

Lamiral, M. 1789. *l'Affrique [sic] et le people affriquain.* Paris: Dessenne.

Raffenel, Anne. 1846. *Voyage dans l'Afrique Occidentale.* Paris: Bertrand.

Sidikou, Aissata G., and Thomas A. Hale, eds. 2011. *Women's Voices from West Africa: An Anthology of Songs from the Sahel.* Bloomington: Indiana University Press.

16

Transformations in Tuareg Tende *Singing*

WOMEN'S VOICES AND LOCAL FEMINISMS

Susan J. Rasmussen

INTRODUCTION: DOES *TENDE* MATTER TODAY?
OTHER SONGS, OTHER FEMINISMS, AND OTHER MODERNITIES

Recently, feminist anthropologists have grappled with representing "other modernities" and "other feminisms" (Mohanty 1991; Collins 1993; Brenner 1998; Rofel 1999; Abu-Lughod 2002). One approach has been to analyze the role of affective and expressive culture—for example, women's songs—in resistance and accommodation to these processes (Abu-Lughod 1986; Trawick 1988). The present essay contributes to these studies by exploring changing meanings of women's song performance in relation to gendered experience of social upheavals among the semi-nomadic, Muslim, and traditionally stratified Tuareg of Niger and Mali.[1] The focus is upon a genre called *tende,* a body of songs performed by women in a variety of performance contexts, accompanied by a drum called by that name. Most *tende* performances traditionally occur at weddings, namedays, spirit possession rituals, and festivals. They are also organized, along with men's camel races, to greet important visitors. Sometimes, they are spontaneously performed, organized at the spur of the moment in late afternoon or evening for young people's gatherings featuring dancing and courtship, or in less structured situations, just for fun. Nowadays, some performances take place at political rallies and on national holidays.

My own exposure to Tuareg women's *tende* singing began early in my research.[2] Several brief performances I saw raised important questions concerning the power of song for these women, its fate in different performance contexts, and its connection to wider events in society. One evening in 1976, during my initial Peace Corps residence in Agadez, Niger, a friend invited me to attend a small musical gathering on the outskirts of town. We extinguished our flashlights to avoid a military vehicle making its rounds nearby. Occasionally, Tuareg were harassed by some outside authorities then posted in the northern regions, at that time marginal to central-state governments and considered "security problems."[3] The gathering was a small spirit possession ritual which features this *tende* drum. Youths in the chorus, somewhat startled and astonished to see me there (I was then a teacher at the local CEG middle school), briefly departed from their "performance frame," but then recovered and returned to their songs. They wove my own name into the song verses, improvising jokes and incorporating them into the possession songs. As outside intruder, I attracted much attention, modifying but not radically transforming this performance, originally intended to be a healing ritual.

Later, in 1983 during my dissertation research on Tuareg spirit possession, I witnessed numerous types of *tende* performances, both in the spirit possession rituals and outside them. Many verses included the refrain: "What is a song? It is not a science, in which I make a mistake and (would be) struck down by a marabout [Islamic scholar]." In an earlier analysis I argued that the spirit possession *tende* songs are defined as "anti-Islamic" and, though not forbidden by Islamic scholars, strike a sensitive nerve: they are non-liturgical and encourage free association between the sexes (Rasmussen 1995).

On many other *tende* occasions since then, I have noticed the cacophonous interplay of different voices and meanings, even in a single performance. Once, when functionaries from Agadez visited a rural community, local residents hastily organized a *tende* song performance by young girls in the village. As soldiers stood by, the singers sang somewhat nervously, some literally shaking, but their songs went well and they drew warm applause.

During my residence in Niamey, capital of Niger, I also encountered *tende* singing, but under contrasting circumstances: this occurred spontaneously, during a visit to my friends. As men played cards and drank tea, women hosting the visit began a good-natured but critical debate on relations between the sexes. A wedding was coming up, and marriage was the topic. One man present had contracted several polygynous marriages and indicated he was considering another: he hoped the women's family would "save" a pretty daughter for him to marry when she grew up. Privately, the women expressed their disapproval of some urban Tuareg men's polygyny, saying, "polygynists do not respect women."[4] Before their male audience, they improvised a *tende* drum with an

empty jerry-can, began drumming, and smiled coyly at the polygynist, insert-
ing his name into their teasing yet sharply critical song verses.

Another interesting early exposure of mine to *tende* came during my attendance of a *Soirée Culturelle* held on a national holiday, Independence Day. This
performance featured a staged version of the Tuareg spirit possession ritual
(called *tende n goumaten*), which, as noted, is one type of *tende* event. Singers
from diverse regions accompanied by a drummer surrounded a dancer representing the "possessed," although here there was neither trance nor illness, nor
was the dancer surrounded by close supportive friends or relatives, customary
in the more intimate ritual therapy. The performance gradually transformed
into a kind of medley of diverse musical traditions from other groups, with
diverse participants, non-Tuareg as well as Tuareg. Of course, I do not imply
this was a "corruption" of "authentic" *tende* music, but rather a creative replay
of it in a more national setting.[5] But nonetheless there was some co-opting of
the therapeutic intent of this type of *tende* singing as locally defined.

More recently, I witnessed additional performances. Once, just before my
departure from a village in Mali where I had conducted research, a small *tende*
was quickly and suddenly organized for me. As I assisted my field hostess and
her female relatives to prepare couscous for our evening meal, they inquired
whether I wished to hear a few *tende* songs. I replied, yes, and they began to
sing, striking the backs of washbasins as improvised drums. These songs, selected verses from longer works, were performed very briefly, with much laughter and "horseplay." We all joked that this was a "*tende n couscous* [*tende* of the
couscous]."

Tuareg women's *tende* performances occur in diverse situations, are entertaining and creative, and have always been surrounded by potentially explosive
social and political dynamics. Over the past twenty-five years, not surprisingly,
there have been striking changes, as well as continuities, in the significance of
the songs, their themes, the effects of the performances, and the roles of the
singers. *Tende* songs are performed at festivals in both rural and urban settings, primarily in northern regions of Niger and Mali. During my residence
and field research in Niger between 1976 and 2002, and more recently, in Mali
in 2002 and 2006, I collected several hundred *tende* songs.[6] The term *tende*
has several meanings. First, it refers to the specific genre of music and singing
accompanied by the instrument called by the same name, the *tende,* a drum
converted from a mortar normally used to crush grain by stretching a thin
goat hide across the top (Card 1978; Rasmussen 1995).[7] The drum is traditionally played by women—in the past, of servile origins, but today of diverse social origins—and, in some regions, by smith/artisan men as well. It is struck

with the hands, its drum patterns vary, and its songs have diverse titles. Titles sometimes describe the drum patterns or rhythms, sometimes describe the singers' or others' states of mind, represent personal names, or refer to other topics of the songs' poetic verses (Rasmussen 1995). Themes include love, travel, marriage, relations between the sexes and the different social strata, intergenerational relationships, and past battles. More recently, songs address wider political themes, such as labor migration and its effect upon women, or local suffering from the violence and atrocities during the 1990–1996 Tuareg nationalist/separatist revolt against the central governments of Mali and Niger and its intermittent resurgences more recently. There is often social commentary, both praise and criticism. There is continued praise of warrior heroes (both precolonial raiders and postcolonial rebel fighters), but also, nowadays, of NGO aid workers. Moreover, professional musical troupes now include some *tende* performances in their repertoires aimed at audiences outside Tuareg communities, such as tourists in the Sahara, government functionaries on official holidays, and expatriates, and some troupes even tour beyond Africa—for example, in France.

Thus *tende* songs are interesting for revealing, over the long term, women's musings over social change. Of course, such musings do not necessarily conform to Western or Euro-American notions of "feminism" (Mohanty 1991). They do, however, offer a local form of feminist discourse analyzed in this essay, not solely for its textual content, but also for its connection to wider, emerging dynamics in performance and society (Hale 1998; B. Hoffman 1995; Wood 1999). More broadly, the songs also offer insights into gender and culture as not finished or static products, but emergent practices (Bourdieu 1978; Giddens 1979; Ortner 1996). Fundamental to *tende* music are its multivocal and dialogical, but also conflictual, aspects. Like song duels and "doing the dozens," many *tende* songs revolve around rivalries and competition. *Tende* also refers generically to all festivals, gatherings, and performances that feature these women's choral songs and soloists accompanied by this drum. In rural communities, these fall into several categories: *tende-n-tagbast,* "the dance *tende,*" held as the standing female chorus and soloist sing and male dancers approach them; *tende-n-emnes,* the camel *tende,* held during men's camel races; and *tende-n-goumaten,* the *tende* of the spirits, when this drum is played during possession of predominantly women by non-Qur'ānic spirits, and accompanies the choral songs associated with this therapeutic ritual. This latter category is analyzed in a previous ethnography (Rasmussen 1995). There are two major styles of performance in *tende* events, which vary according to region and context of *tende.* In some performances, a solo drummer—in the Aïr region of Niger, often a smith man—remains seated and accompanies a standing chorus of women.

During other performances, a group of women sit on the wooden branches weighing down the *tende* and varying its tone, and they drum and sing from this position.

Women's *tende* songs, remarkably, have survived considerable turmoil and upheavals in Tuareg society over the past several decades, albeit not without significant transformations in their meanings, in their themes, and in the roles and styles of their singers, and also some appropriation of them beyond Tuareg culture for commercial and "folkloric" purposes. For example, they coexist, and appear to be holding their own, alongside a new form of music, called *ichumar* or simply "guitar" (Rasmussen 1998, 2000, 2003). The latter songs originated as protest music composed by Tuareg male rebels, and have now swept to popularity among youths in the towns, where these songs have broadened their themes and are currently performed by predominantly (though not exclusively) male guitarists and singers in "rock-style" bands.[8] *Ichumar*/guitar music tends to predominate in the towns, and most (though not all) composers are men; nonetheless, *tende* music remains popular in both rural and urban settings. In the towns, *tende* and *ichumar*/guitar genres are often performed in different phases of the same festival or rite or passage: for example, both are featured at different times at political party rallies.

Thus the question arises, given the complexity and transformation of *tende* performances, and their vulnerability to appropriation by others: exactly why do Tuareg women sing now? Wherein resides the songs' power? Has the past "tradition" of Tuareg women's powerful critical social voice via poetry and song in the local community been "coopted," become diluted, or has it, on the contrary, been amplified to a larger audience, and to greater effect? To what extent has it become integrated with more general Tuareg concerns of local cultural autonomy, praising the local history and memory which have tended to subordinate women to men in the recent military struggles, and to what extent are there still specifically feminine voices in the gendered concerns in these themes?

This essay focuses upon the *tende* performances in terms of their emerging meanings for the singers today, explores some reasons for their enduring popularity among audiences, and also examines changes in the songs' themes and singers' roles, contextualizing them in performance and against the backdrop of wider gendered concerns, and investigating their social consequences. How local "feminist" formulations play out in these processes is of interest for several reasons. Now that *ichumar*/guitar music is rising in popularity, no longer banned after the Peace Accords ending the 1990s rebellions in Niger, I ask, what explains *tende* music's enduring popularity, what have been some of its old and new meanings over the years I have collected these songs, and how do *tende* singers view their art and its gendered themes? What gendered dialogues (and disputes) are addressed in the songs and their performances, and what is their relation to changes during *tende* performances and in the wider society? How do these dialogues among performers and between performers and audience both reflect and shape changing relations between the sexes in times of turmoil? How and why does singing *tende* music matter today?

My method includes analysis of *tende* songs' poetic verses, their performance contexts, and wider and more long-term social, economic, and political processes impinging upon gender and relations between the sexes. There are case studies of several singers. There is also discussion of local notions of speech and verbal art performance in relation to gender and social stratum in this changing society, where the precolonial social hierarchy of endogamous, specialized occupational groups was based on descent, but gender relations stressed prestigious social status and economic independence for most women. In effect, these performances vividly showcase these relations in Tuareg culture. Like other expressive cultural practices, however, they do not perfectly reflect them (Geertz 1973). Although I share the recent recognition, in anthropology of gender, that women are not a unitary or monolithic group (Di Leonardo 1990), nonetheless it is a legitimate goal to foreground some local women's own voices and perspectives of modernity, rather than those of outside observers (Warren and Bourque 1990; Hodgson 2000). The problem is how to "read" (or, more accurately, hear) gendered verbal art performances in terms of what they have to say concerning local African feminisms.

Ideally, *tende* music reflects and reinforces Tuareg women's status. Traditionally, it is one of several sources of women's power. In rural communities, women inherit, own, and manage livestock, build, maintain, and own the tent, and have the right to initiate divorce, travel, and receive male visitors, even after marriage (Murphy 1967; Worley 1991; Claudot-Hawad 1993; Nicolaisen and Nicolaisen 1997; Rasmussen 1995, 1998, 2003). Tuareg speak a Berber language, Tamajaq. Their precolonial stratified social system included an aristocracy, tributaries, Qur'ānic scholars, smith/artisans, and peoples of varying client and servile status. There has been longstanding freedom of interaction between the sexes. Older matrilineal institutions interweave with patrilineal institutions introduced by Islam.[9]

On the other hand, since approximately the early twentieth century, there have been changing bases of property and transformations in the balance of power between the sexes, from drought, war, sedentarization, and colonial and postcolonial nation-state policies of sedentarization, taxation, and limitations of the Saharan caravan trade (Rasmussen 1994, 1995, 2001; Figueiredo 1996). Most women's property primarily consisted of livestock herds, but many herds have been diminished or lost in these upheavals. Yet women continue to exercise much influence through their capacity to publicly ridicule, as well as praise, men. As many become impoverished, men feel greater threats to their masculine pride. The poetry of the *tende* songs, composed and sung by women, alludes to male battle heroes, labor migrants, and Islamic scholars, personal sentiments of love and anger, female kinspersons, friends, and rivals. These themes continue today, but increasingly, there is also commentary on historical and current events, and politics.

Despite some changes in the details of their verses over the past few decades, most *tende* songs continue to alternate, in their general sentiments, between praise, yearning, ridicule, and anger. They retain recurrent images and tropes: metaphoric allusions to orphanhood, the soul, and bitterness, and they contain certain formulaic verses such as greetings, seeking of support from singers, audience, and society, and coaxing for applause. There are allusions to the presence and absence of lovers, support and non-support from fellow singers and more distant "significant others" in the women singers' social universe. There are, however, variations on these motifs and images, which have a relation to changing conditions of interaction between the sexes and to new performance situations and socioeconomic and political contexts.

I show how selected *tende* songs and performances give "voice" to complex feelings concerning the nature of human relations, not always directly, but by means of stylistic variations in the lyrics of their songs. I also show how effective they are in this, and their consequences. I draw from, but also critique, analytic frameworks of polyphony and resistance developed by Bakhtin (1981, 1984), Trawick (1988), and Abu-Lughod (1986, 1993). Among the Tuareg, I argue, feminine and masculine gender constructs still require mutual support and attention for their balanced maintenance, expressed in *tende* performance. While women singers may mock men, there are limits to their power, since women's singing is not considered complete without men's shouts, chants, and general audience applause (Card 1981; Rasmussen 1995).

VERBAL ART AND PERFORMANCE IN TUAREG SOCIETY

Speaking and Singing

Tuareg verbal art and musical performance are surrounded by contradictions (Rasmussen 1995). Music and song in the Sahara enjoy much prestige, and are greatly appreciated, yet there are ambivalent and contradictory feelings about them that derive from religious beliefs, as well as cultural values of reserve (Rasmussen 2000, 136). In rural communities among Tuareg of noble origins, there is great emphasis upon verbal restraint due to fear of *togerchet,* the force of negative gossip, as well as praises from complacency or envy, which can wound people and animals (J. Nicolaisen 1961, 134; Casajus 2000, 32; Rasmussen 2001, 141). Opening the mouth entails risk of this danger, as well as threats from evil spirits. Hence the noble value on *tangalt* (denoting allusion, symbol, metaphor, or indirect speech) in speaking and singing. For example, there is caution about praises addressed to others' families or property. By contrast, smith/artisans and descendants of clients and slaves have always been relatively free from these restrictions. *Tende* singers, as already noted, come from diverse social backgrounds. Thus there are continual negotiations occurring in the expression of themes in *tende* music. Some issues are addressed obliquely, with subtle and covert expression in the tradition of *tangalt*; other themes are more explicitly, even boldly, expressed. To Islamic scholars, all non-liturgical music is suspect. Non-Qurʾānic spirits are believed to be pleased by the music, noise, and jokes pervasive at evening festivals (Rasmussen 1995). The Devil, called Iblis, is present at musical festivals and resides inside the *tende* instrument. Iblis is all the more involved if music is played or sung by a beautiful young woman. Iblis is associated with strong sentiments, in particular love and the sexual force of reproduction (J. Nicolaisen 1961; Rasmussen 1995). Iblis distracts from prayer.[10]

In local body symbolism, the mouth is analogous to the genitals. A proverb says that "the man's face-veil and the trousers are brothers," and one reason men cover their mouths with the turban veil is to display respect toward affines and elders, in particular their mothers-in-law (Murphy 1964). Although Tuareg women do not wear a face-veil, *tende* singers sometimes leave out words and substitute vocables during the later afternoon when affines, with whom they have reserve relationships, are present. After sundown, there is less reserve about singing with the mouth wide open, and fewer vocables are used.

Singing also has powerful political implications. During the French conquest of the Sahara, at Iferouan in the Aïr, the Lamy expeditionary force reported frequent women's singing not solely during everyday and courtship activities, but also in prelude or accompaniment to men's battle attacks and raids (Porch 1984, 171).[11]

The Tende Drum and Tende Singing

The *tende* drum is identified not solely with domestic labor and free sexuality, but also with the earth. The earth has contradictory associations: it is identified with women, who traditionally enjoy high social status and prestige, and their matrilineal spirits, but it is also identified with lower or ambiguous social status: of former slaves, smith/artisans, and other client peoples in the precolonial social system who, until recently, performed most manual and domestic labor that the *tende*'s mortar form iconically represents. The drum's origin may be from Africa south of the Sahara (Card 1978). It evokes the grain of seden-tized farming communities, where Tuareg traded and raided for slaves. Today, women of diverse social backgrounds and smith men, but not noble men, play this drum.

Tende songs, like all popular music, have changed significantly over time. Singers have been exposed to new ideas and technologies. In conversations and interviews, women singers indicated to me that they sing primarily for plea-sure, although sometimes they are now paid by audiences. Most rural singers learned *tende* singing by attending festivals, listening to other singers, often learning from other nomads while at pasture with herds, or from their moth-ers. Some singers, particularly urban singers, learned from the radio. They of-ten practice during rainy season social gatherings. Many indicated they are in-spired by observing some event or person. One stated, "If a gardener or herder kills a jackal, I praise that [action]." She also compared composing songs to inventing a name.

Over the past few decades, singers have indicated that there is greater flexi-bility concerning words in songs; one is no longer obligated to repeat them ac-cording to certain poetic rules.[12] Each singer may invent her own songs, with any drum pattern. This confers more freedom of expression. However, most agreed that song quality still depends on rapport between the singers and the drum-mer. Also, women indicated that a "clear" voice is important. Men expressed preference for a "young, high" voice (Rasmussen 1995). *Tende* singers do in fact tend to be adolescent and single. This makes sense when one recalls that this music is traditionally associated with courtship, as was another instrument, the *anzad* one-stringed bowed lute in the past, and as is the modern guitar now. Many women cease this activity once they marry, particularly women who marry marabouts. *Tende* singers explained that the reason why men do not sing *tende* songs is related to gender typifications: because "in religion [Islam], men usually do not sing non-liturgical music, [just] as men do not wear jewelry." Youths who sing modern *ichumar*/guitar music represent a radical departure from that rule. The women singers explained that, in their opinion, these lat-ter singers sing non-liturgical music "because they are brats," or "because they were fugitive rebels in the mountains, with no women around."

Early *tende* performances I attended functioned primarily to facilitate free relationships between the precolonial social categories, providing an antidote to official, ideally endogamous, and close-cousin marriages arranged by elderly parents (Rasmussen 1995), and providing a forum for individual agency and assertion of power in youth-elder conflicts (Rasmussen 2000, 138). Nonethe-less, *tende* performances have always been carefully orchestrated: they are supposed to encourage flirting, courtship, and conversation, but not sexual relations or marriage, between persons of different social origins: in other words, only jokes and flirting should occur between those who traditionally should not marry. These festivals are neither fully structural, nor fully anti-structural; they collapse the usual communitas and liminal frames, and break down rigid associations of authority with elders and resistance with youths (Rasmussen 2000, 138). For example, many songs at rural festivals express love founded on admiration of individual achievement rather than social origins, and hint at defiance of older persons' authority. At the same time, however, many songs still extoll values of parents in the old noble nomadic warrior culture: courage, respect and reserve, and dignity. *Tangalt* (metaphor) used to predominate more as the ideal style of performance expression for rural noble singers; for example, one noble woman in the 1980s wrote verses praising her lover, a man of servile descent, for his courage and endurance in battle, through the device of lauding his camel (Rasmussen 1995; 2000, 137). In these verses, she also indirectly expressed her resentment toward her lover's father for sending him away from her on caravans.

The *tende* remains identified with, and addresses, the aggregation of disparate forces in Tuareg society: cultural unity and social solidarity across kin and class lines, but also with the risks of indeterminacy in freedom of association at these events. Now, however, there are more external limits to their freedom of expression: during a *tende n goumaten* in the Kidal region of Mali, there were verses accusing a functionary of being a thief; henceforth, these rituals were banned there.

All *tende* performances require highly stylized etiquette. Guests should put on their best clothing and jewelry, but avoid wearing Islamic amulets. In rural areas, performances are held far from the mosque and on the fringes of villages and camps. Nowadays, when these performances are staged on state holiday occasions, they may take place in a kind of central space, near a primary school if there is one in the community. Performers and audience communicate covertly. Male age-mates use special nicknames as forms of address in joking and gossip (Rasmussen 2000, 136). Secret hand greetings indicate favor or disfavor toward suitors' overtures. Relations between the sexes have always featured a degree of license, but also some social restraint; ideally, there is preference for gallant, dignified, subtle, and courteous conduct for men and women.

Recently, however, there have been indications that these gendered meanings of *tende,* the etiquette of its performances, and its effectiveness as a voice protecting women's interests are breaking down (Gast 1992; Figueiredo 1996; Rasmussen 2000, 2001). Despite the textual content of the verses that powerfully asserts singers' sentiments, there is some less-respectful conduct toward women (Gast 1992, 168–170; Rasmussen 2001), occasional violence or gunfire, and even one reported murder (Rasmussen 2001, 289–290). Some outside aid workers, functionaries, and soldiers in the region misinterpret Tuareg sexual mores, and assume that free courtship and open sociability between the sexes imply that Tuareg women are "loose" and available sexually to strangers (Gast 1992, 168–170; Figueiredo 1996). Therefore women's song verses still have the purpose of either praise or covert messages of social commentary, including ridicule and mockery, but the performance and wider social contexts now often contradict their textual messages, which seek to safeguard their interests.

Thus many musical and verbal art performances, while still constituting "carnivalesque" social commentary à la Bakhtin (1984), now also constitute microcosms of recent turmoil and upheaval, and debates over contested values and roles. These processes are shown in greater detail in the following themes of some recent songs, their performance situations, and singers' experiences.

TEXTS AND CONTEXTS OF *TENDE* SONGS

Popular Themes of Selected Verses

One important theme in contemporary *tende* music is commentary on the impact of socioeconomic and political change. In the northern regions of Niger and Mali, women's *tende* singing occurs against the backdrop of drought, monetarization, unemployment, and warfare, which compelled many men to cease long-distance caravan trading and take up oasis gardening, itinerant trading, and labor migration. Many camels were lost in the 1969–1971, 1984, and 2000 droughts, and pastures and rains remain irregular. Other animals were stolen by militia and bandits during the sporadically recurring Tuareg nationalist/ separatist rebellions. The Peace Pacts, despite interruptions by some dissidents resuming conflict, have brought aid organizations, repatriation, and semi-autonomy to the Tuareg regions, but also pressures to sedentarize.

Selected verses from performances by *tende* singers at the end of a political rally for the Amana-UDPS party in Agadez, Niger, in June 1998, sing:

> We have representation in the government / service tables [i.e., positions to serve], for the compatriots / day and night / The route was barred by politics that makes good time / Now we have the freedom to meet with compatriots / Oh, my soul, the good time past / we do not wish for it, Oh, my soul, for politics / The Europeans who invented politics they made a mistake, or those who study it have not succeeded in translating it well . . . / Greetings for the leader of the party and their soldiers, everyone, today, UDPS is animated and it seeks its right in the country of Niger / Federalism [an autonomous region]

is always the dream of the UDPS Amana party, it is the truth / Everybody in our party welcomes you / One welcomes you as you are before [first] / The day to wash [i.e., the day has come that the party can express itself clearly in public, get something off its chest] / The leaders of the party meet in a congress for the election, all ceremonies, our comrades who are in the countryside come back in order to share the work.

Only recently have Tuareg been included in decision-making processes affecting them. In the early twentieth century, French colonization destroyed the Tuareg social order, viewing social hierarchy as unjust, but manipulating it on occasion in order to impose the hierarchy of their own political (colonial) system in French West Africa (Figueiredo 1996, 115). The French created divisions in Tuareg society that were not as rigid before French colonialism. Earlier aid programs were ill-suited to pastoral nomads. For example, some programs installed gasoline-powered pumps and concrete wells in Niger, which disrupted the ecological balance of water. Others attempted to force caravans into rigid time schedules (Camel 2002, 81–89).

Verses from singing at a rural smiths' wedding *tende* in July 1998 feature praises of two Tuareg men, extension agents (called *animateurs*) who work for the IRENEE aid organization: "Ali and Allo, this song it is for the young people who shout from morning to evening / Ali and Allo are teachers of the *animation* [development] / They brought a vision to us people, Ali and Allo / One thanks you, because you made us understand / Ali and Allo, we thank you, and you have animated us . . ."

Following the Peace Pacts, several emergency relief agencies (Africare; *Action Contre la Faim, Aide d'Urgence*) arrived in northern regions in efforts to repatriate the Tuareg. There were attempts to integrate ex-rebels into this, as well as into the armed forces. There were efforts toward greater local autonomy in the decision-making and structuring of the aid agencies. A U.N. refugee agency began compensating individuals for loss of herds. The *Aide d'Urgence Internationale* agency purchased goats from local women to give to schools. Women were working on a tree enclosure project for FAO, and also established economic cooperatives.

At a dance *tende* festival held to honor the *Aide d'Urgence Internationale* workers visiting a rural community with their project, verses praise men who follow traditional ideals of courtship, as follows:

We are for God. One does not belong to ourselves / I call the young people who shout from morning to evening Refrain / I address the young people who have not eaten for seven days if the stomach begins to be empty / they *asserent* the stomach [i.e., she praises their courage, that in the past, when men came to court young women in countryside, they did not eat, from reserve and dignity and to show their strength and endurance] / I am an orphan because there is lacking young people / Everyone has left for the countryside / My Chimo-Chimo on a dromedary with its very pretty cushions / dromedary of two tones (colors) / We are for God / That is a song for the white guests.

These songs praise new male heroes, NGO aid workers, and juxtapose against their praise some subtle critiques of male suitors who abandon traditional politeness standards.

On the same occasion, other songs mention men's absence in labor migration and caravan trade: "Oh, the young girls applaud / You must aid me, what is a song? It is not a study that deceives me / Help in earnest [i.e., do not be distracted] / It is not a sin [*abakat*] so that one perishes, to say that I do sins / All our young people who are present here / Even they who are in Hausa country until the city of Kano."

Singers also mock oasis gardeners, alluding to conflicts between them and herders in their semi-sedentarized community:

This song is for gardeners / when they begin to plant they are very uncertain / They kill goats [an allusion here to conflicts between gardeners and herders; the majority of this village's population are still noble herders, so criticism and praise are mixed; the singer mocks their conflicts] / Even the birds they are against them / When they harvest they shout, very happy, the fumes fly off, burning the thorns [brush, brambles] they are happy / They laugh / Their aromas of garlic and onions / Their boss when he hoes, he is very lazy, as though he had eaten *domanan* [a plant used in the Hausa region that makes one sleepy] / the young girls whom we have here, applaud, shout / their boss who eats the ears of a goat [children cut off ears of goats in order to mark an animal that does damage to the garden, to identify and show the owner's guilt and responsibility].

Official media narratives and aid agency policies have encouraged Tuareg women, as well as men, to sedentarize and become farmers. Local responses to these efforts are mixed. In some regions, until recently there was some social stigma: only slaves and clients gardened. Later, men from diverse social origins took this up, but women did not plant or irrigate. Only elderly women sometimes harvested. I knew some women who did participate in the new programs encouraging women to start their own gardens, but others did not, preferring to make mats to sell on the market and leave oasis gardening to their husbands. Many wives of former caravan traders who now garden felt that, in the past, "there was less food, whereas now there is more food, but we have much more domestic work now than in the past, such as cooking." But some indicated gardener husbands assisted them with housework. They also recognized that oasis gardening brings money in the increasingly monetarized economy.

Another song alludes to Tuareg men who leave their own cultural milieu:

Oh, the girls / Applaud and aid / Something soft I have become a little dizzy / I have become dizzy with fatigue because I lack young people [i.e., others are not participating enough to help with applause and ululating] / They have left for the countries of Europeans for studying, so that they can teach us well / In that epoch, the faces of the Whites [i.e., the white guests are attracting many people to the festival] / You [plural] / the young girls you must encourage this night one does not sleep / There is no rest because we have guests.

At the same event, another song in its verses laments the absence of eligible marriage partners: "Here, oh my soul! / If you know God, you must pray that I do not marry an elder / The men are not here anymore, they have all left for Algeria because they have many debts . . . "

In women's *tende* songs there are mixed sentiments, in themes of amorous deception, but also nostalgia for missed absent lovers. In the 1970s and 1980s, many Tuareg youths left in search of work after the droughts of 1973 and 1984. The unemployed called themselves *ichumeran,* from the French term *chomer,* to be unemployed, or *chomeur,* an unemployed person. Many were adolescents, who normally undergo a local cultural socialization and rite of passage into adulthood through work in herding and caravanning, but these migrations were different: they went from country to country, instead of from tent to tent among female kin. This interrupted their Tuareg education (Figueiredo 1996, 117). They became exposed to other systems of thought.

Starting in 1990, the Tuareg rebellion attracted some of these youthful men. They rallied to seek affiliation for social integration. But their new status derived from outside the Tuareg social system. Some were accused of neglecting religion, and reconversion was also a means some men used to make themselves accepted. But this and even widespread praises of former rebel bravery by many women in their songs did not prevent some men's problems in reintegrating back into Tuareg society.

Tuareg refer to undocumented labor migration in French as *l'exode,* or in slang as *"le travail noir"* ("black work" of Africans). In Tamajaq, the terms are *takagat* or *awezely n agamay* (the latter denotes, literally, "travel of seeking" or "travel in search"). Labor migration is rumored to sometimes include military training in Libya. At one wedding I attended, men danced with axes rather than the usual lances; when I expressed worry and fear, they reassured me, "We know how to hold them, we have had military training." However, this attempt to impress was met with limited success: some women commented with faint mockery that "many dancers here are a bit older than usual for dancing; many of the younger men are away in labor migration and caravans."

Women are worried that men will bring outside gender constructs to their relationships, such as polygyny, more patriarchal property ownership, and perhaps even seclusion. In fact, these values combine with economic pressures to make some more restrictive marriage partners attractive to some families: in the Kidal region of Mali, for example, some Tuareg women marry Kunta Arab men, who require seclusion of wives. When I inquired why, women replied that they looked forward to the relief from arduous household labor such seclusion offers: they no longer need to go to the well, etc. Thus such marriages were not viewed as restriction, but rather offered women opportunities to continue noble patterns of refraining from manual labor. Their parents, for their part, appeared motivated by the higher bridewealth and greater prestige these marriages offer in that region, where approximately 50 percent of the population is Kunta Arab. Similarly, in the Aïr region of Niger, many noble women are being married off at younger ages than in the past, to help relieve their families' poverty.

Men's honor depends on their capacity to return victorious from battle or successful from labor migration. But recently, men have not returned victorious. Many prefer to not return at all, for women's gazes would be insufferable. Women's songs, in fact, can insult as well as praise. They do this by omitting past heroes, or by replacing them with new heroes, as shown in the praises of the local Tuareg NGO workers. Some women even praise non-Tuareg NGO aid workers: in one Malian village, for example, a mother named her baby Amina, after the Ghanaian wife of a European aid agency director. The women also sang his praises for bringing them assistance (compensatory livestock and sacks of rice for their cooperative): "May God make Bernard return one morning / Tana, pregnant, wants something, and Rhaicha is deprived and [consequently] has had a miscarriage [men's causing of a pregnant woman's anger, called *tourgoum*, is believed to bring on either a miscarriage or a birth defect] / Nana has left to complain at the police station, until Bernard arrives." In these poetic song verses, the women jokingly compare their wish for the aid agency director's return to a pregnancy craving which, if denied, may cause reproductive problems.

These praise poems and songs now compete with praises of modern rebel fighters. Praises of husbands on labor migration are contingent upon the money and gifts they bring home. This was shown in the *tende* song of one Aïr Tuareg soloist, when she publically humiliated her lover for not bringing home a radio, as he had promised. On the other hand, some women praise matrilineal male relatives on labor migration, particularly their maternal nephews, as in these verses sung at a *tende-n-goumaten* in Niger in January 2002: "This piece is dedicated to Rhomer who is in Janleda (Libya) / His steps resemble drops of water / His smile resembles gold / Praise song dedicated to Rhomer . . ."

Other song verses, however, are more strident; for example, the following verses mocked men who dress badly: "Oh, my soul! / Hippopotamus! / Bent-over [crouched down] dance, the dance of the hippopotamus [one becomes fat in this dance in order to make people laugh] / She is a bit like the night / The youths dance for Bouna / because one is bent-over." It is, in other words, now more difficult for suitors to dress well for dignified courtship.

A women's wedding *tende* in Agadez, in August 1998, continues similar themes:

> My young girls of Eghaser [village near Iferouan] / All applaud in order to discourage the lazy ones / The performance takes place with the aid of applause / The young girls of my village because I have studied in order not to make a mistake / a father, he must not do evil / your daughters are nearby / Oh, the young girls / Me, I want to congratulate, but I have not seen anything to congratulate / There are others who had the body of a vulture / They left for Hausa country to stay / One of them had the mouth of a crow / He is their boss [i.e., they neglected the traditions of Hausa country; she insults those who stay in Hausa regions for abandoning Tuareg traditions] / Others got into fights because of me / A man and his close relative, they did battle with sabers.

Here, the soloist is proud to be sought after by men, but still expresses disapproval that close relatives, who are not supposed to fight, did battle with swords.

Many fear that far-flung labor migration, military training, and political exile result in abandoning of Tuareg traditions. Unemployment and war have made it difficult for men to assemble bridewealth (*taggalt*) and to support a wife and children. Once they marry, men also experience problems in marriages to more sophisticated women. One man who often sold jewelry in Nigeria had a first wife in rural Aïr. He contracted a polygynous marriage to a second wife in Agadez, but this marriage did not last more than two years. His relatives explained to me that "Agadez wives are hard on a man's pocketbook," alluding to the woman's allegedly expensive tastes. They warned others not to marry Agadez women because "towns' women hurt the wallet" because they have "tastes that drain a man's resources."

This insecurity in masculine gender roles is also shown in informal court-ship situations. In the sedentarized milieu, *tende* gatherings depart from cer-tain conventions of the more nomadic milieu. In the latter, gallant etiquette is practiced, with emphasis on reserve and discretion: lovers had to pass tests, follow special social rules (Gast 1992; Figueiredo 1996; Rasmussen 2000). There was reserve/respect for one's partner. Courtship conversation emphasized poems and oratory which showcased charm. Amorous escapades remained private and in separate feminine and masculine conversations; no one discussed ex-ploits of sexuality from *takarakit* (reserve). Today, conversations discuss amo-rous and sexual relations more openly, in joking and in verbal and even some physical abuse, sometimes even in the presence of elders (Gast 1992; Figueiredo 1996; Rasmussen 2000, 2001). Women's responses to this vary: some women, in particular those of already socially marginal status, marry military and func-tionary men from outside; others leave for towns to become independent and self-supporting. Today these women and their descendants constitute a large part of the sedentary Tuareg population in the larger, more multiethnic Afri-can towns beyond Agadez and Kidal, with some family origins from formerly slave and client descent groups. Consider Latou, one of the women whose *tende* singing mocked the polygynous man earlier in this essay. Latou and her sister, Asalama (pseudonyms), migrated to Niamey, Niger, from Kidal, Mali, during an earlier (1963) tax revolt in northern Mali which was followed by widespread oppression and refugee flight. Their own married daughters could not travel as freely as their mothers, however. Latou by 1998 had divorced her most re-cent husband, who, despite a rather modest income from drawing and toting water from the market pump, had contracted a polygynous marriage. Like most Tuareg women, she was extremely hostile toward polygyny. She lamented, "Men in Niamey do not respect women." Thus women like Latou who move to more multiethnic urban settings face opportunities and constraints: somewhat greater material comfort if their economic position allows it, but also greater restrictions, once they marry, and greater threat of a well-to-do husband's po-lygyny.

However, there are contexts in which the interests of women and men be-come united. Many *tende* singers now also incorporate themes of wider politi-cal resistance into their verses, thereby forging "feminism" into a united front of Tuareg nationalism with men. This theme appeared in other song verses welcoming the *Aide d'Urgence Internationale* workers who reported human rights abuses: "Death, you must distance yourself from young people / The young people who do the dance of horses, you must go to their level [go behind them] / God help / Because of the *Kogritan* [militia attacks on villagers they ac-cused of sheltering former rebels in November 1997], like donkeys, fat donkeys [mocking of authorities or soldiers who attacked villages] that [come] look for the poor in order to punish or do harm [*tchouta*]." Here, in critiques of atrocities by some militia in northern Tuareg regions during and after the rebellion, are emergent themes of cultural survival and regional autonomy.

These songs are broader in their concerns, moving beyond the personal love sentiments predominant in the earlier *tende* music, and even beyond gendered themes of relations between the sexes, toward merging with wider issues of political nationalism and cultural revitalization. There are also now wider audiences, which can mean a wider forum for grievances, or—more ominously— more likely dangers of retaliation. Nonetheless, these issues air women singers' perspectives of problems of violence on their home terrain, which in effect has become a battlefield. There are calls for peace, but also outrage and resistance, as in the following song performed at a *tende n goumaten* possession session in rural Niger in January 2002: "Oh, the young girls, if you know God / you must assist with the festivities, the festivities have become orphaned / This song I have composed for the young people who formerly served in the rebellion [*atawra*] / who were born in Niger, those who rained iron on the tree / the missile that roars like a lion, the *Kalashnikov* that shoots / the young people, I thank you for taking up arms on the shoulders, I tell you / my greetings for you Moussa, Silimane, and Kouche, Atanfa, Abdatan, Kamat, I encourage Ghabdala, who saved a thousand people."

Tende Songs' Impact

The foregoing *tende* song themes and their performance contexts show how women's songs assert longstanding and new forms of resistance (Abu-Lughod 1990), but they also encounter new challenges at the same time. Moreover, the question remains: how effective is all this?

Despite the presence of female heads of local women's organizations, few Tuareg women occupy national political positions. There are divisions between more prominent, cosmopolitan and urban women and their rural counterparts. Many national women's organizations and "development" programs use discourse which describe women and their roles primarily through maternal kinship and wifely and daughterly images.[13]

At the same time, however, women are recognized by most men as fully equal in terms of their competence. Women and men alike tell stories of a few female rebels who performed heroic deeds during the rebellion. There are also a few female *ichumar*/guitar music composers and singers, though they remain outnumbered by men in this latter genre, which emphasizes male rebel heroes.

Most importantly, those mixed-sex, multi-instrument professional musical troupes called *ensembles* or *orchestres* now provide some women and men with opportunities for travel and economic remuneration. One such troupe, named *Ensemble Tartit* (denoting "Union"), whose members are originally from the Goundam and Timbuktoo regions of Mali, has toured internationally, including United States performances. Their first European performance took place in Belgium in 1995. They include a *tende* player alongside players of other instruments, such as the now-rare *anzad* and the *teharden,* a three-stringed lute (sometimes also called the *takamba*). In their public advertisement statement and professional biography, the group emphasizes not solely their music, but also those elements of Tuareg culture they seek to revitalize and present to the outside world: nomadism, the Berber language group and its North African roots, and affinities between the Moor and the Tuareg peoples. *Tartit* was formed at a refugee camp in eastern Mauritania. Originally numbering approximately twenty people, the touring ensemble now numbers eight musicians and one tour manager. The term *Tartit,* they say, "symbolizes the link that exists among these musicians, . . . because these musicians represent the different [pre-colonial political divisions] confederations that [still] make up Tuareg society."[14] In their biography, they describe their refugee plight and commitment to presenting their music to as wide and diverse an audience as possible. The ad/bio continues with a brief review of the importance of music, song, and poetry in Tuareg culture, and in relation to social structure: "Their social structure has traditionally had a great influence on their music: only women of the noble or the vassal [tributary] 'tribes' [*sic*] were once permitted to play the *anzad* . . . Good players of the *anzad* are today becoming rarer and its repertoire is inexorably becoming smaller." They also explain that the *tende,* once played exclusively by "servant" women, is now played by any woman. Hence the rendering, in translation, of local social categories into terms Europeans and Americans can understand. Finally, they explain that the role of music in Tuareg society is, as in much of Africa, "[viewed] as normal . . . as breathing, and not separated into 'performance' as it is in the western world." The ad/bio also explains that members of *Tartit* prefer to be called Kel Tamajaq people and Amazigh, rather than Tuareg and Berber, respectively; for the latter terms were attributed to Tuareg by outsiders. Back home, there is not consensus on this. Thus the *tende* is used as a vehicle for both cultural preservation and change.

These musical tours therefore provide not solely economic remuneration, but also opportunities for a wider cultural "voice" for performers, enabling them to comment to the international community on local concerns of cultural revitalization and human rights. Of course, much of their music is performed strictly for audience pleasure, and many of their song themes undoubtedly lose some of their textual meaning when transplanted so far from home and detached from their local performance context. But they take on new meanings that have consequences for women singers—both in the immediate contexts, and over the longer term.

One cannot underestimate the impact of these wider travels upon Tuareg women, who until recently, despite their nomadism, tended to travel widely less than Tuareg men. Consider the case of a young singer from the Kidal region of Mali, whom I shall call Tita. Tita was approximately eighteen years old, of noble origins, and her mother also was a renowned poet and singer. Unfortunately, following her family's refugee flight to Tamanrasset, Algeria, she suffered an automobile accident there which crushed the bones in her foot and ankle. Following the Peace Pact, Tita returned to Mali and attended secondary school in Gao. There, a French woman aid worker who heard her sing noticed her injury, and took her to France for treatment, where she resided in the woman's home for several months. Later, however, she left: for, according to her own account, the woman grew suspicious that her boyfriend was becoming romantically interested in their houseguest. Tita returned to her home in the Kidal region, and eventually participated with other local singers and musicians in a regional festival competition in Kidal. She related to me with pride that her village's "team" had won out over all other regional teams, including that in Kidal, after the latter had called them "peasants." Here, this singer's career is marked by early upheavals, with intermittent good fortune and triumph. Her uprooting in refugee flight and serious accident injury were followed by medical assistance, but also some social tensions with her host family. Her musical talent survived all this turmoil, and her comments on festival competition reveal that *tende* singing nowadays can also become a vehicle of local regional pride, as well as personal pride in cosmopolitanism.

These musical tours cause additional social tensions between the sexes and social strata back home. There inevitably arise jealousy and divisions. In Niger, a woman from Agadez who sings with another *orchestre/ensemble* group was given jewelry by a male friend to sell for him while she sang on tour in France. Upon her return to Agadez, he accused her (accurately or inaccurately, I do not know) of spending the money from the sales of his jewelry on clothing for herself. He threatened to bring the case to her family, socially prominent in that town. Apparently tensions were diffused, however, because several years later she returned to France again with the musical troupe, unfazed by this business conflict. Her socially prominent family may have offered her some protection from this accusation. In another incident, a famous male dancer was set to travel with an ensemble to Europe. He was much admired for his talent, and attracted a young woman, whom a marabout also loved. The marabout, jealous of the dancer due to tour, allegedly used sorcery to attack him, in the form of a tooth biting into his leg, thereby debilitating the dancer and preventing him from performing. Thus new, more global singing contexts bring performers problems of coping with not failure, but success. Men feel ambivalent about women's newfound independence, and some prominent leaders such as Islamic scholars encounter rivalry from suitors with new sources of prestige in international performances.

CONCLUSION

In *tende* singing in local performance settings, there are indeed expressions of Bakhtin's polyvocality and Abu-Lughod's "dissonent discourses." Many song verses refer collectively to "my female relatives" or "my women friends" or "the girls of my village or neighborhood"; they often appeal to others for support or collaborative performance participation. For *tende* singers in intimate settings, discursive practice often, though not always, represents a collage of multiple articulating voices. As Graham terms Zavante verbal art, "truth is not the universal standard against which individual statements can be measured; truth can be contested, for it is constructed from many voices" (Graham 1995, 142). On the other hand, in the *tende* singing following political leaders' speeches, during aid organizations' visits, and upon "folkloric" presentations of Tuareg cultural "authenticity" to others (Clifford 1988), these more "staged" songs have ambiguous meanings when decontextualized from their local setting. Singers modify themes to suit their purposes before diverse audiences: for example, many *ensembles/orchestres* sing praises of male rebel heroes when they tour internationally, to appeal for support of Tuareg cultural autonomy. But these latter performances, while certainly no "less authentic" than the others, are nonetheless distanced from their local social performance situations. As such, their texts and performance contexts have different gendered meanings, intentions, and effects. Here, representations of both men and women assume political significance as symbols and actors in new scenarios.

Women singers remain prominent as vocal critics of actions by individual men, but they now extend their critiques to institutions such as the state, militia, and NGO agencies. In effect, they conduct a kind of local political economy or anthropology of gender in local feminist perspectives. Their critique does not always translate into actual authority or influence in practice, as shown in emerging courtship, marriage, and property relationships between the sexes. *Tende* song performances suggest women's resistance, but also limitations to their influence. There are contenders in emerging sociopolitical relationships. Some are in danger of losing their places; others are rising in the system to replace them. These songs convey women's reflections on this complex predicament.

NOTES

1. Tuareg today live in Niger, Mali, Algeria, Libya, and Burkina Faso. In addition, there are very small expatriate (but thus far not large immigrant) communities of labor migrants and itinerant traders in Nigeria, and a few students and political exiles in France. Other Tuareg travel on labor migration and to sell art objects, but do not settle permanently, in Italy, Belgium, Germany, and recently, the United States. The spoken language, Tamajaq, has several dialects and is in the Berber group of the Afro-Asiatic language family. Some Tuareg, primarily intellectuals and nationalists, prefer to be called "Kel Tamajaq" because the term Tuareg is of outside origin, perhaps from Arabic; others, however, continue to use "Tuareg." Much of the ethnographic literature uses "Tuareg," so I follow this practice for the sake of consistency here.

2. Data for this essay are based on nearly seven years of cultural/social anthropological field research and residence, between 1976 and 2012, in Niger, first as a teacher with Peace Corps and under local contract for the Ministry of Education, and later as anthropologist, with more recent projects also conducted in Mali and France. I am grateful to Fulbright Hays, Social Science Research Council, Wenner-Gren Foundation, Indiana University, and the University of Houston for support for my research projects on the following topics among the Tuareg: spirit possession; aging and the life course; herbal and diviner healers; comparison of rural and urban smith/artisans; changing urban Tamajaq theatrical plays; and interregional study of the effects of drought, war, and repatriation on changing gender constructs.

3. The northern regions of Niger and Mali are great distances from their respective capital cities, Niamey and Bamako, and until recently Tuareg were marginalized from colonial and independent state governments. As elsewhere in Africa, nation-state boundaries established by European powers were artificial, and have not coincided with cultural/ethnic groupings. French policies, furthermore, tended to foster uneven "development" in different regions of these countries. Until recently, also, most educated elites and leaders have come from southern farming populations. Many nomads in the northern regions tended at first to resist colonial and postcolonial schools, censuses, and taxation as threats to local culture and sources of control. For these reasons, many Tuareg became excluded from jobs in the modern infrastructure. For detailed history of these processes in Niger, see Charlick (1991), Dayak (1992), and Claudot-Hawad (1996b); for discussion of historical relations of Tuareg in Mali, see Boilley (1999), and for Algeria, see Keenan (1977).

4. In contrast to many of their neighbors, most Tuareg practice monogamy, although as Muslims men theoretically have the right to take up to four wives. There is considerable variation and change in marital patterns, according to nomadic/sedentary, rural/urban, and different regional settings, as well as socioeconomic and occupational factors. For example, in my own long-term field research in Niger and more recently Mali, I noticed that some prominent Islamic scholars (popularly called marabouts or *ineslemen*)—both Tuareg and Kunta Arab—often become polygynous. Among some confederations, such as the Kel Ewey of the Aïr Mountains of northeastern Niger and the Kel (E)suk in the Adar and Kidal regions of Mali, these marabouts are quite influential and numerous, inheriting their occupation in clans, some of whom claim descent from the Prophet. In some more sedentarized and urban communities, also, polygyny

appears more widespread, despite the greater expense, among those who can afford it: namely, prosperous oasis gardeners and merchants. A few caravanners have for many years had "secret wives" in the south, where they spend approximately half the year. Many Tuareg women, however, vehemently oppose their husbands' polygyny, and until recently most of them demanded divorce rather than tolerate it. Most women who do accept a polygynous match insist on separate villages of residence for co-wives.

5. Regarding such terms as "original," "authentic," and "real," I agree with some other theorists (Clifford 1988; Davis 1999) about the need to critically deconstruct them and recognize their highly subjective and relative meanings, subject to creative manipulation in the art-culture system. See also Rasmussen (2003) for some discussion of these issues in the recent "diaspora" of Tuareg smith/artisans and their tourist art.

6. In the course of many visits to and long-term residence in Tuareg communities, I collected numerous examples of verbal art: poetry, *tende* and other song genres such as *ichumar*/guitar and *anzad*, folk tales, riddles, life histories, and other oral traditions, especially during my research on spirit possession and smith/artisans (who, among some but not all Tuareg groups, play roles similar to those of *griots*). In my early research, I photographed and audiotaped these performances; later, I videotaped them, always with local permission, of course. Transcription, translation, and textual analysis (local exegesis) were conducted with several different "key informants/assistants/ consultants," both men and women, singers and non-singers, and insofar as possible, persons of diverse social origins. We wrote verses initially in Tamajaq (in the Roman rather than Tifinagh alphabet) and French. Later, I translated these materials into English. I played most recordings back for local residents for more informal commentary. I have attempted to minimize problems of orthography, but there is continuing disagreement among Tuareg intellectuals of different regions and confederations (who speak very different dialects) concerning rules for transliteration. Some more cosmopolitan Tuareg know the international phonetic alphabet, but most of my assistants worked with me "on the ground" and were from the local (usually rural) communities where I collected my data, and, while very skilled and knowledgeable of local traditions, tended to have minimal formal education. Outsiders, while more cosmopolitan and formally educated, tended to be less trusted by local residents as assistants than persons from the local community, particularly in the countryside.

7. For analysis of this instrument in relation to other local instruments, and discussion of connections between Tuareg music and social stratum and region from an ethnomusicological perspective, see Card (1978) and Borel (1988); for symbolic and aesthetic analysis of *tende* songs specifically associated with the *tende n goumaten* spirit possession exorcism ritual, see Rasmussen (1995), chapter 6.

8. Thus far, there is a paucity of studies of the new *ichumar*/guitar music, except in some biographical and promotional materials of Tuareg musical ensembles. Bourgeot (1990, 150) includes brief mention of these "revolutionary" protest songs in an early work on the Tuareg nationalist/separatist rebellion. There is an essay on this music's performance context and its implications for intergenerational relationships (Rasmussen 2000). It is difficult to ascertain this music's current meanings, but like some Western popular music—for example, punk—these songs appear to be gradually moving away from their protest messages, which were once banned in Niger and Mali, although even now at urban festivals many retain political themes, such as praise of former rebel

heroes. The few women *ichumar* composers and singers generally sing the poetry, but do not usually play the electric guitar, bass, or drum. Some bands and singers—for example, Abdullah—have recorded cassettes professionally.

9. Matrilineal institutions among the Tuareg have become submerged, to different degrees and in varied ways, in diverse regions and confederations. In some groups, such as among the Ifoghas of the Adar n Ifoghas region in northern Mali, "living milk" inheritance or endowment (in which property goes only to sisters, nieces, and daughters) remains important, and NGO and UN compensation of herds attempts to preserve these principles (personal communication, Aicha Belco, director of women's association), and in some confederations, such as the Kel Geres in southern Niger, succession still goes from maternal uncle to sister's son. In others, Qurʾānic influence and patrilineal inheritance, descent, and succession are more important today. Among the Kel Ewey of the Aïr region of Niger, Islamic scholars require written wills with witnesses, or consider inheritance to be Qurʾānic (*takachit*). In many confederations (precolonial political and regional groups headed by a sultan or *amenukal*) as well as clans, there are origin myths tracing descent back to female founding ancestresses/culture heroes, matrilineal images in healing rituals (in particular, herbalism), and some matrilineal naming practices (women use *welet,* "daughter of," rather than *ag,* "son of")—though this is discouraged by some marabouts, schools, voting registration policies, and post offices.

10. These attitudes are expressed in a tale I collected near Mt. Bagzan in the Aïr region of Niger about Iblis, the Devil, and the Prophet Aghaly, in which Aghaly ties up Iblis after being interrupted by Iblis from praying at the mosque, but this causes all the men to cease sexual relations with their wives. Once Aghaly unties Iblis, the men resume normal sexual relations with their wives.

11. For instance, women stopping to sing their slow regular songs, always the same five flat notes, beat out on a "primitive" drum or simply by clapping hands (Porch 1984, 171). Lamy also wrote that he heard "a great rumble, some piercing cries, and an indescribable hubbub" some yards from his military camp: he next saw a "dark mass of humanity rumbling forward . . . the Tuareg on camels and the 'blacks' on foot, some actually clinging to the tails of the camels and urging them forward by thrusting knives into their haunches" (Porch 1984, 172–173).

12. In the past, noble descent groups had a kind of "copyright" over certain poems, songs, and drum-patterns. There were precise rules concerning who could perform them, when, where, and in what style. Smith/artisans attached to noble families often performed them. Nowadays, these rules have relaxed and anyone may compose and perform any poetry and music, and styles are more individually shaped according to performer and audience preference. In the countryside, there remains emphasis upon women and men "pleasing" each other in performances, however; for example, women's songs still are not considered complete without men's shouts and applause (Card 1978; Rasmussen 1995).

13. For example, many national women's organizations headquartered in the capital cities of Niamey and Bamako tend to discuss in their newsletters' editorials women's contributions using metaphors of daughters and sisters. Likewise, a female radio performer with a program on gender and "development" issues in Agadez appeals to female kinship roles and relationships, including wifely duties, in her broadcasts.

14. *Touring, Ensemble Tartit* publicity statement/brochure, March/April 2003.

WORKS CITED

Abu-Lughod, Lila. 1986. *Veiled Sentiments: Honor and Poetry in a Bedouin Society.* Berkeley: University of California Press.

———. 1990. The romance of resistance. In *Beyond the Second Sex,* ed. Peggy Sanday and Ruth Goodenough, 311–337. Philadelphia: University of Pennsylvania Press.

———. 1993. *Writing Women's Worlds: Bedouin Stories.* Berkeley: University of California Press.

———. 2002. Do Muslim women really need saving? *American Anthropologist* 104 (3): 783–790.

Bakhtin, Mikhail. 1981. *The Dialogic Imagination: Four Essays.* Ed. M. Holquist. Trans. C. Emerson and M. Holquist. Austin: University of Texas Press.

———. 1984 [1965]. *Rabelais and His World.* Trans. Helene Iswolsky. Bloomington: Indiana University Press.

Boilley, Pierre. 1999. *Les Kel Adar: Dépendances et révoltes: du Soudan français au Mali contemporain.* Paris: Karthala.

Borel, François. 1988. Rhythmes de passage chez les Touaregs de l'Azawagh (Niger). In *Cahiers de musiques traditionnelles,* vol. 1. Geneva: Ateliers d'ethnomusicologie.

Bourdieu, Pierre. 1978. *Outline of a Theory of Practice.* Cambridge: Cambridge University Press.

Bourgeot, André. 1990. Identité touaregue: de l'aristocratie à la révolution. *Etudes Rurales* 120 (Oct.–Dec.): 129–162.

Brenner, Suzanne April. 1998. *The Domestication of Desire: Women, Wealth, and Modernity in Java.* Princeton: Princeton University Press.

Camel, Florence. 2002. Voyage sous contrôle colonial: les caravanes de sel des Kel Aïr dans la première moitié du Xxième siècle. In *Voyager d'un point de vue nomade,* ed. Hélenè Claudot-Hawad, 81–89. Paris: Editions Paris-Mediterranee, IREMAM.

Card, Caroline. 1978. Tuareg Music and Social Identity. PhD diss., Indiana University.

———. 1981. Some problems of field recording for research purposes. In *Discourse in Ethnomusicology: Essays in Honor of George List,* ed. Caroline Card, John Hasse, Roberta L. Singer, and Ruth M. Stone, 53–65. Bloomington: Ethnomusicology Publications Group, Indiana University.

Casajus, Dominique. 2000. *Gens de Parole.* Textes à l'appui/série anthropologie. Paris: Editions la Découverte.

Charlick, Robert. 1991. *Niger: Personal Rule and Survival in the Sahel.* Boulder: Westview.

Claudot-Hawad, Hélenè. 1993. *Touareg, Portrait en fragments.* Aix-en-Provence: Edisud.

———, ed. 1996a. *Touaregs et autres Sahariens entre plusieurs mondes.* Aix-en-Provence: Edisud.

———, ed. 1996b. *Touaregs, Voix solitaires sous l'horizon confisqué.* Aix-en-Provence: Edisud.

Clifford, James. 1988. *The Predicament of Culture.* Cambridge, Mass.: Harvard University Press.

Collins, P. H. 1993. Toward an Afrocentric feminist epistemology. In *Feminist Frameworks,* ed. A. M. Jaggar and P. S. Rotenberg, 93–103. New York: McGraw Hill.

Davis, Elizabeth A. 1999. Metamorphosis in the culture market of Niger. *American Anthropologist* 101 (3): 485–501.

Dayak, Mano. 1992. *Touareg, La Tragédiè*. Paris: Editions Jean-Claude Lattès.

Di Leonardo, Micaela. 1990. *Gender at the Crossroads of Knowledge*. Berkeley: University of California Press.

Figueiredo, Christina. 1996. Identité et concitoyenneté: La réélaboration des relations entre hommes et femmes aux marges de la société Kel Adagh (Mali). In *Touaregs et autres Sahariens entre plusieurs mondes,* ed. Hélenè Claudot-Hawad, 113–137. Aix-en-Provence: Edisud.

Gast, Marcel. 1992. Les relations amoureuses chez les Kel Ahaggar. In *Amour, Phantasmes et sociétés en Afrique du nord et au Sahara,* ed. Tassadit Yacine, 151–173. Paris: l'Harmattan-Awal.

Geertz, Clifford. 1973. *The Interpretation of Cultures*. New York: Basic.

Giddens, Anthony. 1979. *Central Problems in Social Theory: Action, Structure, and Contradiction in Social Analysis*. Berkeley: University of California Press.

Graham, Laura. 1995. *Performing Dreams*. Austin: University of Texas Press.

Hale, Thomas A. 1998. *Griots and Griottes*. Bloomington: Indiana University Press.

Hodgson, Beverly. 2000. *Rethinking Pastoralism in Africa*. Oxford: James Currey; Athens: Ohio University Press.

Hoffman, Barbara. 1995. Power, structure, and Mande jeliw. In *Status and Identity in West Africa: Nyamakalaw of Mande,* ed. David C. Conrad and Barbara E. Frank, 36–57. Bloomington: Indiana University Press.

Keenan, Jeremy. 1977. *Tuareg: People of Ahaggar*. London: Allen Lane.

Mohanty, Chandra Talpade. 1991. Under Western eyes: Feminist scholarship and colonial discourses. In *Third World Women and the Politics of Feminism,* ed. Chandra Talpade Mohanty, Ann Russo, and Lourdes Torres, 51–80. Bloomington: Indiana University Press.

Murphy, Robert. 1964. Social distance and the veil. *American Anthropologist* 66:1257–1274.

———. 1967. Tuareg kinship. *American Anthropologist* 69:163–170.

Nicolaisen, Ida, and Johannes Nicolaisen. 1997. *The Pastoral Tuareg*. Copenhagen: The Carlsberg Foundation.

Nicolaisen, Johannes. 1961. Essai sur la religion et la magie touaregues. *Folk* 3:113–160.

Ortner, Sherry B. 1996. *Making Gender: The Politics and Erotics of Culture*. Boston: Beacon.

Porch, Douglas. 1984. *The Conquest of the Sahara*. New York: Knopf.

Rasmussen, Susan. 1994. Female sexuality, social reproduction, and medical intervention: Kel Ewey Tuareg perspectives. *Culture, Medicine, and Psychiatry* 18:433–462.

———. 1995. *Spirit Possession and Personhood among the Kel Ewey Tuareg*. Cambridge: Cambridge University Press.

———. 1998. Within the tent and at the crossroads: Travel and gender identity among the Tuareg of Niger. *Ethos* 26 (2): 153–182.

———. 2000. Between several worlds: Images of youth and age in Tuareg popular performances. *Anthropological Quarterly* 73 (3): 133–145.

———. 2001. *Healing in Community: Medicine, Contested Terrains, and Cultural Encounters among the Tuareg*. Westport, Conn.: Bergin and Garvey.

———. 2003. When the field space comes to the home space: New constructions of ethnographic knowledge in a new African diaspora. *Anthropological Quarterly* 76 (1): 7–32.

Rofel, Lisa. 1999. *Other Modernities: Gender in China after Socialism.* Berkeley: University of California Press.

Trawick, Margaret. 1988. Spirits and voices in Tamil songs. *American Ethnologist* 15 (2): 193–216.

Warren, Kay, and Susan C. Bourque. 1990. Women, technology, and international development ideologies: Analyzing feminist voices. In *Gender at the Crossroads of Knowledge,* ed. Micaela Di Leonardo, 278–312. Berkeley: University of California Press.

Wood, John. 1999. *When Men Are Women.* Madison: University of Wisconsin Press.

Worley, Barbara. 1991. Women's War Drum, Women's Wealth. PhD Diss., Columbia University.

17

Income Strategies of a Jelimuso in Mali and France

Nienke Muurling

INTRODUCTION

Remittances are a major source of income in Mali. It is estimated that the yearly amount of money sent by Malian emigrants exceeds 100 million euros, of which at least 50 million euros are sent by Malians who reside in France.[1] One indicator of the importance of these France-Mali remittances is the fact that France provides approximately 60 million euros a year in aid to Mali (Gubert 2003). The "French money" sent by relatives is used for the purchase agricultural equipment. The funds are also invested in social relationships. Although these transfers of funds may appear at first to operate outside the framework of traditional customs because they are initiated in France rather than in Mali, other participants, in particular professional female singers known as *jelimusow*,[2] also participate. The question is how these women, involved locally in activities that involve money (rewards for performances and other services), participate in the larger financial network linking France and Mali.

In their praise songs *jelimusow* forge relations between people by connecting them to their ancestors and relatives. At the same time they emphasize the unique and wealthy position of the subject, often in the presence of a large public—for example, at a major event such as a wedding or an installation of a chief. The subject of the songs appreciates the lyrics of the *jelimusow* because they heighten the reputation of the patron, who in turn will remunerate them with a gift such as jewelry, cloth, or money. Money, then, purchases not only luxury goods but also personal and family fame. During her performance, the jelimuso not only establishes or strengthens relations between people present but also confirms a people's identity in relation to others, thus creating a kind of transparency in networks.

But what about the *jelimusow* themselves? What are their income and distribution strategies? How do they make ends meet? And how do they handle the problems all women have to cope with when living in a large city such as Bamako? Where do their financial operations fit into the larger network of transfers from France to Mali? How does increasing anonymity, caused by migration and the growing size of Bamako, contribute to family problems? What is the impact of the relatively new development of neolocal settlement of husband and wife upon marriage, and in particular the decline of the extended family as a basis for socio-economic organization? (Brand 2000, 45, 59 and 90–93). One outcome is that people become more dependent on new networks, as demonstrated by an increasing proportion of gifts received from friends (Vaa et al. 1989), which easily transcends national boundaries. In this rapidly changing context, it is the involvement of the *jelimuso* with the social services she offers that may provide partial solutions, or at least some hope, to individuals and families.

In Bamako, the capital of Mali, it is not unusual that a local and fairly well-known *jelimuso* earns up to 200,000 Communauté financière africaine (CFA) francs a day, the equivalent of 300 euros, when performing at a life course celebration such as a naming ceremony or a wedding. This leads one to ask, what is the source of this money in a country as poor as Mali? And why are people willing to invest in something seemingly immaterial like social relationships? The answer to the second question is that by investing in relations people are building social capital and enlarging the network on which they can call in times of necessity. Here I follow Annelet Harts-Broekhuis, who states that "social obligations towards families and others of the same social or cultural group play a major role in the allocation of work, housing, and income. These ties are not only important for ensuring integration into the urban structure but also function as a help network during periods of economic depression" (1997, 107). As for the first question, it appears that the lion's share comes from abroad, primarily from France, where a rather large Malian community exists,[3] but also from countries such as Ivory Coast and Gabon. For example, Madu Diawara, one of my informants, who has been living in France since November 2001 and who works as a security agent, assured me that he sends at least 80 percent of his monthly salary of €1000 to his relatives in Mali. This money is invested in both communal and individual projects. Half of it is meant to nourish his father's family, to pay his monthly electricity and cable television bills and to provide his father as well as his paternal uncles with cash for daily needs. The

other half is destined for his fiancée and the construction of his own compound. Although young Malian bachelors in Paris live very economically and
do not demand much luxury,[4] I suspect that it is impossible to live on 200 euros
per month without other sources of support. My informant for instance regularly receives pocket money from his mother, who lives in Paris as well, while
others may be provided with Malian goods to sell in Paris and thus establish a
revenue-producing trade.[5] Next to the regular remittances this same informant
also sent 100,000 CFA francs to cover the expenses of his engagement ceremony, held in August 2002. At least half of this amount was intended for his
fiancée and her sisters to reward the *jelimusow* who performed at the engagement party.

Although *jelimusow* are crucial in shaping and reshaping social relations in
Mali, and thus receive a great deal of "French money," they themselves are operating in a context of transnational networks too. In Paris, for instance, there
are many *jelimusow* who followed their patrons (*jatigiw*), or better, who are
flown in by them to take care of their ceremonies and to encourage and embel-
lish them with their powerful words. This is a very lucrative business because
a *jelimuso* can easily earn up to €100 per song in Paris! Even though we might
expect, due to the distance, that pressure on these *jelimusow* to share income
received from families living in Paris is not as great as it is in Mali, I believe that
a rather large part of the rewards given to these performers is directly invested
in Mali.

To understand the micropolitics of giving and receiving within the space
limitations of a short essay, it is useful to examine the income and distribution
strategies of a *jelimuso* operating in a context of transnational migration, more
precisely between Kela, Bamako, and Paris.

A SUITABLE SPOUSE

Sanungwe Kouyate, born in Kangaba somewhere around 1953, is the eldest
daughter of Siramori Diabate, Mali's most legendary *jelimuso* from Kela (see
Jansen 1996), and Nankoman Kouyate, a skillful *balafon* player from Heremankono, a small village on the other side of the Niger river in the region of
Kangaba. Contrary to Mande customs in which a wife moves into her husband's family (patrilocal and virlocal settlement patterns), Siramori had established her own compound in Kangaba. This indicates the special situation in
which Sanungwe grew up.

Despite the fact that in the past, *jeliw* were endogamous and were not supposed to marry so-called *horonw* (freeborn people; on Mande status categories
see Conrad and Frank 1995), Sanungwe was a very beloved and desirable wed-

ding candidate because she was Siramori's daughter, had inherited her prestige, and was gifted with a beautiful voice. Therefore, during her adolescence, Sanungwe was highly sought after by different young men from the region, until the day that Zoumana Diawara arrived on the spot. Zoumana's father, Jemory Diawara,[6] was a Soninke who came from Kinki in the west of Mali but decided to settle in the Kangaba region and set up a trade in gold, kola nuts, and donkeys. Thanks to this flourishing business he became very much appreciated by his Maninka neighbors. His son Zoumana, who was born in Kangaba, followed in his footsteps, searched for adventure, and became a succesful trader too, in particular buying and selling cloth. After several years of traveling between Bamako, Dakar, Abidjan, and Conakry he decided to return to Kangaba to search for an appropriate bride. Being successful, of *horon* origin, and rather distinguished himself, he was an attractive and suitable spouse for the eldest daughter of Siramori. And thus, Zoumana married Sanugwe. Soon after their marriage they migrated to Bouaké, Ivory Coast, where their son Madu was born around 1973. However, suddenly the times changed and Zoumana's income began to fall. At this moment, it is said, Siramori instructed her daughter to come back to Kangaba and to divorce her husband. Sanungwe agreed, despite the fact that she had two small children.

Concern about money was apparently the main reason for the divorce. But there was another, more basic reason for the breakup, as Sanungwe explained to me. The *horon* origin of Zoumana's family meant that it was impossible for Sanungwe to broaden her knowledge because there were no *jeliw* in her immediate surroundings. Moreover, in this particular Diawara family, members did not perform *jeli* tasks such as mediating and singing at wedding ceremonies. This contradicted the desire on the part of Sanungwe and above all her mother that the young woman should become a professional singer. Soon after her divorce she married the talented guitarist Madusilla Kouyate from Komankera, a small village near the Guinean border. They formed an ideal couple as they performed together and gained a living as *jeliw,* though they never had children together. I assume that this childlessness points to the independence of Sanungwe, being evidently in control of her own fertility (see Brand 2000). Her autonomy in the domain of reproduction can also be seen as a money-saving strategy.

A SUCCESSFUL CAREER

In the early years of her marriage with Madusilla Kouyate, Sanungwe decided to settle in Bamako, but she always maintained contacts with her region of origin. In the beginning of the 1980s, Bamako grew rapidly and could therefore be seen as an enormous field of opportunity for Sanungwe and many other *jelimu-sow*. Every weekend there were and still are many marriages to be celebrated, and it is precisely at these kinds of life course events that *jelimusow* perform and are able to "find" money. The fact that Malian marriages can be regarded as big businesses will be illustrated by the following present-tense description of a successful and lucrative wedding (*konyo*) celebrated in September 1999.

One Sunday morning Jimiya Kouyate, Sanungwe's sister-in-law who lives in the same compound in Djikoroni Dontème, proposes to join her in going to Hamdallaye, another quarter in Bamako.[7] She explains to me that Sanungwe herself has to leave early this morning because she was invited to accompany the marrying couple and both their families to see the mayor. Musicians are preparing themselves, children are waiting and having fun, while suddenly many cars turn the corner. In the middle of the crowd I recognize Sanungwe, but she does not pay attention to me because she has to follow the newly married couple to the courtyard. There the bride's family and in-laws are waiting in the presence of many other *jelimusow*. While the *jelimusow* are praising their patrons and soliciting gifts, the elders are indicating to the bride how to be a suitable wife and good mother.

The *jelimusow* stop singing approximately fifteen minutes later. Everybody leaves the courtyard and returns to the street to look for a chair beneath a canvas. Sanungwe takes a seat next to the musicians, who are all *jeliw* too. She is the main praise singer today, and being in this position she will direct this wedding party. In her right hand she holds a note, which the mother of the bride, who is appointed as organizer of the feast, gave her earlier this morning. On this tiny note a list of names has been written. One can be sure that those on the list will be praised. First the mothers (*denbaw*) of the bride are welcomed. The biological mother as well as the aunts and other mothers (for instance the co-wives of the biological father) belong to this group. They distinguish themselves from others with their "uniform."[8] For the special occasion of the marriage of their daughter they agreed to wear a dress made of the same cloth. This can be seen as an expression of their solidarity, but wearing a "uniform" has a practical reason too: it is much cheaper to buy cloth together. Another distinguishing aspect is the *denbajala,* a narrow cloth of gold (or yellow) thread in which their patronymic, the family name inherited through the father, and their husband's patronymic have been woven. The women wear the *denbajala* around their headscarf, where it symbolizes womanhood or the importance of a woman.

When the musicians start the widely known tune of *denko* (child affair), Sanungwe praises the mothers with the following words: "A husband can give you money, gold, and houses, but the only precious thing he can give is a child."

In Mali children are important, because it is only through being a mother that a woman can achieve full womanhood (see Brand 2000 and Grosz-Ngaté 1989). Moreover, children are of importance not only for their own mothers but also for the society at large. While hearing these words the women rise and form a circle. Dancing and moving in a row, they pass by the group of *jelimusow*. Meanwhile it is striking that a large amont of money (*wari*) is circulating: from the hands of the mothers through the hands of the biological mother, who is dancing in front of them all, to Sanungwe, who receives the best part of it. The women are also giving money to the other *jelimusow* present, who form the background chorus. It is difficult for an outsider to follow and to take account of who is giving what to whom, principally because there are several gift-giving relationships: not only between *jatigimusow* (patron, hostess, giver) and *jelimusow* (client, female praise singer, receiver) but also between the *jatigimusow* themselves. The women are seemingly loaded with money; they even throw it on a plaid cloth in front of the feet of the *jelimusow*. Apparently, the latter receive most all of it, and thus they put it into their collective bag to keep until they can count and distribute it at the end of the day. Before hiding the money the *jelimusow* show off the banknotes to the public and thank the generous givers with words such as *n be kanu barika da i ye, nison ni juguson* or *n te nyina koroman ko abada*, meaning, respectively, "I thank you for your friendship," "Giver of presents to friends and enemies" and "I will never forget the old things."

Following the list names Sanungwe continues to praise her public one by one until dusk. She often has to compete for the microphone, for the other *jelimusow* want to be heard as well. In this case, to be heard means to be remunerated.

The marriage in Hamdallaye described above is a fine illustration of a successful marriage because afterwards it appeared that Sanungwe and her musicians had collected at least 200,000 CFA francs. Of course Sanungwe had to share this amount with the musicians and other *jelimusow*, but she took half of it. Including the price of the contract between Sanungwe and the organizing Feita family, she had earned up to 150,000 CFA francs. Compared to the fixed minimum wage of 23,000 CFA francs per month in Mali, this is a very high income. Nevertheless, it has to be said that this was a lucrative wedding for her, as are most of the other ceremonies she attends, but this is not the case for every *jelimuso*.

Sanungwe is successful because she is able to make a living from performing. Apart from her clear voice and talent Sanungwe's special position is related to the fact that she has a very prestigious mother through whom she is directly affiliated to the Kela *jeliw*. They possess the privilege and authority to recount the epic of Sunjata during the Kamabolon ceremony every seven years to mark both the link between past and present and the unity of the Mande world (see Jansen 1998). Her mother's own reputation gives Sanungwe an advantage in her work because she is regarded as Siramori's heiress. Sanungwe uses this reputation and has become fortunate in her own way, too. She manages her own household and makes her own decisions. Although she has a high income, one cannot ignore the reality that she must devote a significant portion of her rewards to meet the needs of many people. She explained that she had to solve not only her own problems and the problems of her compound, the reason why I would like to call her a female household head, but also the financial problems of her two younger brothers, Sidiki, who lives in Kangaba, and Tayiru, who also lives in Bamako, as well as those of their families, her younger sister Bintan, who resides in Kela, and the family of her deceased father in Heremankono. Apart from these close relatives people seem to find her easily when she performs at a marriage or naming ceremony. It struck me that she is always visited by many people in the course of the day after her performance. She takes her visitors into her room to give them some money in private. In these circumstances, her money does not last more than a few days before she loses everything she has earned. Saving is not possible, she reported to me, because many people in Bamako and the surrounding area depend on her income.

For the Maninka in Bamako, Sanungwe not only represents but also personifies the "old" Kela tradition, and hence I would argue that she is bridging the gap between the city, characterized by the loosening of family networks, and the village, where everybody seems to know one another. Sanungwe herself claims that Kela is her main source of knowledge and that she could not be in Bamako without going to the countryside, more specifically of course Kangaba, Kela, and their surroundings, every one or two months to visit her relatives and to perform at their ceremonies. For a performance in the village she would not charge the organizers of the celebration. First, she and they are linked through family ties. Second, there is less cash in the countryside. Finally, as her son argued, she stills loves her village. Next to this expressed love for her region of origin, it appears that it is a strategic move to associate herself with the countryside because in Mali it is believed that the strongest knowledge originates in or relates to the bush, far away from civilization.

While Sanungwe personifies the Kela tradition in Bamako, she represents Mande tradition and perhaps even Mali itself in Paris. In 1989 she went to Paris for the very first time, together with her husband, to perform, among other things, at a conference about oral traditions (Jansen 1991, 12). In Paris she also contacted Salif Keita, the reknowned singer from Djoliba, a village on the road from Bamako to Kela, who had married a French woman. He helped her to get in contact with Ibrahim Sylla, an established producer of West African music cassettes. Together with the assistance of Salif he produced her first album, "Balendala Djiby" (Kouyate 1990).

After a while, Sanungwe went back to Bamako to live with her husband, but several years later, in the middle of the nineties, she was invited by one of her *jatigiw* to come to Germany and France again. She accepted the invitation and went to spend another period in Europe. Now her life is divided between her patrons living in two continents. She used to travel back and forth, but fortunately for me, in 1999, the year in which I conducted my fieldwork in Mali, she found herself in Bamako. I followed her wherever I could and in the meantime she showed me Mali's capital through the eyes of a *jelimuso*, taking me to a range of different naming and marriage ceremonies, where I was confronted with the ostentatious display of wealth, described earlier. In the course of my fieldwork, however, these displays underscored the fact that praise and prestige can only be achieved by people with money. The wealthy are able to reward the *jelimusow* for their powerful words that inflate the reputations of their subjects and their ancestors. This contributes to the growing gap between the rich and those who do not have the means to attract praises from the *jelimusow*. The following lyrics of a praise song sung by Sanungwe emphasize this problem:

Ah! Jama bara labò,	Ah! When the crowd comes out
jelitigi ni jelintan tè kelen di.	The one who has a griot and the one who does not are not the same.
Jama bara labò,	Ah! When the crowd comes out
mògòtigi ni mògòntan tè kelen di.	The one who has followers and the one who does not are not the same.
Jama bara labò,	Ah! When the crowd comes out
waritigi ni warintan tè kelen di.	The one who has money and the one who does not are not the same.
Iye! Awa, nin lawilitò jigi le ma,	Iye! Awa, this is caused by hope. Awa,
denba nyuman.	Good mother.[9]

Having money or not, or having a large and developed network of people surrounding you, certainly matters for those involved in transnational migration. In 2000 Sanungwe was invited once again to come to live in Europe with one of her *jatigimusow* with whom she maintained a good and long-lasting relationship. Ideally, a woman should ask permission from her husband if she plans to travel, but in Sanungwe's case this is not compulsory. As indicated earlier, she is a female head of household obtaining her own income, sharing it with whomever she thinks needs help, and making her own decisions. One of these decisions was whether to go to Paris. Two months after I returned to Holland, Sanungwe traveled to Europe.

In February 2000 she moved to the Parisian suburb Montreuil. Just after her arrival she called me to explain that the main reason for coming to Europe, apart from the invitation, was medical treatment, possibly because she might have been diabetic. Later, she argued that it was the production of a new album that kept her in France. Asetou Keita, one of her other *jatigimusow* in Paris who was the patron of the famous Kandia Kouyate from Kita, proposed that Sanungwe work with the producer Japi Diawara. There was most likely another reason for her presence in Europe: she was able to earn a large amount of money by performing at Malian ceremonies and concerts.[10] Malian people in France have more money to spend, as evidenced from the rewards she received. For example, in one year she was given three cars and two round-trip air tickets to Mali. But if she earns more than in Bamako, she must send money back home. Nevertheless, she is able to put aside more than she ever could have saved in Bamako. With this money she constructed her own house and compound in Bamako. When the day of her departure arrives, she will use one of the tickets she received and fly back home. But it is also plausible that she may stay in France longer because of the attraction of earning and saving more money.

CONCLUSION

From the example of Sanungwe, which is in many ways typical, it appears that *jelimusow* also contribute to the transfer of "French money" from France to Mali. These performers, like other migrants, add to funds for both communal projects and individual purposes. But unlike the other migrants, she develops her own distinctive income and distribution strategies. One of the outcomes is the construction of houses, of course, but next to that is her investment in social relationships. Here *jelimusow* play an essential role. In an era of weakening family ties and greater dependency on new networks that transcend national boundaries with great ease, a *jelimuso* may give hope, for she is able to confirm the identity of her subjects in her songs, to connect them with others, and to emphasize the generosity of the praised one. Her life story also reveals the way a skillful *jelimuso* is able to negotiate her own fame as well as that of her mother. By paying close attention to the choice of a suitable spouse and to the development of her rather successful career one can see how she illustrates yet another of the many dimensions of the *jeliw* profession.

NOTES

1. Estimations like these are difficult to make because remittances are mostly transferred outside the official banking systems. Next to the approximately 11 million in-

habitants of Mali itself the Malian diaspora is composed of 4 million people, of whom 1 million live in Ivory Coast and about 120,000 in France. Other Malian immigration countries are Senegal, Gabon, Congo-Brazzaville (Republic of the Congo), and the United States, where they principally live in New York. For an historic perspective on Malian, and more specifically Soninke, migration see Manchuelle (1997); for literature on Malian migration towards France see Daum (1998), Findley (1989) and also Sargent and Cordell (2003).

2. A *jelimuso* is a female praise singer or bard. *Jeli,* a Mande term, can be translated as "griot," a widely used regional term, whereas the suffix *muso* means "woman." In Bamana, a major member of the Mande family of languages, a *w* is added to indicate the plural. In the literature (Hale 1998; Jansen 1996; Janson 2002) the term *griotte* is often used. In order to avoid confusion, I will follow Hale's recommendation that ethno-specific terms rather than *griotte,* of unclear origin and filtered through French, be employed when the focus is largely on a particular group or family of languages.

3. In note 1 I already mentioned that there are some 120,000 Malians living in France, mainly in the Paris region of Île-de-France. However, only one-third of them possess a residence permit, meaning that some 80,000 are living there illegally—based on estimates, not on facts provided by the French government. These illegal Malians and other Africans are often called "sans-papiers" (*Le Monde* 2003 and Gubert 2003).

4. According to Madu Diawara, young Malian celibates in France do not need very much: they often squat in empty buildings or share an apartment with relatives and refrain from luxuries. But as soon as they are married and have managed to bring wives to France, this thrifty lifestyle is said to finish, as do the regular high remittances to Mali, because then there are more personal expenses to cover such as rent and the needs of the wife.

5. This idea was suggested to me by Jan Jansen (personal communication, March 2003) and merits further study.

6. According to both Sanungwe Kouyate and her son Madu Diawara, Jemory Diawara was the elder brother of Madusilla Diawara, to whom the well-known song *Julafundo Madusilla* is dedicated. Julafundo is a village near Kangaba. One of the daughters of Madusilla Diawara, called Naberete, was married to Banjugu Kouyate from Komankera in the region of Narena. Their son, named after his grandfather, is now married to Sanungwe.

7. The following description is based on field notes which I made at the wedding party of Ayisa Keita on 5 September 1999. Ayisa is the youngest daughter of Fama Keita, who is one of the patrons (*jatigikèw*) of my main informant, Sanungwe Kouyate. From 1 August till 30 November I lived in the compound of Sanungwe and conducted fieldwork for my MA thesis.

8. A Maninka term for the word *uniform* is unknown to me because women in Bamako only use the French term *uniforme*. Barbara Hoffman also uses the same term. According to her, each woman is free to have the cloth cut to her own taste: the "uniformity" or solidarity, she writes, is in the cloth itself, not in the composition of the cloth (2000, 25n22).

9. Maninka translated first into French by Ouna Faran Camara from DNAFLA in Bamako. These lines were sung by Sanungwe Kouyate from Djikoroni Dontème/ Bamako at the marriage ceremony of Ayisa Keita, the youngest daughter of Sanungwe's

jatigi; recorded on 5 September 1999 in Hamdallaye/Bamako. The song was dedicated to Awa Kone, one of the mothers (*denbaw*) of the bride.

10. In addition to the regular Malian life course celebrations in Paris Sanungwe also performed several times in the Netherlands. For the first series of concerts (2000, organized in cooperation with PAN records) she was accompanied by her brother Lansine Kouyate, the skilled *jenbe* player Fodekaba Diabate from Kela, and the guitarist Fedjala Diawara. Her brother plays the *balafon* and lives in Paris too. A second performance was given with Ballake Cissoko, the famous *kora* player from Bamako, and his group in early 2003, where she was accompanied by the *kora* player Layiba Diawara, originally from Guinea but residing in the Netherlands.

WORKS CITED

Brand, Saskia. 2000. *Mediating Means and Fate: A Socio-Political Analysis of Fertility and Demographic Change in Bamako, Mali.* Leiden: Brill.

Conrad, David, and Barbara Frank, eds. 1995. *Status and Identity in West Africa:* Nyamakalaw *of Mande.* Bloomington: Indiana University Press.

Daum, Christophe. 1998. *Les associations de Maliens en France: Migration, développement et citoyenneté.* Paris: Karthala.

Findley, S. E. 1989. Choosing between African and French destinations: The role of family and community factors in migration from the Senegal River Valley. In *Working Papers in African Studies no. 142,* 1–21. Boston: Boston University African Studies Center.

Grosz-Ngaté, Maria. 1989. Hidden meanings: Explorations into a Bamanan construction of gender. *Ethnology* 28 (2): 167–183.

Gubert, F. 2003. L'Aide à la réinsertion offerte aux immigrés est un leurre: Ces immigrés qui vont vivre le Mali. *Le Monde,* 19 February, 10.

Hale, Thomas A. 1998. *Griots and Griottes. Masters of Words and Music.* Bloomington: Indiana University Press.

Harts-Broekhuis, Anelet. 1997. How to sustain a living? Urban households and poverty in the Sahelian town of Mopti. *Africa: Journal of the African Institute* 67:106–129.

Hoffman, Barbara G. 2000. *Griots at War: Conflict, Conciliation, and Caste in Mande.* Bloomington: Indiana University Press.

Jansen, Jan. 1991. *Siramuri Diabate et ses enfants: une étude sur deux générations des griots Malinke.* Utrecht: ISOR.

———. 1996. "Elle connaît tout le Mande": A tribute to the griotte Siramori Diabate.' *Research in African Literatures* 27 (4): 180–197.

———. 1998. Hot issues: The Kamablon ceremony in Kangaba (Mali). *The International Journal of African Historical Studies* 31 (2): 253–278.

Janson, Marloes. 2002. *The Best Hand Is the Hand That Always Gives: Griottes and Their Profession in Eastern Gambia.* Leiden: CNWS.

Kouyate, Sanungwe. 1990. *Balendala Djibé.* Msimby, MS 001. Album produced by Ibrahim Sylla and Salif Keita.

Manchuelle, François. 1997. *Willing Migrants: Soninke Labor Diasporas, 1848–1960.* Athens: Ohio University Press; London: James Currey.

Monde, Le. 2003. Quelque 120,000 Maliens en France, dont un tiers légalement. 11 February.

Muurling, Nienke. 2004. *Relaties smeden: Een studie naar de rol en functie van een* je-limuso *(griotte) tussen Bamako en Paris* [Forging relations: A study of the role and function of a *jelimuso* (griotte) between Bamako and Paris]. Amsterdam: Aksant.

Sargent, C., and D. Cordell. 2003. Polygamy, disrupted reproduction, and the state: Malian migrants in Paris, France. *Social Science and Medicine* 56 (9): 1961–1972.

Vaa, M., S. E. Findley, and A. Diallo. 1989. The gift economy: A study of women mi-grants' survival strategies in a low-income Bamako neighborhood. *Labour, Capital and Society* 22 (2): 234–260.

Index

Contributors

Brahima Camara is lecturer in the Department of German Language at the Université du Mali, Bamako. He works in Mande hunters' oral literature and has published articles on the history and representations of *tirailleurs,* African riflemen who served in the French armed services in Africa.

Ariane Deluz (d. 2010) was Director of Research at the Centre National de la Recherche Scientifique (CNRS) and a member of the Laboratoire d'Anthropologie Sociale. She was editor (with Colette Le Cour Grandmaison and Anne Retel-Laurentin) of *Vies et paroles de femmes africaines* (2001). She was also editor (with Stephen Belcher) of *Mande Studies.*

Bah Diakité is Cabinet Chief in the Malian Ministry of Culture. He is author of the essay "Tradition, Music, and Dance of Mali," which is included in *The Spirit's Dance in Africa,* edited by Esther A. Dagan (1997).

Marame Gueye is Assistant Professor of English at Eastern Carolina University. Of *gewel* origin herself, she studies songs by women in Senegal and is working on a book about how African women negotiate voice and space through verbal art.

Thomas A. Hale is Edwin Erle Sparks professor emeritus of African, French, and Comparative Literature at The Pennsylvania State University. He is editor (with Aissata Sidikou) of *Women's Voices from West Africa* (Indiana University Press, 2011). His other publications include *Griots and Griottes: Masters of Words and Music* and *Oral Epics from Africa: Vibrant Voices from a Vast Continent,* which are also available from Indiana University Press.

Jan Jansen is a professor in the Department of Cultural Anthropology and Development Sociology at the University of Leiden. He is author of *Epopée, Histoire, Société: Le cas de Soundjata (Mali-Guinée)* (2001) and *The Griot's Craft:*

An Essay on Oral Tradition and Diplomacy (2000). He is co-editor of the book series African Sources for African History.

Marloes Janson is a researcher at Zentrum Moderner Orient (Centre for Modern Oriental Studies) in Berlin. She is author of *The Best Hand Is the Hand That Always Gives: Griottes and their Profession in Eastern Gambia* (2002) and has edited a special issue of *Africultures*.

George Joseph is Professor of French and Francophone Studies at Hobart and William Smith Colleges. His work has been published in *Research in African Literatures, Diagonales,* and *The American Journal of Semiotics.* He contributed an essay to *Understanding Contemporary Africa,* edited by April A. Gordon and Donald L. Gordon.

Kirsten Langeveld is a policy analyst for the city of Amsterdam. She earned her PhD from the University of Utrecht and has published her work in *Mande Studies.*

Beverly B. Mack is Professor of African Studies at the University of Kansas. She is author of *Muslim Women Sing: Hausa Popular Song* (Indiana University Press, 2004), and (with Jean Boyd) *One Woman's Jihad: Nana Asma'u, Scholar and Scribe* (Indiana University Press, 2000).

Fatima Mounkaïla is Professor of Comparative Literature at the Université Abdou Moumouni Dioffo in Niamey. She is author of *Mythe et Histoire dans la Geste de Zabarkane* (1988) and has contributed to *Women Writing Africa: West Africa and the Sahel* (2005).

Nienke Muurling is a junior lecturer in the Department of Sociology and Anthropology at the University of Amsterdam. She is author of *Relaties smeden. De rol van een jelimuso (griotte) in Mali* (*Forging relations: The role of a* jelimuso *[griotte] in Mali*) (2003).

Boubé Namaïwa is Professor of Philosophy at the Université Cheikh Anta Diop, Dakar. He is editor (with Diouldé Laya and Jean-Dominique Penel) of *Boubou Hama: un homme de culture nigérien* and (with Nicole Moulin, Marie-France Roy, and Bori Zamo) *Lougou et Saraounya* (2007).

Aissata Niandou is an associate professor of English and Head of the English Department at the Université Abdou Moumouni Dioffo of Niamey. She has